Curr Lib
QA135.5 .M36765 2002
gr.2
Mathematics.

D0517868

ACSI

MATHEMATICS

GRADE TWO

Life in the Air

WITHDRAWN
MURDOCK LEARNING RESOURCE CENTER
GEORGE FOX UNIVERSITY
NEWBERG, OR. 97132

Association of Christian Schools International
Dr. Ken Smitherman, President
Post Office Box 35097 Colorado Springs, CO 80935-3509
www.acsi.org

© Copyright 1999 ACSI Mathematics Grade 2

ACSI ENABLING EDUCATORS SERIES

Life in the Air

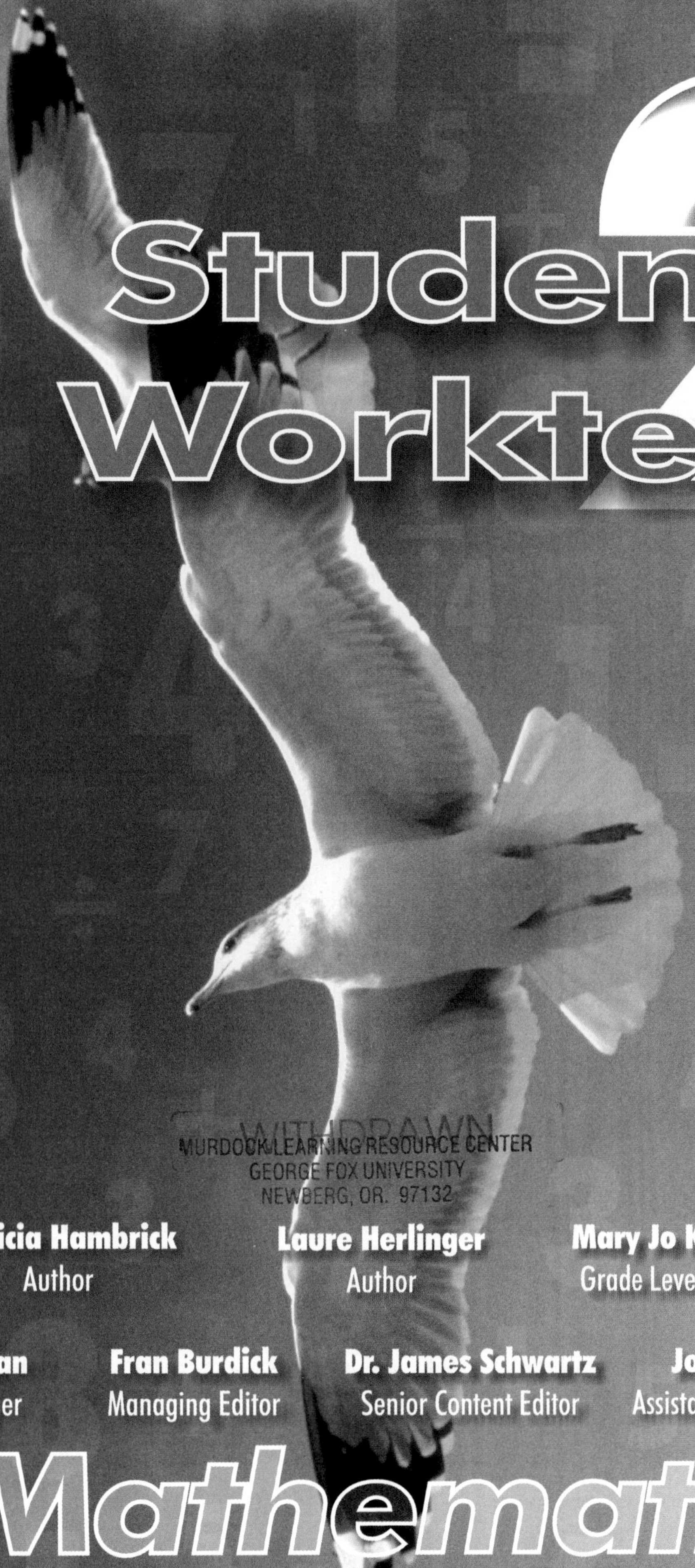

Student Worktext 2

WITHDRAWN
MURDOCK LEARNING RESOURCE CENTER
GEORGE FOX UNIVERSITY
NEWBERG, OR. 97132

Patricia Hambrick
Author

Laure Herlinger
Author

Mary Jo Kynerd
Grade Level Editor

Thom Hoyman
Graphic Designer

Fran Burdick
Managing Editor

Dr. James Schwartz
Senior Content Editor

JoAnn Keenan
Assistant Managing Editor

Mathematics

To enable Christian educators and schools worldwide to effectively prepare students for life

www.acsi.org

© 1999 Association of Christian Schools International

All rights reserved. No portion of this book, except for blackline masters and drill sheets, may be reproduced in any way without prior written permission of the Association of Christian Schools International.

Publishing is a function of the Academic Affairs Department of ACSI. As an organization, ACSI is committed to the ministry of Christian school education, to enable Christian educators and schools worldwide to effectively prepare students for life. As a publisher of books, textbooks, and other resources, ACSI endeavors to produce biblically sound materials that reflect Christian scholarship and stewardship, and that address the identified needs of Christian schools around the world.

For additional information write ACSI, Academic Affairs Department, PO Box 35097, Colorado Springs, CO 80935-3509.

Scripture taken from the New King James Version of the Bible. Copyright © 1982 by Thomas Nelson, Inc. Used by permission. All rights reserved.

References to literature books, computer software, and other ancillary resources in this Series are not endorsements by ACSI. These materials were selected to provide teachers with additional resources appropriate to the math concepts being taught and to promote student understanding and enjoyment.

Printed in the United States of America

ACSI Elementary Mathematics Grade Two
ISBN 1-58331-182-3 Student Worktext Catalog #7212
ISBN 1-58331-183-1 Teacher Edition Catalog #7213

Table of Contents

Chapter One   Patterns and Place Value

Chapter Two   Addition and Subtraction Facts

Chapter Three   Geometry And Measurement

Chapter Four Place Value to 999

Chapter Five Time and Money

Chapter Six Addition and Subtraction Facts to 18

Chapter Seven Fractions and Measurement

(continued on the next page)

© Copyright 1999 Mathematics Grade 2

Chapter Eight   Two-Digit Addition with Regrouping

Chapter Nine   Two-Digit Subtraction with Regrouping

Chapter Ten   Place Value, Addition, and Subtraction

(continued on the next page)

Chapter Eleven   Multiplication and Division

Chapter Twelve   Mixed Review

© Copyright 1999   Mathematics Grade 2

CHAPTER 1

Patterns and Place Value

As an eagle stirs up its nest,
Hovers over its young,
Spreading out its wings, taking them up,
Carrying them on its wings,
So the LORD alone led . . .

Deuteronomy 32:11,12

Dear Parents,

We are embarking on an exciting year of second grade math. Each level of the ACSI mathematics series concentrates on one facet of God's creation. Our book's theme is *Life in the Air*. Your child will enjoy this special focus on flying things created by God (eagles, toucans, owls) and flying machines men invented with God's help.

In each chapter we will study mathematical concepts that are developmentally appropriate for your child's age and ability level. In the first chapter we will study patterns, attributes, classifying, and place value.

Take some time to show your child the fun of mathematics at home. Count and sort your groceries. Listen to your child count by 2's, 5's, and 10's. Ask questions of your child that will allow him or her to compare and order numbers and shapes.

We will discover a wealth of spiritual meaning in mathematics: number patterns, time, and order. The world of mathematical precision is truly God's world. We will celebrate each opportunity to praise God as we enjoy mathematics together.

© Copyright 1999

Classifying

Classify the toys.

1. Write your name on the green toy box.

2. Draw lines from the toys you would choose to your toy box.

3. Draw lines from the toys you did not choose to Austin's toy box.

4. Write three ways to classify the toys.

5. Write the name of another toy for each group.

_____ ⇒ _____

_____ ⇒ _____

_____ ⇒ _____

© Copyright 1999 ACSI Mathematics Grade 2

Review   Find the patterns.

1. Draw what comes next.

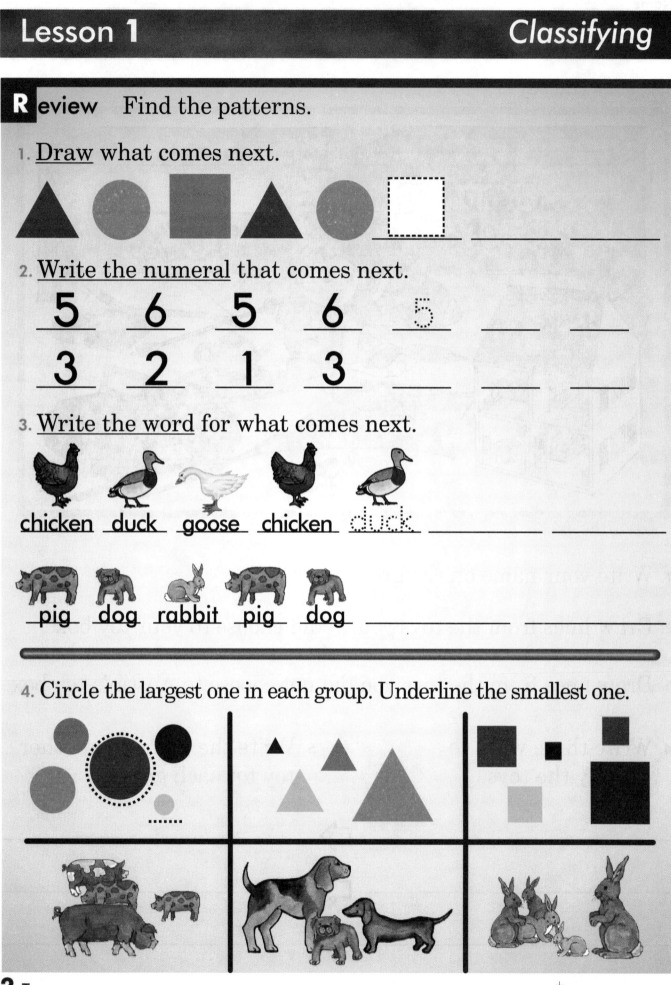

2. Write the numeral that comes next.

$$5 \quad 6 \quad 5 \quad 6 \quad 5 \quad \underline{\hspace{1cm}} \quad \underline{\hspace{1cm}}$$

$$3 \quad 2 \quad 1 \quad 3 \quad \underline{\hspace{1cm}} \quad \underline{\hspace{1cm}} \quad \underline{\hspace{1cm}}$$

3. Write the word for what comes next.

chicken   duck   goose   chicken   duck   _____   _____

pig   dog   rabbit   pig   dog   _____   _____

4. Circle the largest one in each group. Underline the smallest one.

© Copyright 1999 ✠ACSI Mathematics Grade 2

Calendar Math   Lesson 2

Write the name of the current month. Write the numerals.

Sunday	Monday	Tuesday	Wednesday	Thursday	Friday	Saturday

Use the calendar. Write the answers.

1. Count by 10's. Write the numbers. __10__ _____ _____

2. Count by 5's. Write the numbers. _5_ _10_ ___ ___ ___ ___

3. Count by 2's. Write the numbers.

   _2_ ___ _6_ ___ ___ ___ ___ ___ ___ ___

4. Count by 3's. _3_ ___ ___ _12_ ___ ___ _21_ ___ _27_ ___

5. Write your name on your favorite date on the calendar.

6. Draw a picture on any Monday on the calendar.

© Copyright 1999 ACSI Mathematics Grade 2

Use the Word Banks. Write the answers.

Word Bank

Sunday

Monday

Tuesday

Wednesday

Thursday

Friday

Saturday

7. What is the first day of
the week?_____

8. _____ is the fourth
day of the week.

9. Sunday comes after _____.

10. _____comes just before Wednesday.

11. Two days after Wednesday is _____.

12. The day between Wednesday and
Friday is _____.

13. _____ is the
second day of the week.

14. Write the ordinal numbers for the days of the week.

Sunday_____ first _____

Monday _____

Tuesday _____

Wednesday _____

Thursday _____

Friday _____

Saturday _____

Word Bank

sixth

second

third

first

seventh

fifth

fourth

© Copyright 1999   Mathematics Grade 2

Counting by 2's, 5's, and 10's — Lesson 3

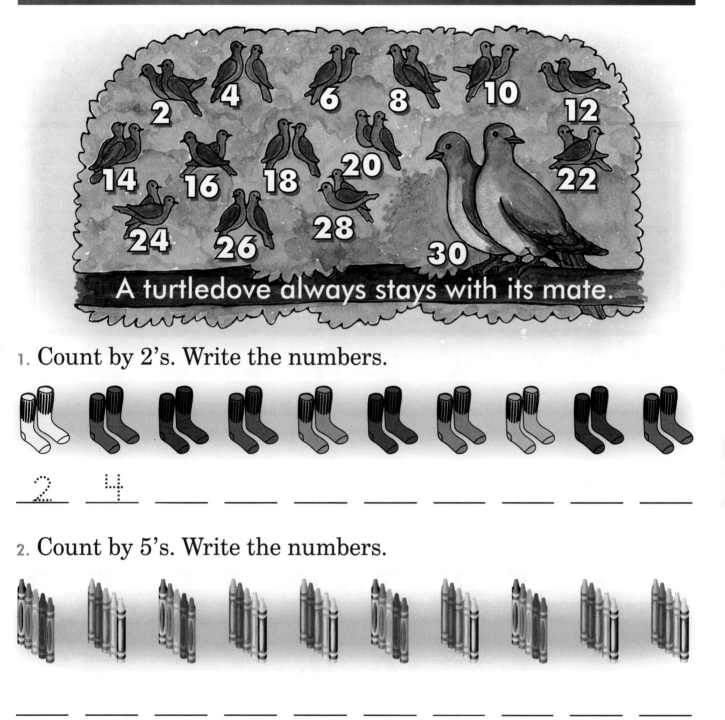

A turtledove always stays with its mate.

1. Count by 2's. Write the numbers.

2   4   __   __   __   __   __   __   __   __

2. Count by 5's. Write the numbers.

__   __   __   __   __   __   __   __   __   __

3. Count by 10's. Write the numbers.

__   __   __   __   __   __   __   __   __   __

4. Use the Word Bank. Write the second word for these famous pairs.

Word Bank		
paper	spoon	socks
stars	butter	eggs

moon and _stars_	fork and _____	pencil and _____
shoes and _____	**bread and** _____	**bacon and** _____

5. Write three more word pairs that you know.

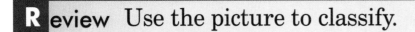

_____   **and**   _____   _____   **and**   _____   _____   **and**   _____

Review   Use the picture to classify.

1. Write on the signs 2 ways to classify the activities.

2. Draw lines from the people to the signs.

© Copyright 1999 ACSI Mathematics Grade 2

Comparing and Ordering Numbers Lesson 4

1. Number the animals.

___ ___ ___ ___ ___ ___ ___ ___ ___ ___ ___ ___ ___ ___

2. Write the number that comes between.

8 _9_ 10   26 ___ 28   43 ___ 45

17 ___ 19   10 ___ 12   38 ___ 40

3. Write the number that comes before and after.

___ 25 ___   ___ 8 ___   ___ 41 ___

___ 13 ___   ___ 29 ___   ___ 17 ___

4. Which is greater? Write the numbers in the blanks.

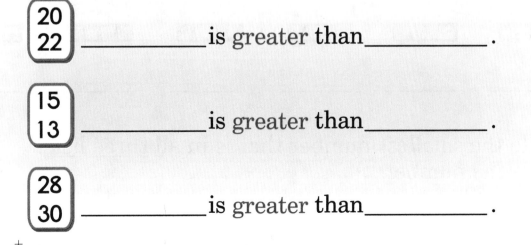

20
22   _____ is greater than _____ .

15
13   _____ is greater than _____ .

28
30   _____ is greater than _____ .

© Copyright 1999 ACSI Mathematics Grade 2

5. Circle all the numbers in each shape that are greater than the number below the shape.

Review Count.

1.

_2_ _4_ ___ ___ ___ ___ ___

2.

___ ___ ___ ___ ___ ___ ___

3.

___ ___ ___ ___ ___ ___

4. Circle the smallest number that is in <u>all</u> <u>three</u> <u>lists</u>. Write the number.

_____

© Copyright 1999   Mathematics Grade 2

Name ___________________________________

Graphing — Lesson 5

Bar graphs show number information by using bars of different lengths.

Ruth
Seth
Thomas

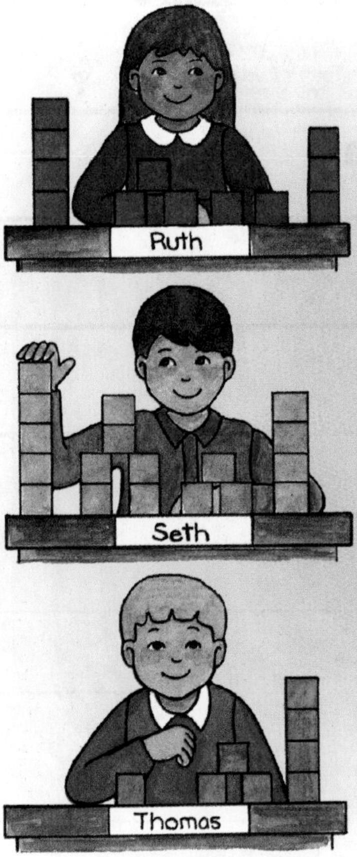

Ruth
Seth
Thomas

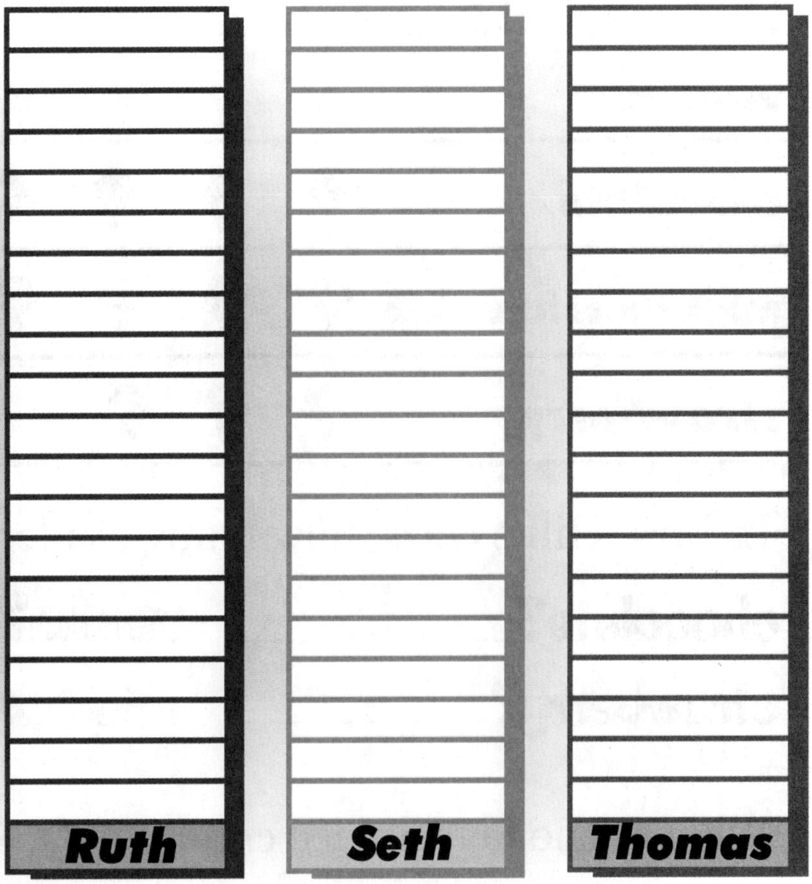

Count and color.

1. How many cubes does Ruth have? ___12___ cubes

2. How many cubes does Seth have? _________ cubes

3. How many cubes does Thomas have? _________ cubes

4. ___Seth___ has more cubes than ___Ruth___ or ___Thomas___.

   __________ has more cubes than __________.

5. __________ has fewer cubes than __________ or __________.

   __________ has fewer cubes than __________.

6. __________ has the most cubes of all.

© Copyright 1999 ACSI Mathematics Grade 2

Read the pictograph. Write the answers.

Favorite Flavors

vanilla	🍦 🍦 🍦 🍦 🍦 🍦 🍦 🍦 🍦
chocolate	🍦 🍦 🍦 🍦 🍦
mint chocolate chip	🍦 🍦 🍦 🍦
strawberry	🍦 🍦 🍦

7. In Mrs. Hill's class, how many students like:

chocolate?_____5_____   vanilla?_____

strawberry?_____   mint chocolate chip?_____

8. What is the favorite ice cream of the class?_____

9. What is the flavor chosen by the fewest students?_____

10. What is your favorite ice cream flavor?_____

Review   Add.

| 1. $\begin{array}{r} 6 \\ +2 \\ \hline \end{array}$ | 2. $\begin{array}{r} 2 \\ +3 \\ \hline \end{array}$ | 3. $\begin{array}{r} 5 \\ +5 \\ \hline \end{array}$ | 4. $\begin{array}{r} 4 \\ +2 \\ \hline \end{array}$ | 5. $\begin{array}{r} 3 \\ +4 \\ \hline \end{array}$ |
| 6. $\begin{array}{r} 3 \\ +3 \\ \hline \end{array}$ | 7. $\begin{array}{r} 7 \\ +2 \\ \hline \end{array}$ | 8. $\begin{array}{r} 5 \\ +3 \\ \hline \end{array}$ | 9. $\begin{array}{r} 4 \\ +4 \\ \hline \end{array}$ | 10. $\begin{array}{r} 6 \\ +3 \\ \hline \end{array}$ |

© Copyright 1999   Mathematics Grade 2

Identifying Same and Different   Lesson 6

1. Draw lines to match sets of birds that have the same number.

Fill in the blanks.

2. The duckling that is different is _____ in line.

3. The duckling is different because it is _____. The

   other ducklings are _____.

4. Name one way all sets in the picture are the same. _____

   _____

5. Choose two sets in the picture and name one way they are

   different. _____ are different from _____ because

   _____.

6. Count each kind of bird. Draw a set of objects with the same number.

cardinals   swans   bluebirds

Mark two in each section that do not belong.
The first one has been done for you.

© Copyright 1999 Mathematics Grade 2

Review   Count by 2's, 5's, and 10's. Fill in the blanks.

1. __2__ __4__ __6__ ____ ____ ____ __14__ ____ ____ ____

2. __5__ ____ ____ ____ __25__ ____ ____ __40__ ____ ____

3. __10__ ____ ____ ____ ____ ____ ____ ____ __100__

Pennies, Nickels, and Dimes　　　　Lesson 7

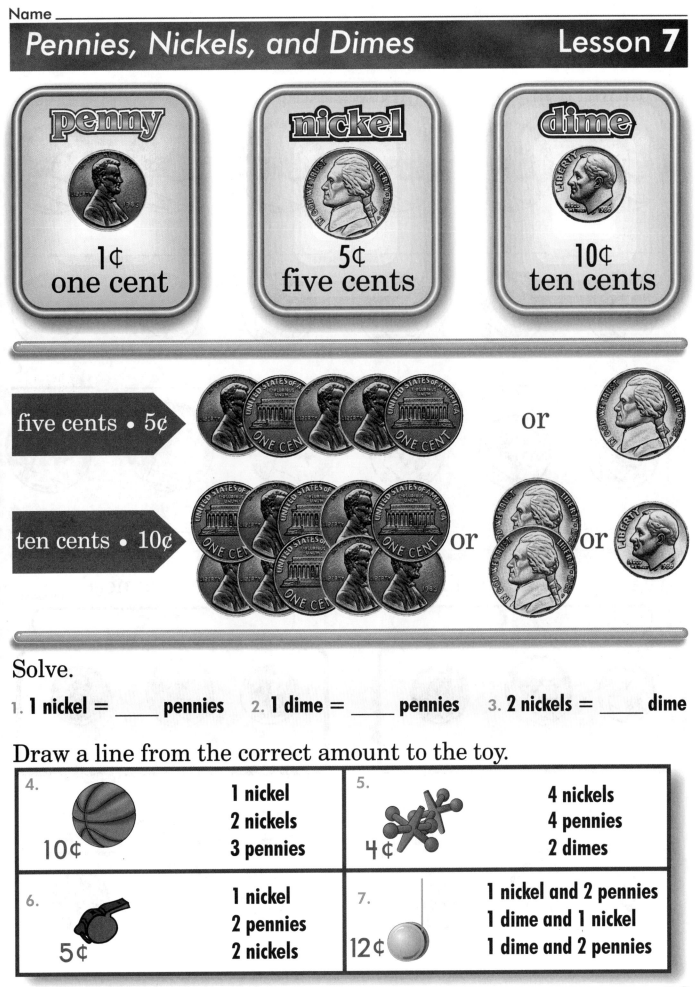

penny

1¢
one cent

nickel

5¢
five cents

dime

10¢
ten cents

five cents • 5¢

or

ten cents • 10¢

or　or

Solve.

1. **1 nickel = _____ pennies**　　2. **1 dime = _____ pennies**　　3. **2 nickels = _____ dime**

Draw a line from the correct amount to the toy.

4. 10¢	1 nickel 2 nickels 3 pennies	5. 4¢	4 nickels 4 pennies 2 dimes
6. 5¢	1 nickel 2 pennies 2 nickels	7. 12¢	1 nickel and 2 pennies 1 dime and 1 nickel 1 dime and 2 pennies

Count up. Write the amounts.

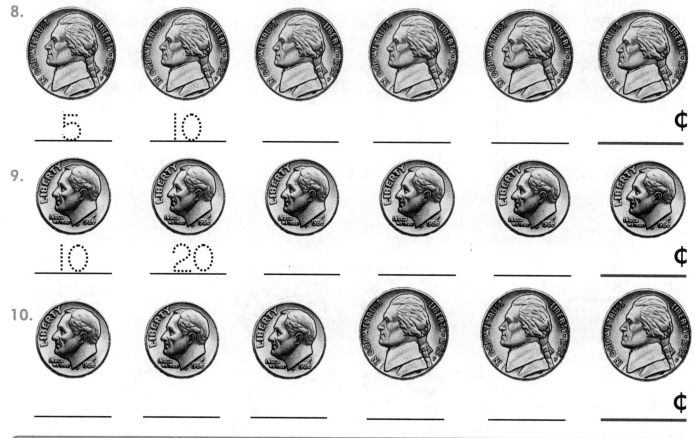

8. _5_ _10_ ___ ___ ___ ___ ¢

9. _10_ _20_ ___ ___ ___ ___ ¢

10. ___ ___ ___ ___ ___ ___ ¢

Write the number of dimes, nickels, and pennies you need.

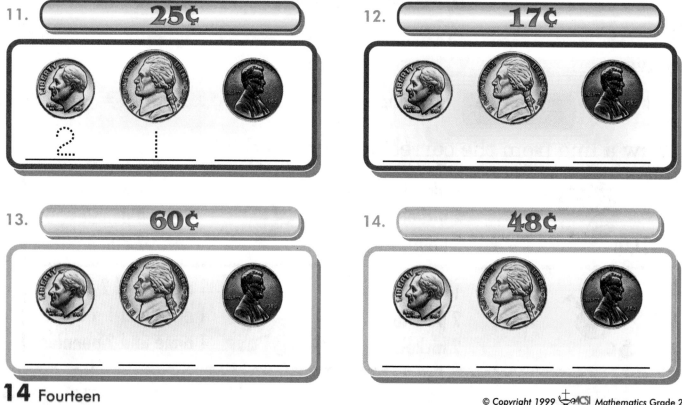

11. **25¢**   _2_ _1_ ___

12. **17¢**   ___ ___ ___

13. **60¢**   ___ ___ ___

14. **48¢**   ___ ___ ___

© Copyright 1999 Mathematics Grade 2

Use the colored numbers to write each sequence.
Continue by repeating the number pattern.

$$7 \quad {}^1 \quad 4 \quad {}^3 \quad 6 \quad {}^5 \quad 8 \quad 2$$

large blue	large green	large red	large yellow			
1. 2	4	6	8	2	___	___

small blue	small green	small red	small yellow			
2. ___	___	___	___	___	___	___

large yellow	small yellow	large red	small red			
3. ___	___	___	___	___	___	___

small blue	large blue	large green	large yellow			
4. ___	___	___	___	___	___	___

5. Continue the number pattern. Finish the sentence.

__10__ __20__ __30__ ___ ___ ___ ___ ___ ___

This pattern is _____.

6. Write numbers in a pattern. Begin with the number 5. Ask a
   partner to find your pattern and add the next number.

5 _____

How are these things related?
Draw one more object that fits each group.

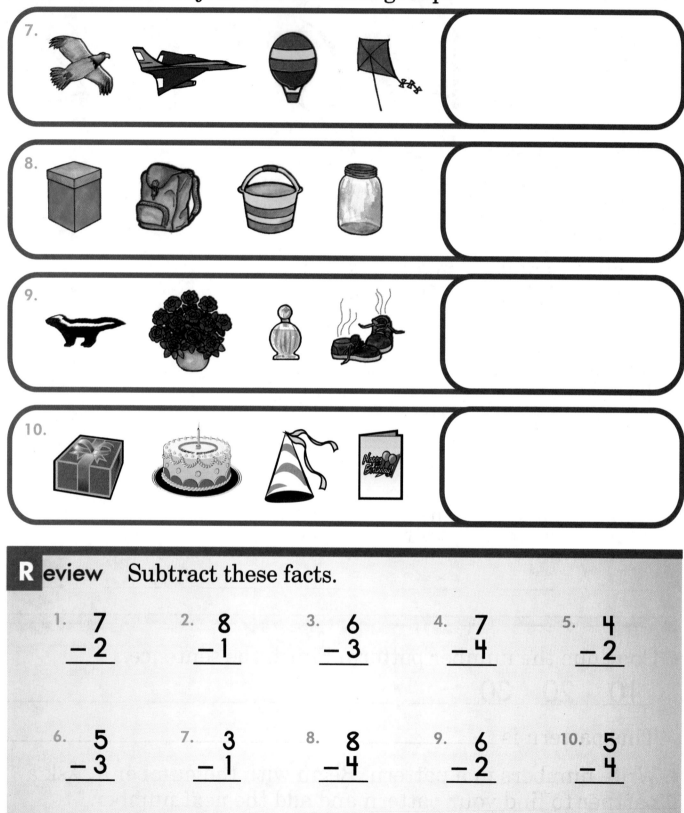

7.

8.

9.

10.

Review   Subtract these facts.

1. $\begin{array}{r} 7 \\ -2 \\ \hline \end{array}$	2. $\begin{array}{r} 8 \\ -1 \\ \hline \end{array}$	3. $\begin{array}{r} 6 \\ -3 \\ \hline \end{array}$	4. $\begin{array}{r} 7 \\ -4 \\ \hline \end{array}$	5. $\begin{array}{r} 4 \\ -2 \\ \hline \end{array}$
6. $\begin{array}{r} 5 \\ -3 \\ \hline \end{array}$	7. $\begin{array}{r} 3 \\ -1 \\ \hline \end{array}$	8. $\begin{array}{r} 8 \\ -4 \\ \hline \end{array}$	9. $\begin{array}{r} 6 \\ -2 \\ \hline \end{array}$	10. $\begin{array}{r} 5 \\ -4 \\ \hline \end{array}$

© Copyright 1999 ACSI Mathematics Grade 2

Even and Odd Numbers   Lesson 9

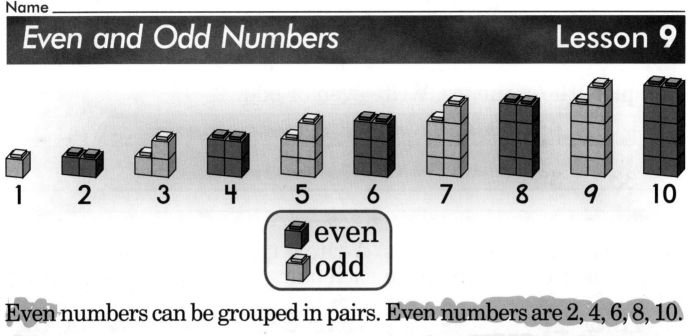

🔲	even
🔲	odd

Even numbers can be grouped in pairs. Even numbers are 2, 4, 6, 8, 10.

Odd numbers have one cube left over. Odd numbers are 1, 3, 5, 7, 9.

Count each group. Circle odd or even.

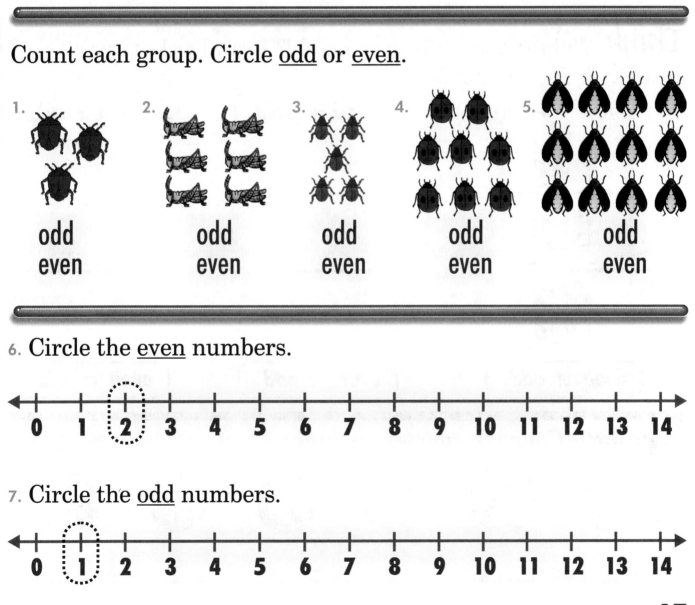

1. odd even

2. odd even

3. odd even

4. odd even

5. odd even

6. Circle the even numbers.

0 1 (2) 3 4 5 6 7 8 9 10 11 12 13 14

7. Circle the odd numbers.

0 (1) 2 3 4 5 6 7 8 9 10 11 12 13 14

Complete the sequence. Write <u>even</u> or <u>odd</u>.

8. __12__　__14__　__16__　_____　_____　_____　　__even__

9. __33__　__35__　_____　_____　_____　_____　　_____

Write **<u>e</u>** under even numbers. Write **<u>o</u>** under odd numbers.
Circle the greater number in each pair.

10. (**28**) or **21**　　　11. **35** or **37**　　　12. **64** or **67**

　　_e_　_o_　　　　　　_____ _____　　　　　　_____ _____

Think Will the answer be even or odd? Draw blocks to prove your answer. Circle <u>even</u> or <u>odd</u>.

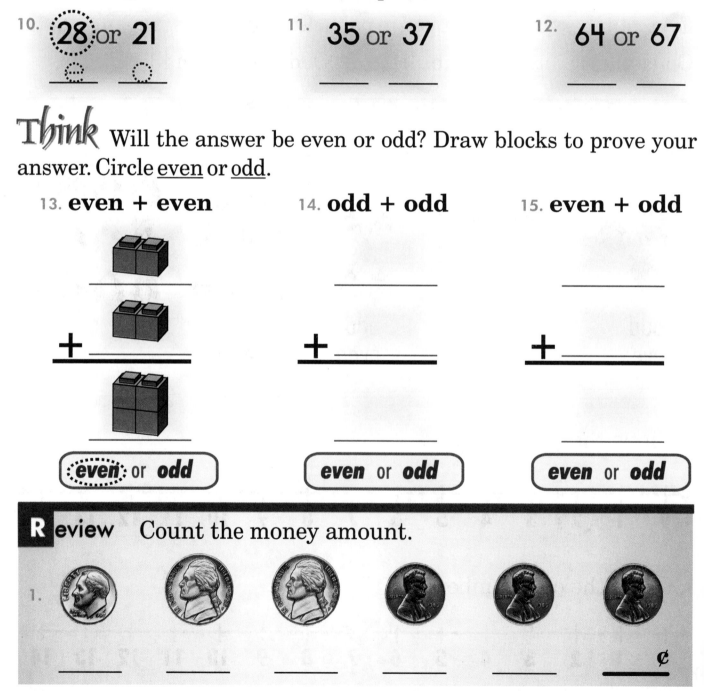

13. **even + even**　　14. **odd + odd**　　15. **even + odd**

13. _____　　14. _____　　15. _____

+ _____　　　　+ _____　　　　+ _____

_____　　　　_____　　　　_____

((**even**) or **odd**)　　(**even** or **odd**)　　(**even** or **odd**)

Review　Count the money amount.

1.

_____ _____ _____ _____ _____ _____ ¢

© Copyright 1999 　ACSI Mathematics Grade 2

Count up. Write the amounts.

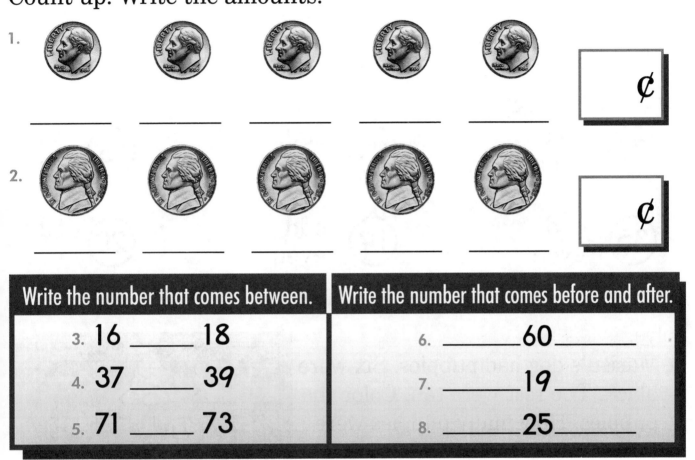

1. _____ _____ _____ _____ _____   [ ] ¢

2. _____ _____ _____ _____ _____   [ ] ¢

Write the number that comes between.	Write the number that comes before and after.
3. 16 _____ 18	6. _____ 60 _____
4. 37 _____ 39	7. _____ 19 _____
5. 71 _____ 73	8. _____ 25 _____

Continue the pattern. Write the numbers.

9. __44__ __45__ __46__ __47__ __48__ _____ _____ _____

10. __4th__ __5th__ __6th__ _____ _____ __9th__ _____ _____

11. __25__ __30__ _____ _____ _____ _____ _____

Continue the pattern. Draw the shapes.

12. ▲ ▲ ■ ▲ _____

13. ⬡ ■ ▲ ⬡ ■ _____

Circle the greater number.

14. **47** or **50**   15. **100** or **99**   16. **43** or **34**

Circle <u>odd</u> or <u>even</u>.

17. (77) odd
          even

18. (84) odd
          even

19. (16) odd
          even

20. (35) odd
          even

21. (19) odd
          even

22. (20) odd
          even

Solve.

23. Marisu's dog had puppies. Six were black. The rest were tan. Color the puppies. How many puppies were tan?

_____

24.

is _____ puppies.

Moments in Careers

"My dad works as a financial manager. In his work he uses math to process loans, prepare budgets, calculate interest, and in many other ways."

Spencer
Memphis, TN

Introducing Place Value

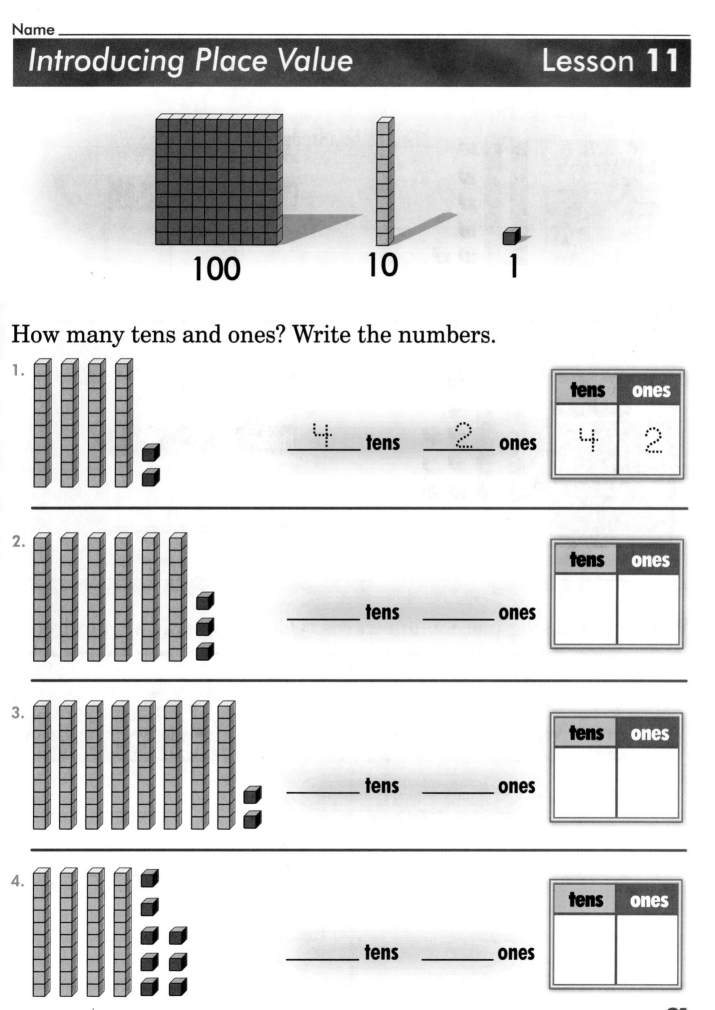

100   **10**   **1**

How many tens and ones? Write the numbers.

1.

_____4_____ tens   _____2_____ ones

tens	ones
4	2

2.

_____ tens   _____ ones

tens	ones

3.

_____ tens   _____ ones

tens	ones

4.

_____ tens   _____ ones

tens	ones

Write the numbers.

5. _____ hundreds _____ tens _____ ones

hundreds	tens	ones

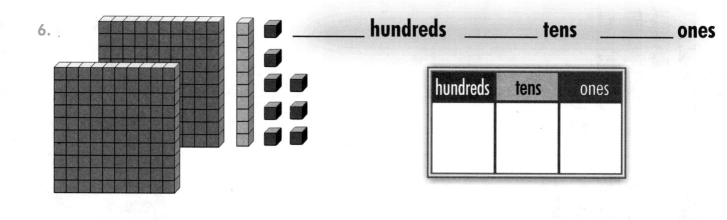

6. _____ hundreds _____ tens _____ ones

hundreds	tens	ones

Write the missing place value words. Use <u>ones</u>, <u>tens</u>, or <u>hundreds</u>.

7. 278	8. 453
What do these numbers mean?	
The 7 means 7 ___tens___.	The 3 means 3 _____.
The 2 means 2 _____.	The 4 means 4 _____.
The 8 means 8 _____.	The 5 means 5 _____.

© Copyright 1999 　　 Mathematics Grade 2

Making Tens and Ones   Lesson 12

Count the tens and ones. Write the number.

1.

2.

_____ ladybugs

4.

_____ grapes

Count the tens and ones.

#400   10-19-2009 7:49PM
Item(s) checked out to Widmer, Amy Jo.

TITLE: Scott Foresman-Addison Wesley mat
BARCODE: 35212001313584
DUE DATE: 11-16-09

TITLE: Math by all means : money, grades
BARCODE: 35212002012078
DUE DATE: 11-16-09

TITLE: Mathematics.
BARCODE: 35212002531820
DUE DATE: 11-16-09

TITLE: Mathematics.
BARCODE: 35212002531903
DUE DATE: 11-16-09

TITLE: Nimble with numbers : engaging ma
BARCODE: 35212002016020
DUE DATE: 11-16-09

TITLE: Mathematics.
BARCODE: 35212002531895
DATE: 11-16-09

5.

54
6.

42
7.

29
8.

Write the missing numbers.

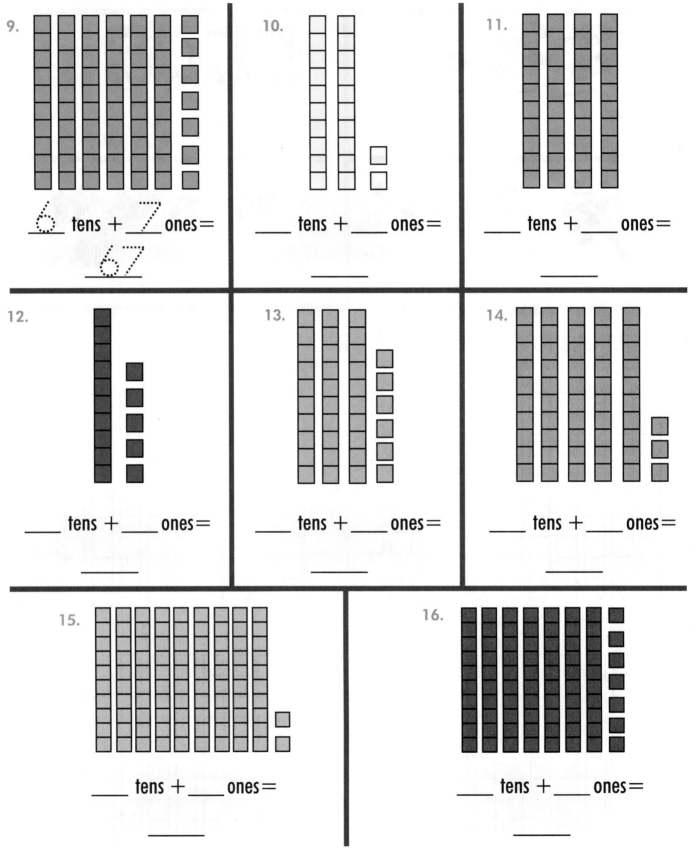

9. __6__ tens + __7__ ones =

    __67__

10. ____ tens + ____ ones =

    ____

11. ____ tens + ____ ones =

    ____

12. ____ tens + ____ ones =

    ____

13. ____ tens + ____ ones =

    ____

14. ____ tens + ____ ones =

    ____

15. ____ tens + ____ ones =

    ____

16. ____ tens + ____ ones =

    ____

© Copyright 1999 ACSI Mathematics Grade 2

Two-Digit Numbers

Cut the numerals apart. The dragonfly picture makes a puzzle.

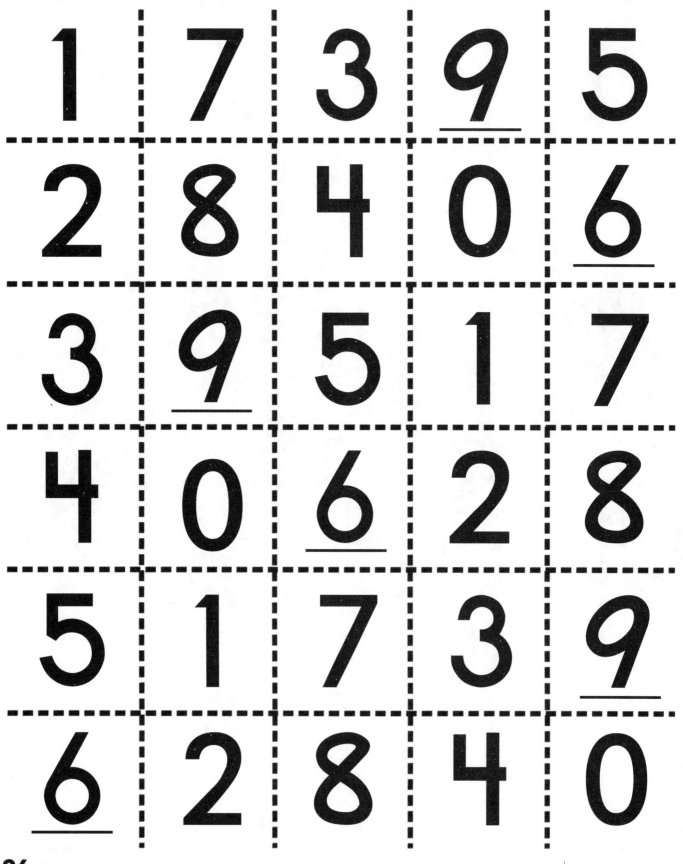

© Copyright 1999   Mathematics Grade 2

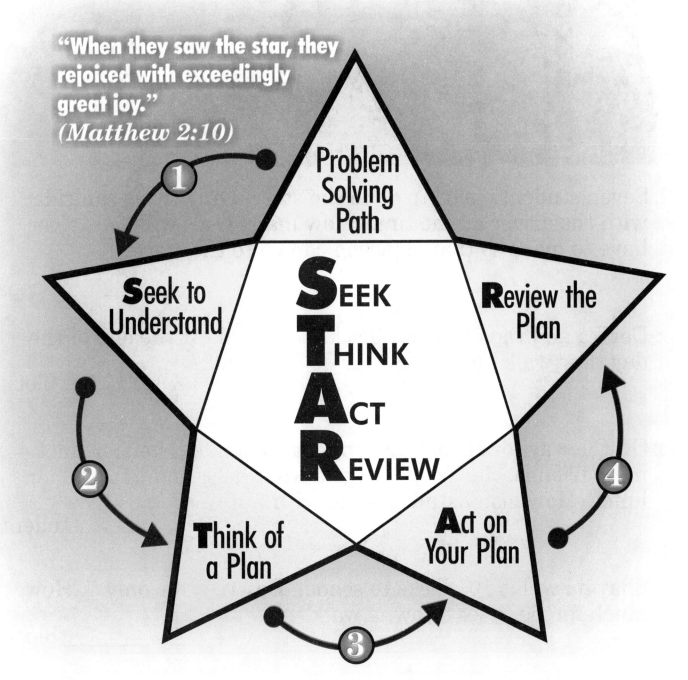

"When they saw the star, they rejoiced with exceedingly great joy."
(Matthew 2:10)

Problem Solving Path

Seek to Understand

Review the Plan

SEEK
THINK
ACT
REVIEW

Think of a Plan

Act on Your Plan

Complete the following sentences and circle the main word in each step.

Problem Solving Path

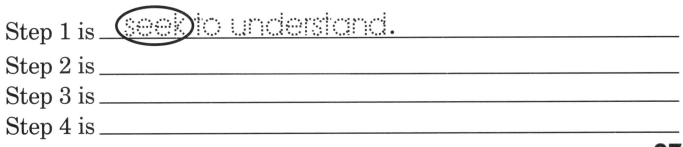

Step 1 is ___(seek) to understand.___

Step 2 is _____

Step 3 is _____

Step 4 is _____

1. Seven students need to go to the store. Only three can ride with the driver at one time. How many trips will the driver have to make so that all seven can go to the store?

_____ trips

2. Derika and David walk 4 blocks to school. At the end of the day they walk home. How far do they walk?

_____ blocks

3. On the way to school Carmen met 3 friends. Then she met 4 more friends. Her friend Angela went back home to get her lunch. How many students are with Carmen?

_____ students

4. Shawna walks 10 blocks to school. Dawn walks only 7. How much farther does Shawna walk?

_____ blocks

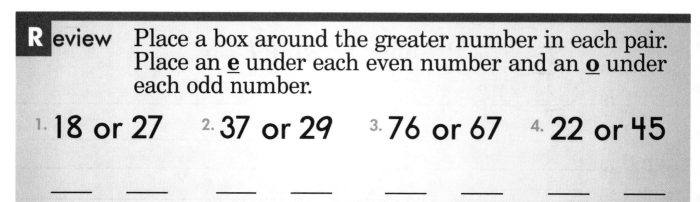

Review   Place a box around the greater number in each pair. Place an **e** under each even number and an **o** under each odd number.

1. 18 or 27   2. 37 or 29   3. 76 or 67   4. 22 or 45

___ ___   ___ ___   ___ ___   ___ ___

© Copyright 1999 Mathematics Grade 2

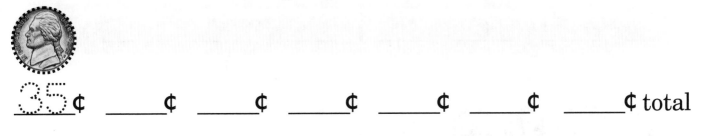

Listen to the story about Jonathan. Be ready to answer the questions.

1. Draw nickels and count by fives to show how much money Jonathan had after each group boarded the bus.

35¢ ____¢ ____¢ ____¢ ____¢ ____¢ ____¢ total

2. How many students were on the bus altogether? _____

3. If Jonathan traded nickels for dimes how many would he have?

 _____ dimes and _____ nickel

4. Write your own problem about Jonathan's trip.

_____

_____

_____

5. Write how many.

_____   _____   _____   _____

6. Count by 10's.

  ___ ___ ___ ___ ___ ___

7. Count by 2's.

2 ___ ___ ___ ___ ___ ___

8. Continue the pattern.

_____ _____ _____

9. Write the amount of money in each set.

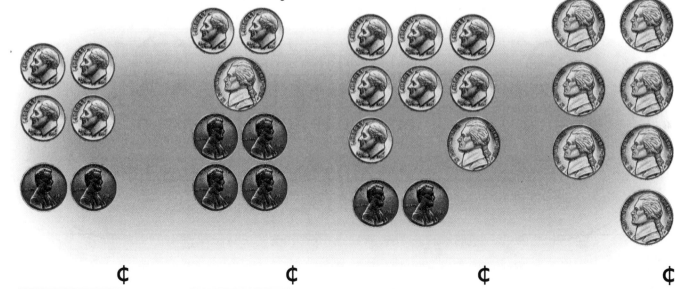

_____ ¢   _____ ¢   _____ ¢   _____ ¢

© Copyright 1999 Mathematics Grade 2

CHAPTER 2

Addition and Subtraction Facts

. . . the birds of the heavens have their habitation;
They sing among the branches.

Psalm 104:12

Dear Parents,

Your child has completed Chapter One of our math book. It is exciting to see how much the students have already learned about patterns, place value, counting, and comparing numbers. In Chapter Two we will use strategies to learn addition and subtraction facts. Our goal will be to develop *number sense*, a conceptual understanding of number relationships. The use of manipulatives will be an essential part of this process.

A variety of fact strategies will be used to make memorization of the facts as easy as possible. By using the order property (that is, by knowing that the sum of 4 + 6 is the same as the sum of 6 + 4) the memory load is reduced by nearly half. Learning the "doubles" and "near-doubles" and thinking of facts as "families" further reduces the number of facts to be memorized. If you want to help your child learn the facts at home, consider that it is better to concentrate on a few facts during short, frequent sessions, than to try to learn many facts at one time. Remember also, that in the beginning accuracy is more important than speed. The use of games and computer software programs that encourage speedy recall of basic facts are also useful.

You may reinforce math skills by using pictures to suggest problems. Using the picture shown, you might ask:

How many birds do you see?

How many nests are there?

Use the groups of birds to count by 2's.

Use the eggs in the nests to count by 3's.

What is the total number of eggs?

If all but one egg hatches, how many baby birds will there be?

Please call me if you have any questions about your child's progress.

© Copyright 1999

Counting On to Add
Lesson 16

Follow the flamingo as he counts on to add. Write the addends and the sum.

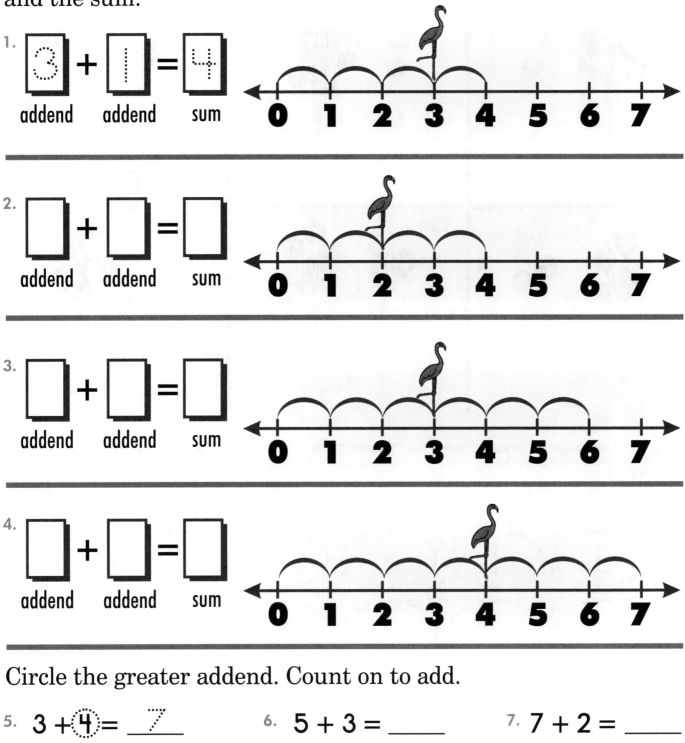

1. $3 + 1 = 4$
    addend addend sum

2. ☐ + ☐ = ☐
    addend addend sum

3. ☐ + ☐ = ☐
    addend addend sum

4. ☐ + ☐ = ☐
    addend addend sum

Circle the greater addend. Count on to add.

5. $3 + (4) = \underline{7}$

6. $5 + 3 = \underline{}$

7. $7 + 2 = \underline{}$

8. $8 + 2 = \underline{}$

9. $3 + 6 = \underline{}$

10. $5 + 2 = \underline{}$

11. $1 + 7 = \underline{}$

12. $2 + 6 = \underline{}$

13. $1 + 8 = \underline{}$

Count the balloons. Write down the greater number first.
Write down the lesser number then count on to add.

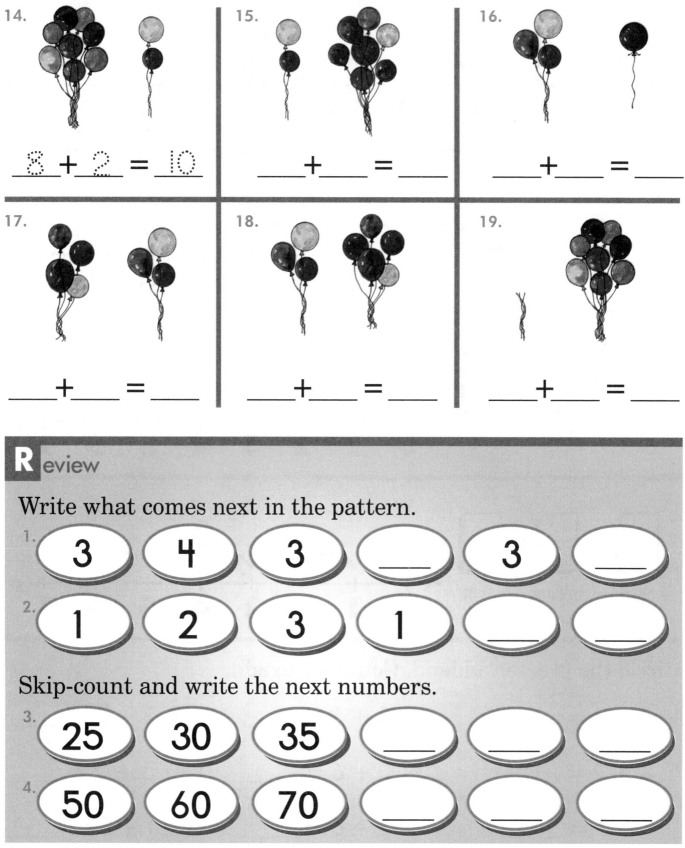

14. $\underline{8} + \underline{2} = \underline{10}$

15. $\underline{} + \underline{} = \underline{}$

16. $\underline{} + \underline{} = \underline{}$

17. $\underline{} + \underline{} = \underline{}$

18. $\underline{} + \underline{} = \underline{}$

19. $\underline{} + \underline{} = \underline{}$

Review

Write what comes next in the pattern.

1. 3   4   3   ___   3   ___

2. 1   2   3   1   ___   ___

Skip-count and write the next numbers.

3. 25   30   35   ___   ___   ___

4. 50   60   70   ___   ___   ___

© Copyright 1999   Mathematics Grade 2

Addition Facts to 10　　　Lesson 17

Write all the addition facts for each sum.

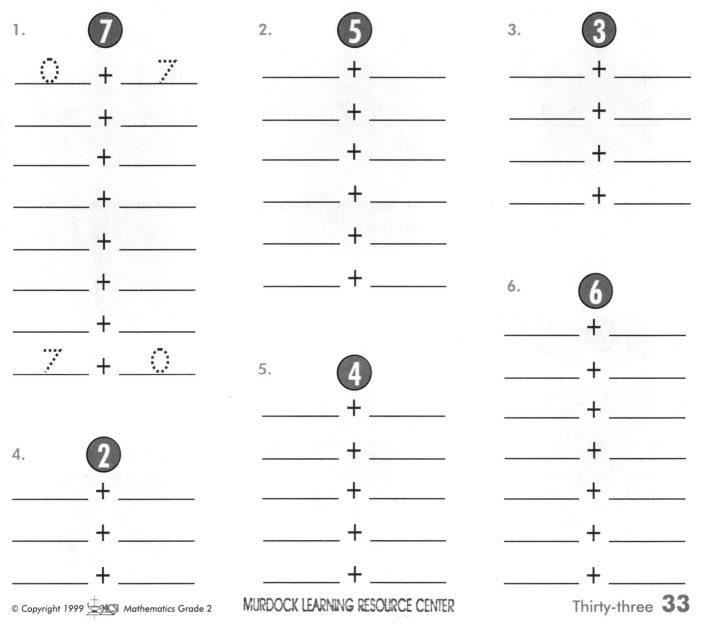

1.　**7**

___0___ + ___7___

_____ + _____

_____ + _____

_____ + _____

_____ + _____

_____ + _____

___7___ + ___0___

2.　**5**

_____ + _____

_____ + _____

_____ + _____

_____ + _____

_____ + _____

_____ + _____

3.　**3**

_____ + _____

_____ + _____

_____ + _____

_____ + _____

6.　**6**

_____ + _____

_____ + _____

_____ + _____

_____ + _____

_____ + _____

4.　**2**

_____ + _____

_____ + _____

_____ + _____

5.　**4**

_____ + _____

_____ + _____

_____ + _____

_____ + _____

Add.

7. 3
   + 2

    5

8. 5
   + 2
   ----

9. 1
   + 3
   ----

10. 6
   + 2
   ----

11. 2
   + 2
   ----

12. 5
   + 3
   ----

13. 4
   + 3
   ----

14. 4
   + 2
   ----

15. 6
   + 1
   ----

16. 3
   + 3
   ----

17. 2
   + 7
   ----

18. 4
   + 4
   ----

19. 3
   + 6
   ----

20. 4
   + 5

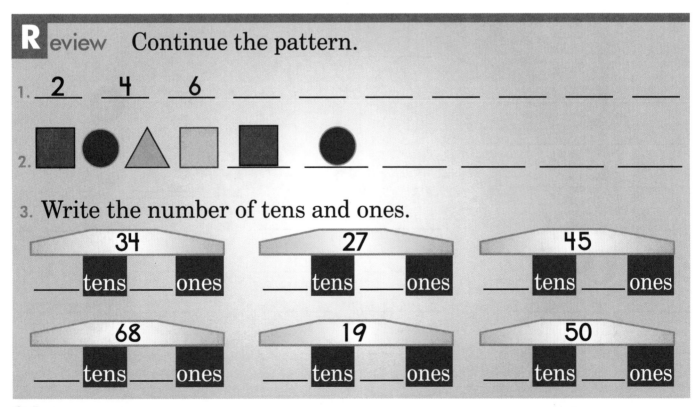

Review   Continue the pattern.

1. 2   4   6   ___ ___ ___ ___

2. ___ ___ ___ ___

3. Write the number of tens and ones.

34
___ tens ___ ones

27
___ tens ___ ones

45
___ tens ___ ones

68
___ tens ___ ones

19
___ tens ___ ones

50
___ tens ___ ones

© Copyright 1999 ACSI Mathematics Grade 2

Counting Back to Subtract

Listen to the story. Count back to subtract.

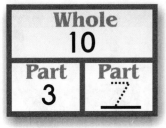

Whole
10

Part	Part
3	7

Think 10. Count back **9, 8, _7_.**

$10 - 3 = \underline{7}$ The difference is **7.**

Think the number (the whole). Count back the number you need to subtract (the part). The other part is the <u>difference</u>.

Count back to find the difference.

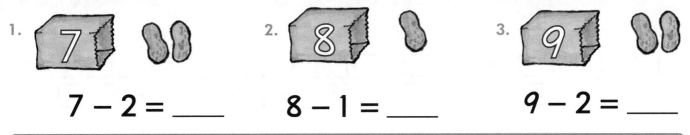

1. $7 - 2 = \underline{}$

2. $8 - 1 = \underline{}$

3. $9 - 2 = \underline{}$

Follow the crow as he counts back to subtract.

4.

7	−	4	=	3
sum		addend		addend

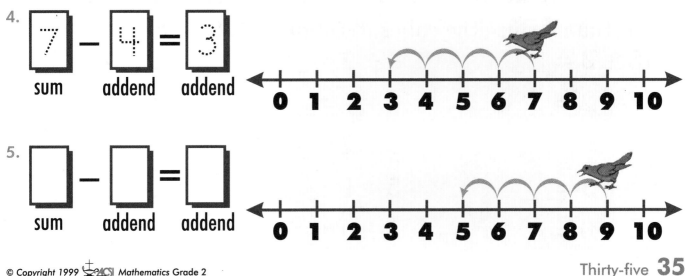

5.

	−		=	
sum		addend		addend

Use a pencil and a paper clip to make a spinner.

Spin and add.

6. $4 + \underline{\hspace{1cm}} = \underline{\hspace{1cm}}$

7. $5 + \underline{\hspace{1cm}} = \underline{\hspace{1cm}}$

8. $7 + \underline{\hspace{1cm}} = \underline{\hspace{1cm}}$

9. $6 + \underline{\hspace{1cm}} = \underline{\hspace{1cm}}$

Spin and subtract.

10. $9 - \underline{\hspace{1cm}} = \underline{\hspace{1cm}}$

11. $7 - \underline{\hspace{1cm}} = \underline{\hspace{1cm}}$

12. $8 - \underline{\hspace{1cm}} = \underline{\hspace{1cm}}$

13. $10 - \underline{\hspace{1cm}} = \underline{\hspace{1cm}}$

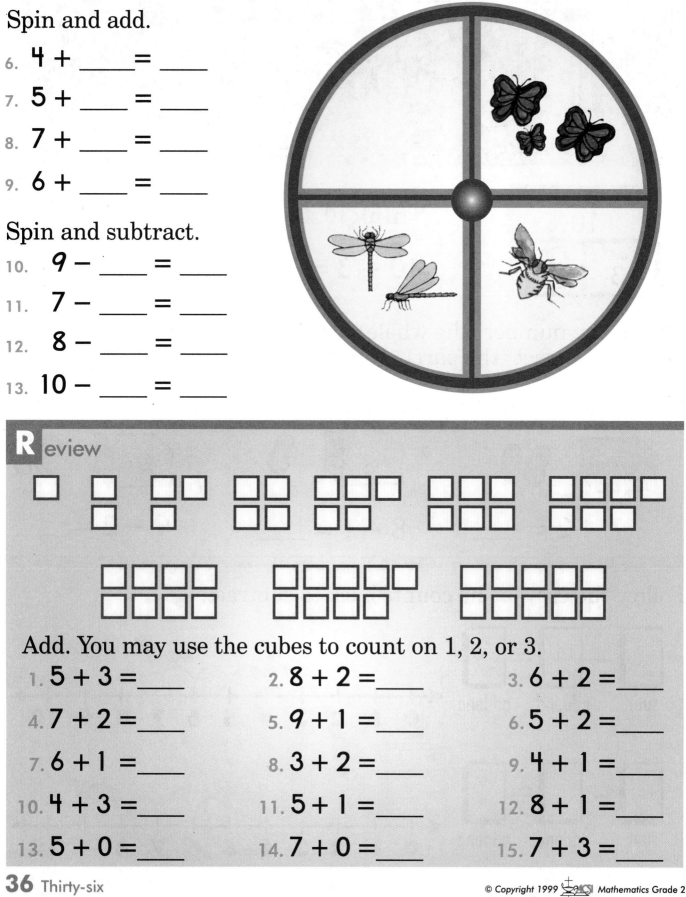

Review

Add. You may use the cubes to count on 1, 2, or 3.

1. $5 + 3 = \underline{\hspace{1cm}}$ 2. $8 + 2 = \underline{\hspace{1cm}}$ 3. $6 + 2 = \underline{\hspace{1cm}}$

4. $7 + 2 = \underline{\hspace{1cm}}$ 5. $9 + 1 = \underline{\hspace{1cm}}$ 6. $5 + 2 = \underline{\hspace{1cm}}$

7. $6 + 1 = \underline{\hspace{1cm}}$ 8. $3 + 2 = \underline{\hspace{1cm}}$ 9. $4 + 1 = \underline{\hspace{1cm}}$

10. $4 + 3 = \underline{\hspace{1cm}}$ 11. $5 + 1 = \underline{\hspace{1cm}}$ 12. $8 + 1 = \underline{\hspace{1cm}}$

13. $5 + 0 = \underline{\hspace{1cm}}$ 14. $7 + 0 = \underline{\hspace{1cm}}$ 15. $7 + 3 = \underline{\hspace{1cm}}$

© Copyright 1999   ACSI Mathematics Grade 2

Subtraction Facts to 10   Lesson 19

Write the sum in the diamond. Write subtraction facts for each dot card.

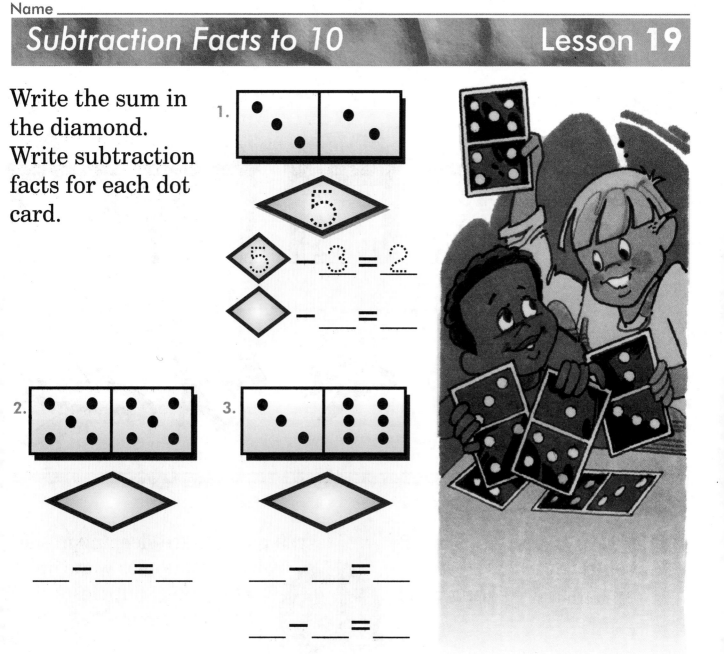

1.

5

$5 - 3 = 2$

___ − ___ = ___

2.

___ − ___ = ___

3.

___ − ___ = ___

___ − ___ = ___

Draw dots to make an addition fact. Write subtraction facts to match.

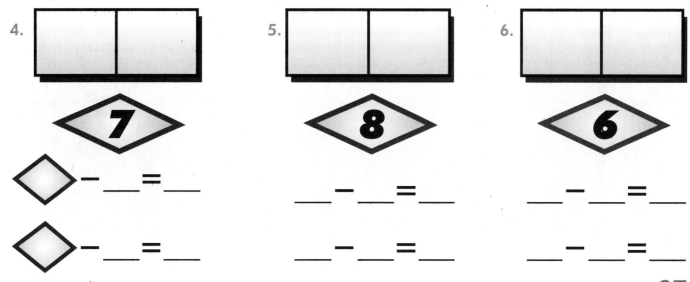

4.

7

___ − ___ = ___

___ − ___ = ___

5.

8

___ − ___ = ___

___ − ___ = ___

6.

6

___ − ___ = ___

___ − ___ = ___

7. Draw a line from the hangar to the airplane with the correct answer.

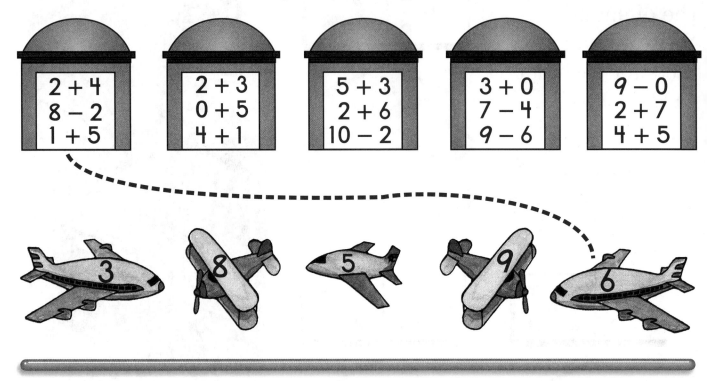

Solve.

8. There are 10 horses eating. 2 horses gallop away. How many horses are eating now?

_____

9. 9 puppies are sleeping in the barn. 3 puppies wake up. How many puppies are still sleeping?

_____

Review Add.

1. 3
   + 4

2. 5
   + 2

3. 6
   + 3

4. 6
   + 1

5. 3
   + 5

6. 4
   + 1

7. 6
   + 2

8. 3
   + 0

9. 7
   + 2

10. 4
    + 6

© Copyright 1999 Mathematics Grade 2

Adding in Any Order — Lesson 20

Write fact combinations. Let the pictures help you.

1. Write all the facts for sums of 9.

_0_ + _9_   ___ + ___   ___ + ___

___ + ___   ___ + ___   ___ + ___

___ + ___   ___ + ___   ___ + ___

          ___ + ___

2. Write all the facts for sums of 10.

_0_ + _10_   ___ + ___   ___ + ___

___ + ___   ___ + ___   ___ + ___

___ + ___   ___ + ___   ___ + ___

___ + ___   ___ + ___

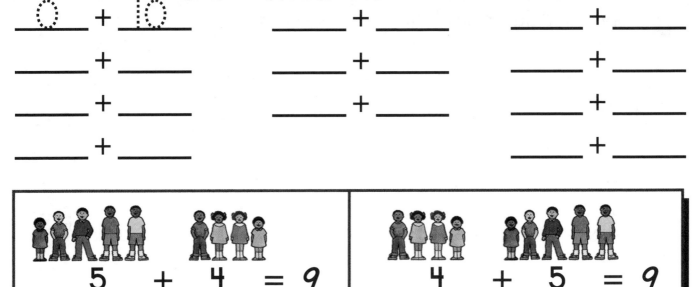

$5 + 4 = 9$
addends   sum

$4 + 5 = 9$
addends   sum

The order of the addends does not change the sum.

3. Follow the path to the cross on the hill. Choose the path by coloring only problems with a sum of 10.

↓ Start Here

3+7	3+3	7+0	5+2	3+5	1+6	4+4		
7+0	8+2	5+2	3+4	6+1	5+1	2+6		
3+1	5+5	4+3	1+7	4+4	2+3	4+6	7+2	7+1
5+3	6+4	2+7	6+5	3+3	10+0	4+4	4+5	6+2
1+4	3+7	2+1	2+2	2+8	5+3	3+8	5+2	5+1
2+2	1+6	1+9	5+5	1+8	3+6	2+6	4+5	4+3

Review   Add or subtract.

| 1. | 3 | 2. | 4 | 3. | 5 | 4. | 9 | 5. | 7 |
| | +2 | | +6 | | −3 | | −1 | | +3 |

| 6. | 7 | 7. | 4 | 8. | 3 | 9. | 8 | 10. | 4 |
| | −2 | | −1 | | +0 | | −5 | | +5 |

11. Complete the number pattern.

| 31 | | 51 | 61 | | | 91 |

© Copyright 1999   Mathematics Grade 2

Fact Families: Sums to 10

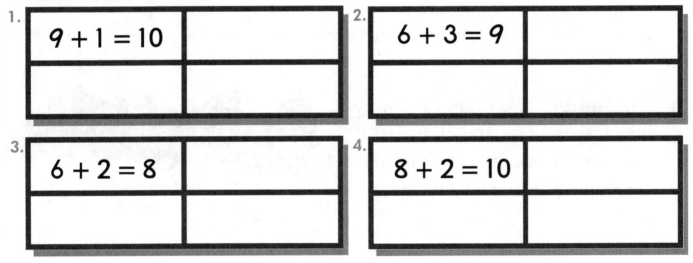

Part + Part = Whole

Whole − Part = Part

Whole 7		$5 + 2 = 7$	$2 + 5 = 7$
Part 5	Part 2	$7 - 5 = 2$	$7 - 2 = 5$

You can make four related sentences with these numbers.
This is a fact family.

1.

$9 + 1 = 10$	

2.

$6 + 3 = 9$	

3.

$6 + 2 = 8$	

4.

$8 + 2 = 10$	

Write the family facts for each picture.

5. $3 + 1 = 4$

_____

_____

_____

6. $4 + 5 = 9$

_____

_____

_____

Write the family facts.

7. $4 + 2 = 6$

$2 + 4 = 6$

_____

_____

8. $10 - 6 = 4$

_____

_____

_____

9. $7 - 2 = 5$

_____

_____

_____

10. $10 - 7 = 3$

_____

_____

_____

11. **Challenge:** Are there family facts for sums greater than 10? If you can think of an example, write it on the line below.

_____

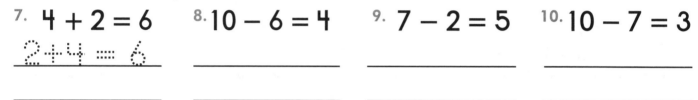

Review   Add or subtract.

1. $\begin{array}{r} 6 \\ +3 \\ \hline \end{array}$

2. $\begin{array}{r} 4 \\ -2 \\ \hline \end{array}$

3. $\begin{array}{r} 5 \\ +1 \\ \hline \end{array}$

4. $\begin{array}{r} 7 \\ -3 \\ \hline \end{array}$

5. $\begin{array}{r} 5 \\ +5 \\ \hline \end{array}$

6. $\begin{array}{r} 10 \\ -2 \\ \hline \end{array}$

7. $\begin{array}{r} 9 \\ -4 \\ \hline \end{array}$

8. $\begin{array}{r} 6 \\ +3 \\ \hline \end{array}$

9. $\begin{array}{r} 3 \\ +7 \\ \hline \end{array}$

10. $\begin{array}{r} 9 \\ -5 \\ \hline \end{array}$

© Copyright 1999 *Mathematics Grade 2*

Adding Doubles

When the two parts are the same, the numbers are called doubles.
Write the parts and add.

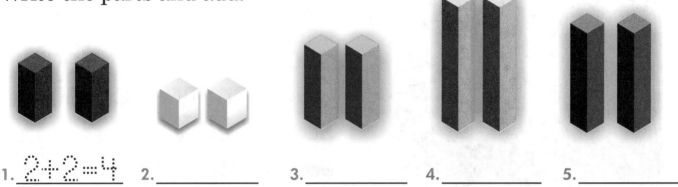

1. _2+2=4_   2. _____   3. _____   4. _____   5. _____

Circle and add the problems that are doubles.

6. 3 +2	7. 4 +4	8. 5 +5	9. 2 +2	10. 6 +3	11. 3 +3	12. 1 +1
___	_8_	___	___	___	___	___

The wrapped boxes contain the same objects as the opened boxes.
Write the parts and add.

13.

14.

15.

_3+3=6_   _____   _____

16.

17.

_____   _____

"Thus Noah did;
according to all that
God commanded him,
so he did."

Genesis 6:22

Use the Scripture to complete the sentence.

18. _____ should do _____ _____ commands.
      (Your name)

Use the animals in the picture to count by twos.

19. ____ ____ ____ ____ ____ ____ ____ ____ ____

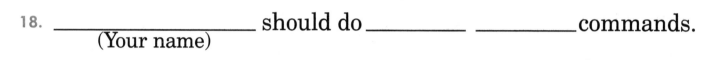

Use the animals to write doubles problems.

kangaroo ears   **squirrel feet**

20. ☐ + ☐ = ☐   21. ☐ + ☐ = ☐

elephant trunks   **chicken toes**

22. ☐ + ☐ = ☐   23. ☐ + ☐ = ☐

Complete the pattern.

24.

| 1 | 1 | 2 | 2 | 2 | 4 | 3 | 3 | 6 | | | | | | |

© Copyright 1999   Mathematics Grade 2

Review: Addition and Subtraction Facts — Lesson 23

Read the story and solve.

Joel started with 7¢. He lost 3¢ then found 6¢. He bought candy for 5¢. How much money does he have now?

Circle the signs (+ or −). Enter the numbers.

1. $\boxed{7¢} \; {}^+_-\; \boxed{} = \boxed{} \; {}^+_-\; \boxed{} = \boxed{} \; {}^+_-\; \boxed{} = \boxed{}$

Write all the facts for each sum.

2. **5**

0 + 5 = 5
_____
_____
_____
_____
_____

3. **3**

_____
_____
_____
_____

4. **2**

_____
_____
_____

5. **6**

_____
_____
_____
_____
_____
_____

Circle problems that have a sum or difference of 6.

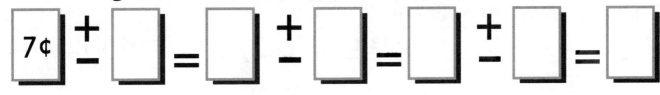

6. (3 + 3)   7. 8 − 2   8. 7 + 3   9. 10 − 4

10. 5 + 4   11. 4 + 4   12. 7 − 1   13. 9 − 3

1 2 3 4 5 6 7 8 9 10 11 12 13 14

Count on or count back. Write the number.

14. **Begin with:**	Count on 3
7	10
6	_____
5	_____

15. **Begin with:**	Count back 2
10	_____
6	_____
8	_____

16. **Begin with:**	Count on 2
5	_____
6	_____
8	_____

Write the other family facts.

17. $8 - 3 = 5$

$8 - 5 = 3$

_____

_____

18. $4 + 3 = 7$

_____

_____

_____

19. $10 - 1 = 9$

_____

_____

_____

20. **Bonus:** How many different combinations of addends are there in the sum of 7? _____ What is the rule? _____

_____ .

Add or subtract.

21. $\begin{array}{r} 3 \\ +6 \\ \hline \end{array}$ 22. $\begin{array}{r} 8 \\ -2 \\ \hline \end{array}$ 23. $\begin{array}{r} 5 \\ +4 \\ \hline \end{array}$ 24. $\begin{array}{r} 9 \\ -4 \\ \hline \end{array}$ 25. $\begin{array}{r} 5 \\ +5 \\ \hline \end{array}$ 26. $\begin{array}{r} 7 \\ +2 \\ \hline \end{array}$

27. $\begin{array}{r} 10 \\ -6 \\ \hline \end{array}$ 28. $\begin{array}{r} 3 \\ +3 \\ \hline \end{array}$ 29. $\begin{array}{r} 8 \\ -6 \\ \hline \end{array}$ 30. $\begin{array}{r} 6 \\ -2 \\ \hline \end{array}$ 31. $\begin{array}{r} 2 \\ +6 \\ \hline \end{array}$ 32. $\begin{array}{r} 9 \\ +0 \\ \hline \end{array}$

© Copyright 1999 Mathematics Grade 2

Adding and Subtracting to 12 — Lesson 24

+	1				5	6
1	2					
5						
6						12

1. Complete the addition block.

2. Find and color a number pattern.

3. Explain the pattern you found. _____

_____

_____

4. Complete the subtraction block.

5. Find and color a number pattern.

6. Explain the pattern you found. _____

_____

_____

−	12	11	10	9	8	7
1	11					
5						
6						1

7.
$$\begin{array}{r} 3 \\ +\ 9 \\ \hline \end{array}$$

8.
$$\begin{array}{r} 11 \\ -\ 7 \\ \hline \end{array}$$

9.
$$\begin{array}{r} 8 \\ +\ 3 \\ \hline \end{array}$$

10.
$$\begin{array}{r} 12 \\ -\ 4 \\ \hline \end{array}$$

11.
$$\begin{array}{r} 12 \\ -\ 5 \\ \hline \end{array}$$

12.
$$\begin{array}{r} 6 \\ +\ 5 \\ \hline \end{array}$$

When the pet store closed at 5:00 p.m., the animals found a way to play. Solve the pet store problems.

13. There were 12 cats in all. Two escaped from their cages. How many cats were left in cages?

_____

14. 3 goldfish were in bowls. 9 goldfish were in a large tank. How many goldfish altogether?

_____

Review   Count the colored shapes.
Use the shapes to add and subtract.

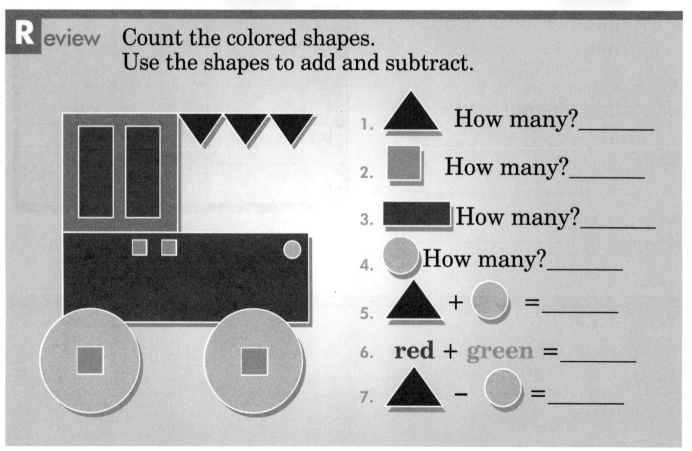

1. How many?_____
2. How many?_____
3. How many?_____
4. How many?_____
5. ▲ + ● = _____
6. **red** + green = _____
7. ▲ – ● = _____

© Copyright 1999   Mathematics Grade 2

Problem Solving: Addition and Subtraction   Lesson 25

Circle the correct operation word and sign. Write the problem and solve.

1. 3 ducks and 5 geese. How many birds?

   add

   subtract _____ ⊞ _____ = _____
   (+ / −)

2. 7 pigs and 3 horses.
   How many more pigs than horses?

   add

   subtract _____ ⊞ _____ = _____
   (+ / −)

3. Julio has 6 balloons. Karen gives him 2 more.
   How many balloons does he have in all?

   add

   subtract _____ ⊞ _____ = _____
   (+ / −)

4. 10 glasses. 4 are full. The rest are empty.
   How many glasses are empty?

   add

   subtract _____ ⊞ _____ = _____
   (+ / −)

Think 5 houses. 3 windows and one door on each house.

5. Total windows:_____   6. Total doors:_____

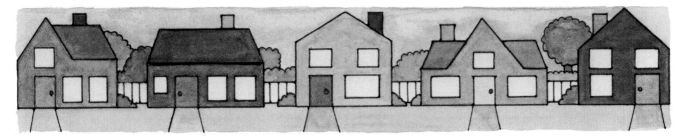

© Copyright 1999 ACSI Mathematics Grade 2

Look at the playground picture. Make up two problems to solve.

7. _____ $\begin{array}{c}+\\-\end{array}$ _____ = _____   8. _____ $\begin{array}{c}+\\-\end{array}$ _____ = _____

Draw the remaining boxes to make doubles problems.

9. $4 +$ _____ = _____   10. _____ $+$ _____ = _____   11. _____ $+$ _____ = _____

Draw your own doubles problem and solve.

12. _____ $+$ _____ = _____

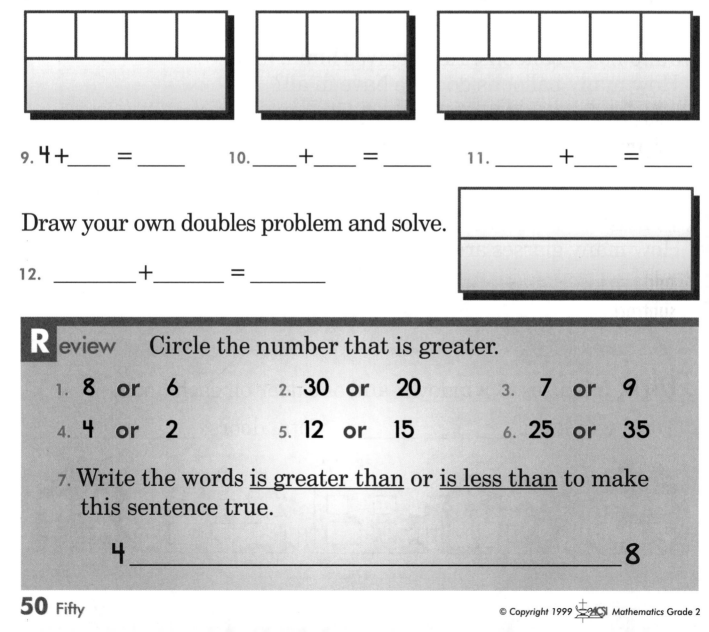

Review   Circle the number that is greater.

1. **8 or 6**   2. **30 or 20**   3. **7 or 9**

4. **4 or 2**   5. **12 or 15**   6. **25 or 35**

7. Write the words <u>is greater than</u> or <u>is less than</u> to make this sentence true.

    4 _____ 8

© Copyright 1999   Mathematics Grade 2

Facts Practice: Sums to 12 Lesson 26

Match the pictures to the correct problems. Write the letter of the problem on the line. Write the numbers in the boxes.

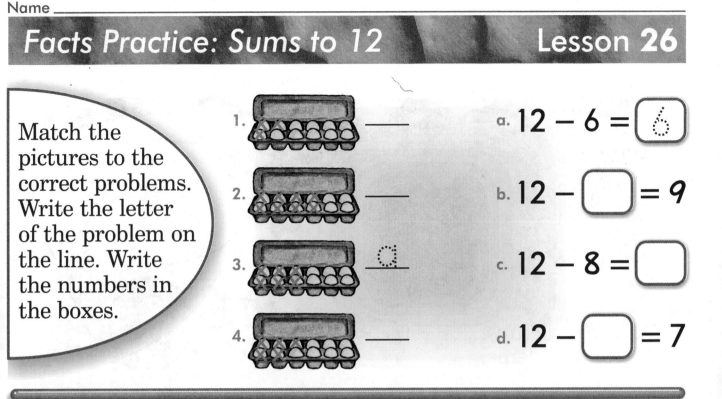

1. _____

2. _____

3. __a__

4. _____

a. $12 - 6 = \boxed{6}$

b. $12 - \boxed{} = 9$

c. $12 - 8 = \boxed{}$

d. $12 - \boxed{} = 7$

Mark off the eggs to show these problems, then solve.

5. $12 - 3 =$ ___

6. $12 - 7 =$ ___

Write the subtraction problems shown by the egg cartons.

7. _____

8. _____

9. _____

10. _____

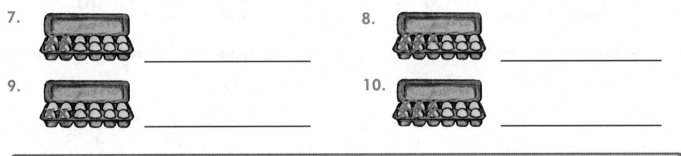

11. Draw a picture to show the problem. Write the number sentence and solve it.

Six eggs were found on Monday. 5 were gathered on Tuesday. How many eggs altogether?

$\boxed{} \; \square \; \boxed{} = \boxed{}$

Look at the picture.
Write the problems.

12. 10 baby chicks.
5 chicks are dry.
_____chicks are
getting wet.

$$\boxed{}-\boxed{}=\boxed{}\text{ chicks}$$

13. 5 chicks are under the mother
hen's wings. 1 chick is under her
right wing. _____chicks are
under her left wing.

$$\boxed{}-\boxed{}=\boxed{}\text{ chicks}$$

Review   Add.

1.	2.	3.	4.	5.	6.
8 + 2	4 + 6	7 + 4	2 + 9	5 + 7	6 + 3

7.	8.	9.	10.	11.	12.
6 + 6	8 + 4	3 + 5	7 + 5	5 + 4	9 + 3

13.	14.	15.	16.	17.	18.
4 + 4	6 + 4	5 + 5	2 + 7	5 + 6	3 + 8

© Copyright 1999　ACSI Mathematics Grade 2

Doubles Plus One

Listen to the story. Use counters to show the problem.

$5 + 5 = 10$

$5 + 6 =$ _____

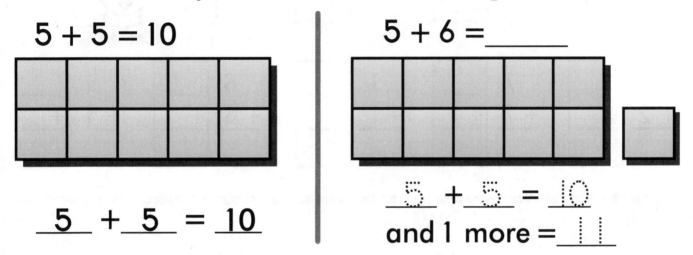

_5_ + _5_ = _10_

_5_ + _5_ = _10_
and 1 more = _11_

Add. Write the doubles facts that can help you solve the problems.

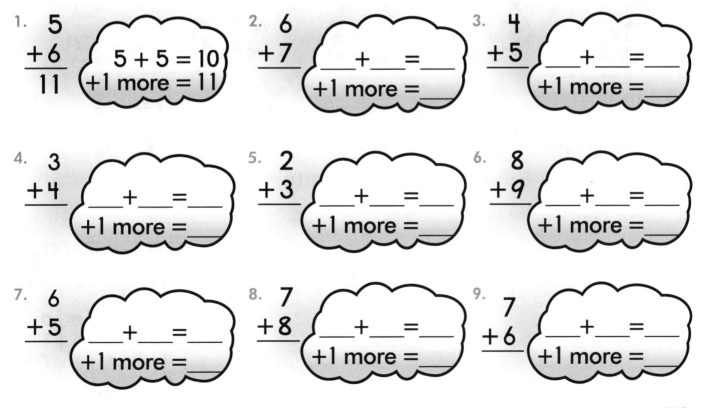

1. 5
   +6
   ‾‾
   11   5 + 5 = 10
          +1 more = 11

2. 6
   +7
   ‾‾   ___ + ___ = ___
          +1 more = ___

3. 4
   +5
   ‾‾   ___ + ___ = ___
          +1 more = ___

4. 3
   +4
   ‾‾   ___ + ___ = ___
          +1 more = ___

5. 2
   +3
   ‾‾   ___ + ___ = ___
          +1 more = ___

6. 8
   +9
   ‾‾   ___ + ___ = ___
          +1 more = ___

7. 6
   +5
   ‾‾   ___ + ___ = ___
          +1 more = ___

8. 7
   +8
   ‾‾   ___ + ___ = ___
          +1 more = ___

9. 7
   +6
   ‾‾   ___ + ___ = ___
          +1 more = ___

Solve the doubles facts. Next to each problem write a <u>doubles</u> <u>plus</u> <u>1</u> fact.

> 4 + 5 = ?
> 4 + 4 = 8
> +1 more = 9

10.
$$5 \\ +5 \over 10$$
$$5 \\ +6 \over 11$$

11.
$$6 \\ +6$$
$$\underline{} \\ +$$

12.
$$3 \\ +3$$
$$\underline{} \\ +$$

13.
$$2 \\ +2$$
$$\underline{} \\ +$$

14.
$$7 \\ +7$$
$$\underline{} \\ +$$

15.
$$1 \\ +1$$
$$\underline{} \\ +$$

16.
$$8 \\ +8$$
$$\underline{} \\ +$$

17.
$$4 \\ +4$$
$$\underline{} \\ +$$

R eview

5 fish are in each of 5 bowls. How many fish altogether? What will help you solve the problem?

1. Count by?_____ 2. _____ _____ _____ _____ _____

Make letters worth money and write the value of words.

3. bus = 2 + 1 + 4 = _____ cents

4. star = _____ + _____ + _____ + _____ = _____ cents

5. Which is worth more, the word "math" or the word "rich?"_____

6. How much is your first name worth?_____

7. Your last name?_____

1¢	2¢	3¢	4¢	5¢
A	B	C	D	E
F	G	H	I	J
K	L	M	N	O
P	Q	R	S	T
U	V	W	X	Y
Z				

© Copyright 1999   ACSI Mathematics Grade 2

Doubles Minus One   Lesson 28

Count the boxes to show doubles minus one.

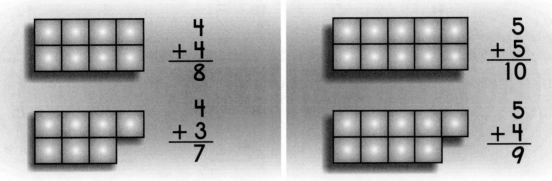

$$\begin{array}{r} 4 \\ +\,4 \\ \hline 8 \end{array}$$

$$\begin{array}{r} 4 \\ +\,3 \\ \hline 7 \end{array}$$

$$\begin{array}{r} 5 \\ +\,5 \\ \hline 10 \end{array}$$

$$\begin{array}{r} 5 \\ +\,4 \\ \hline 9 \end{array}$$

Draw boxes to show the doubles minus one method of addition.

1. 8 + 7 = _____

2. 5 + 4 = _____

3. 6 + 5 = _____

4. 7 + 6 = _____

Draw dots to change the double to a double minus one problem. Solve.

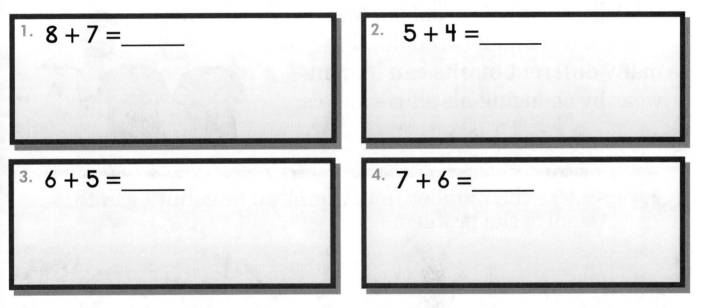

5.   14   →   13

$$\begin{array}{r} 7 \\ +\,7 \\ \hline 14 \end{array}$$

$$\begin{array}{r} 7 \\ +\,6 \\ \hline 13 \end{array}$$

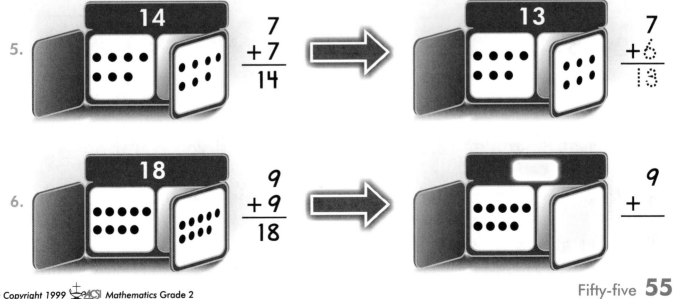

6.   18   →

$$\begin{array}{r} 9 \\ +\,9 \\ \hline 18 \end{array}$$

$$\begin{array}{r} 9 \\ +\, \\ \hline \end{array}$$

Look for doubles to solve the problems.

7.	8.	9.	10.	11.	12.
5 + 5	4 + 4	3 + 4	5 + 4	1 + 1	7 + 6

13.	14.	15.	16.	17.	18.
2 + 3	2 + 2	6 + 5	1 + 2	8 + 9	8 + 7

19. **Think** Solve this problem. Martin has 3 shirts and 2 baseball caps. How many different outfits can Martin wear by changing his shirts and caps?

_____

Review   Use the number line. Count on or count back to solve the problems.

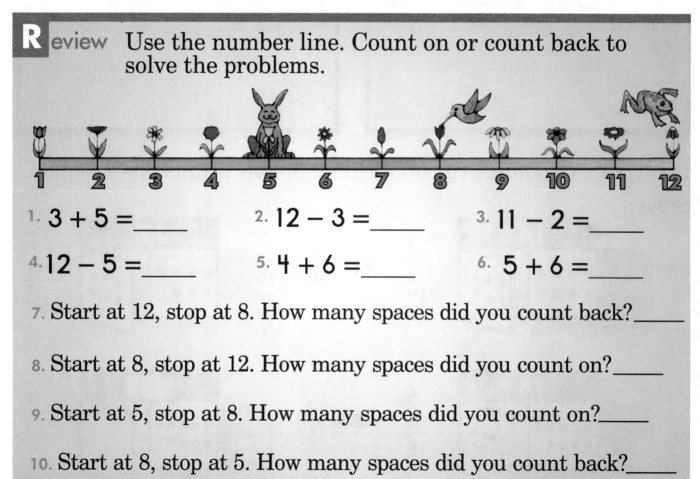

1. $3 + 5 =$ ____

2. $12 - 3 =$ ____

3. $11 - 2 =$ ____

4. $12 - 5 =$ ____

5. $4 + 6 =$ ____

6. $5 + 6 =$ ____

7. Start at 12, stop at 8. How many spaces did you count back? ____

8. Start at 8, stop at 12. How many spaces did you count on? ____

9. Start at 5, stop at 8. How many spaces did you count on? ____

10. Start at 8, stop at 5. How many spaces did you count back? ____

© Copyright 1999   Mathematics Grade 2

Solving Picture Problems   Lesson 29

BEFORE

Samantha and
her father went
bowling.

AFTER

Here's how the pins looked
before Samantha's first turn.

Next is how the pins
looked after the turn.

1. Write the numbers and signs to show what happened on her first turn.

_____ ◯ _____ ◯ _____

BEFORE

Samantha had
another turn. Here
is what happened.

AFTER

2. Write the numbers and signs to show what happened on her second turn.

_____ ◯ _____ ◯ _____

The pins are colored in **red** for the first turn and **blue** for the second
turn. Color Samantha's pins to record her two turns. Count her father's
pins. Write the numbers in the blanks.

3.

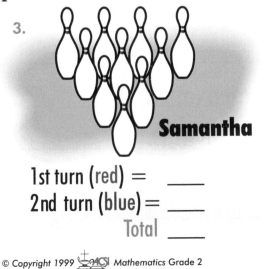

Samantha

1st turn (red) = _____
2nd turn (blue) = _____
    Total _____

4.

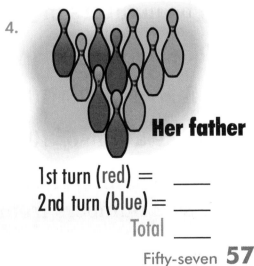

Her father

1st turn (red) = _____
2nd turn (blue) = _____
    Total _____

© Copyright 1999 Mathematics Grade 2

Write a number sentence for each picture problem.

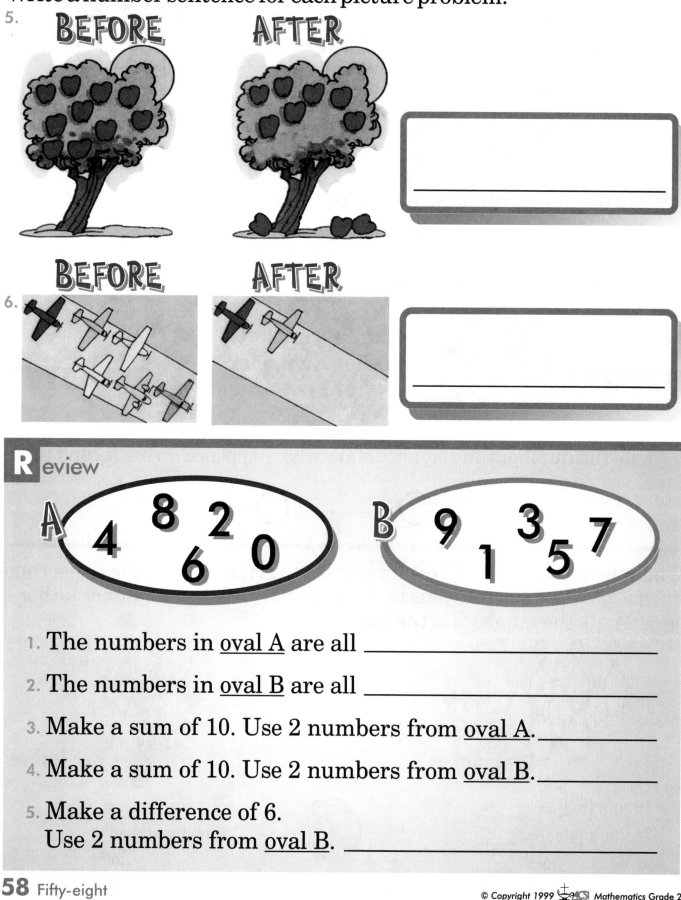

5. **BEFORE**   **AFTER**

_____

6. **BEFORE**   **AFTER**

_____

Review

A   4   8   2   6   0

B   9   3   7   1   5

1. The numbers in <u>oval A</u> are all _____

2. The numbers in <u>oval B</u> are all _____

3. Make a sum of 10. Use 2 numbers from <u>oval A</u>. _____

4. Make a sum of 10. Use 2 numbers from <u>oval B</u>. _____

5. Make a difference of 6.
   Use 2 numbers from <u>oval B</u>. _____

© Copyright 1999   Mathematics Grade 2

1. Circle problems with answers greater than 6.

$3 + 4$ $5 + 4$ $2 + 6$ $8 - 4$

$9 - 3$ $1 + 5$ $10 - 3$ $2 + 4$

1 — 2 — 3 — 4 — 5 — 6 — **7** — 8 — 9 — 10 — 11 — 12 — 13 — 14 — 15 — 16 — 17 — 18 — 19 — 20

Solve only problems with answers of 9.

2. $\begin{array}{r} 6 \\ + 6 \\ \hline \end{array}$ 3. $\begin{array}{r} 3 \\ + 6 \\ \hline \end{array}$ 4. $\begin{array}{r} 7 \\ + 1 \\ \hline \end{array}$ 5. $\begin{array}{r} 2 \\ + 7 \\ \hline \end{array}$ 6. $\begin{array}{r} 3 \\ + 5 \\ \hline \end{array}$ 7. $\begin{array}{r} 9 \\ - 0 \\ \hline \end{array}$

8. $\begin{array}{r} 10 \\ - 1 \\ \hline \end{array}$ 9. $\begin{array}{r} 5 \\ + 5 \\ \hline \end{array}$ 10. $\begin{array}{r} 7 \\ + 2 \\ \hline \end{array}$ 11. $\begin{array}{r} 4 \\ + 5 \\ \hline \end{array}$ 12. $\begin{array}{r} 4 \\ + 4 \\ \hline \end{array}$ 13. $\begin{array}{r} 1 \\ + 8 \\ \hline \end{array}$

31 — 30 — 29 — 28 — 27 — 26 — 25 — 24 — 23 — 22 — 21 — 20

32
33
34
35
36
37

Solve. Fill the circle to identify the type of problem.

14. $\begin{array}{r} 9 \\ + 8 \\ \hline 17 \end{array}$ ○ Doubles   ○ Doubles +1   ● Doubles −1

15. $\begin{array}{r} 2 \\ + 2 \\ \hline \end{array}$ ○ Doubles   ○ Doubles +1   ○ Doubles −1

16. $\begin{array}{r} 4 \\ + 5 \\ \hline \end{array}$ ○ Doubles   ○ Doubles +1   ○ Doubles −1

17. $\begin{array}{r} 3 \\ + 4 \\ \hline \end{array}$ ○ Doubles   ○ Doubles +1   ○ Doubles −1

18. $\begin{array}{r} 7 \\ + 7 \\ \hline \end{array}$ ○ Doubles   ○ Doubles +1   ○ Doubles −1

19. $\begin{array}{r} 6 \\ + 5 \\ \hline \end{array}$ ○ Doubles   ○ Doubles +1   ○ Doubles −1

38 — 39 — 40 — 41 — 42 — 43 — 44 — 45 — 46 — 47 — 48 — 49 — 50

20. Use the number chain to count by 7's. Color the numbers lightly as you count. Write the numbers.

7 ___ ___ ___ ___ ___ ___

© Copyright 1999
Mathematics Grade 2

Use shape addition. Write the sums.

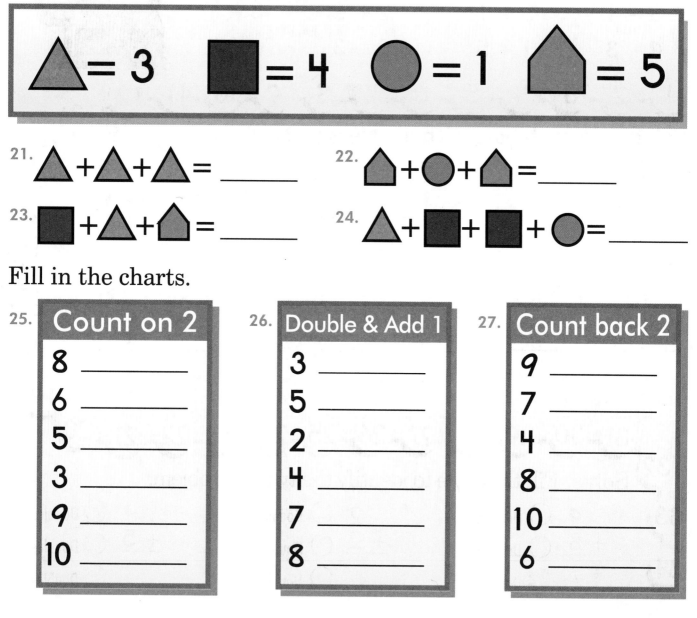

△ = 3   ■ = 4   ◯ = 1   ⬠ = 5

21. △ + △ + △ = _____

22. ⬠ + ◯ + ⬠ = _____

23. ■ + △ + ⬠ = _____

24. △ + ■ + ■ + ◯ = _____

Fill in the charts.

25.

Count on 2	
8	_____
6	_____
5	_____
3	_____
9	_____
10	_____

26.

Double & Add 1	
3	_____
5	_____
2	_____
4	_____
7	_____
8	_____

27.

Count back 2	
9	_____
7	_____
4	_____
8	_____
10	_____
6	_____

28. Write all the subtraction facts for 10.

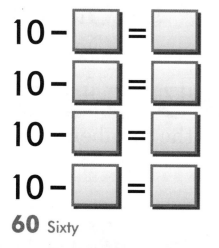
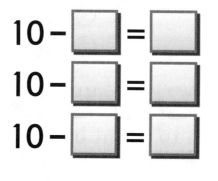
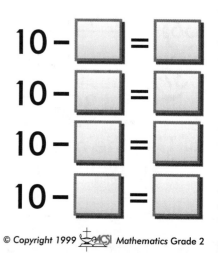

10 − ☐ = ☐   10 − ☐ = ☐   10 − ☐ = ☐

10 − ☐ = ☐   10 − ☐ = ☐   10 − ☐ = ☐

10 − ☐ = ☐   10 − ☐ = ☐   10 − ☐ = ☐

10 − ☐ = ☐   10 − ☐ = ☐

© Copyright 1999 ACSI Mathematics Grade 2

CHAPTER 3

Geometry and Measurement

For behold,
He who forms mountains,
And creates the wind...
The LORD God of hosts is His name.

Amos 4:13

Dear Parents,

A new friend will join us in Chapter Three of our math book. Your child will be invited to do measuring and shape activities with "Math Dog." Math Dog is a real-life dog that lives in San Diego, California. Locate San Diego on a map. Math Dog loves to play in the Pacific Ocean! Have your child locate a spot on the coast where Math Dog might swim.

As your child works on the lessons in this chapter, there are things you can do at home to promote understanding of geometry and measurement. As you go for a walk, ask your child to look for triangles, rectangles, and squares in fences, brick walls, or in signs.

Talk about how you use measuring at home; for example, in the kitchen, in the workshop, etc. Help your child measure the size of a room, the porch, or a garden. Have the child tell you whether his or her bed will fit in a different location in the bedroom. It is important to share ways that you use math both at home and at work. Thank you for your help in making math meaningful and fun for your child.

Math in Second Grade is going to be fun all year long!

© Copyright 1999

Classifying Shapes

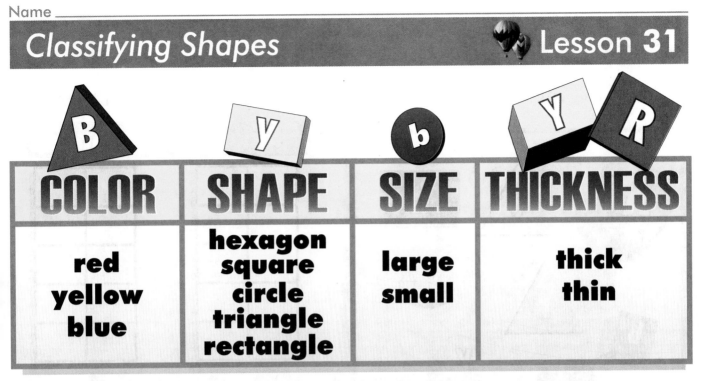

COLOR	SHAPE	SIZE	THICKNESS
red yellow blue	hexagon square circle triangle rectangle	large small	thick thin

Mark off the two blocks in each set that do not belong.

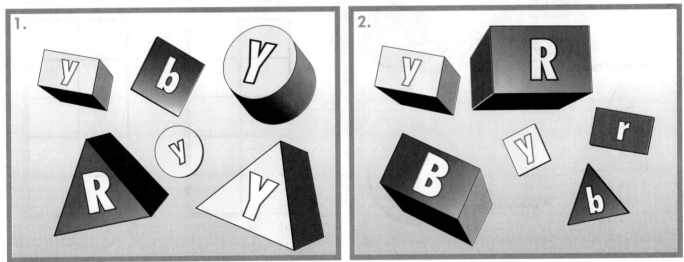

1.

2.

Circle the blocks that could go in the box.

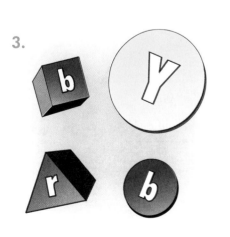

3.

4. Count the thick and thin shapes. Color blocks on the graph to match.

Thick and Thin Shapes

In the tens column put the numbers from triangle **A** in order from **least** to **greatest**. In the ones column put the numbers from triangle **B** in order from **greatest** to **least**. Write the numbers you made.

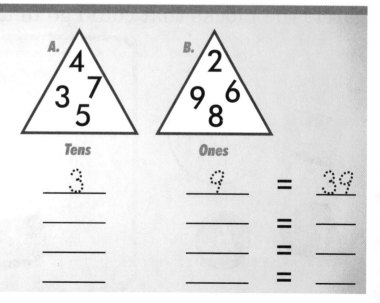

A. 4 3 7 5

B. 2 9 6 8

Tens   Ones

3   9   =   39

___   ___   =   ___

___   ___   =   ___

___   ___   =   ___

© Copyright 1999   Mathematics Grade 2

Circles and Spheres

Locate and underline all circles ⬤ and spheres ⬤.

The Circle family can win prizes for finding circular items.

1. Write the total number of circular items found. _____

2. Each item is worth five points. How many points does the Circle family have? _____

3. The Grand Prize, a stuffed lion, takes 75 points. Does the Circle family have enough points? _____

Count the number of circles and spheres in the flower.

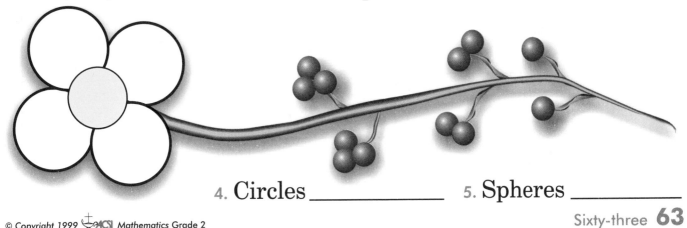

4. Circles _____   5. Spheres _____

6. Mark off objects that are circles.

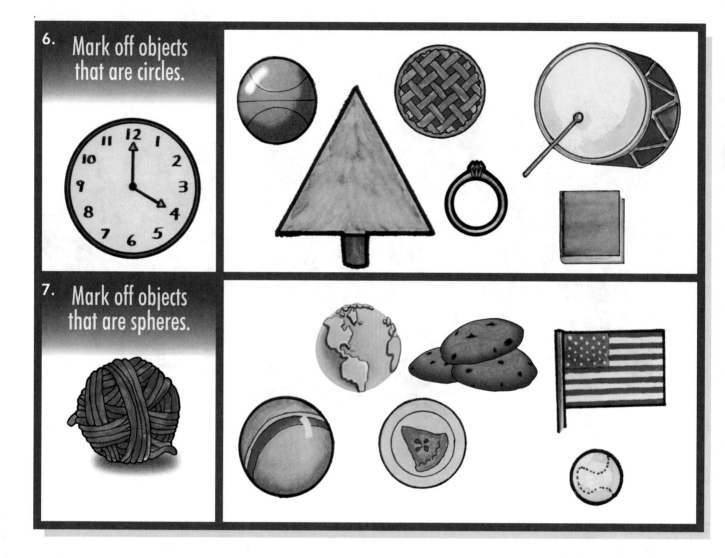

7. Mark off objects that are spheres.

Review

Look at the buttons. List 4 ways to classify them.

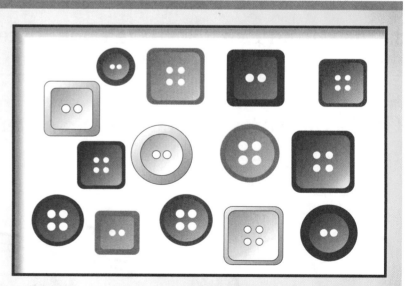

1. _____

2. _____

3. _____

4. _____

5. Draw a line from one button to another that shows a match by one or more attributes.

© Copyright 1999 Mathematics Grade 2

Triangles
Lesson 33

Use pattern blocks to cover Math Dog's picture. First estimate the number, then find the actual count.

	ESTIMATE	ACTUAL
1.	_____	_____
2.	_____	_____
3.	_____	_____
4.	_____	_____
5.	_____	_____

What shape does Math Dog's face remind you of?

Count the triangles.

6. _____ **large triangle**

7. _____ **medium triangles**

8. _____ **small triangles**

9. _____ **total triangles**

10. Continue the triangle pattern.

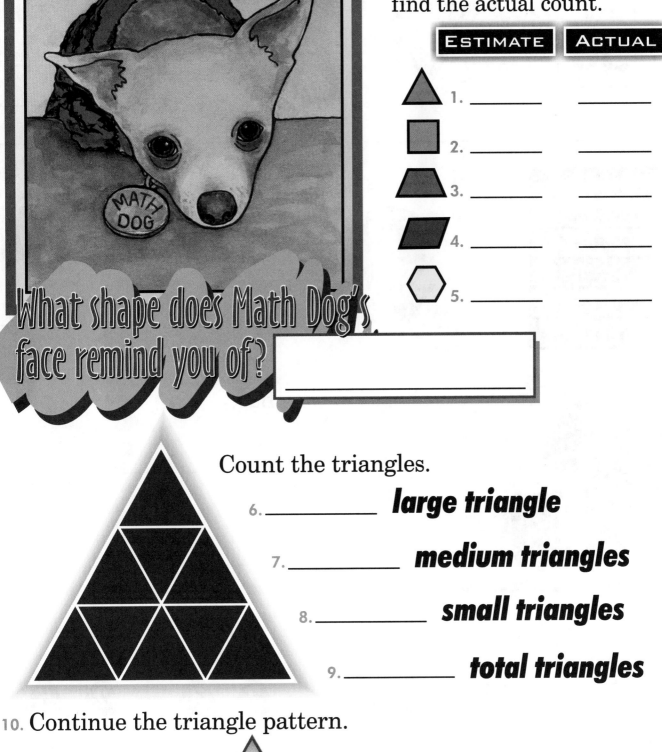

Write the name of the shape of the frame around each sign.

11. SPEED LIMIT 50

12. YIELD

13. DANGER HARD HAT AREA

14.

_____

_____   _____   _____

Word Bank
rectangle
square
circle
hexagon
triangle

Write the name of each shape.

15. _____

16. _____

_____

_____

Name the shapes in each flag.

17. _____   _____

18. _____   _____

Review

Use the triangles to make one addition and one subtraction fact.

1. 9 6 3

$6 + \square = \square$

$9 - 6 = \square$

2. 10 7 3

$\square + \square = \square$

$\square - \square = \square$

3. 7 2 5

$\square + \square = \square$

$\square - \square = \square$

© Copyright 1999 Mathematics Grade 2

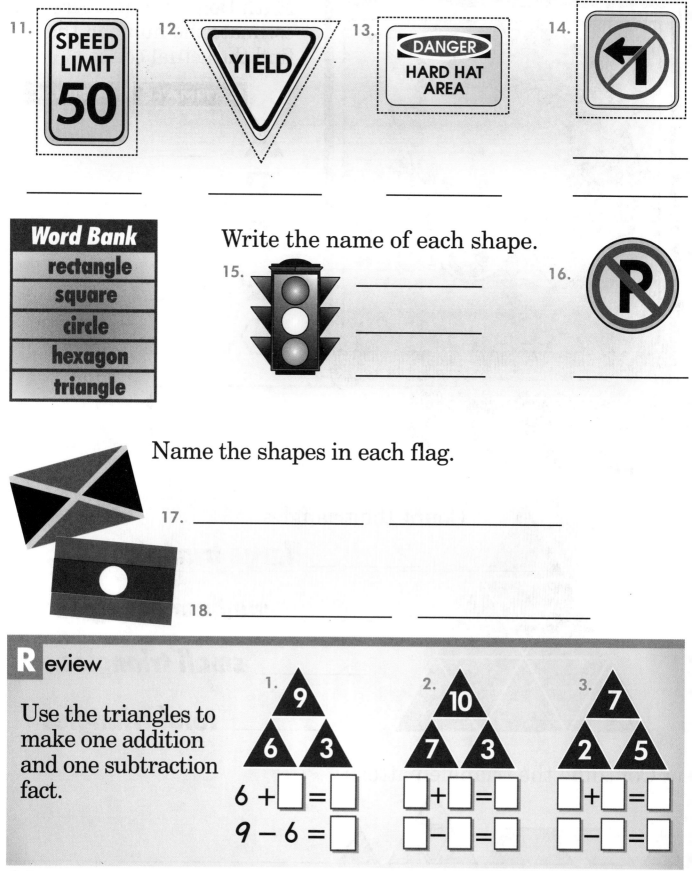

Four-Sided Shapes

Check each word that fits.

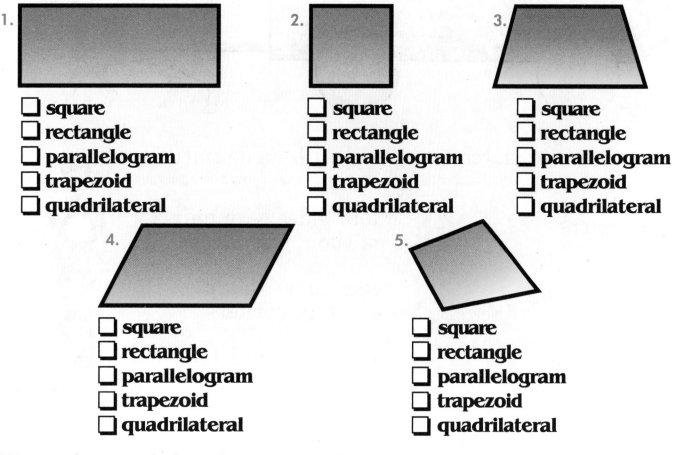

1.
- ☐ square
- ☐ rectangle
- ☐ parallelogram
- ☐ trapezoid
- ☐ quadrilateral

2.
- ☐ square
- ☐ rectangle
- ☐ parallelogram
- ☐ trapezoid
- ☐ quadrilateral

3.
- ☐ square
- ☐ rectangle
- ☐ parallelogram
- ☐ trapezoid
- ☐ quadrilateral

4.
- ☐ square
- ☐ rectangle
- ☐ parallelogram
- ☐ trapezoid
- ☐ quadrilateral

5.
- ☐ square
- ☐ rectangle
- ☐ parallelogram
- ☐ trapezoid
- ☐ quadrilateral

Write the word that describes <u>all</u> the above shapes.

6.

Write the number of each shape.

7._____

8._____

9._____

10._____

11._____

12._____

Draw a line to match each word with its definition.

13. **square**

14. **rectangle**

15. **trapezoid**

• four sides with only 2 of them parallel.

• four equal sides and 4 straight corners.

• four sides and 4 straight corners.

Review   Write the numbers.

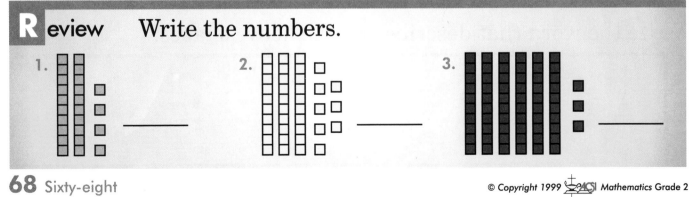

1. _____

2. _____

3. _____

© Copyright 1999 ACSI Mathematics Grade 2

Squares and Rectangles

Lesson 35

One unit is the distance <u>between</u> two pegs. Make each design on your own geoboard first. Then draw geobands on these pegs.

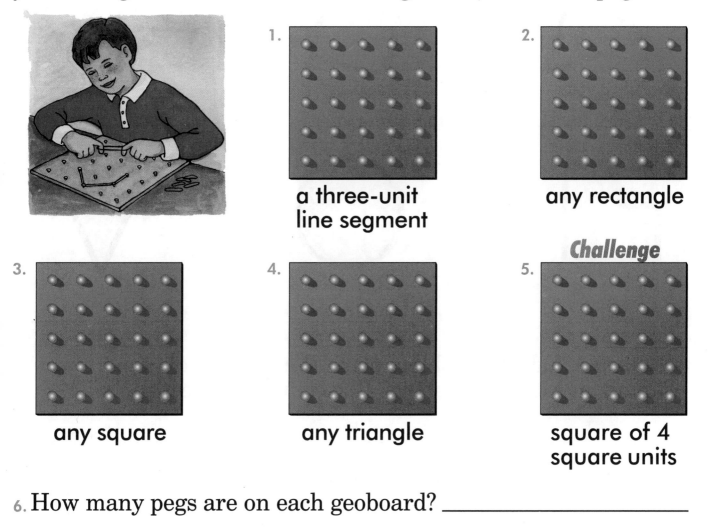

1. a three-unit line segment

2. any rectangle

3. any square

4. any triangle

5. **Challenge** square of 4 square units

6. How many pegs are on each geoboard? _____

Fill in the blanks.

squares   rectangles

7. Squares and rectangles are the <u>same</u> in 2 ways. Both have _____ sides and _____ square corners.
_{number}   _{number}

8. A rectangle with all sides the same length is a _____.

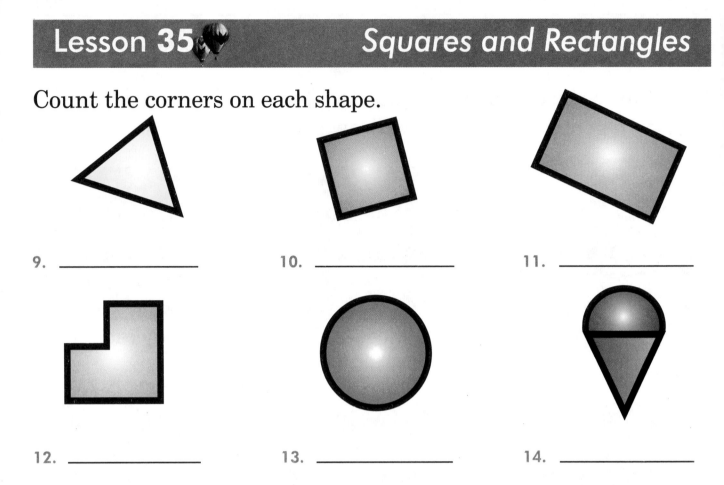
Count the corners on each shape.

9. _____

10. _____

11. _____

12. _____

13. _____

14. _____

15. Make an addition problem using the number of corners you found on each shape above. Use counters if needed.

____ + ____ + ____ + ____ + ____ + ____ = ____ corners

16. Draw 3 rectangles of different sizes in this space.
Use 3 different crayons to color.

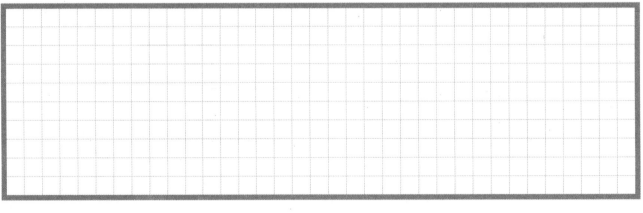

Moments in Careers

"My dad works as an engineer. In his work, he uses math to design buildings."   **Steven**, Corvallis, OR

© Copyright 1999 ACSI Mathematics Grade 2

Angles

When the sides of shapes meet, they form angles.

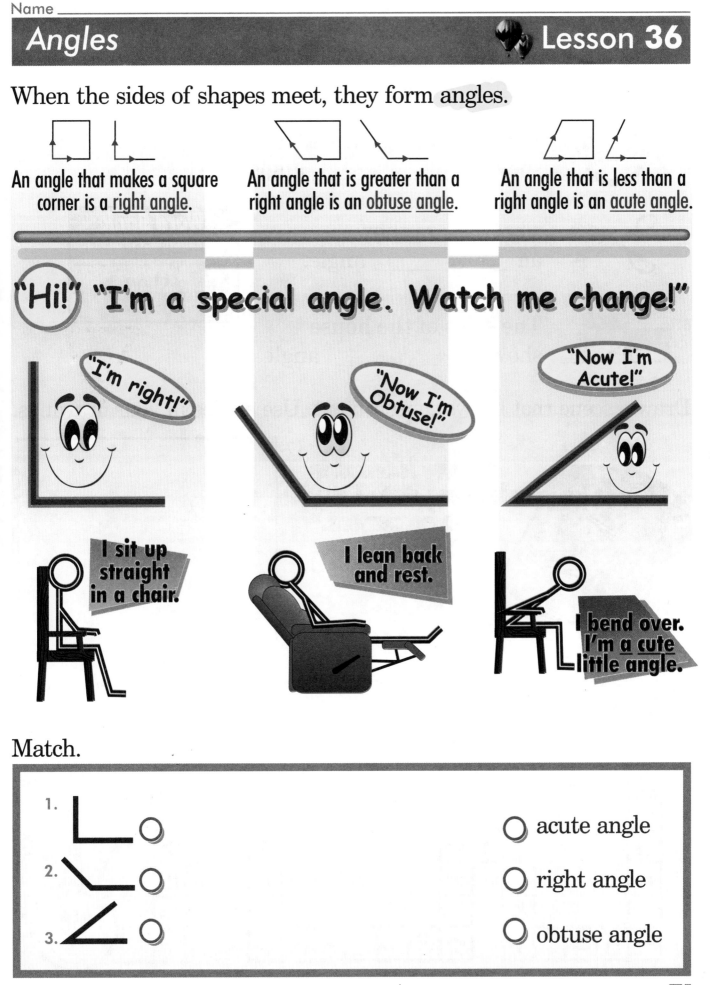

An angle that makes a square corner is a <u>right</u> angle.

An angle that is greater than a right angle is an <u>obtuse</u> angle.

An angle that is less than a right angle is an <u>acute</u> angle.

"Hi!" "I'm a special angle. Watch me change!"

"I'm right!"

"Now I'm Obtuse!"

"Now I'm Acute!"

I sit up straight in a chair.

I lean back and rest.

I bend over. I'm a cute little angle.

Match.

1. ◯
2. ◯
3. ◯

◯ acute angle

◯ right angle

◯ obtuse angle

© Copyright 1999 Mathematics Grade 2

Use the Word Bank to answer the questions.

4.  The hands of the clock show an _____ angle.

Word Bank
right
obtuse
acute

5. The scissors show an _____ angle.

6. The sides of the house show a _____ angle.

Draw a scene that shows contentment. Use angles in your drawings.

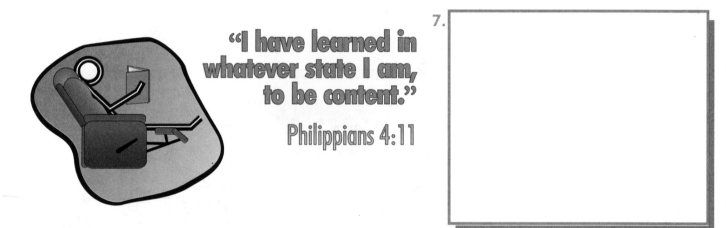

"I have learned in whatever state I am, to be content."

Philippians 4:11

7.

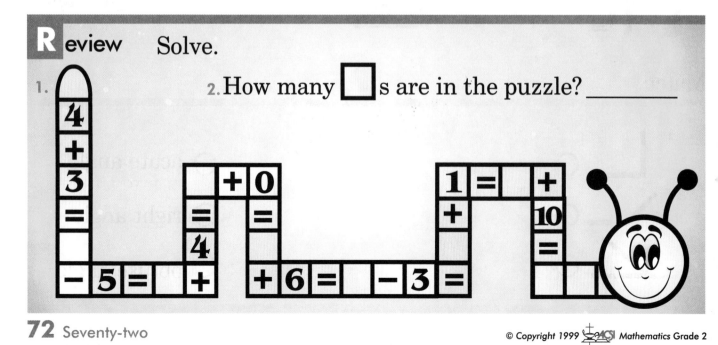

Review   Solve.

1.

2. How many ☐s are in the puzzle? _____

© Copyright 1999 Mathematics Grade 2

Patterns and Shapes in Our World  Lesson 37

Write the name of the shapes you see. Write the number you counted.

1. _____ _____

2. _____ _____

3. _____ _____

4. _____ _____

Word Bank
circle
triangle
square
rectangle

Circle the name of the shape.

5.

square
triangle

6.

circle
square

7.

circle
triangle

8.

circle
rectangle

9.

triangle
rectangle

10.

square
circle

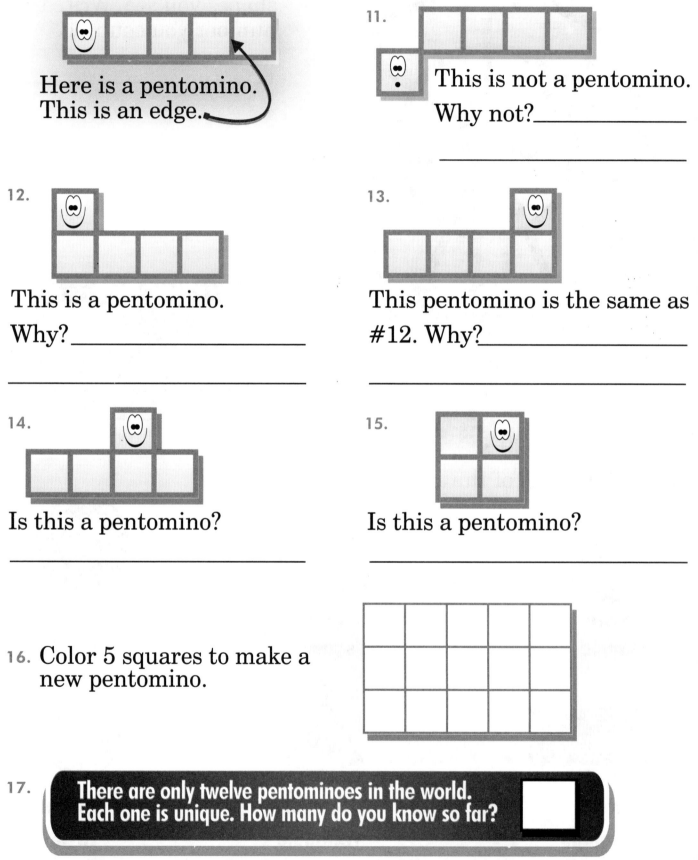
A pentomino has five squares connected by at least one edge.

Here is a pentomino.
This is an edge.

11. This is not a pentomino.
Why not?_____

_____

12. This is a pentomino.
Why?_____

_____

13. This pentomino is the same as
#12. Why?_____

_____

14. Is this a pentomino?

_____

15. Is this a pentomino?

_____

16. Color 5 squares to make a
new pentomino.

17. There are only twelve pentominoes in the world.
Each one is unique. How many do you know so far?

© Copyright 1999 Mathematics Grade 2

Shapes Review

Terry, Mick, and Dave are playing on the "shapes bars."

1. **Check the shapes you see.**

- ⬭ triangle
- ⬭ square
- ⬭ hexagon
- ⬭ rectangle
- ⬭ circle
- ⬭ trapezoid

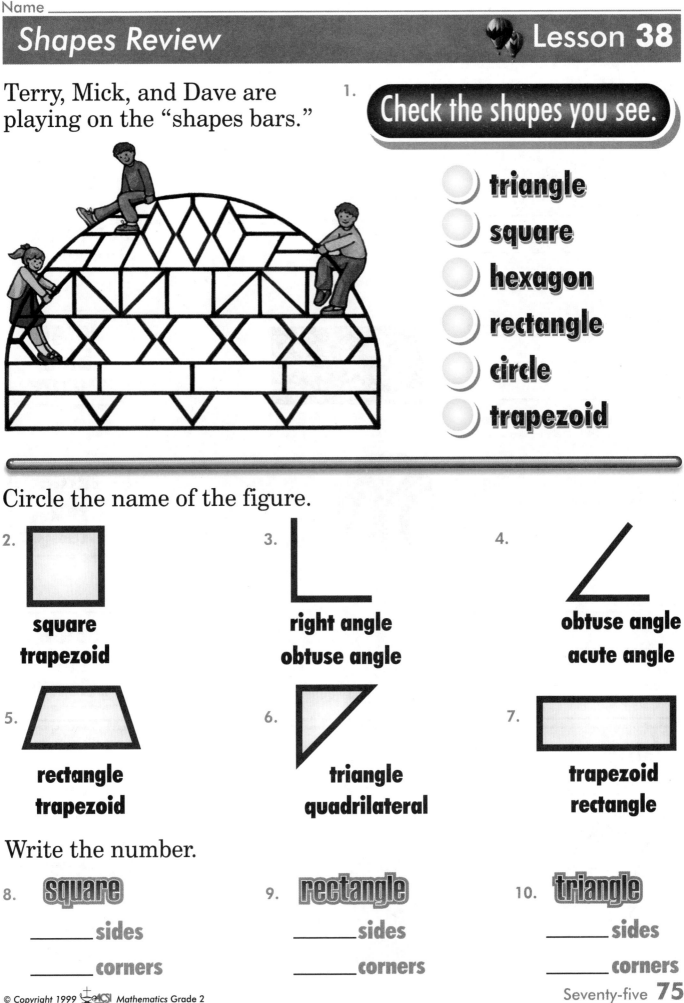

Circle the name of the figure.

2.
square
trapezoid

3.
right angle
obtuse angle

4.
obtuse angle
acute angle

5.
rectangle
trapezoid

6.
triangle
quadrilateral

7.
trapezoid
rectangle

Write the number.

8. **square**

_____ sides

_____ corners

9. **rectangle**

_____ sides

_____ corners

10. **triangle**

_____ sides

_____ corners

Write the 3 attributes of each shape on the lines. Connect the shapes to the boxes that are <u>one attribute different</u>.

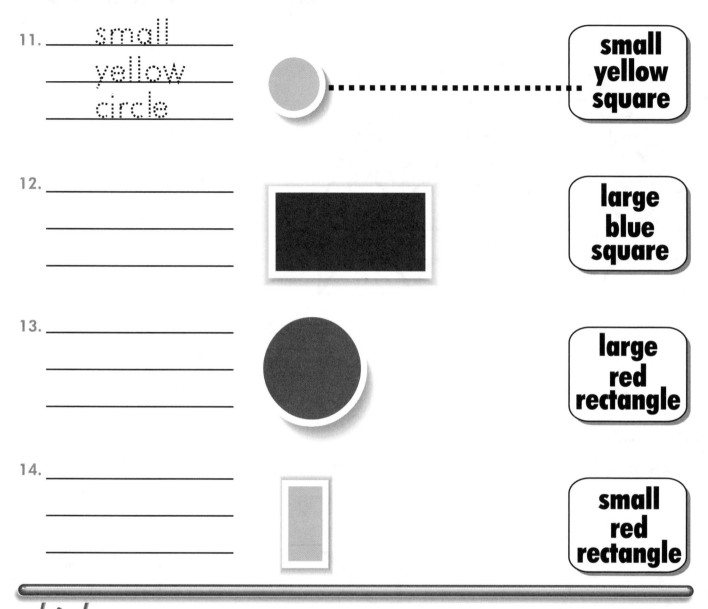

11. small
    yellow
    circle

small
yellow
square

12. _____
    _____
    _____

large
blue
square

13. _____
    _____
    _____

large
red
rectangle

14. _____
    _____
    _____

small
red
rectangle

Think Three children each have one shape. Cindy's shape has no corners, John's shape is not small and Henry's shape has 3 sides. Who has what shape? Write the names.

large, red square

small, green circle

large, green triangle

_____   _____   _____

© Copyright 1999   Mathematics Grade 2

Measurement: Inches   Lesson 39

INCHES	1	2	3	4	5	6

1. Circle objects less than one inch.

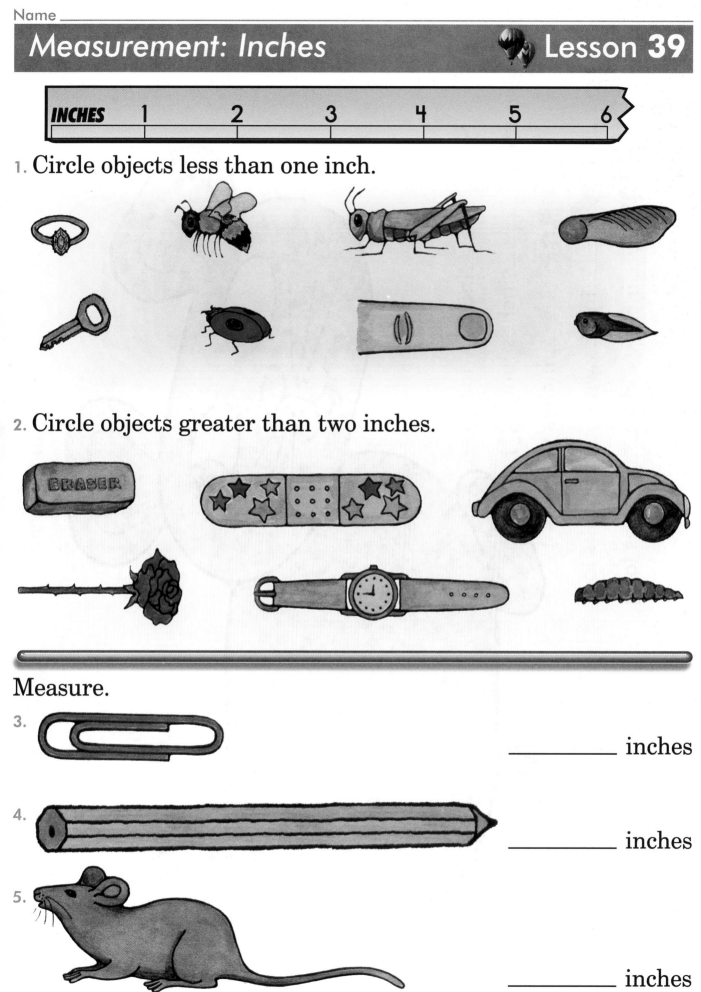

2. Circle objects greater than two inches.

Measure.

3. _____ inches

4. _____ inches

5. _____ inches

© Copyright 1999 Mathematics Grade 2

Measure each part of the mouse to the nearest inch. Measure wide ←——→ , long ↕ .

6. **Eye** ____ inches wide (←——→)

7. **Ear** ____ inches long (↕)

8. **Whisker** ____ inches wide (←——→)

9. **Head** ____ inches wide ____ inches long

10. **Body** ____ inches wide ____ inches long

11. **Tail** ____ inches long

Write more or less.

12. Is the mouse's foot more or less than two inches wide?

_____

© Copyright 1999   Mathematics Grade 2

Measurement: Feet Lesson 40

We use <u>inches</u> to measure short lengths. We use <u>feet</u> to measure longer lengths. 12 inches equal one foot.

How many feet long and wide do you think these blankets are?

1. What shapes and figures do you see? _____

_____

Would these real-life objects be more or less than one foot long?

2. **more**
    less

3. **more**
    less

4. **more**
    less

5. **more**
    less

6. **more**
    less

7. **more**
    less

© Copyright 1999 ACSI Mathematics Grade 2

Use your ruler to measure.

Draw your foot inside this foot. Measure your foot in inches.

8. **How <u>wide</u> (⟷) is your foot?**

_____ inches

9. **How <u>long</u> (↕) is your foot?**

_____ inches

10. **How <u>wide</u> is this foot?**

about _____ inches

11. **How <u>long</u> is this foot?**

about _____ inches

One foot is 12 inches long. Find 3 things in the classroom that are more than one foot in length. Write their names.

12. _____

13. _____

14. _____

Review Write the amount of money in each group.

1.

[   ] ¢

2.

[   ] ¢

© Copyright 1999 ACSI Mathematics Grade 2

Measurement: Yards — Lesson 41

1. Which family members would be taller than one yard? Make a ✔.

☐ **Dad**　　☐ **young boy**　　☐ **baby**

☐ **Mom**　　☐ **young girl**　　☐ **Math Dog**

☐ **teenager**

Circle the correct answer.

2. **A foot is:**　10 inches　　6 inches　　12 inches

3. **A yard is:**　12 feet　　3 feet　　6 feet

4. **A yard is:**　36 inches　　12 inches　　10 inches

Measure in inches.

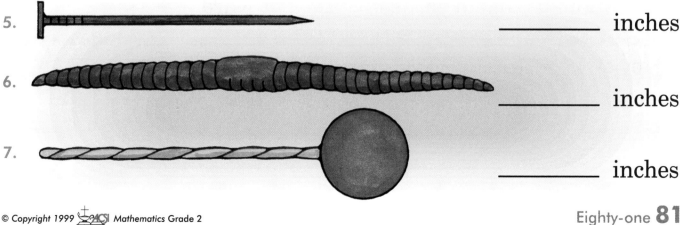

5. _____ inches

6. _____ inches

7. _____ inches

© Copyright 1999 ACSI Mathematics Grade 2

Circle each comparison word. Write a comparison story using the Word Bank.

Word Bank
horse
snake
man
river
cow
car
puppy
mouse

8. A _____ is taller than a _____.

9. A _____ is longer than a _____.

10. A _____ is larger than a _____.

11. **I am shorter than a** _____.

12. How can you measure this yarn? _____

13. How long is this yarn? _____ inches

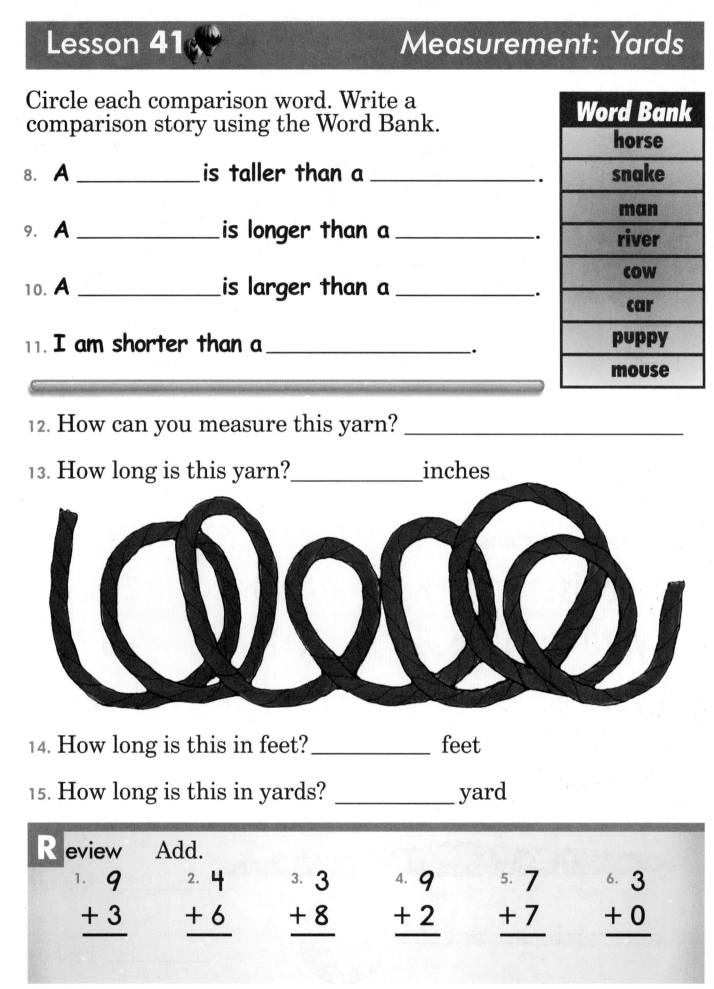

14. How long is this in feet? _____ feet

15. How long is this in yards? _____ yard

Review   Add.

1. 9	2. 4	3. 3	4. 9	5. 7	6. 3
+ 3	+ 6	+ 8	+ 2	+ 7	+ 0

© Copyright 1999 ACSI Mathematics Grade 2

Measurement: Centimeters

Circle the distance between the Centi-bees.

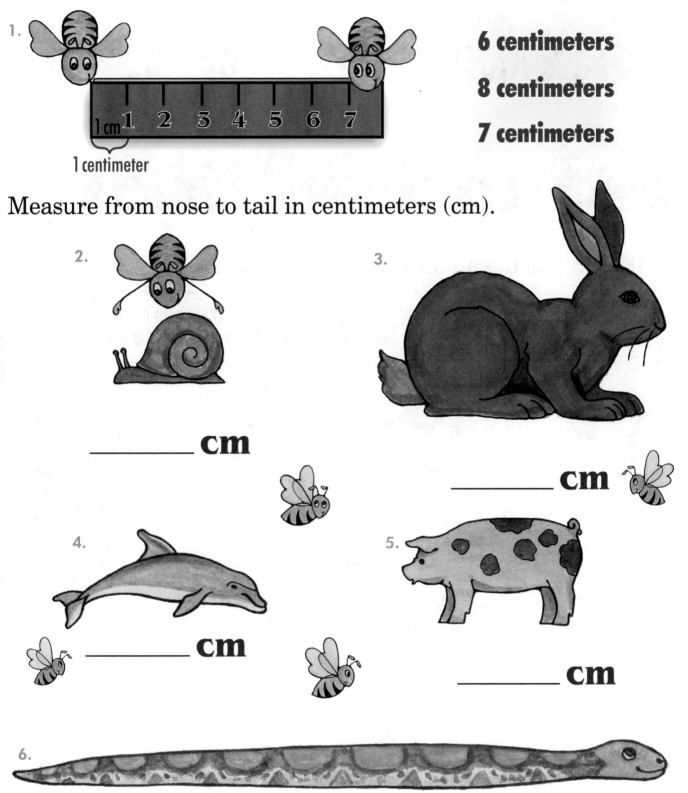

1.

6 centimeters

8 centimeters

7 centimeters

Measure from nose to tail in centimeters (cm).

2.

_____ **cm**

3.

_____ **cm**

4.

_____ **cm**

5.

_____ **cm**

6.

_____ **cm**

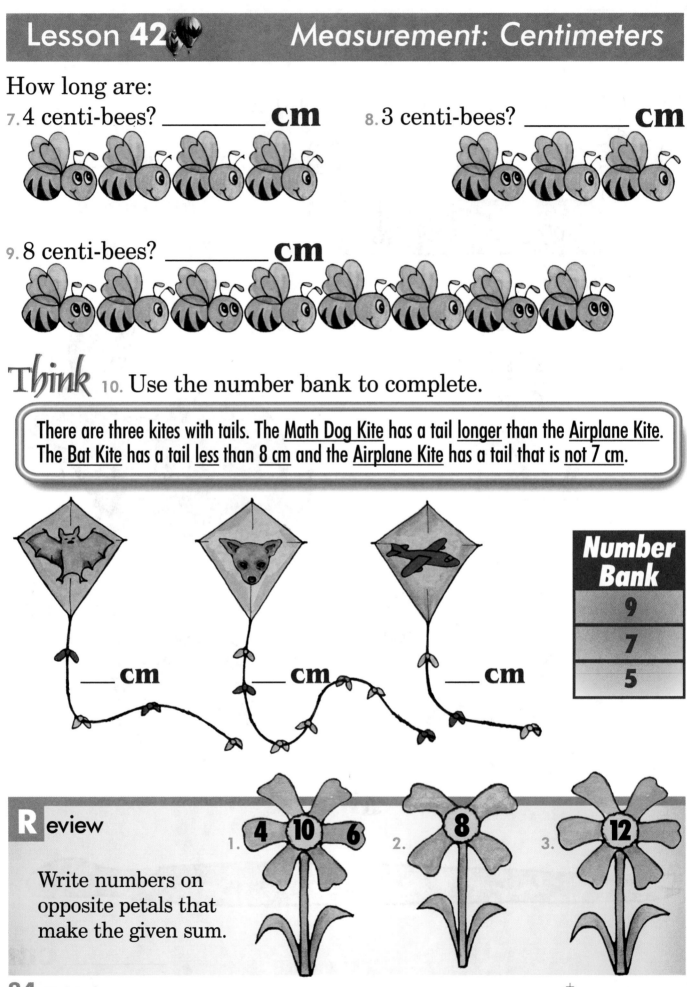

How long are:

7. 4 centi-bees? _____ **cm**

8. 3 centi-bees? _____ **cm**

9. 8 centi-bees? _____ **cm**

Think 10. Use the number bank to complete.

> There are three kites with tails. The <u>Math Dog Kite</u> has a tail <u>longer</u> than the <u>Airplane Kite</u>. The <u>Bat Kite</u> has a tail <u>less</u> than <u>8 cm</u> and the <u>Airplane Kite</u> has a tail that is <u>not 7 cm</u>.

___ cm   ___ cm   ___ cm

Number Bank

9
7
5

Review

Write numbers on opposite petals that make the given sum.

1. 4 10 6

2. 8

3. 12

© Copyright 1999 ACSI Mathematics Grade 2

one centimeter   one decimeter

0   10

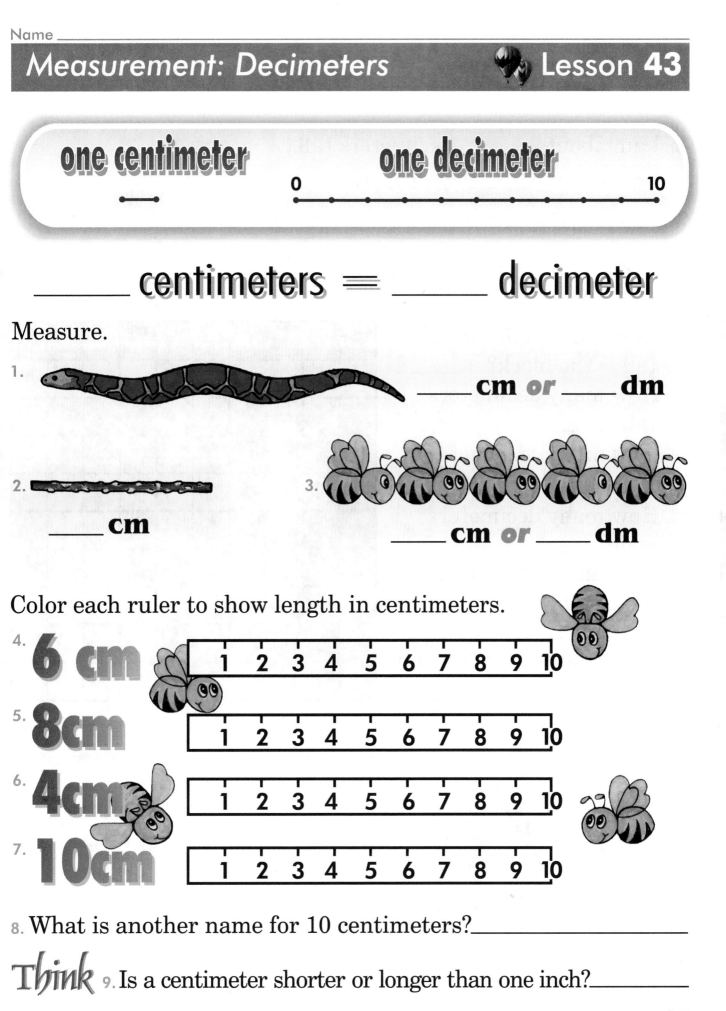

_____ centimeters ≡ _____ decimeter

Measure.

1.

_____ cm or _____ dm

2.

_____ cm

3.

_____ cm or _____ dm

Color each ruler to show length in centimeters.

4. **6 cm**

| 1 | 2 | 3 | 4 | 5 | 6 | 7 | 8 | 9 | 10 |

5. **8cm**

| 1 | 2 | 3 | 4 | 5 | 6 | 7 | 8 | 9 | 10 |

6. **4cm**

| 1 | 2 | 3 | 4 | 5 | 6 | 7 | 8 | 9 | 10 |

7. **10cm**

| 1 | 2 | 3 | 4 | 5 | 6 | 7 | 8 | 9 | 10 |

8. What is another name for 10 centimeters?_____

Think 9. Is a centimeter shorter or longer than one inch?_____

10. I am about _____ decimeters tall.

11. I am about _____ centimeters tall.

(Count by tens to show how tall you are in centimeters. Stop at the closest 10.)

10 20 ___ ___ ___ ___ ___ ___ ___ ___ ___ ___ ___

12. How many centimeters tall is the block?_____

13. How many decimeters tall?_____

14. How many centimeters wide is the block?_____

15. How many decimeters wide? _____

16. How many centimeter squares in the block?_____

17. How many decimeter rods fit into the block? _____

Review   Complete the pattern.

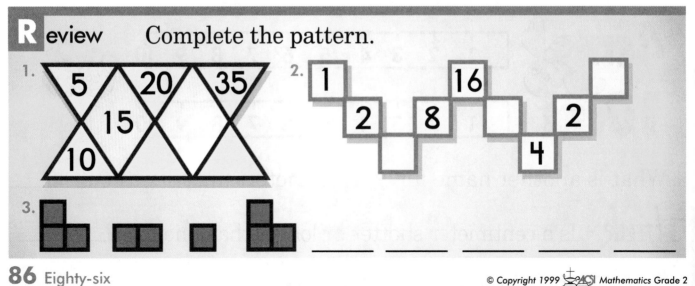

1. 5   20   35   15   10

2. 1   16   2   8   2   4

© Copyright 1999   Mathematics Grade 2

Measurement: Meters

1 **meter** is 100 centimeters.

1 **meter** is 10 decimeters.

I am about 2 meters (m) tall.

1 METER

How tall am I?

1. About how tall is the basketball player?_____ m
2. About how tall is the child?_____ m
3. About how high is the basket?_____ m

What unit would you use to measure these real-life objects?
Circle the best answer.

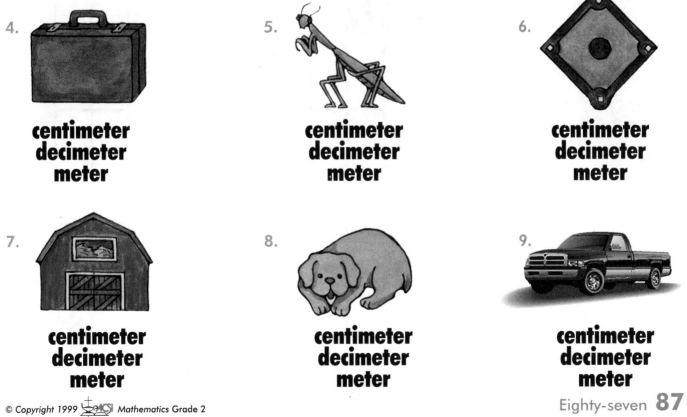

4.
**centimeter
decimeter
meter**

5.
**centimeter
decimeter
meter**

6.
**centimeter
decimeter
meter**

7.
**centimeter
decimeter
meter**

8.
**centimeter
decimeter
meter**

9.
**centimeter
decimeter
meter**

Circle the best answer.

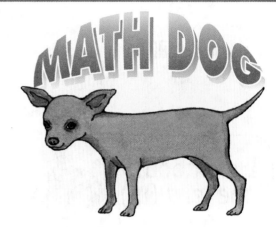

10. Math Dog's ears
    centimeter OR **decimeter**

11. Math Dog's tail
    centimeter OR **meter**

12. Math Dog's body
    decimeter OR **meter**

13. Math Dog's legs
    centimeter OR **decimeter**

Answer.

14. **One meter=** _____ **centimeters**

15. **One meter=** _____ **decimeters**

16. **One decimeter=** _____ **centimeters**

Review

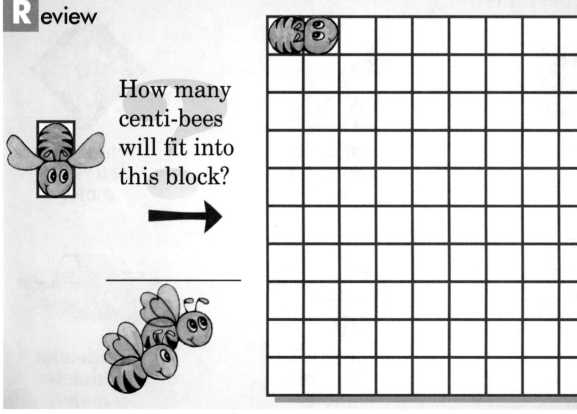

How many centi-bees will fit into this block?

_____

© Copyright 1999 Mathematics Grade 2

Name the shapes.

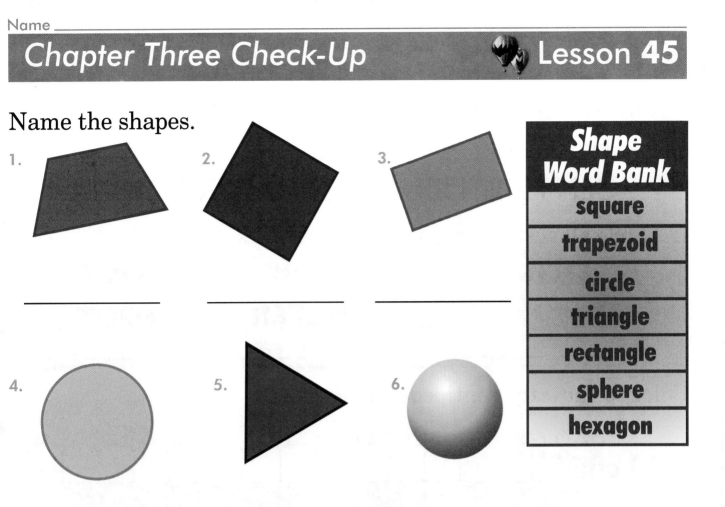

1. _____

2. _____

3. _____

4. _____

5. _____

6. _____

Shape Word Bank

square
trapezoid
circle
triangle
rectangle
sphere
hexagon

Mark off ☒ the pairs that match by at least one attribute. Write the attribute on the line.

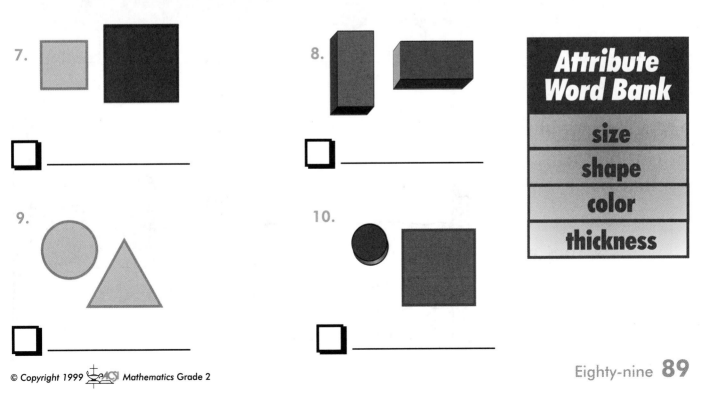

7. ☐ _____

8. ☐ _____

9. ☐ _____

10. ☐ _____

Attribute Word Bank

size
shape
color
thickness

11. Circle all metric measurement units.

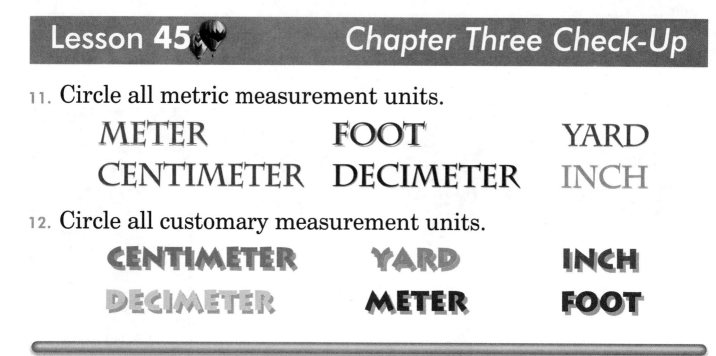

METER   FOOT   YARD

CENTIMETER   DECIMETER   INCH

12. Circle all customary measurement units.

CENTIMETER   YARD   INCH

DECIMETER   METER   FOOT

Color to show the centipedes' lengths.

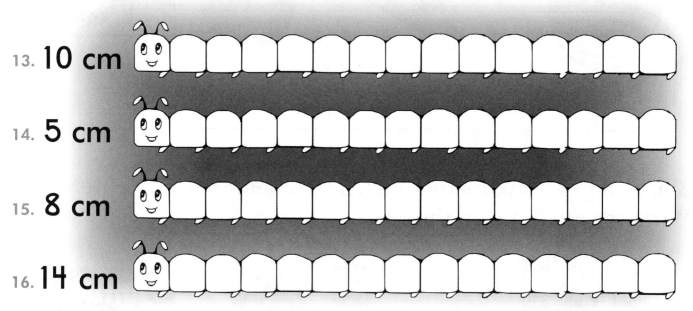

13. **10 cm**

14. **5 cm**

15. **8 cm**

16. **14 cm**

Measure the length of the bed in inches.

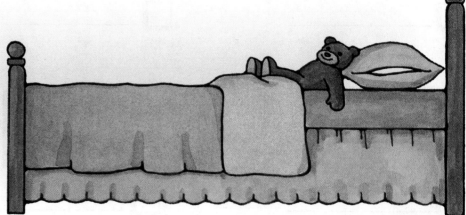

17. _____ inches

© Copyright 1999   Mathematics Grade 2

CHAPTER 4

Place Value to 999

Praise the LORD from the earth,
Creeping things and flying fowl.

Psalm 148:7a and 10b

Dear Parents,

BIG, BIG, BIG numbers are the focus of Chapter Four. This chapter is designed to help students understand and identify place value of ones, tens, and hundreds. To promote understanding, your child will use base ten blocks to form 3-digit numbers. The students will learn to read, write, compare, and order numbers to 999.

One way that place value will be reinforced is through the use of games. You can play place value games at home by writing each number (0 through 9) on three sets of index cards. The directions for one game, which is played with a partner, follow:

• Mix the 30 cards; place them facedown.
• Each player will take turns drawing from the pile until they have three cards.
• The players will use their cards to make a number, then compare the ones, tens, and hundreds. For example, Player A might make the number 462. Player B might form the number 835.
• Scoring will be done by assigning points for the greater number in each place: 1 point for the greater number of ones, 2 points for the greater number of tens, and 3 points for the greater number of hundreds. According to this, Player A would receive 2 points for having the greater number of tens; Player B would receive 5 points (4 for the greater number of hundreds plus 1 point for the greater number of ones).
• Play is continued. The first person to reach 20 points is the winner.

You can use the same cards for another activity. Put the cards in a basket or bag. Have your child draw three cards and make the greatest three-digit number possible. Have him or her draw three more cards and make the least number possible. Later in the year the cards can be used to form three-digit numbers for adding and subtracting.

Have your child listen and watch for large numbers. Ask questions such as, *"Is that more or less than 500? What is the number that comes just before and after that number?"*

We are going to work hard, but we will have fun with BIG numbers!

© Copyright 1999 Mathematics Grade 2

Introduction to 3- and 4-Digit Numbers — Lesson 46

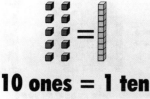

10 ones = 1 ten

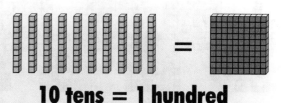

10 tens = 1 hundred

Mr. Murphy's second grade students are collecting data about the school library. The librarian told Robbie that on Monday students in grades 1 through 5 checked out two hundred eighty-five books. What does this number mean, and what should Robbie write down?

hundreds	tens	ones
2	8	5

You need three places for hundreds.

Read the number:
        two hundred eighty-five

Write the number: 285

Count the hundreds, the tens, and the ones. Write the number.

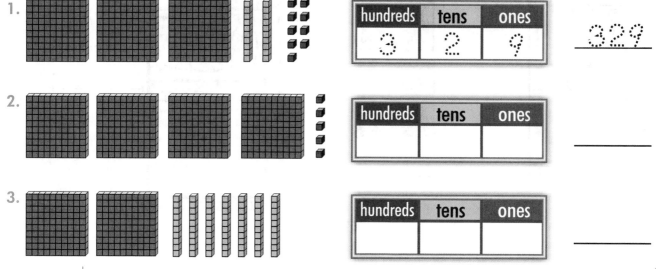

1.

hundreds	tens	ones
3	2	9

329

2.

hundreds	tens	ones

_____

3.

hundreds	tens	ones

_____

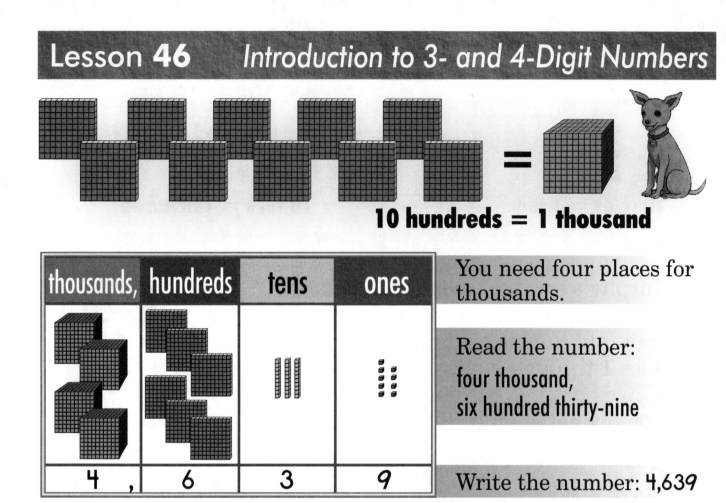

10 hundreds = 1 thousand

thousands,	hundreds	tens	ones
4 ,	6	3	9

You need four places for thousands.

Read the number:
four thousand,
six hundred thirty-nine

Write the number: 4,639

Think 4. What is the largest four-digit number you can make?

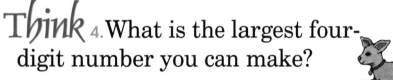

Review   Help Goldilocks measure each bed in centimeters. Write if the bed belongs to <u>Momma</u> Bear, <u>Poppa</u> Bear, or <u>Baby</u> Bear.

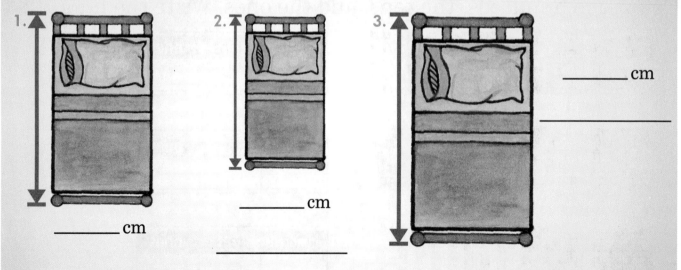

1. _____ cm

_____

2. _____ cm

_____

3. _____ cm

_____

© Copyright 1999   *Mathematics Grade 2*

Building Numbers to 100 — Lesson 47

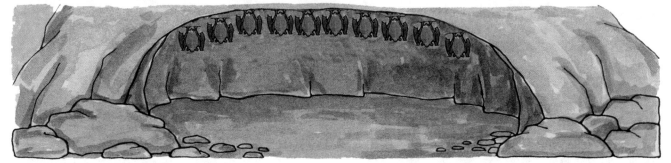

Write the numbers.

1. ____ **tens** ____ **ones**   2. ____ **tens** ____ **ones**

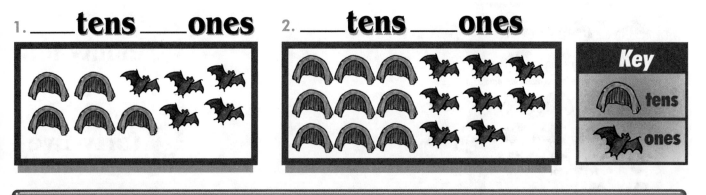

Key

tens

ones

Write the number.

3. ____   4. ____   5. ____

Draw caves and bats to build these numbers.

6. 37   7. 60   8. 82

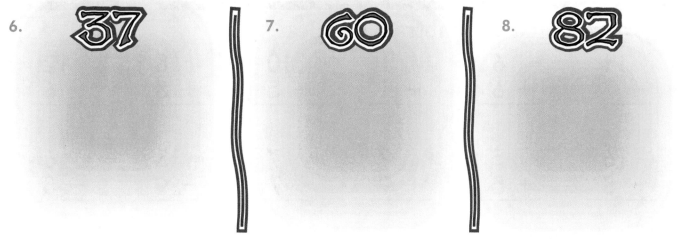

© Copyright 1999 ACSI Mathematics Grade 2

Match the picture to the number word.

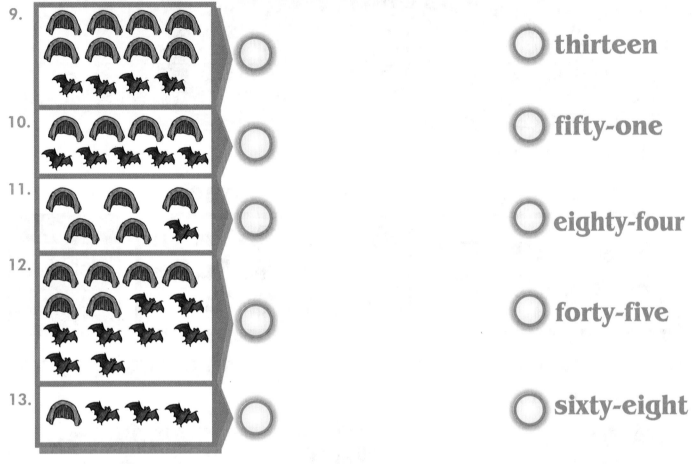

9.

10.

11.

12.

13.

○ thirteen

○ fifty-one

○ eighty-four

○ forty-five

○ sixty-eight

SOLVE. 14. There are fifty stars on the United States flag. How many tens and ones are there?_____

15. If there were 29 bats in a barn and 9 flew out, how many groups of ten would be left?_____

Review   Add and subtract doubles.

1. 14	2. 6	3. 4	4. 10	5. 8	6. 12
− 7	+ 6	+ 4	− 5	+ 8	− 6

7. 16	8. 5	9. 9	10. 7	11. 18	12. 6
− 8	+ 5	+ 9	+ 7	− 9	− 3

© Copyright 1999 Mathematics Grade 2

Building Numbers to 200 — Lesson 48

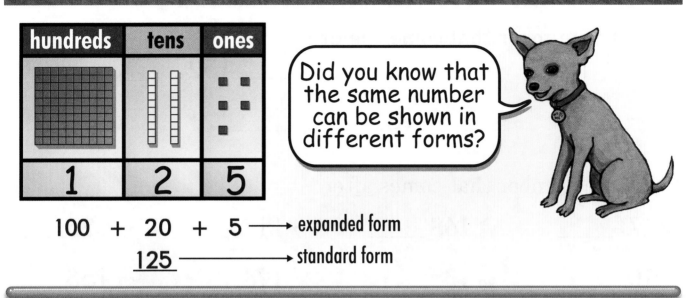

hundreds	tens	ones
1	2	5

Did you know that the same number can be shown in different forms?

100 + 20 + 5 ⟶ expanded form

125 ⟶ standard form

Write each number in expanded and standard form.

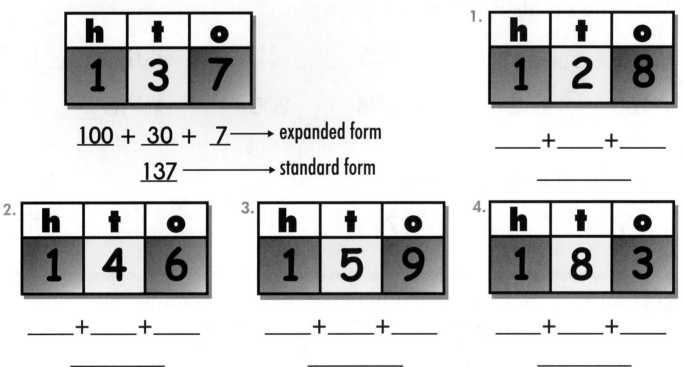

h	t	o
1	3	7

100 + 30 + 7 ⟶ expanded form

137 ⟶ standard form

1.

h	t	o
1	2	8

___+___+___

_____

2.

h	t	o
1	4	6

___+___+___

_____

3.

h	t	o
1	5	9

___+___+___

_____

4.

h	t	o
1	8	3

___+___+___

_____

SOLVE.

5. On Tuesday the school library loaned 100 picture books, 70 chapter books, and 9 animal books. How many books were checked out?

_____

6. On Wednesday, 100 books were returned by second graders. 60 were returned by third graders. How many books were returned on Wednesday?

_____

Write the number that comes <u>before</u>.

7. __112__ 113   8. _____ 130   9. _____ 152   10. _____ 109

11. _____ 167   12. _____ 181   13. _____ 124   14. _____ 146

Write the number that comes <u>after</u>.

15. 171 _____   16. 168 _____   17. 149 _____   18. 125 _____

19. 107 _____   20. 134 _____   21. 198 _____   22. 153 _____

Write the number that comes <u>between</u>.

23. 114 _____ 116   24. 129 _____ 131   25. 187 _____ 189

26. 160 _____ 162   27. 198 _____ 200   28. 145 _____ 147

Write the missing numbers.

29. 174 _____ _____ 177   30. 138 _____ _____ 141

Review   Draw caves and bats to show these numbers.

= 10   = 1

26	45

© Copyright 1999   Mathematics Grade 2

Make 10 three-digit numbers **less than 300**. Choose one digit from each part of the pretzel to make your numbers.

1. 163
2. _____
3. _____
4. _____
5. _____

6. _____
7. _____
8. _____
9. _____
10. _____

Think

11. What is the smallest three-digit pretzel number you can make?

_____

12. What is the largest three-digit pretzel number you can make?

_____

13. What number can be made that is closest to 300? _____

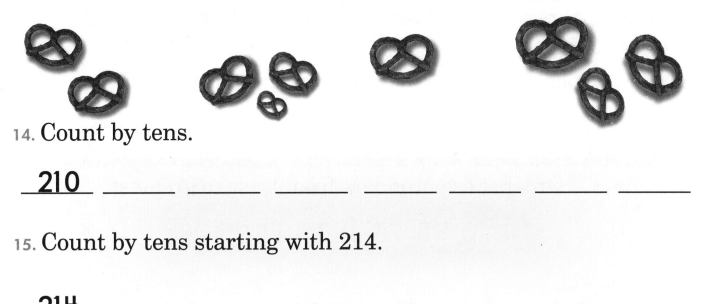

14. Count by tens.

210 ___ ___ ___ ___ ___

15. Count by tens starting with 214.

214 ___ ___ ___ ___ ___

Pretzel Time Game

Roll a number cube labeled twice with 1, 2, and 3. Use a penny as a marker. Record the path you take by making three-digit numbers.

Continue playing until you find Home.

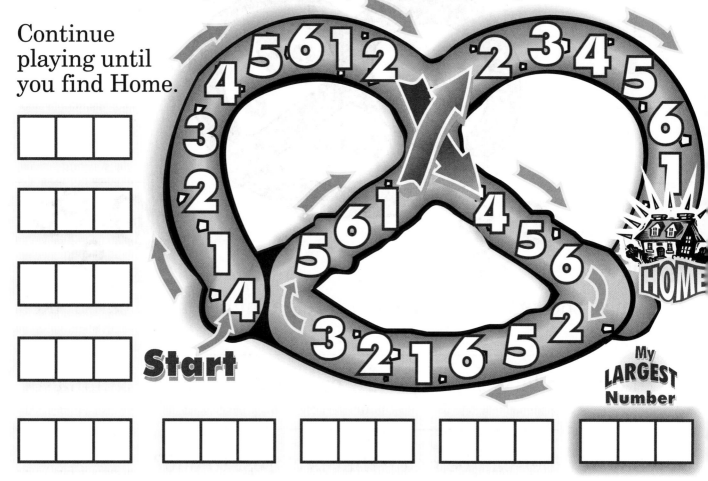

Start

How many three-digit numbers did you make before reaching "Home?"_____

How many numbers did you make that were greater than 300?_____

How many numbers did you make that were less than 300?_____

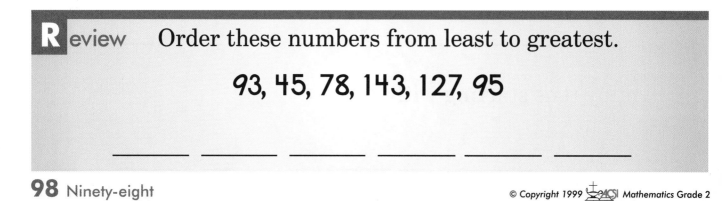

Review   Order these numbers from least to greatest.

93, 45, 78, 143, 127, 95

____ ____ ____ ____ ____ ____

© Copyright 1999 ACSI Mathematics Grade 2

Building Numbers to 400 | Lesson 50

1. <u>Circle</u> the numbers between 300 and 400. <u>Mark off</u> numbers less than 300. <u>Draw boxes</u> around numbers greater than 400.

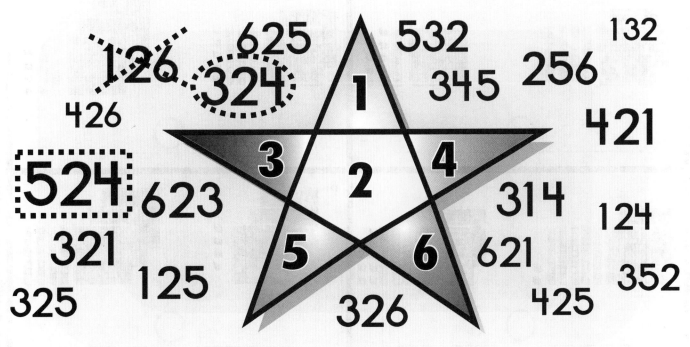

2. Place these numbers on the snake in order from least to greatest.

102   201   278   258   53   47   95   25

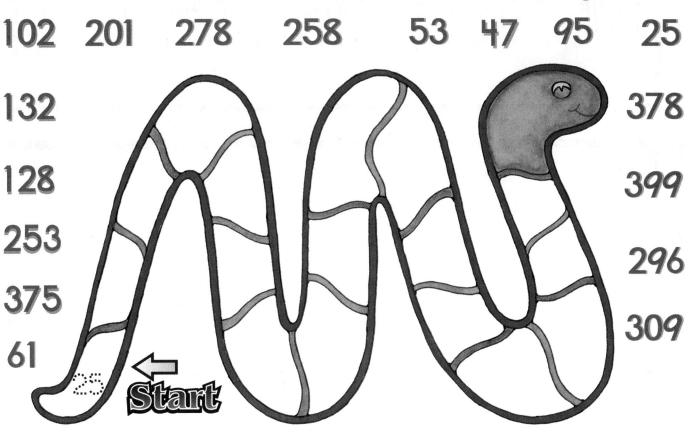

© Copyright 1999 ACSI Mathematics Grade 2

Write the number. Write < or > in each circle.

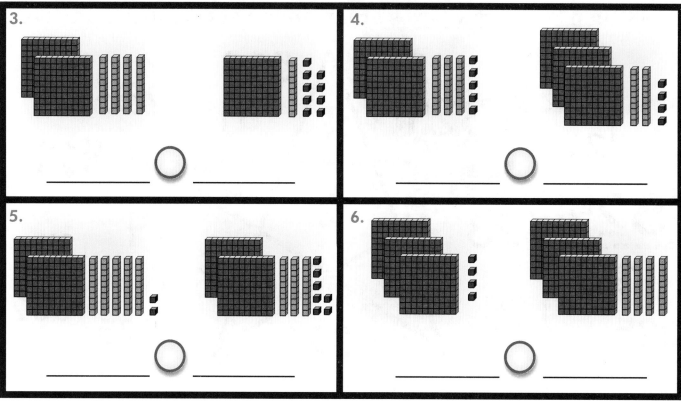

3. _____ ◯ _____

4. _____ ◯ _____

5. _____ ◯ _____

6. _____ ◯ _____

7. **SOLVE.** Evan scored 332 points playing the Place Value Game. Jason scored 311 points. Which boy scored higher?

_____

Review   Add and subtract.

1. 7
   +6

2. 12
   − 3

3. 8
   +9

4. 14
   − 7

5. 5
   +7

6. 6
   +4

Complete.

7. 34 = _____ tens and _____ ones

8. 245 = _____ hundreds _____ tens and _____ ones

© Copyright 1999 ACSI Mathematics Grade 2

Write the number on each fish above the correct boat.

1. _95_ _____

2. _____ _____

3. _____ _____

_____ _____   _____ _____   _____ _____

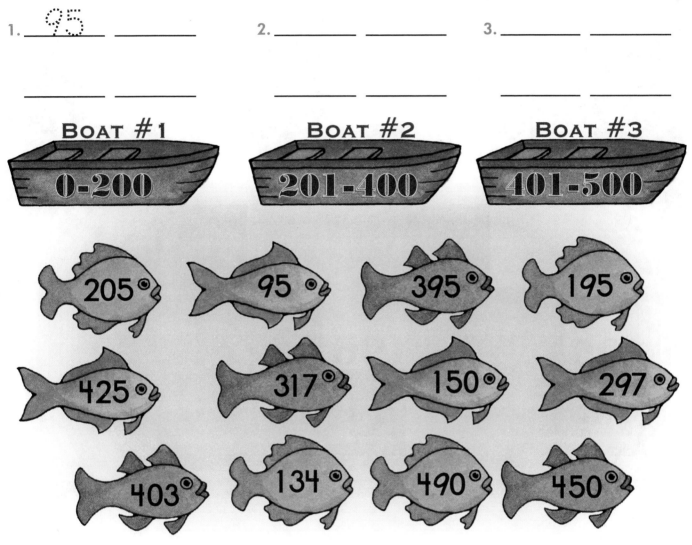

BOAT #1   BOAT #2   BOAT #3

0-200   201-400   401-500

205   95   395   195

425   317   150   297

403   134   490   450

Compare the number pairs using greater than > or less than < signs.

4. 347 _____ 253   5. 148 _____ 167

6. 468 _____ 499   7. 234 _____ 423

8. 200 _____ 199   9. 199 _____ 165

Help Susie climb the steps. Write numbers that go higher on each step.

500

350

10. **105**

11. **196**

Count by 10's.

12. **420 430** _____ _____ _____ _____

13. **260** _____ _____ _____ _____ _____

Count by 100's.

14. **130** _____ _____ _____ _____

15. **70** _____ _____ _____ _____

© Copyright 1999   Mathematics Grade 2

Building Numbers to 600 Lesson 52

1. Connect the dots.
Start with zero.

349 • • 0 **START**

325 •

320 •

50 •

125 •

75 •

145 •

135 •

175 •

315 •

301 •

310 •

300 •

302 •

303 •

285 •

275 •

261 •

274 •

250 •

230 •

210 •

200 •

295 •

290 •

2. Lasso only the numbers you would say if
you counted by tens starting at 10.

430 **(30)** **278** **190**

275 **235** **87**

225

450

70 **50** **76** **165**

© Copyright 1999 Mathematics Grade 2

Write the missing numbers.

3.
102		104	
202			
	303		
			405
		504	
	603		**605**

4.

5.

6.

7.

8.

Use the balloons to make 3-digit numbers.

9. _____ 10. _____
   greatest   **least**

Write the number of hundreds.

11. 20 tens = _____ hundreds

12. 50 tens = _____ hundreds

13. 10 tens = _____ hundreds

14. 30 tens = _____ hundreds

Write the number of tens.

15. four hundred = _____ tens

16. six hundred = _____ tens

Review   Write the numbers that come before and after.

1. _____ 36 _____

2. _____ 29 _____

3. _____ 150 _____

4. _____ 290 _____

5. _____ 417 _____

6. _____ 399 _____

© Copyright 1999 Mathematics Grade 2

Fact Families: Sums of 13 and 14   Lesson 53

Because of the order property, there are only <u>five</u> new combinations to learn for sums of 13 and 14.

Whole 13	
Part	**Part**
4	9

$4 + 9 = 13$ $13 - 4 = 9$
$9 + 4 = 13$ $13 - 9 = 4$

Write the fact families.

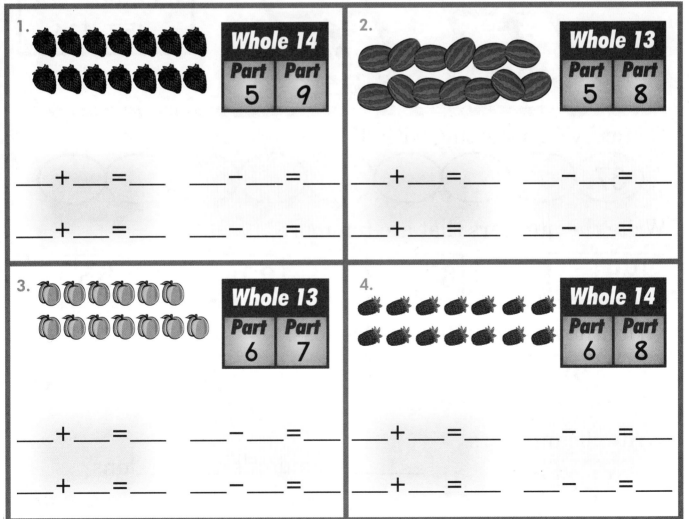

1.

Whole 14	
Part	**Part**
5	9

___ + ___ = ___   ___ − ___ = ___

___ + ___ = ___   ___ − ___ = ___

2.

Whole 13	
Part	**Part**
5	8

___ + ___ = ___   ___ − ___ = ___

___ + ___ = ___   ___ − ___ = ___

3.

Whole 13	
Part	**Part**
6	7

___ + ___ = ___   ___ − ___ = ___

___ + ___ = ___   ___ − ___ = ___

4.

Whole 14	
Part	**Part**
6	8

___ + ___ = ___   ___ − ___ = ___

___ + ___ = ___   ___ − ___ = ___

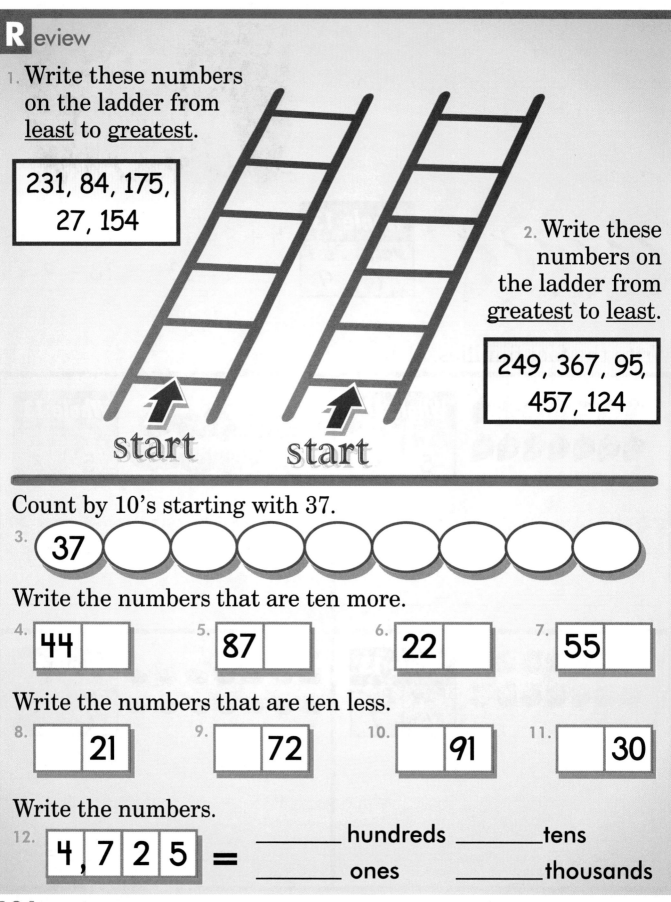

Review

1. Write these numbers on the ladder from <u>least</u> to <u>greatest</u>.

231, 84, 175, 27, 154

2. Write these numbers on the ladder from <u>greatest</u> to <u>least</u>.

249, 367, 95, 457, 124

start   start

Count by 10's starting with 37.

3. 37

Write the numbers that are ten more.

4. 44
5. 87
6. 22
7. 55

Write the numbers that are ten less.

8. 21
9. 72
10. 91
11. 30

Write the numbers.

12. 4,725 = _____ hundreds _____ tens _____ ones _____ thousands

© Copyright 1999   Mathematics Grade 2

Building Numbers to 700 — Lesson 54

Write the three-digit numbers.

1.

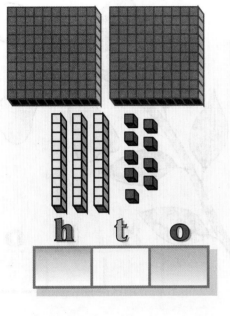

h   t   o

2.

h   t   o

3.

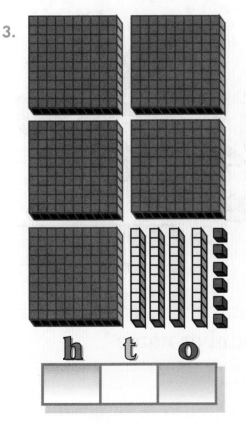

h   t   o

4.

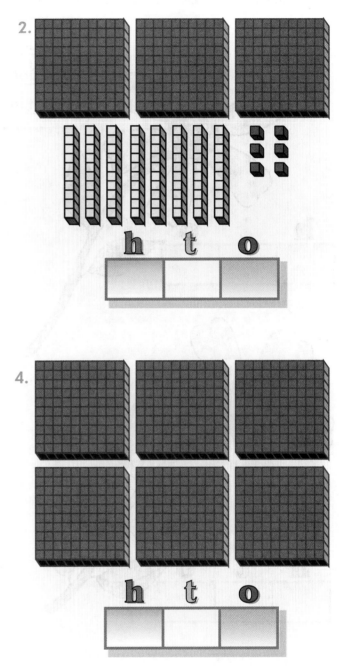

h   t   o

5. Mark only the number words that match the numbers above.

- ○ three hundred
- ○ four hundred eighty
- ○ two hundred thirty-nine
- ○ six hundred
- ○ two hundred twenty-nine
- ○ three hundred eighty-six
- ○ five hundred forty-one
- ○ five hundred forty-six

© Copyright 1999 Mathematics Grade 2

Write the number name for each flower.

Each <u>petal</u> = 100
Each <u>dot</u> = 10
Each <u>leaf</u> = 1

6. | h | t | o |
|---|---|---|
| | | |

7. | h | t | o |
|---|---|---|
| | | |

8. | h | t | o |
|---|---|---|
| | | |

9. | h | t | o |
|---|---|---|
| | | |

10. Draw your own flower and write the number name.

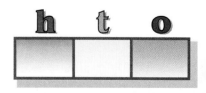

h	t	o

© Copyright 1999   Mathematics Grade 2

Building Numbers to 800   Lesson 55

Listen to the story. Write the answers.

1. What was the strong man's score?

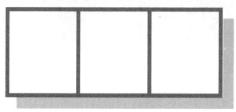

Name Bank
Strong Man
John _____
José _____
Reggie _____

2. Who had the lowest score? _____

3. Who had the highest score? _____

4. What was the lowest possible score? _____

5. Write the four scores in order from least to greatest.

_____   _____   _____   _____

6. List all the 3-digit numbers you can find. <u>Read across, down, or corner-to-corner</u>. Do not read backward.

_____   _____   _____

_____   _____   _____

_____   _____   _____

7. Write the numbers you found that were between:

101 and 200	201 and 300	301 and 500	501 and 800

© Copyright 1999 ⌁ACSI *Mathematics Grade 2*

Guess my number.

My number has an even number > 6 in the ones place.

MY NUMBER HAS A 5 IN THE TENS PLACE.

My number has the number of letters in my name in the hundreds place.

Alex

1. What is my number? ☐☐☐

Match.

2. **708** ○   ○ six hundred ten

3. **610** ○   ○ one hundred sixty

4. **780** ○   ○ seven hundred eight

5. **160** ○   ○ seven hundred eighty

6. Write your own three-digit number and the number word.

☐☐☐ _____

7. Match.

More than 200 ⃝   **Less than 200** ⃝

Review

Number Fun

1. Look at this number. | 3 | 5 | 4 |
   What two-digit numbers could you make if you first <u>added</u> two digits?

2. Look in each shape for two addends that make a sum of 10. Circle the shapes.

© Copyright 1999 · Mathematics Grade 2

Exploring Thousands — Lesson 57

Lakeview Christian School is collecting school supplies for a *sister school* in Central America. The second grade is packing tablets.

First, the tablets are counted in groups of 10.

Next, 10 groups of 10 are packed in each box. How many tablets are there in each box?

Finally, 10 boxes are packed in each carton. How many tablets are there in each carton? There are 10 hundreds in each carton. There are 1 thousand tablets in each carton.

100 TABLETS 100 TABLETS 100 TABLETS 100 TABLETS 100 TABLETS
100 TABLETS 100 TABLETS 100 TABLETS 100 TABLETS 100 TABLETS

Ones, tens, hundreds, and thousands are related.

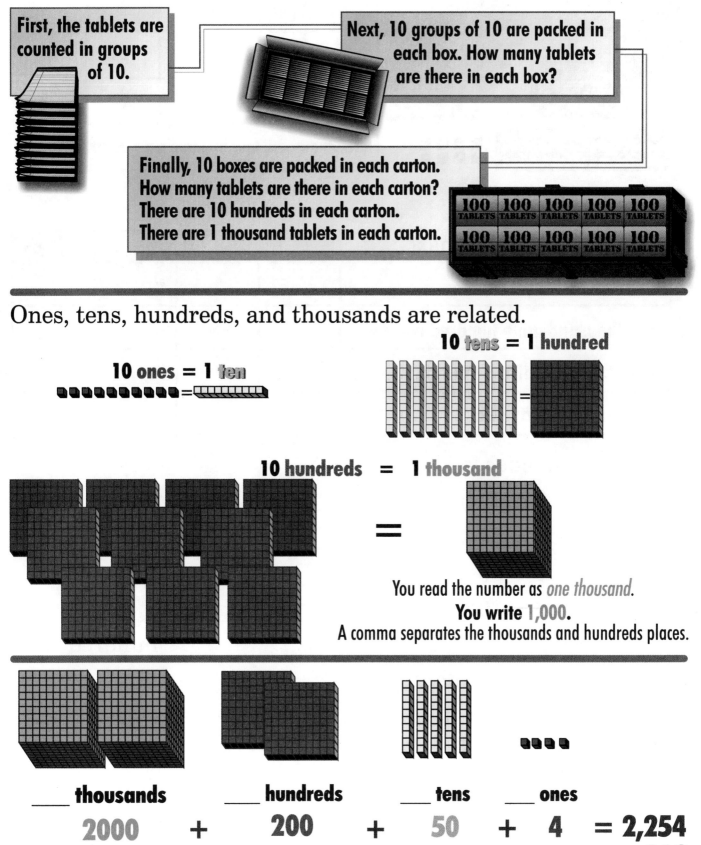

10 ones = 1 ten

10 tens = 1 hundred

10 hundreds = 1 thousand

You read the number as *one thousand*.
You write 1,000.
A comma separates the thousands and hundreds places.

____ **thousands**   ____ **hundreds**   ____ **tens**   ____ **ones**

2000   +   200   +   50   +   4   = **2,254**

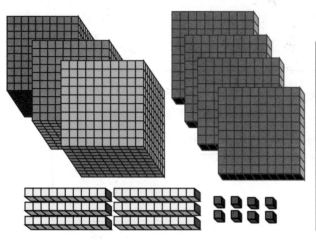

These blocks show a number.

thousands,	hundreds	tens	ones	
3,	**4**	**6**	**8**	Standard form
3,000 +	400 +	60 +	8	Expanded form
three thousand, four hundred sixty-eight				

Write each number in standard form in the chart.

	thousands,	hundreds	tens	ones
1. six hundred seventy-three	,			
2. four thousand, nine hundred twenty	,			
3. eight thousand, five hundred sixty-six	,			
4. two hundred thirty-two	,			

Write each number in standard form.

5. $5,000 + 700 + 50 + 1 =$ _____

6. $7,000 + 600 + 80 + 7 =$ _____

7. $4,000 + 300 + 60 =$ _____

8. $1,000 + 800 + 10 + 5 =$ _____

9. A thousand is how many hundreds? _____ hundreds

10. A hundred is how many tens? _____ tens

11. Write this number in standard form and expanded form:
    three thousand, two hundred seventy-eight

    Standard form: _____

    Expanded form: _____ + _____ + _____ + _____

© Copyright 1999   Mathematics Grade 2

Roll the hula-hoop with your hands. How high can your partner count before the hula-hoop falls?

My estimate_____

Actual_____

Twist the hula-hoop around your waist. How high can your partner count before the hula-hoop falls?

My estimate_____

Actual_____

Write a question to fit the story. Write your answer.

1. Donna has 300 stickers. Keesha has 100 more than Donna.

_____

_____

2. Luke collected $600 in play money to use for a board game. He needs $800.

_____

_____

3. Ben has collected 268 baseball cards. Alan has collected 286 baseball cards.

_____

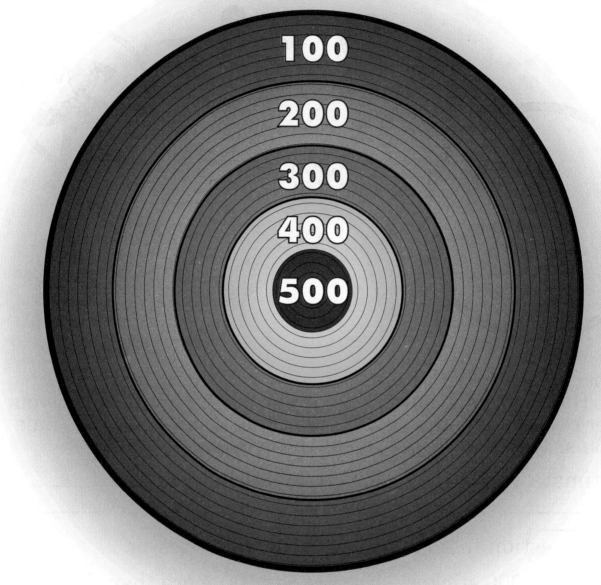

Maribeth and Jake are playing bean bag toss. They each get <u>three tosses</u>. Maribeth lands on **purple**, yellow, **and orange**. Jake lands on **red**, **purple**, and green.

4. Who is the winner?_____

5. How could you get a score of 800 in three turns?_____

_____

6. Which would be more, a score of orange + orange + yellow, or yellow
   + green + orange? _____

7. What is the highest possible score?_____

8. What would be the score if the three bags landed on orange, orange,
   and green? _____

     © Copyright 1999 *Mathematics Grade 2*

Listen to the story of the
Eiffel Tower.

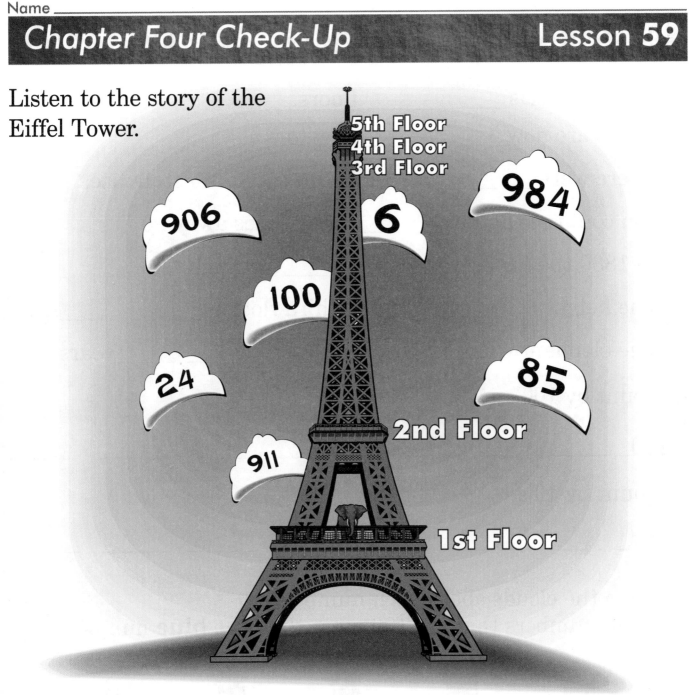

Look at the numbers on the clouds.

1. Use the clouds below to write the numbers in order from
   least to greatest.

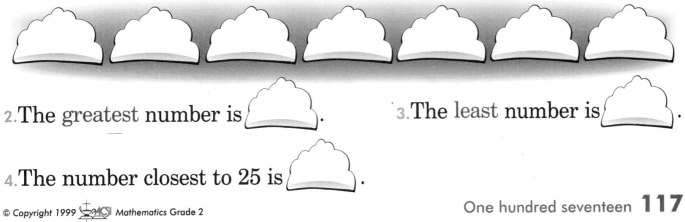

2. The greatest number is ⬭.

3. The least number is ⬭.

4. The number closest to 25 is ⬭.

5. The tower has_____floors.

6. There are now_____elevators.

7. There were_____steps on the spiral staircase.

8. You could see lights_____miles away.

9. In 1889 the tower was_____feet high.

10. The height of the tower at the third floor is_____feet.

11. The elephant who climbed the tower was_____years old.

12. Count by 100's.

__200__ _____ _____ _____ _____ _____ _____

13. Count by 10's.

__310__ _____ _____ _____ _____ _____ _____

Write in the clouds above each number.
14. Write numbers that are <u>100 more</u> than the **blue** numbers.

640   340   220   500   870   180

15. Write numbers that are <u>10 less</u> than the **green** numbers.

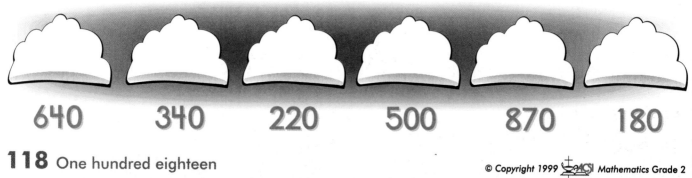

640   340   220   500   870   180

          © Copyright 1999 Mathematics Grade 2

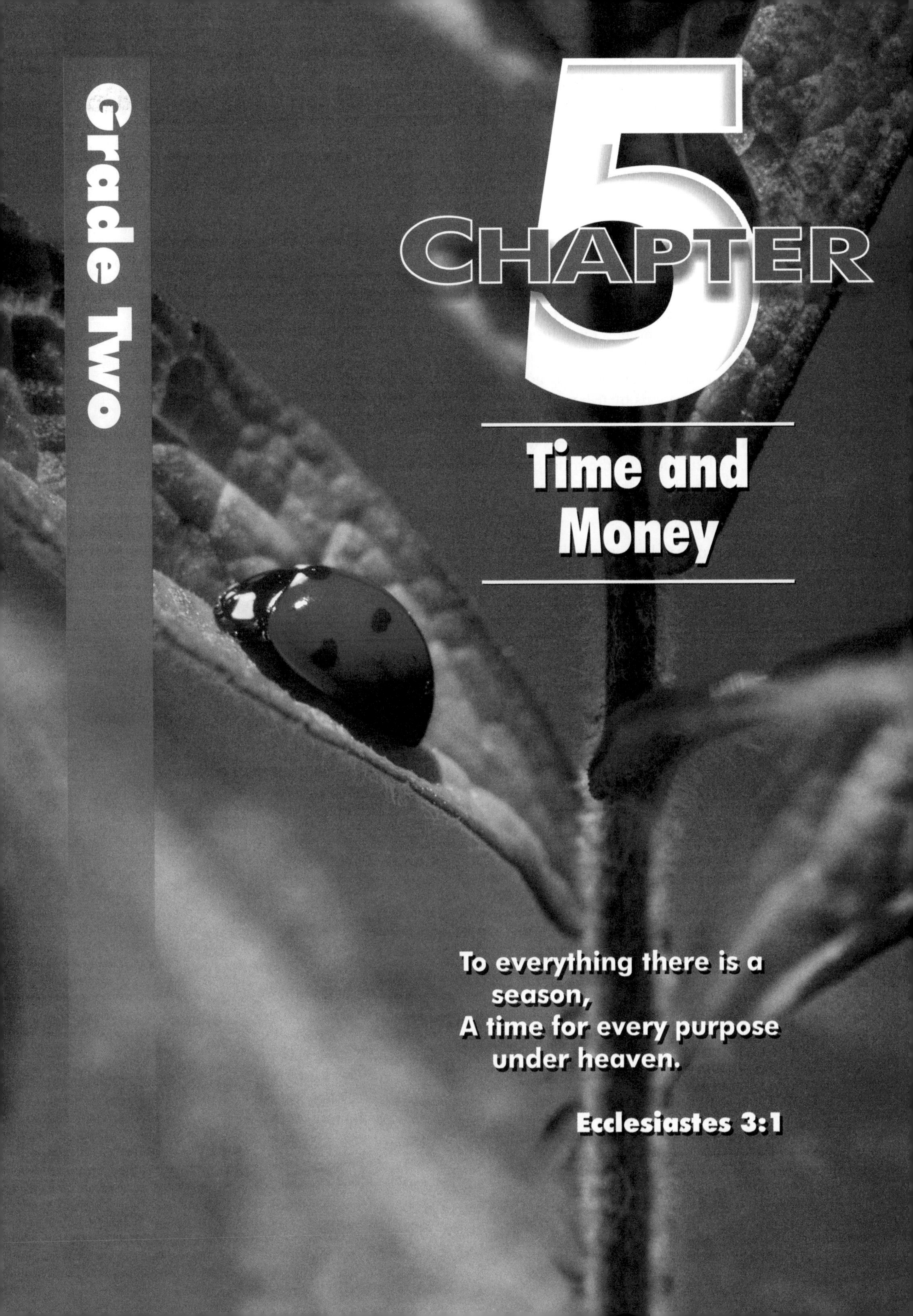

Grade Two

Chapter 5

Time and Money

To everything there is a
season,
A time for every purpose
under heaven.

Ecclesiastes 3:1

Dear Parents,

What an exciting time we have had in math class so far this year! I appreciate all the help you have given to make sure your child practices math skills and completes math homework.

There are two important learning goals for this chapter: the practical everyday applications of telling time and using money. Your child will learn to tell time to five-minute intervals on both standard and digital clocks. Through solving problems with elapsed time, he or she will develop a better idea of the concept and passage of time. Your child will read and complete a daily schedule and find that even Math Dog has a schedule!

At home, you can help your child practice telling time by asking him or her to identify times on the clock. Help your child develop "time sense" by asking which of two activities would take longer: getting dressed or reading a book, writing a story or making a bed, etc.

The second learning goal involves money. Counting money is a very important skill. You can help your child become competent at counting coin values by practicing counting by fives, tens, twenty-fives, and by counting on these amounts. For example, show your child one quarter, one dime, two nickels, and three pennies. Help him or her to count on beginning with 25, then by ten to 35, by fives for 40 and 45, then by ones, for 46, 47, 48. In order to help your child learn which sets of coins have equivalent values you may have him or her practice trading coins (five pennies for one nickel, two nickels for one dime, two dimes and one nickel for a quarter, etc.).

You can take a handful of coins from your pocket or purse and ask your child to help count the money. Point out grocery item prices to help build your child's awareness of math in daily life.

© Copyright 1999 ☩ACSI Mathematics Grade 2

Math Dog's Morning Schedule

6:00 a.m.   **Gets up**
6:01 a.m.   **Goes outside to play**
6:30 a.m.   **Comes in**
6:31 a.m.   **Eats breakfast**
7:00 a.m.   **Is taken for a walk**
9:00 a.m.   **Plays outside**
10:00 a.m. **Sleeps in a sunbeam**
11:00 a.m. **Plays with dog friend**

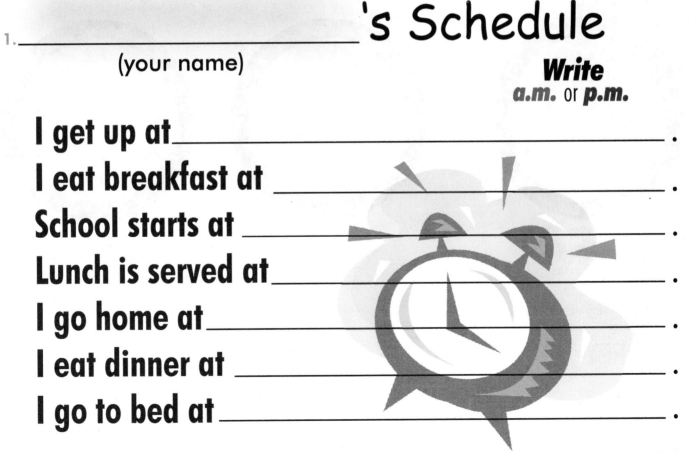

's Schedule

1._____

(your name)

Write
a.m. or **p.m.**

I get up at_____ .
I eat breakfast at _____ .
School starts at _____ .
Lunch is served at_____ .
I go home at_____ .
I eat dinner at _____ .
I go to bed at_____ .

Write the time shown on the clock.

2.
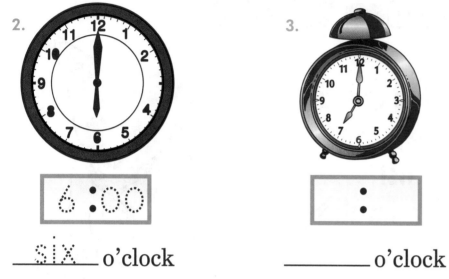

```
6 :00
```

__six__ o'clock

3.

```
  :
```

_____ o'clock

4.
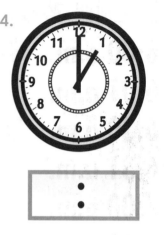

```
  :
```

_____ o'clock

5. Use your own clock to show a friend these times:

12:00, 4:00, and 11:00

Draw hands to show the time.

6. **3:00**

7. **8:00**

8. **2:00**

9. Complete the sentence.

A happy time for me is when I _____

_____

© Copyright 1999 Mathematics Grade 2

Time to the Half Hour   Lesson 61

There are 30 minutes in a half hour.

Practice with your own clock.
Make three different times.
Write them on the lines.

_____

_____

_____

Write the time.

1.

| 10:30 |

__ten thirty__

2.

| : |

_____

3.

| : |

_____o'clock

4.

| : |

_____

5.

| : |

_____o'clock

6.

| : |

_____

7. When the minute hand is on six and the hour hand is between 12 and 1, what time is it? _____

Lesson 61 Time to the Half Hour

Use a clock to find how much time has passed.

START STOP

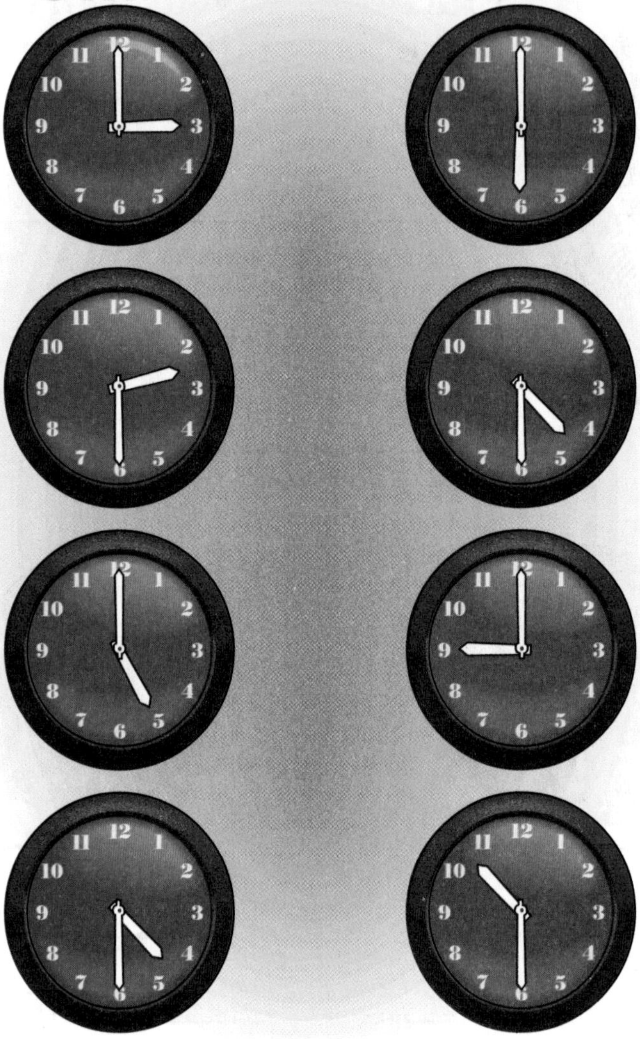

Write how much time has passed.

8. ___3___ *hours*

9. ________ *hours*

10. ________ *hours*

11. ________ *hours*

12. Marceley and her mother went to the store at four o'clock. They stopped at the sandwich shop at six o'clock. They got home at eight o'clock. How much time passed? ________________

Review Complete the pattern.

1. ______ ______ ______ ______

2. 234 345 456 ______ ______ ______

© Copyright 1999 ACSI Mathematics Grade 2

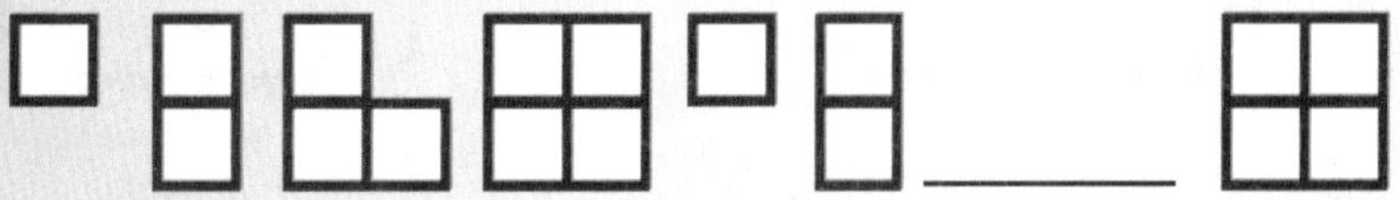

Time in Fifteen-Minute Intervals Lesson 62

There are 15 minutes in a quarter hour.

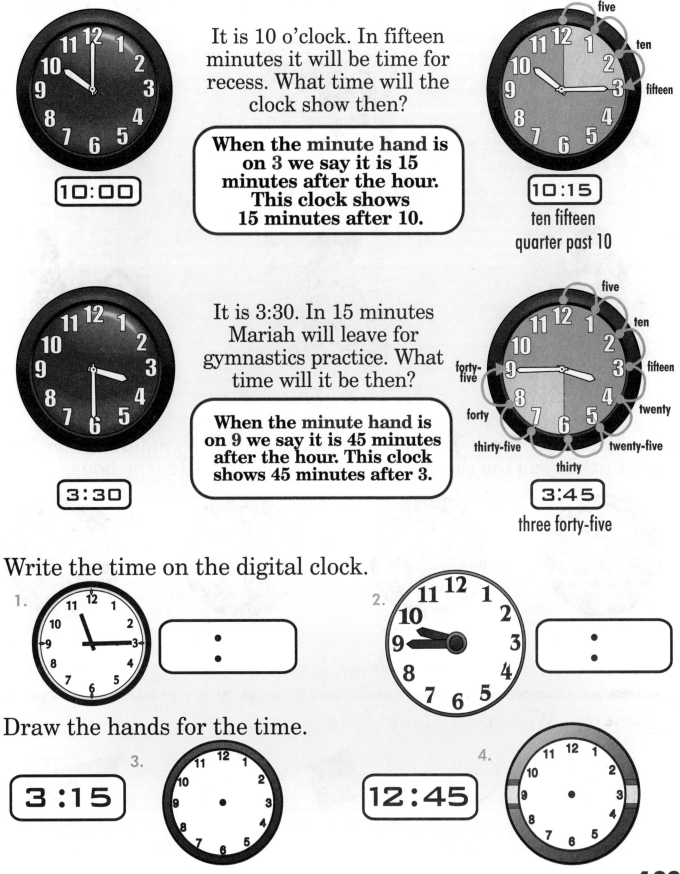

It is 10 o'clock. In fifteen minutes it will be time for recess. What time will the clock show then?

When the minute hand is on 3 we say it is 15 minutes after the hour. This clock shows 15 minutes after 10.

`10:00`

`10:15`
ten fifteen
quarter past 10

It is 3:30. In 15 minutes Mariah will leave for gymnastics practice. What time will it be then?

When the minute hand is on 9 we say it is 45 minutes after the hour. This clock shows 45 minutes after 3.

`3:30`

`3:45`
three forty-five

Write the time on the digital clock.

1.

2.

Draw the hands for the time.

3. `3:15`

4. `12:45`

The time between midnight and noon is called a.m. The time between noon and midnight is called p.m. Write <u>a.m.</u> or <u>p.m.</u> for each picture.

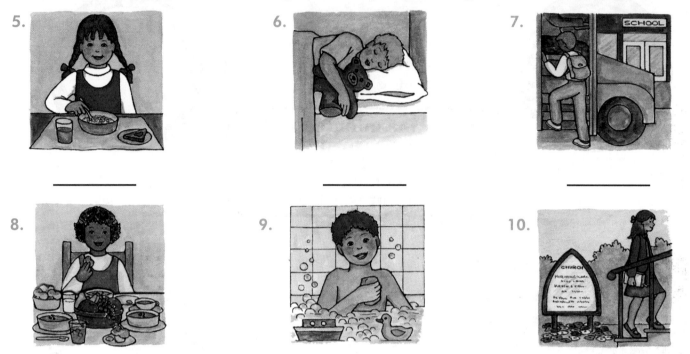

5. _____

6. _____

7. _____

8. _____

9. _____

10. _____

Write the times. Put a ☆ on the clock that shows 15 minutes after the hour. Put a 🌙 on the clock that shows 45 minutes after the hour.

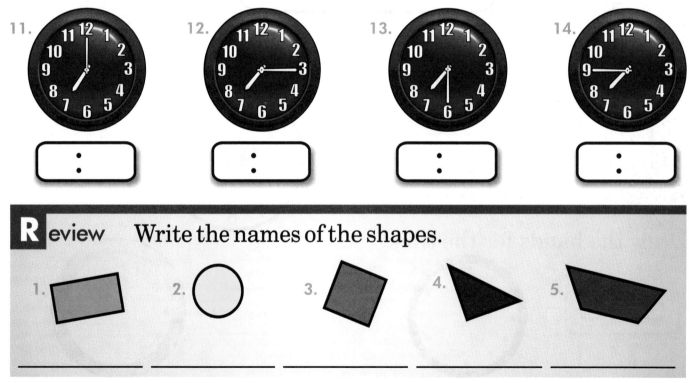

11. [:]

12. [:]

13. [:]

14. [:]

Review　Write the names of the shapes.

1. _____ 2. _____ 3. _____ 4. _____ 5. _____

© Copyright 1999　Mathematics Grade 2

Time in Five-Minute Intervals   Lesson 63

1. Read the story. Draw hands to show the correct time on each clock.

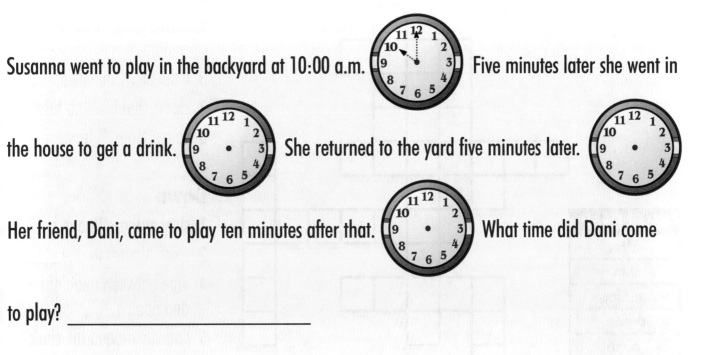

Susanna went to play in the backyard at 10:00 a.m. Five minutes later she went in

the house to get a drink. She returned to the yard five minutes later.

Her friend, Dani, came to play ten minutes after that. What time did Dani come

to play? _____

Write the time on the digital clock.

2.

3.

4.

5.

6.

7.

8.

9.

10. Complete the crossword puzzle.

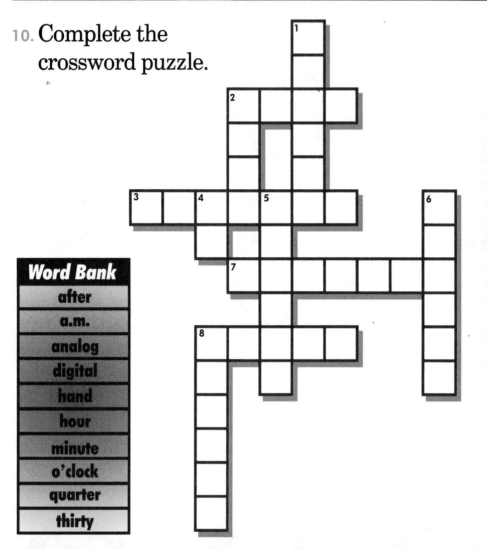

Word Bank

| after |
| a.m. |
| analog |
| digital |
| hand |
| hour |
| minute |
| o'clock |
| quarter |
| thirty |

Across

2. points to the hour or minute
3. a set of 15 minutes
7. clocks that have no faces
8. called "past" time

Down

1. sixty of these in one hour
2. sixty minutes in one_____
4. time between midnight and noon
5. halfway around the clock
6. tells the hour of the day
8. a regular clock face

Review   Put a <u>box</u> around each number.
Put the numbers in order from <u>least</u> to <u>greatest</u>.

- A Siberian tiger traveled 620 miles in one day to search for food.
- The heaviest Siberian tiger weighed 850 pounds.
- A cheetah weighs up to 130 pounds.
- A cheetah is the fastest of all land mammals. It sprints over 60 miles an hour.
- A Nile crocodile weighs over 1,500 pounds.
- The longest Nile crocodile was over 25 feet long.

_25_ _____ _____ _____ _____ _____

© Copyright 1999   *Mathematics Grade 2*

Holidays and the Calendar — Lesson 64

DECEMBER _____
(year)

Sunday	Monday	Tuesday	Wednesday	Thursday	Friday	Saturday

1. Fill in the dates.

2. Draw small pictures for the December holidays and special events.

3. Listen to the clue. When is Math Dog's birthday?_____

4. What day of the week is the last day of this month?_____

5. What day of the week will start the next month?_____

6. Write three December holiday names. _____

    _____   _____

7. Write three pairs of calendar dates that have a sum of 14.

    _____ and _____   _____ and _____   _____ and _____

8. What date is one week later than December 8th?_____

9. Write all odd numbers between the 17th and 31st.

    _____ _____ _____ _____ _____ _____ _____

Use a calendar to answer the questions.

10. There are _____ days in March.

11. Each month has about _____ weeks.

12. The first day of the week is _____.

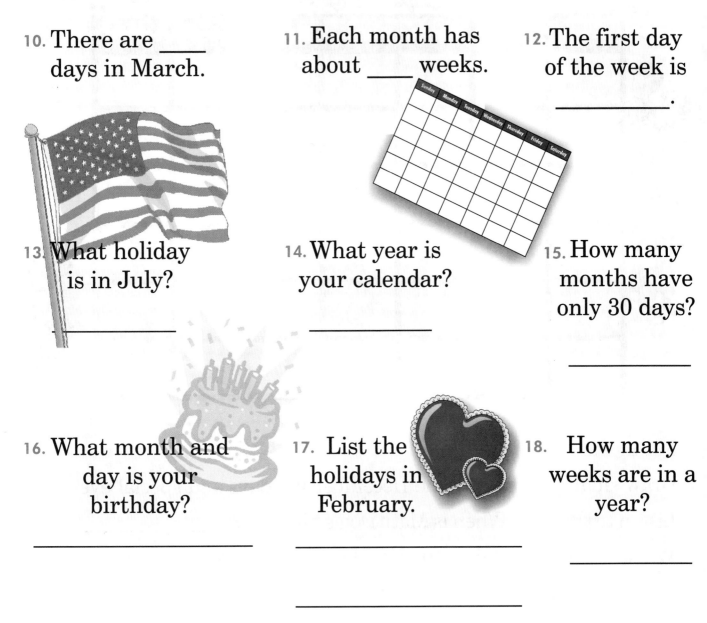

13. What holiday is in July?

_____

14. What year is your calendar?

_____

15. How many months have only 30 days?

_____

16. What month and day is your birthday?

_____

17. List the holidays in February.

_____

_____

18. How many weeks are in a year?

_____

19. How many months are there in a year?

_____

20. What is your favorite month? Why?

_____

_____

_____

© Copyright 1999   Mathematics Grade 2

Seasons and the Calendar — Lesson 65

To everything there is a season. A time for every purpose under heaven.

Ecclesiastes 3:1

Name the seasons.

1. _____ 2. _____ 3. _____ 4. _____

5. In North America the weather in winter is _____ and the weather in summer is _____.

Use a 12-month calendar to find the first day of:

6. spring _____

7. summer _____

8. fall _____

9. winter _____

Word Bank
September
June
December
March

These are Fahrenheit thermometers. Fill in the blanks with the number of degrees and the word hot, warm, or cold.

10. **A** shows _____ degrees. The temperature is _____.

11. **B** shows _____ degrees. The temperature is _____.

12. **C** shows _____ degrees. The temperature is _____.

A   B   C

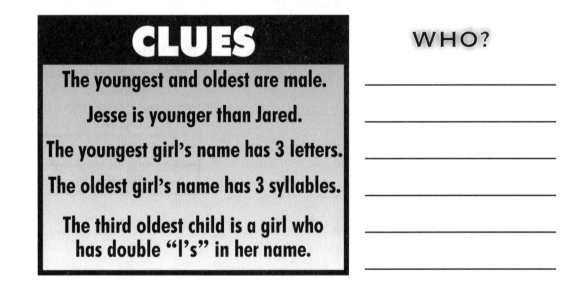

There are six children in the Wilson family. Their names are Johanna, Jared, Jesse, Janelle, Julie, and Joy.

13. Match the name of each child with the correct date of his or her birth.

CLUES

The youngest and oldest are male.

Jesse is younger than Jared.

The youngest girl's name has 3 letters.

The oldest girl's name has 3 syllables.

The third oldest child is a girl who has double "l's" in her name.

WHO?	WHEN?
_____	August 17, 1983
_____	November 22, 1985
_____	September 11, 1988
_____	December 25, 1990
_____	October 23, 1992
_____	December 26, 1994

14. Who is the youngest child?_____

15. Who is the oldest girl?_____

16. In how many different months of the year do their birthdays occur?_____

17. How many years are there between the youngest and the next to the youngest child?_____

Problem Solving: Calendars and Time　Lesson 66

1. Write the dates. Use the calendar to answer the questions.

FEBRUARY

Sunday	Monday	Tuesday	Wednesday	Thursday	Friday	Saturday

2. What holidays are celebrated in February? _____

_____

3. What date is the second Saturday of the month? _____

4. How many Sundays are there in February? _____

5. What day will it be on February 8th? _____

6. February is the _____ month of the year.

7. What month comes just before this month? _____

- -

8. John and Roman were cleaning their rooms. They started at 10:00 a.m. John finished at 10:45. Roman finished at 10:40.

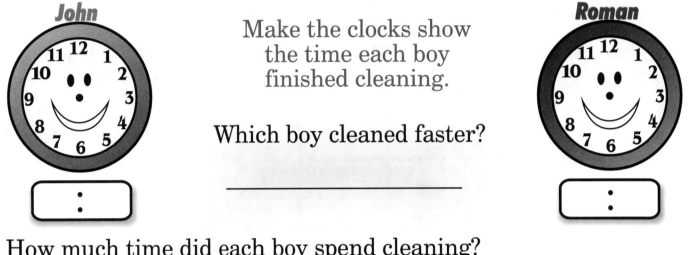

Make the clocks show the time each boy finished cleaning.

Which boy cleaned faster?

_____

How much time did each boy spend cleaning?

John _____ minutes   **Roman** _____ minutes

9. Make the clocks below show the time Suzette finished playing at each attraction. Write the time on each line as you read.

Suzette went to the park at 11:00. She played on the swing until 11:15. Suzette went to the slide for 10 minutes. Next, she stayed 20 minutes on the monkey bars. Finally, she played 10 minutes on the merry-go-round.

© Copyright 1999   Mathematics Grade 2

Review: Telling Time
Lesson 67

Draw hands on Timothy Time-Teller to show the time. Circle a.m. or p.m.

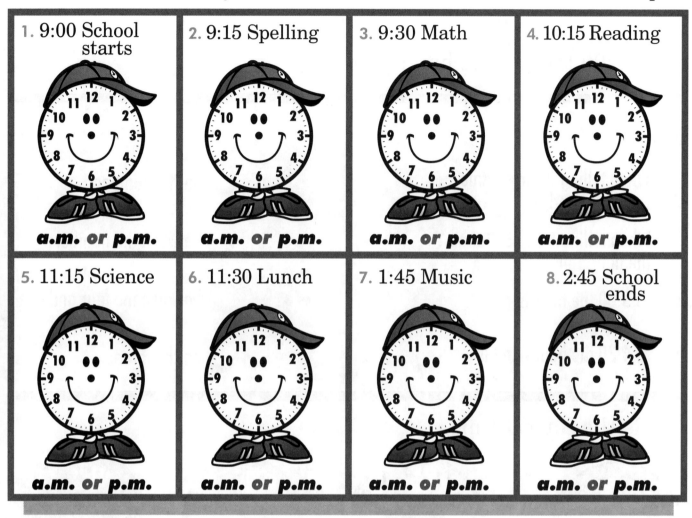

1. 9:00 School starts
a.m. or p.m.

2. 9:15 Spelling
a.m. or p.m.

3. 9:30 Math
a.m. or p.m.

4. 10:15 Reading
a.m. or p.m.

5. 11:15 Science
a.m. or p.m.

6. 11:30 Lunch
a.m. or p.m.

7. 1:45 Music
a.m. or p.m.

8. 2:45 School ends
a.m. or p.m.

Write the time in words.

9. **12:30**

10. **11:15**

11. **3:45**

twelve thirty _____ _____

How much time has passed?

		Starts	Ends	Time
12.	Recess	11:50	12:10	
13.	Breakfast	8:00	8:15	
14.	Homework	4:00	6:00	

Fill in the blanks.

15. At 12:30 the minute hand is on _____ .

16. At 1:00 the minute hand is on _____ .

Match.

17. When telling "thirty" time, the hour hand is

18. When telling "o'clock" time, the hour hand is

19. At 3:00 the hour hand is

20. At 4:30 the hour hand is

on the number

between the numbers

between the four and five

on the three

Circle the correct time.

21.

3:25 or 3:35

22.

8:10 or 7:50

23.

7:15 or 6:45

24.

4:05 or 2:20

25.

Think

My time is after school is dismissed.
It is p.m. time.
It is half-way between 4 o'clock and 6 o'clock.
What time is it? _____

© Copyright 1999 Mathematics Grade 2

Write the total amount of money.

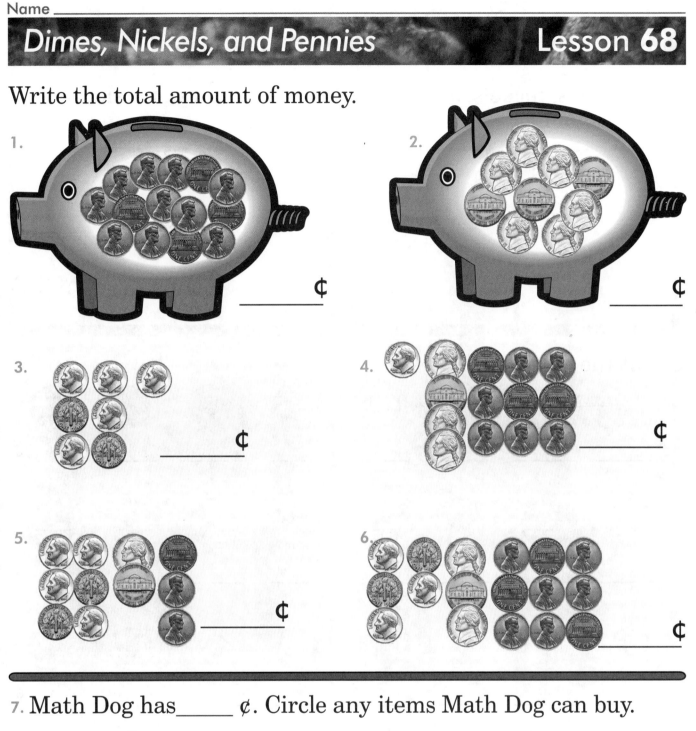

1. _____ ¢

2. _____ ¢

3. _____ ¢

4. _____ ¢

5. _____ ¢

6. _____ ¢

---

7. Math Dog has _____ ¢. Circle any items Math Dog can buy.

75¢

39¢

74¢

69¢

49¢

58¢

Use pennies, nickels, and dimes. Draw two ways to make each money amount.

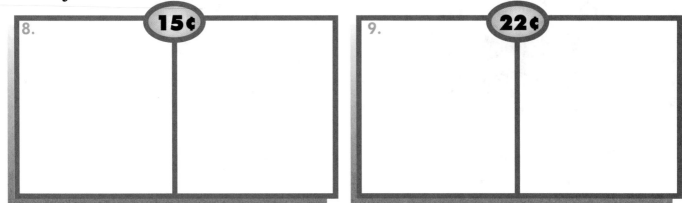

8. **15¢**

9. **22¢**

Count the money.

10. _____ ¢

11. _____ ¢

12. _____ ¢

Which is more? Circle your answer.

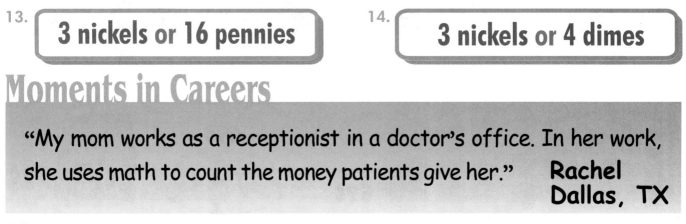

13. **3 nickels or 16 pennies**

14. **3 nickels or 4 dimes**

Moments in Careers

"My mom works as a receptionist in a doctor's office. In her work, she uses math to count the money patients give her." **Rachel Dallas, TX**

© Copyright 1999   Mathematics Grade 2

Quarters, Dimes, Nickels, and Pennies   Lesson 69

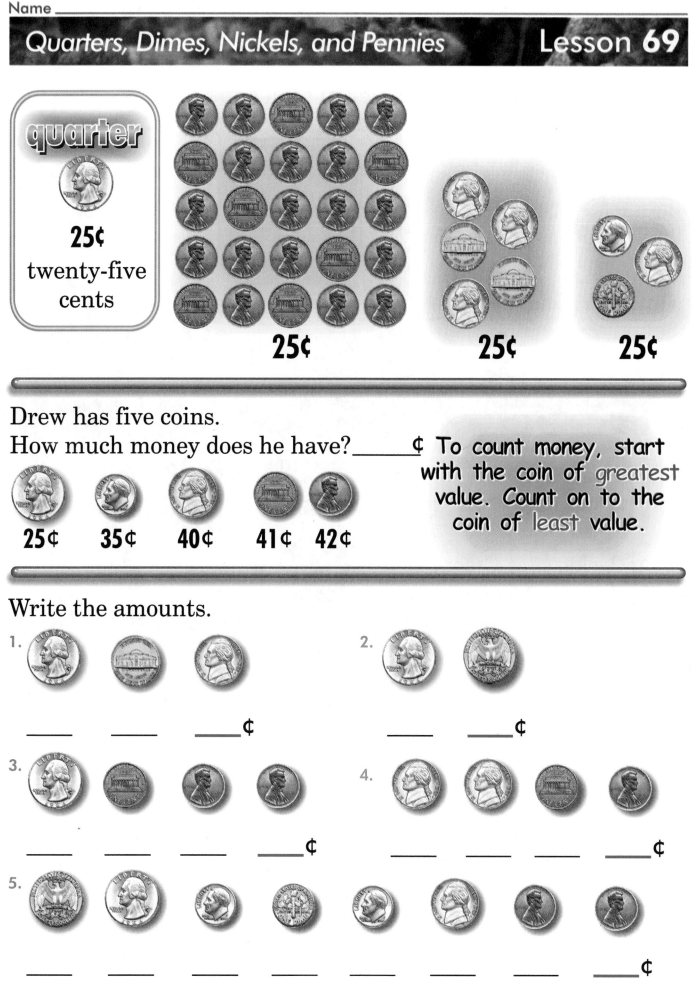

quarter

25¢
twenty-five
cents

25¢

25¢

25¢

Drew has five coins.
How much money does he have? _____ ¢

To count money, start with the coin of greatest value. Count on to the coin of least value.

25¢   35¢   40¢   41¢   42¢

Write the amounts.

1. ____ ____ ____ ¢

2. ____ ____ ¢

3. ____ ____ ____ ____ ¢

4. ____ ____ ____ ____ ¢

5. ____ ____ ____ ____ ____ ____ ____ ____ ¢

Write the total amount of money in each bank.

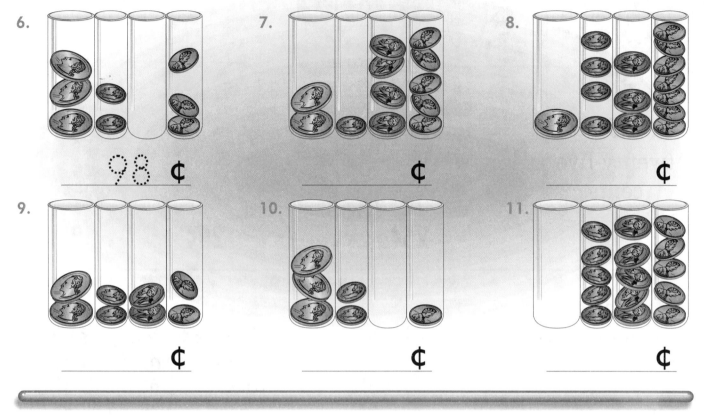

6. _98_ ¢

7. _____ ¢

8. _____ ¢

9. _____ ¢

10. _____ ¢

11. _____ ¢

12. At Jackie's Ice-Cream Store each flavor costs a different amount and you pay for the cone. How much does this ice-cream cone cost?_____ ¢

chocolate = 25¢

vanilla = 20¢

strawberry = 15¢

cone = 10¢

Think 13. Draw the coins. Find the total.

Math Dog has 4 dishes and 8 coins (pennies, nickels, dimes, and quarters). Dish 1 has more value than dish 2. Dish 2 has more value than dish 3 and dish 3 has more value than dish 4. The two coins in each dish are the same. Each dish holds a different type of coin. The value of all dishes is 82¢. Draw the coins above each dish.

© Copyright 1999   Mathematics Grade 2

Draw 3 different ways to make twenty-five cents.

1.	2.	3.

Draw 3 different ways to make fifty cents.

4.	5.	6.

Draw the <u>one</u> <u>coin</u> <u>needed</u> to buy the food.

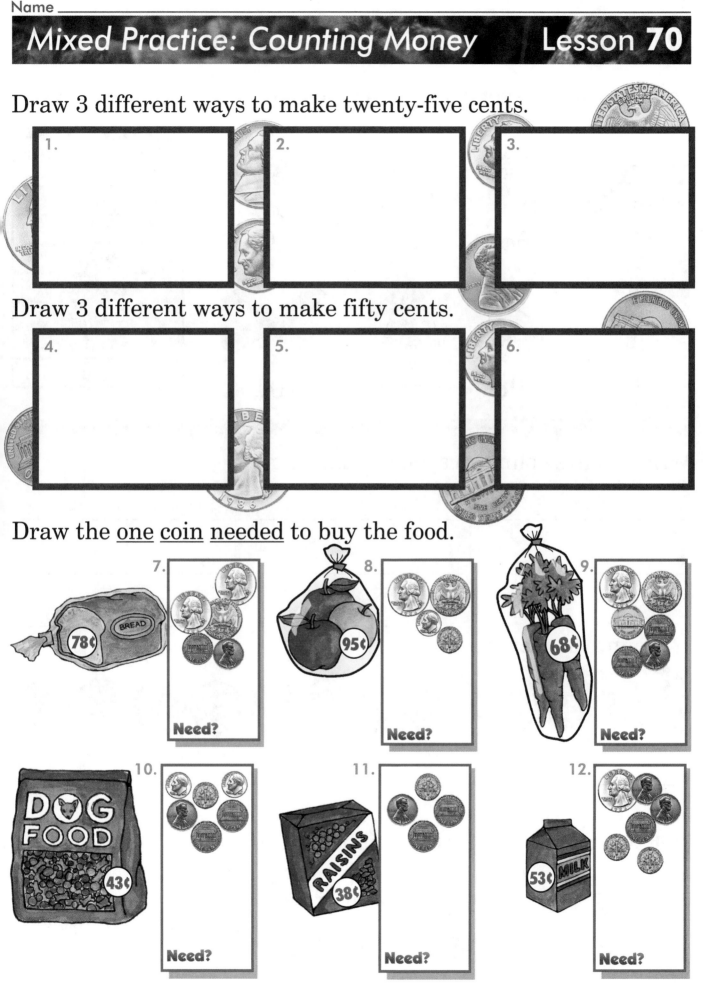

7. BREAD 78¢   Need?

8. 95¢   Need?

9. 68¢   Need?

10. DOG FOOD 43¢   Need?

11. RAISINS 38¢   Need?

12. MILK 53¢   Need?

John has 18¢ to spend at Joey's yard sale. What are some ways John can spend exactly 18¢?

15¢   3¢   6¢   10¢

5¢   9¢   8¢   10¢

Word Bank
car
card
ball
bunny
soldier
dinosaur
doll
plane

Write 3 ways John can spend all his money.

13. _____
+ _____

14. _____
+ _____

15. _____
+ _____
+ _____

16. Count the money.

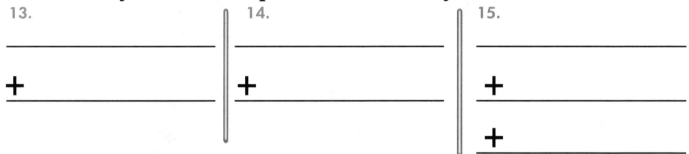

___ ___ ___ ___ ___ ___ ___ ___ ___ ___ ___ ¢
Total

17. Exchange for the fewest number of coins.

_____ quarters
_____ dimes
_____ nickels
_____ pennies

Exchanging Coins for Dollars   Lesson 71

Mark off any box of coins that totals exactly one dollar.

7. Draw coins to put one dollar in the jar.

How many coins =

8. _____ **dimes**

9. _____ **nickels**

10. _____ **quarters**

11. _____ **pennies**

12. _____ **quarters = $5.00**

Would the item cost **more** or **less** than $1.00? Circle <u>more</u> or <u>less</u>.

13.

more or less

14.

more or less

15.

more or less

16.

more or less

17.

more or less

18.

more or less

Think   Four children have money to spend at the fun center. Chris has <u>the most</u> money. Zachary has <u>some pennies</u>. Jamie has <u>only one type</u> of coin. Sierra has <u>the least</u> amount of money. Draw lines to match the child to the correct amount. Write the total amount of money beside each name.

19. Sierra $____.____ ◯   ◯ 6 quarters

20. Zachary $____.____ ◯   ◯ 8 quarters, 5 dimes

21. Chris $____.____ ◯   ◯ 3 quarters, 2 dimes, 1 nickel, 1 penny

22. Jamie $____.____ ◯   ◯ 4 quarters, 10 dimes, 7 pennies

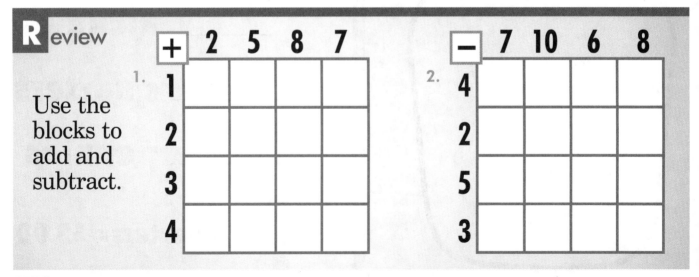

Review

Use the blocks to add and subtract.

1.

+	2	5	8	7
1				
2				
3				
4				

2.

−	7	10	6	8
4				
2				
5				
3				

© Copyright 1999   Mathematics Grade 2

Half Dollar and Dollar

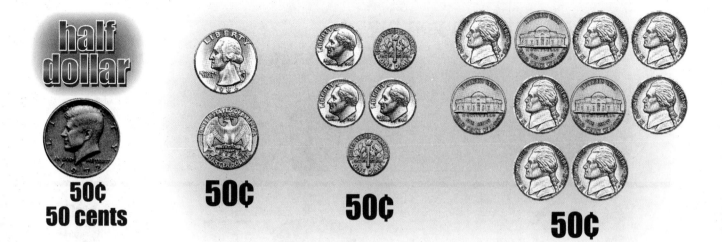

half dollar

50¢
50 cents

50¢

50¢

50¢

Count the money. Circle the set with the greatest amount.

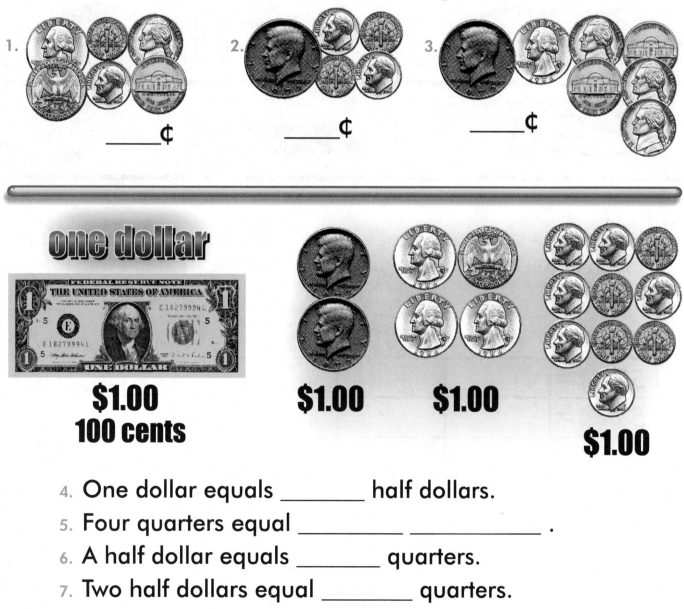

1. _____ ¢

2. _____ ¢

3. _____ ¢

one dollar

$1.00
100 cents

$1.00

$1.00

$1.00

4. One dollar equals _____ half dollars.

5. Four quarters equal _____ _____ .

6. A half dollar equals _____ quarters.

7. Two half dollars equal _____ quarters.

Write the amount. Can you buy it?

You have		Snack shop menu	Can you buy it?

8. _____ 75¢ **Yes No**

9. _____ 17¢ **Yes No**

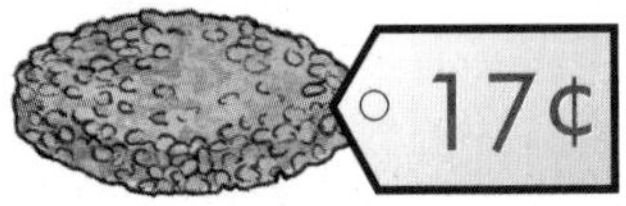

10. _____ 35¢ **Yes No**

11. _____ 75¢ **Yes No**

Think Write the number of each type of coin or bill that equals the given amount. Draw a smiley face if there is no answer for that space.

	nickel	dime	quarter	half dollar	dollar
12. 50 ¢ =			2		☺
13. 5 ¢ =					☺
14. 25 ¢ =					
15. 30 ¢ =		3			
16. 60 ¢ =	12				
17. 100 ¢ =					

© Copyright 1999 Mathematics Grade 2

Problem Solving with Money — Lesson 73

1. Color only the "money" with the correct answer.

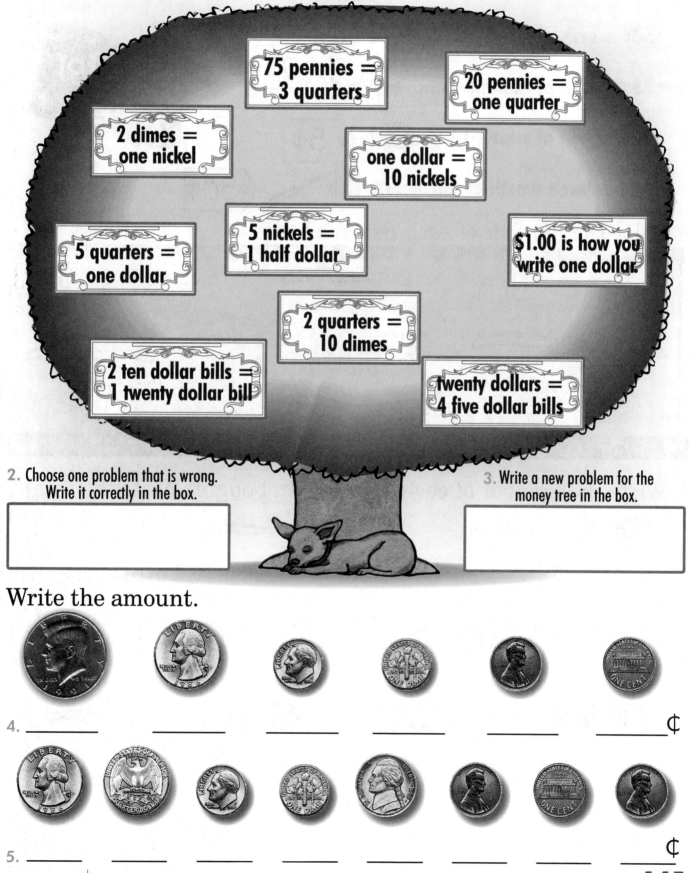

75 pennies =
3 quarters

20 pennies =
one quarter

2 dimes =
one nickel

one dollar =
10 nickels

5 quarters =
one dollar

5 nickels =
1 half dollar

$1.00 is how you
write one dollar.

2 quarters =
10 dimes

2 ten dollar bills =
1 twenty dollar bill

twenty dollars =
4 five dollar bills

2. Choose one problem that is wrong.
Write it correctly in the box.

3. Write a new problem for the
money tree in the box.

Write the amount.

4. _____ _____ _____ _____ _____ _____ ¢

5. _____ _____ _____ _____ _____ _____ ¢

Kristin went to Aquarama to buy fish. <u>She bought</u>:

- **50¢ worth of tigerfish**

- **75¢ worth of hammerhead**

- **25¢ worth of spotted fish**

- **one dollar's worth of glowworm fish**

6. Color the number of each fish she bought.

7. Write the number of each fish Kristin bought. Write the total.

_____   _____   _____   _____   **Total:** _____ fish

8. Draw the <u>fewest number of coins</u> needed to buy each group of fish. Then write the total amount Kristin spent.

Total: _____

© Copyright 1999   *Mathematics Grade 2*

Draw the hands on each clock. Write the time.

15 minutes later   15 minutes later   15 minutes later   15 minutes later

1.   2.   3.   4.   5.

10:30   _____   _____   _____   _____

Write whether each clock above shows o'clock, thirty, or after.

thirty   _____   _____   _____   _____

Fill in the blanks. Then draw hands on each clock.

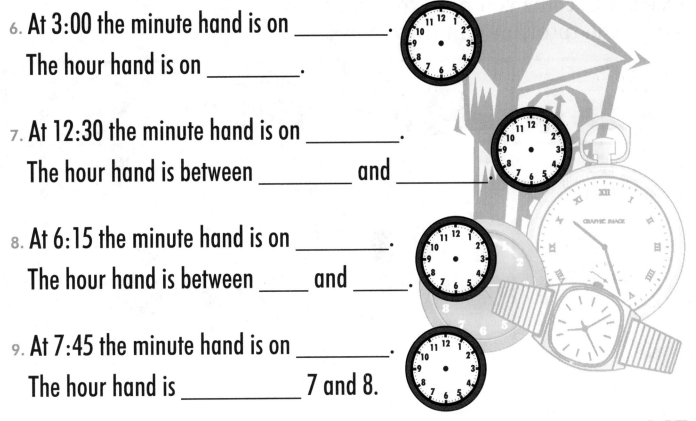

6. At 3:00 the minute hand is on _____.
The hour hand is on _____.

7. At 12:30 the minute hand is on _____.
The hour hand is between _____ and _____.

8. At 6:15 the minute hand is on _____.
The hour hand is between _____ and _____.

9. At 7:45 the minute hand is on _____.
The hour hand is _____ 7 and 8.

Math Dog and his pal Phil have money in their pouches. They always carry the same <u>kind</u> of coins but not the same number. Draw the missing coins in the boxes.

	TOTAL MONEY	PHIL	MATH DOG
10.	75¢	25¢	
11.	80¢		40¢
12.	$1.00	75¢	
13.	30¢		10¢

Circle the coins you need to buy the item.
Write the total amount in each set.

14. 38¢	15. 97¢	16. 88¢	17. 43¢
Total: $___.___	Total: $___.___	Total: $___.___	Total: $___.___

© Copyright 1999 ACSI Mathematics Grade 2

CHAPTER 6

Addition and Subtraction Facts to 18

The heavens are Yours, the earth also is Yours.

Psalm 89:11a

Dear Parents,

Second grade mathematics continues to be an adventure! Your child has worked with numbers to 999, learned addition and subtraction facts to 14, used a calendar, learned to tell time, count money, and much more.

During Chapter Six your child will learn addition and subtraction facts to 18 and the addition and subtraction of two-digit numbers. Here's an idea you can use at home to help your child practice math facts.

Cut the attached cards apart to play a fact game with your child. Have the child turn over two cards at a time. Take turns asking your child to add the numbers or subtract the smaller number from the larger. Have him or her hold up the correct card to show the answer to an addition or subtraction fact. Later, you will be able to turn over three cards at a time and have your child add three addends.

You can also use the cards to review comparing numbers. Have the child choose two or three cards and then form the greatest or least two- or three-digit number possible.

To practice adding and subtracting 2-digit numbers without regrouping, remove all the cards with the numerals 5 through 9. Have the child draw four cards and use them to form two 2-digit numbers. Ask him or her to add or subtract. (After we complete chapters eight and nine you will be able to make problems with all the digits 0-9.)

Read Psalm 89:11 (the first part of which is printed on the other side of this page) with your child. It is a wonderful comfort to know that God has been, is, and will be in control of the world and everything in it. God is so good!

Thanks for helping your child learn to love mathematics and appreciate that only God could have created such an orderly and interesting system.

© Copyright 1999

Reviewing Facts to 14 — Lesson 75

You can use pictures to add.

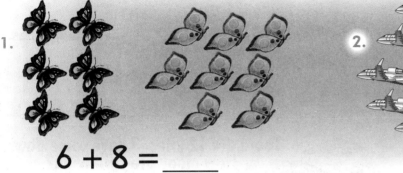

1.

2.

$6 + 8 =$ ____

$7 + 5 =$ ____

You can use the number line to add.

$$\begin{array}{ccccccccccccccc} 0 & 1 & 2 & 3 & 4 & 5 & 6 & 7 & 8 & 9 & 10 & 11 & 12 & 13 & 14 \end{array}$$

$9 + 2 = 11$

3.	4.	5.	6.	7.	8.
3 +8	2 +8	6 +8	7 +7	7 +5	6 +6

9.	10.	11.	12.	13.	14.
7 +4	5 +8	6 +4	9 +4	3 +9	5 +5

You can add in any order. The sum is the same.

15.		16.		17.	
9 +2	2 +9	9 +5	5 +9	4 +8	8 +4

18.		19.		20.	
5 +6	6 +5	6 +7	7 +6	3 +8	8 +3

You can use pictures to subtract.

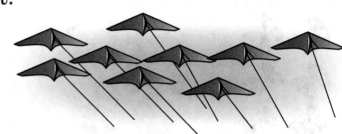

There are 11 birds. 4 fly away. How many are left?

There are 12 kites. 3 have come down. How many are still flying?

21. $11 - 4 =$ _____

22. $12 - 3 =$ _____

You can use the number line to subtract.

```
◄——┼——┼——┼——┼——┼——┼——┼——┼——┼——┼——┼——┼——┼——┼——►
   0  1  2  3  4  5  6  7  8  9  10 11 12 13 14
```

$$11 - 6 = 5$$

23. $12 - 3 =$ _____   24. $12 - 6 =$ _____   25. $13 - 5 =$ _____

26. $14 - 5 =$ _____   27. $10 - 5 =$ _____   28. $13 - 4 =$ _____

Subtract.

29. $\begin{array}{r} 10 \\ -\ 6 \\ \hline \end{array}$ 30. $\begin{array}{r} 11 \\ -\ 8 \\ \hline \end{array}$ 31. $\begin{array}{r} 11 \\ -\ 3 \\ \hline \end{array}$ 32. $\begin{array}{r} 12 \\ -\ 7 \\ \hline \end{array}$ 33. $\begin{array}{r} 11 \\ -\ 2 \\ \hline \end{array}$ 34. $\begin{array}{r} 11 \\ -\ 9 \\ \hline \end{array}$

35. $\begin{array}{r} 11 \\ -\ 6 \\ \hline \end{array}$ 36. $\begin{array}{r} 12 \\ -\ 9 \\ \hline \end{array}$ 37. $\begin{array}{r} 12 \\ -\ 3 \\ \hline \end{array}$ 38. $\begin{array}{r} 12 \\ -\ 8 \\ \hline \end{array}$ 39. $\begin{array}{r} 9 \\ -\ 2 \\ \hline \end{array}$ 40. $\begin{array}{r} 11 \\ -\ 7 \\ \hline \end{array}$

© Copyright 1999   Mathematics Grade 2

Find the addition patterns.

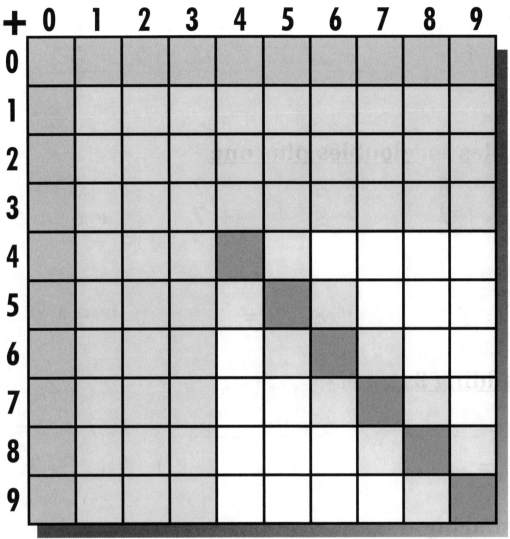

Congratulations! You are almost there! You can use these fact strategies to add.

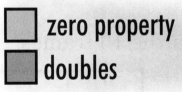 zero property   ☐ counting on 1, 2, or 3

☐ doubles   ☐ doubles plus one

1. Write the sums in the shaded squares.
2. Use the <u>adding 9</u> strategy. Write the sums in the squares. Color.
3. Use the <u>sharing</u> strategy. Write the sums in the squares. Color.
4. Use the <u>make a 10</u> strategy. Write the sums in the squares. Color.

Add by **counting on**.

5.　$\begin{array}{r} 2 \\ + 9 \\ \hline \end{array}$　　6.　$\begin{array}{r} 8 \\ + 1 \\ \hline \end{array}$　　7.　$\begin{array}{r} 7 \\ + 2 \\ \hline \end{array}$　　8.　$\begin{array}{r} 3 \\ + 8 \\ \hline \end{array}$　　9.　$\begin{array}{r} 9 \\ + 3 \\ \hline \end{array}$　　10.　$\begin{array}{r} 2 \\ + 8 \\ \hline \end{array}$

Add **doubles** and **doubles plus one**.

11.　$\begin{array}{r} 6 \\ + 6 \\ \hline \end{array}$　　12.　$\begin{array}{r} 8 \\ + 7 \\ \hline \end{array}$　　13.　$\begin{array}{r} 8 \\ + 8 \\ \hline \end{array}$　　14.　$\begin{array}{r} 7 \\ + 7 \\ \hline \end{array}$　　15.　$\begin{array}{r} 5 \\ + 6 \\ \hline \end{array}$　　16.　$\begin{array}{r} 7 \\ + 6 \\ \hline \end{array}$

17. $5 + 5 = $ _____　　18. $8 + 9 = $ _____　　19. $9 + 9 = $ _____

Use the **adding 9** strategy.

20. $4 + 9 = $ _____　　21. $6 + 9 = $ _____　　22. $7 + 9 = $ _____

$(3 + 10 = $____$)$　　$(__ + 10 = $___$)$　　$(__ + 10 = $___$)$

Use the **sharing** strategy.

23. $6 + 4 = $ __10__　　24. $8 + 6 = $ _____　　25. $5 + 7 = $ _____

$(5 + 5 = $ __10__ $)$　　$(__ + __ = $____$)$　　$(__ + __ = $____$)$

Use the **make a 10** strategy. Draw beans in the 10 frames.

26.

27.

28.

$8 + 5 = $ _____　　$7 + 4 = $ _____　　$8 + 4 = $ _____

© Copyright 1999　Mathematics Grade 2

A.J. had 15 small collector cars. He gave 6 to his friend Frankie.
How many cars did he keep?

$15 - 6 = 9$ A.J. kept 9 cars.

Mark off to find the difference.

1.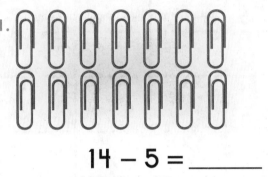

$14 - 5 = $ _____

2.

$16 - 7 = $ _____

Use connecting cubes to make the whole. Break off a part. Find the part that is left.

3. 13 whole
    − 6 part

    _____ part

4. 15 whole
    − 7 part

    _____ part

5. 14 whole
    − 8 part

    _____ part

6. 17 whole
    − 9 part

    _____ part

Subtract.

7. 18
    − 9

8. 13
    − 5

9. 12
    − 7

10. 16
    − 8

11. 17
    − 8

12. 15
    − 8

13. 14
    − 5

14. 15
    − 9

15. 13
    − 9

16. 11
    − 8

17. 13
    − 7

18. 16
    − 9

19.

11 − 2	11 − 3	11 − 4	11 − 5	11 − 6	11 − 7	11 − 8	11 − 9

20.

12 − 3	12 − 4	12 − 5	12 − 6	12 − 7	12 − 8	12 − 9

21.

13 − 4	13 − 5	13 − 6	13 − 7	13 − 8	13 − 9

Subtract.

What patterns do you see in the answers?

22.

14 − 5	14 − 6	14 − 7	14 − 8	14 − 9

23.

15 − 6	15 − 7	15 − 8	15 − 9

27. _____

_____

28. _____

24.

16 − 7	16 − 8	16 − 9

_____

29. _____

25.

17 − 8	17 − 9

_____

Review   Read and solve.

Carissa has piano lessons after lunch on Saturday.
Her mother shops while Carissa has her lesson.
She leaves Carissa at her lesson at 1:15 and picks her up at 2:00.

26.

18 − 9

1. Is the lesson during a.m. or p.m. time?_____

2. How long does Carissa's lesson last?_____

© Copyright 1999 　 Mathematics Grade 2

Adding Three Numbers — Lesson 78

Cameron is trying to count the puppies at the pet store. He counted 8, 7, and 2. How many puppies are there altogether?

$$8 \quad + \quad 7 \quad + \quad 2 = \underline{\quad}$$

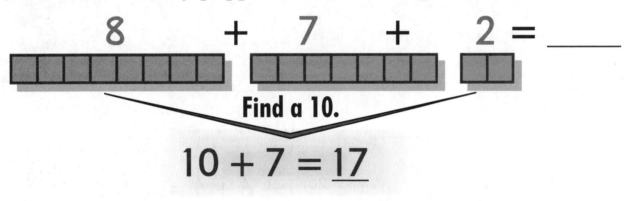

Find a 10.

$$10 + 7 = \underline{17}$$

Use connecting cubes to add. ➡ $6 + 4 + 5 = \underline{\quad}$

Changing the order of the addends does not change the sum. Circle two numbers that equal 10. Add the third number.

1. $7 + 3 + 8 = \underline{\quad}$ 2. $5 + 7 + 5 = \underline{\quad}$ 3. $2 + 4 + 8 = \underline{\quad}$

4. $4 + 3 + 6 = \underline{\quad}$ 5. $6 + 5 + 4 = \underline{\quad}$ 6. $8 + 6 + 2 = \underline{\quad}$

7. $5 + 9 + 1 = \underline{\quad}$ 8. $3 + 8 + 7 = \underline{\quad}$ 9. $2 + 5 + 5 = \underline{\quad}$

Draw lines if there is a 10. Add.

10.
$$\begin{array}{r} 4 \\ 3 \\ + 6 \\ \hline \end{array}$$

11.
$$\begin{array}{r} 3 \\ 8 \\ + 7 \\ \hline \end{array}$$

12.
$$\begin{array}{r} 6 \\ 2 \\ + 5 \\ \hline \end{array}$$

13.
$$\begin{array}{r} 2 \\ 4 \\ + 8 \\ \hline \end{array}$$

14.
$$\begin{array}{r} 6 \\ 5 \\ + 6 \\ \hline \end{array}$$

15. Color groups of ten on the number bug.

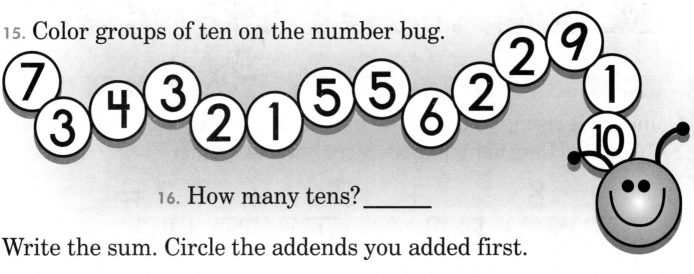

16. How many tens? _____

Write the sum. Circle the addends you added first.

17. $3 + 5 + 5 =$ _____   18. $6 + 4 + 4 =$ _____

19. $7 + 4 + 7 =$ _____   20. $1 + 6 + 6 =$ _____

21. $8 + 8 + 2 =$ _____   22. $3 + 3 + 7 =$ _____

Review

Color the flower petals equal to the center number.

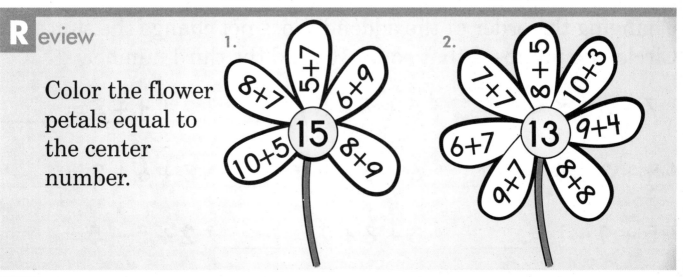

© Copyright 1999   ACSI Mathematics Grade 2

Two-Digit Addition

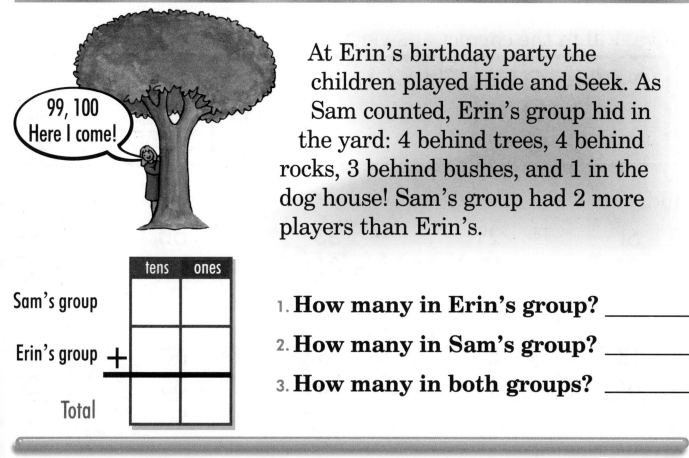

99, 100
Here I come!

At Erin's birthday party the children played Hide and Seek. As Sam counted, Erin's group hid in the yard: 4 behind trees, 4 behind rocks, 3 behind bushes, and 1 in the dog house! Sam's group had 2 more players than Erin's.

	tens	ones
Sam's group		
Erin's group +		
Total		

1. **How many in Erin's group?** _____

2. **How many in Sam's group?** _____

3. **How many in both groups?** _____

Use base ten blocks to add.

4.
tens	ones
2	3
+ 1	4
3	7

5.
tens	ones
3	6
+ 2	3

6.
tens	ones
5	2
+ 3	7

7. 47
   + 32

8. 21
   + 15

9. 14
   + 74

10. 25
    + 70

11. 44
    + 35

12. $51 + 7 =$ _____ tens _____ ones = _____

13. $29 + 30 =$ _____ tens _____ ones = _____

© Copyright 1999 ACSI Mathematics Grade 2

Solve. Fill in the correct answer.

14. 10 + 8 = ○ 108 ○ 18 ○ 8

15. 12 + 11 = ○ 122 ○ 121 ○ 23

16.
$$\begin{array}{r} 23 \\ + 32 \\ \hline \end{array}$$
○ 55 ○ 45 ○ 52

Add.

17.
$$\begin{array}{r} 61 \\ + 26 \\ \hline \end{array}$$

18.
$$\begin{array}{r} 24 \\ + 15 \\ \hline \end{array}$$

19.
$$\begin{array}{r} 33 \\ + 36 \\ \hline \end{array}$$

20.
$$\begin{array}{r} 50 \\ + 40 \\ \hline \end{array}$$

21.
$$\begin{array}{r} 80 \\ + 17 \\ \hline \end{array}$$

22.
$$\begin{array}{r} 18 \\ + 61 \\ \hline \end{array}$$

23.
$$\begin{array}{r} 53 \\ + 10 \\ \hline \end{array}$$

24.
$$\begin{array}{r} 16 \\ + 13 \\ \hline \end{array}$$

25.
$$\begin{array}{r} 60 \\ + 38 \\ \hline \end{array}$$

26.
$$\begin{array}{r} 59 \\ + 20 \\ \hline \end{array}$$

27.
$$\begin{array}{r} 24 \\ + 23 \\ \hline \end{array}$$

28.
$$\begin{array}{r} 62 \\ + 36 \\ \hline \end{array}$$

29.
$$\begin{array}{r} 81 \\ + 18 \\ \hline \end{array}$$

30.
$$\begin{array}{r} 63 \\ + 24 \\ \hline \end{array}$$

31.
$$\begin{array}{r} 71 \\ + 26 \\ \hline \end{array}$$

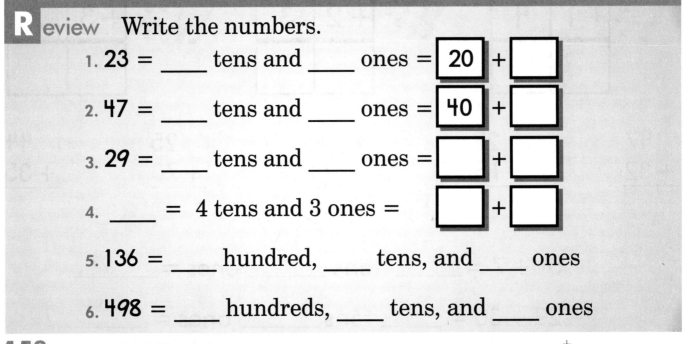

Review   Write the numbers.

1. 23 = _____ tens and _____ ones = [20] + [   ]

2. 47 = _____ tens and _____ ones = [40] + [   ]

3. 29 = _____ tens and _____ ones = [   ] + [   ]

4. _____ = 4 tens and 3 ones = [   ] + [   ]

5. 136 = _____ hundred, _____ tens, and _____ ones

6. 498 = _____ hundreds, _____ tens, and _____ ones

© Copyright 1999   Mathematics Grade 2

Two-Digit Subtraction   Lesson **80**

Scott's mother made 28 cupcakes for the class party. The students ate 16. How many were left?

_____cupcakes

To find out, take away 16 from 28.

$$\begin{array}{r} 28 \\ -\ 16 \\ \hline 12 \end{array}$$

28 is 2 tens and 8 ones.

16 is 1 ten and 6 ones.

First, take away the ones.
8 ones − 6 ones = 2 ones

Then take away the tens.
2 tens − 1 ten = 1 ten

1.	tens	ones
	6	2
−	3	1
	3	

2.	tens	ones
	5	7
−	4	3

3.	tens	ones
	9	5
−	2	1

4.	tens	ones
	7	9
−	3	1

5.	tens	ones
	8	6
−	7	6

Subtract.

6. $\begin{array}{r} 80 \\ -\ 50 \\ \hline \end{array}$
7. $\begin{array}{r} 90 \\ -\ 20 \\ \hline \end{array}$
8. $\begin{array}{r} 28 \\ -\ 16 \\ \hline \end{array}$
9. $\begin{array}{r} 49 \\ -\ 29 \\ \hline \end{array}$
10. $\begin{array}{r} 96 \\ -\ 43 \\ \hline \end{array}$
11. $\begin{array}{r} 55 \\ -\ 34 \\ \hline \end{array}$

12. 36 − 22 = _____ tens _____ ones = _____

13. 90 − 40 = _____ tens _____ ones = _____

© Copyright 1999 ACSI Mathematics Grade 2

Trouble in the garden!

65 ladybugs

49 grasshoppers

87 flies

42 roses

34 sunflowers

31 pansies

Subtract flowers from bugs.

$$
\begin{array}{r}
65 \text{ ladybugs} \\
- 42 \text{ roses} \\
\hline
23
\end{array}
$$

Use another piece of paper to write as many problems as you can.

Subtract.

14. $\begin{array}{r} 68 \\ -57 \\ \hline \end{array}$

15. $\begin{array}{r} 98 \\ -77 \\ \hline \end{array}$

16. $\begin{array}{r} 76 \\ -63 \\ \hline \end{array}$

17. $\begin{array}{r} 37 \\ -12 \\ \hline \end{array}$

18. $\begin{array}{r} 62 \\ -42 \\ \hline \end{array}$

19. $\begin{array}{r} 36 \\ -21 \\ \hline \end{array}$

20. $\begin{array}{r} 25 \\ -11 \\ \hline \end{array}$

21. $\begin{array}{r} 50 \\ -30 \\ \hline \end{array}$

22. $\begin{array}{r} 44 \\ -32 \\ \hline \end{array}$

23. $\begin{array}{r} 62 \\ -40 \\ \hline \end{array}$

24. $\begin{array}{r} 77 \\ -63 \\ \hline \end{array}$

25. $\begin{array}{r} 85 \\ -64 \\ \hline \end{array}$

Review

Add the numbers in each letter. Write the sum of each letter on the line.

Color letters with sums <16 orange. Color letters with sums = to or >16 green.

© Copyright 1999 ACSI Mathematics Grade 2

Checking Addition and Subtraction — Lesson 81

You can use <u>subtraction</u> to check your work in <u>addition</u>.

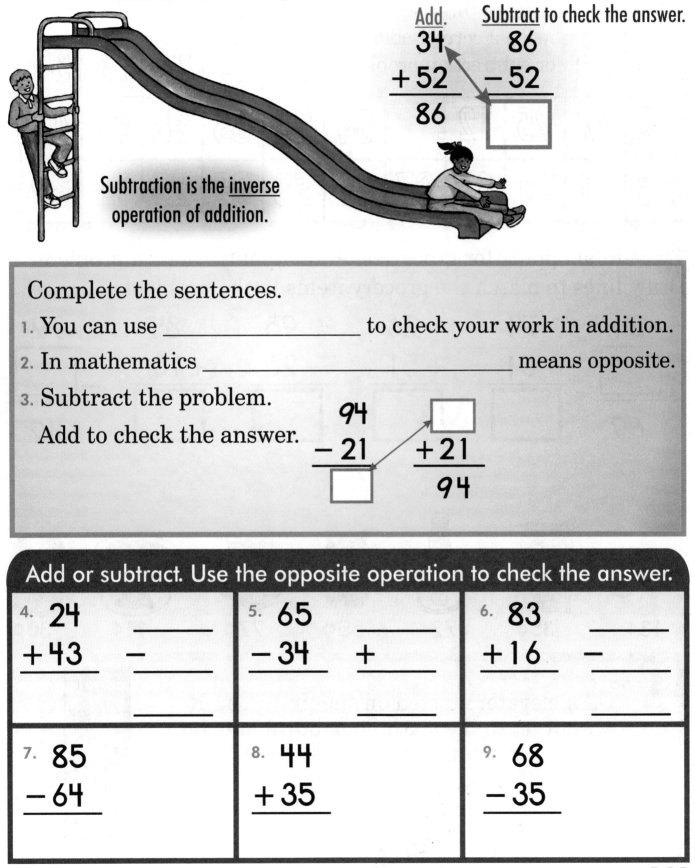

Add.   <u>Subtract</u> to check the answer.

$$34 + 52 = 86$$

$$86 - 52 = \boxed{}$$

Subtraction is the <u>inverse</u> operation of addition.

Complete the sentences.

1. You can use _____ to check your work in addition.

2. In mathematics _____ means opposite.

3. Subtract the problem.
   Add to check the answer.

$$\begin{array}{r} 94 \\ -21 \\ \hline \boxed{} \end{array} \qquad \begin{array}{r} \boxed{} \\ +21 \\ \hline 94 \end{array}$$

Add or subtract. Use the opposite operation to check the answer.

4. $\begin{array}{r} 24 \\ +43 \\ \hline \end{array}$ $-$ ___	5. $\begin{array}{r} 65 \\ -34 \\ \hline \end{array}$ $+$ ___	6. $\begin{array}{r} 83 \\ +16 \\ \hline \end{array}$ $-$ ___
7. $\begin{array}{r} 85 \\ -64 \\ \hline \end{array}$	8. $\begin{array}{r} 44 \\ +35 \\ \hline \end{array}$	9. $\begin{array}{r} 68 \\ -35 \\ \hline \end{array}$

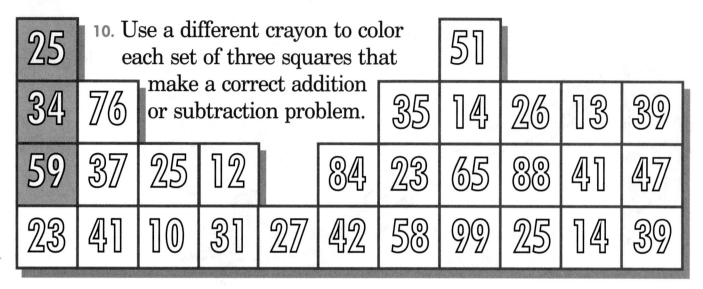

10. Use a different crayon to color each set of three squares that make a correct addition or subtraction problem.

Ty went shopping for groceries. Add or subtract each problem. Draw lines to match the grocery items to the problems.

11. 34
+ ☐
―――
69

12. 74
− 61
―――
☐

13. 26
+ 51
―――
☐

14. 95
− 23
―――
☐

15. 84
+ 10
―――
☐

16. 72
− ☐
―――
42

13¢   35¢   72¢   55¢   77¢   94¢   30¢

Review

An elevator started on the first floor. It went up to the sixth floor, down one, up three, and down four floors. What floor did it land on?

The elevator landed on the _____ floor.

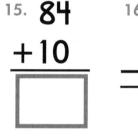

© Copyright 1999   Mathematics Grade 2

Review: Facts to 18　　　　Lesson 82

Write the sum in the ◯. Example:

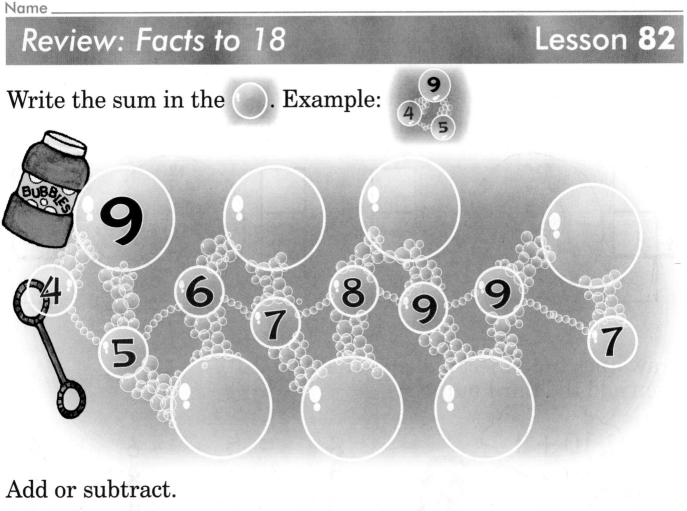

Add or subtract.

1. $14 - 9 =$ ☐
4. $18 - 9 =$ ☐
7. $10 + 10 =$ ☐

2. $7 + 7 =$ ☐
5. $12 - 6 =$ ☐
8. $5 + 7 =$ ☐

3. $7 + 10 =$ ☐
6. $4 + 9 =$ ☐
9. $16 - 8 =$ ☐

10. Write all the addition facts for the sum of fourteen.

$0 + 14 = 14$ _____

_____　　_____　　_____

_____　　_____　　_____

_____　　_____　　_____

_____　　_____　　$14 + 0 = 14$

11. Write the fact family problems for **7 + 6**.

_____ _____　　_____ _____

Add the numbers on each snail.
Check your work by making a subtraction problem.

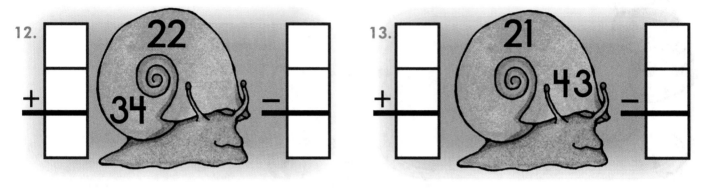

12. ▢
　 ＋▢ ⟶ 22 34 ⟶ ▢ －▢

13. ▢
　 ＋▢ ⟶ 21 43 ⟶ ▢ －▢

Draw lines to connect addends that equal 10.
Then add the third number.

(thought bubble) 10 + 4

3
4 ⟩ 10
＋7
――――
14

14.　8
　　2
　＋9
――――

15.　5
　　1
　＋9
――――

16.　6
　　8
　＋4
――――

17.　9
　　8
　＋1
――――

Review　Circle the tens. Draw squares around the hundreds.

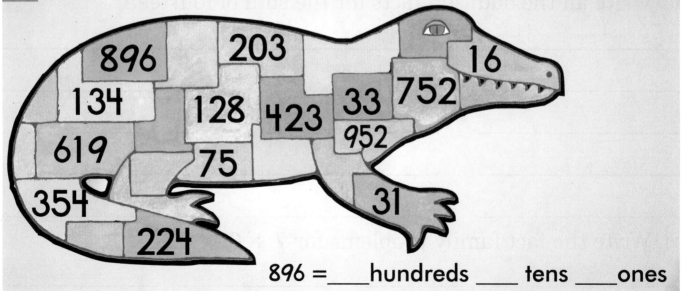

896　203　16
134　128　423　33　752
619　952
354　75　31
224

896 = ____ hundreds ____ tens ____ ones

© Copyright 1999 　 *Mathematics Grade 2*

Trading Ones for Tens

Fill in the blanks.

1.

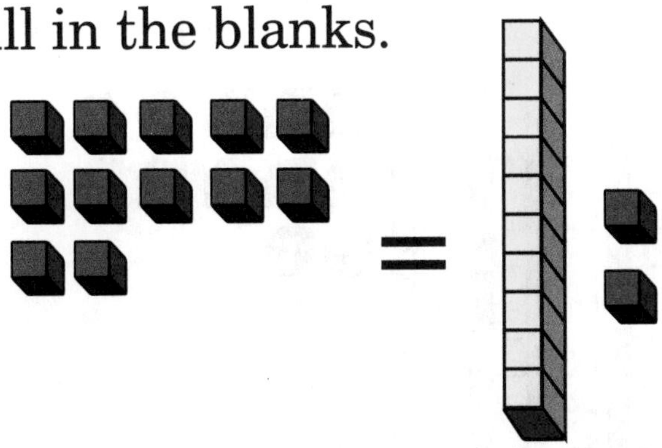

12 ones = _____ ten _____ ones

2.

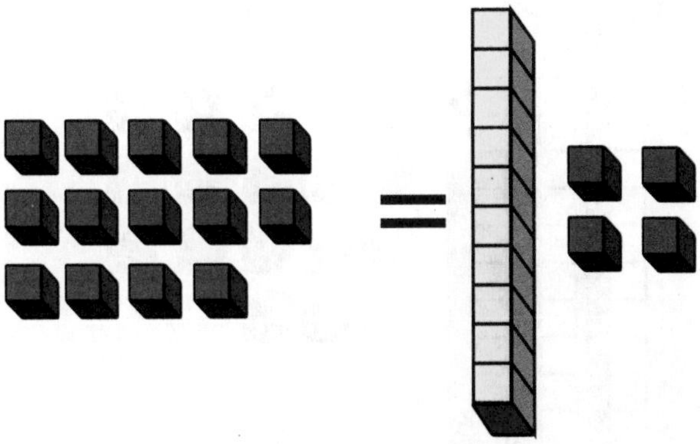

_____ ones = _____ ten _____ ones

3.

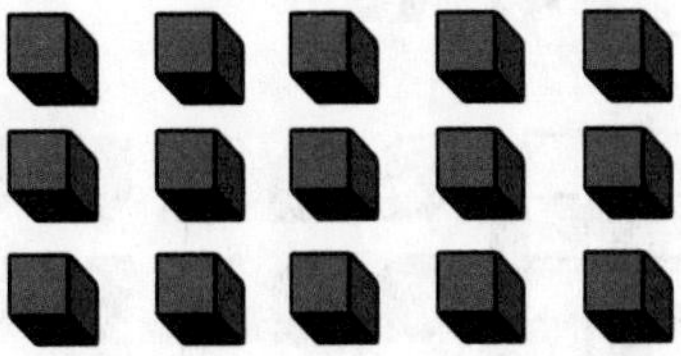

= _____ **ones,** or _____ **ten** and _____ **ones**

Use base ten blocks to make another ten.

4. **3 tens and 17 ones = _____ tens _____ ones = _____**

5. **6 tens and 19 ones = _____ tens _____ ones = _____**

6. **2 tens and 13 ones = _____ tens _____ ones = _____**

7. **7 tens and 10 ones = _____ tens _____ ones = _____**

SOLVE.

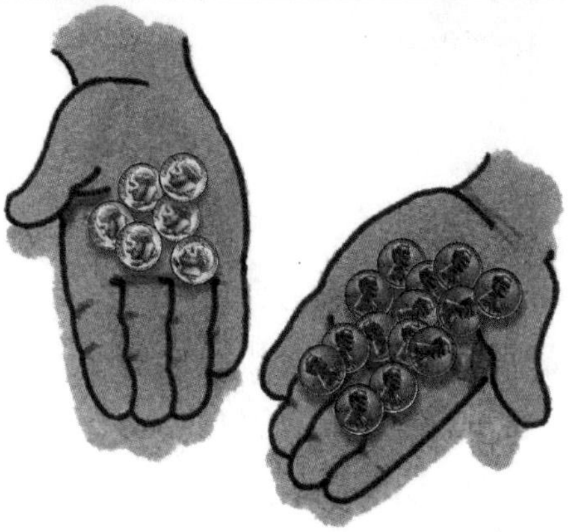

8. Sydney has 14 pennies and 6 dimes. Regroup to find out how much money he has.

6 dimes and 14 pennies = _____ dimes _____ pennies = _____ ¢

Make necessary trades. Fill in the blanks. Circle <u>yes</u> or <u>no</u>.

9.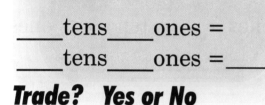

_____tens_____ones =
_____tens_____ones =_____

Trade? Yes or No

10.

_____tens_____ones =
_____tens_____ones =_____

Trade? Yes or No

11.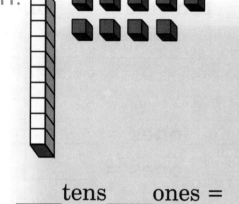

_____tens_____ones =
_____tens_____ones =_____

Trade? Yes or No

12.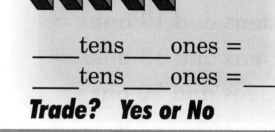

_____tens_____ones =
_____tens_____ones =_____

Trade? Yes or No

Review

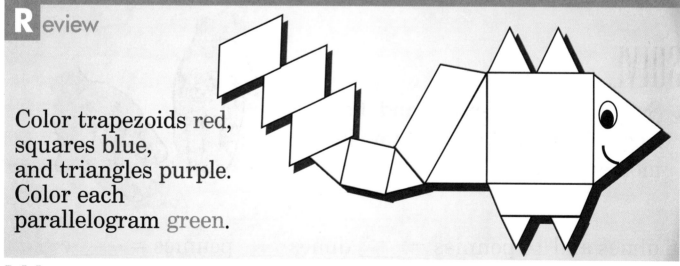

Color trapezoids red,
squares blue,
and triangles purple.
Color each
parallelogram green.

© Copyright 1999   Mathematics Grade 2

Understanding Regrouping Lesson 84

Tens and Ones City

1. Building 1 = _____ tens _____ ones
2. Building 2 = _____ tens _____ ones, or _____ tens _____ ones
3. Building 3 = _____ tens _____ ones
4. Building 4 = _____ tens _____ ones
5. Building 5 = _____ tens _____ ones
6. Use base ten blocks to find the total.

Total = _____ hundreds

_____ tens _____ ones

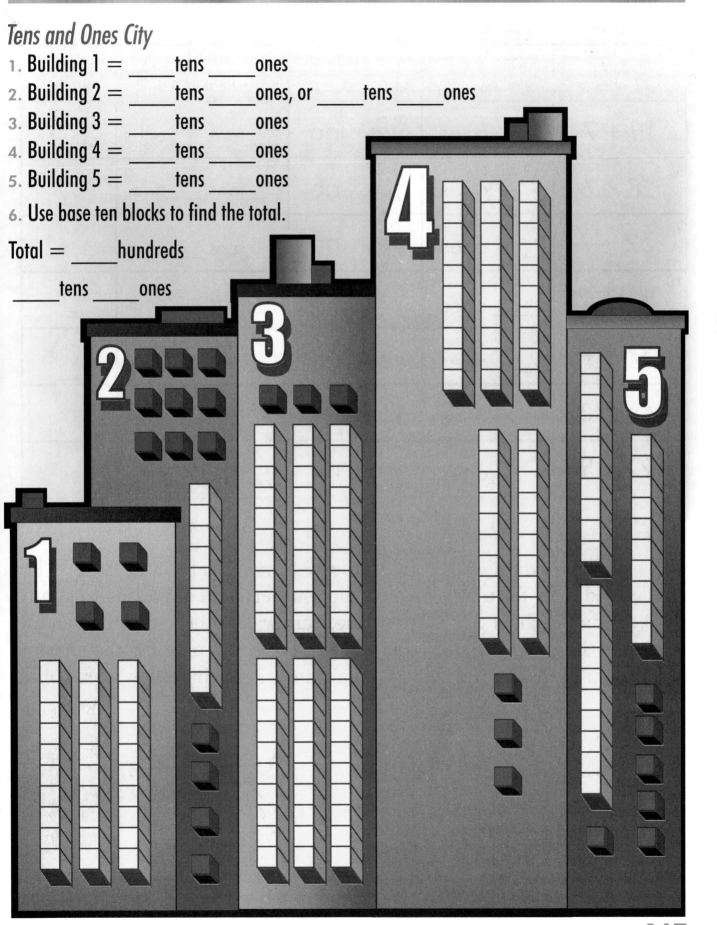

Complete the table.

Show:	Combine the ones. Write how many.	Do you regroup? Circle yes or no.	Combine the tens. Write how many.	Write the number.
7. $19 + 7$	__16__ ones	(yes) no	__2__ tens __6__ ones	26
8. $28 + 6$	_____ ones	yes no	___ tens ___ ones	
9. $52 + 7$	_____ ones	yes no	___ tens ___ ones	
10. $45 + 28$	_____ ones	yes no	___ tens ___ ones	
11. $37 + 14$	_____ ones	yes no	___ tens ___ ones	
12. $64 + 33$	_____ ones	yes no	___ tens ___ ones	
13. $22 + 49$	_____ ones	yes no	___ tens ___ ones	

Think

14. There were three sea gull brothers, Simon, Sam, and Stan. They planned to fly from Key West on the southern end of Florida to Miami, Daytona Beach, or Saint Augustine. Sam was in the lead, but Stan had the farthest to fly. Simon was a slow flyer so he planned the shortest trip. On the lines write the sea gulls' names and where they were going.

_____   _____   _____

_____   _____   _____

© Copyright 1999 — Mathematics Grade 2

Problem Solving: Addition and Subtraction   Lesson 85

There are many ways to solve a problem. Sometimes writing a number sentence can help.

Frog and Toad take a walk in the woods. Toad loses a button. The friends look for it. If Frog finds 23 buttons and Toad finds 26, how many do they both find? _____

$23 + 26 =$ _____

$$\begin{array}{r} 23 \\ + 26 \\ \hline 49 \end{array} \text{ buttons}$$

Write the number sentences. Add or subtract.

1. The second grade is collecting buttons for a puppet project. On Tuesday, Bill's mom brings in 46 buttons. Art's mom sends in 51 buttons. How many buttons does the class receive on Tuesday? _____

2. Of all the buttons collected on Tuesday, 30 are red and 24 are green. How many are red and green? _____
How many are other colors? _____
   Step 1   **Step 2**

3. The students look at each button carefully. They find 15 buttons are too large and 22 are too small. How many are too large and small? ____ The rest are the right size to use. How many are the right size? _____
   Step 1   **Step 2**

4. The puppets are ready for the show. 42 first graders and 53 third graders come to enjoy the second grade puppet show. How many first and third graders are there? _____

Write the number sentences. Add or subtract.

5. Tony took 29 steps on the tires before falling off. Mindy took 18 steps. How many more steps did Tony take than Mindy? _____ **steps**

6. On Monday Mrs. Ward's class is able to play outside for 20 minutes. On Tuesday they play for 25 minutes. How many minutes does the class play on these two days?

_____ **minutes**

7. Three friends emptied their bags of marbles. 37 landed inside the circle. 21 landed outside the circle. How many more marbles landed inside than outside the circle?

_____ **marbles**

8. The second grade played Four Square during recess. On Wednesday they played for 15 minutes. On Thursday they had 5 minutes longer to play. How many minutes did they play on Wednesday and Thursday?

_____ **minutes**

© Copyright 1999 *Mathematics Grade 2*

Using Shapes to Add and Subtract — Lesson 86

Use the key to solve the shape problems.

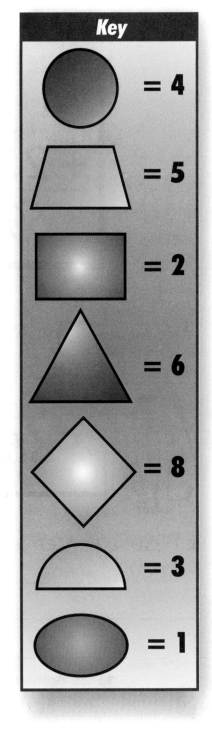

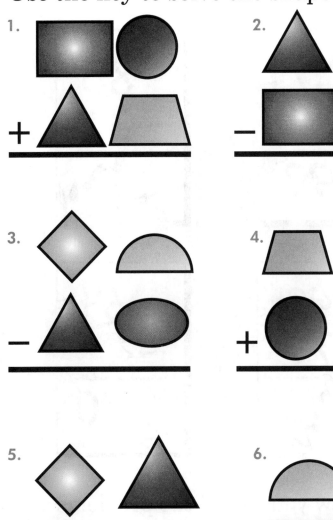

1.

2.

3.

4.

5.

6.

Key

○ = 4

▱ = 5

▭ = 2

△ = 6

◇ = 8

◠ = 3

⬭ = 1

Draw a shape problem for each sum.

7.
+
2 3

8.
+
9 8

9.
+
5 5

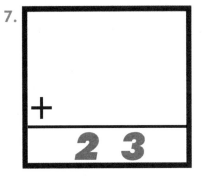

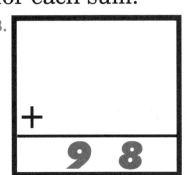

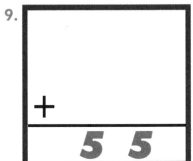

© Copyright 1999 Mathematics Grade 2

Math Dog ate my homework! Help me find the missing numbers.

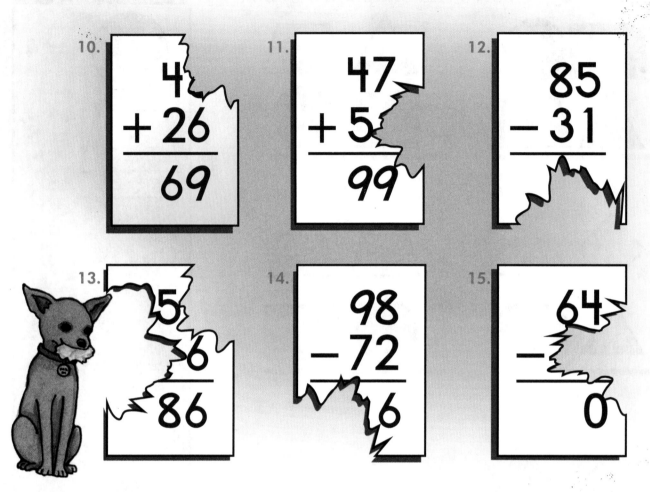

10.
$$4$$
$$+\,26$$
$$\overline{69}$$

11.
$$47$$
$$+\,5$$
$$\overline{99}$$

12.
$$85$$
$$-\,31$$

13.
$$5$$
$$6$$
$$\overline{86}$$

14.
$$98$$
$$-\,72$$
$$\overline{6}$$

15.
$$64$$
$$-$$
$$\overline{0}$$

16. Write a sentence to describe how you solved the problems above. _____

_____

_____

Review Read and think. Write the month for each person's birthday.

Zack's birthday was two months before Charlotte's. Alfred's birthday was four months after Zack's. Marissa's birthday was two months before Zack's and falls on Saint Patrick's day.

Zack   **Charlotte**   **Alfred**   **Marissa**

_____   _____   _____   _____

"Let your light so shine before men, that they may see your good works and glorify your Father in heaven." Matthew 5:16

List 3 sources of earthly light.

List 3 ways your "light" can shine.

_____   _____

_____   _____

_____   _____

If the answer is correct, color the light bulb. If the answer is not correct, write the problem beside the lamp and solve it.

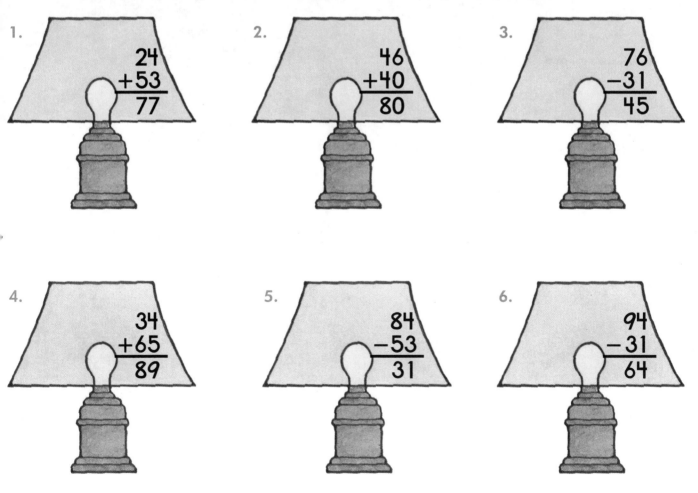

1.
```
  24
+ 53
----
  77
```

2.
```
  46
+ 40
----
  80
```

3.
```
  76
- 31
----
  45
```

4.
```
  34
+ 65
----
  89
```

5.
```
  84
- 53
----
  31
```

6.
```
  94
- 31
----
  64
```

Read the clues to find where each child lives.

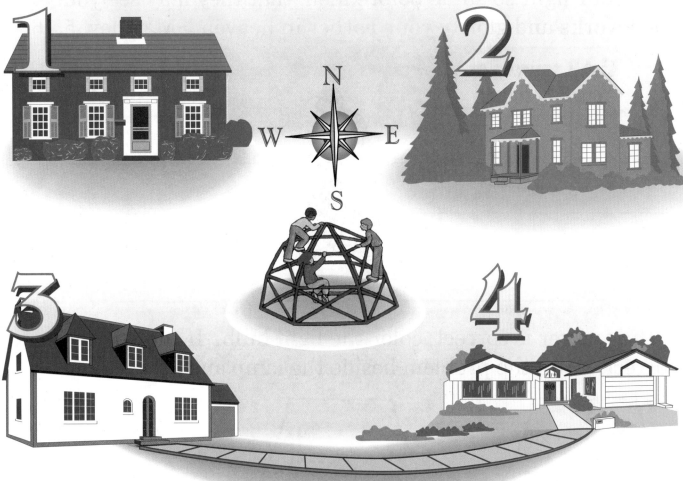

- Ted's house is north of Matthew's.
- Tracy's house is twelve giant steps from Matthew's.
- Amy's house is in the northwest corner.

Where does everyone live? Write the house numbers under the children's faces.

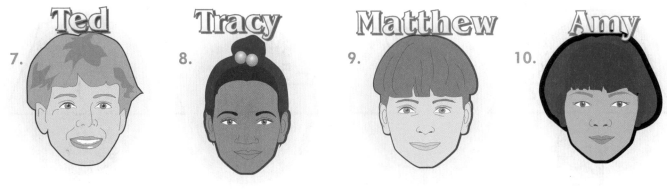

7. Ted

8. Tracy

9. Matthew

10. Amy

© Copyright 1999 ACSI Mathematics Grade 2

Name _____

Adding and Subtracting Money

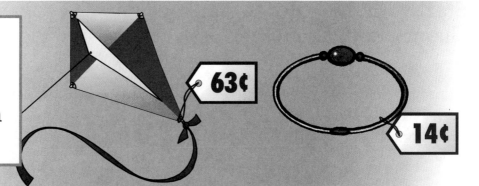

Carlita bought a kite for 63¢. She bought a bracelet for 14¢. How much did Carlita spend?

To add money you can use the cents sign.

$$\begin{array}{r} 63¢ \\ + 14¢ \\ \hline 77¢ \end{array}$$

Another way to show money is to use a dollar sign and a decimal point.

$$\begin{array}{r} \$0.63 \\ + 0.14 \\ \hline \$0.77 \end{array}$$

Write another way to show each money problem.

1.
$$\begin{array}{r} 40¢ \\ + 34¢ \\ \hline 74¢ \end{array}$$
$$\begin{array}{r} \$0.40 \\ + 0.34 \\ \hline \$0.74 \end{array}$$

2.
$$\begin{array}{r} 26¢ \\ + 33¢ \\ \hline \end{array}$$
+

3.
$$\begin{array}{r} \$0.51 \\ + 0.38 \\ \hline \end{array}$$
+

4.
$$\begin{array}{r} 95¢ \\ - 22¢ \\ \hline \end{array}$$
−

5.
$$\begin{array}{r} \$0.78 \\ - 0.44 \\ \hline \end{array}$$
−

6.
$$\begin{array}{r} 69¢ \\ - 14¢ \\ \hline \end{array}$$
−

Find any two items that total 94¢. Draw lines to connect the objects.

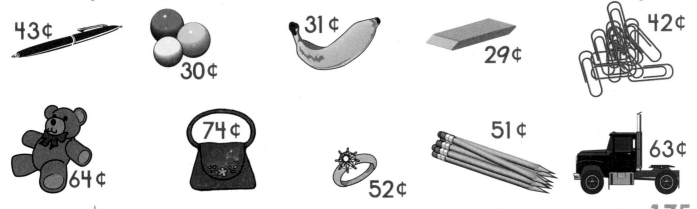

43¢   30¢   31¢   29¢   42¢
64¢   74¢   52¢   51¢   63¢

© Copyright 1999 Mathematics Grade 2   One hundred seventy-five **175**

Start with the center amount. Add the yellow amounts. Subtract the blue amounts. Write the answer in the outside ring.

Color the toy if its price is one of the answers on the disk.

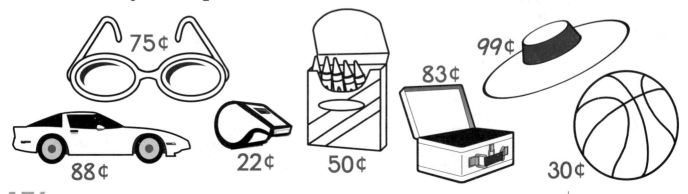

© Copyright 1999 ACSI Mathematics Grade 2

Chapter Six Check-Up   Lesson 89

Find the sums of 18. Color the numbers on each star.

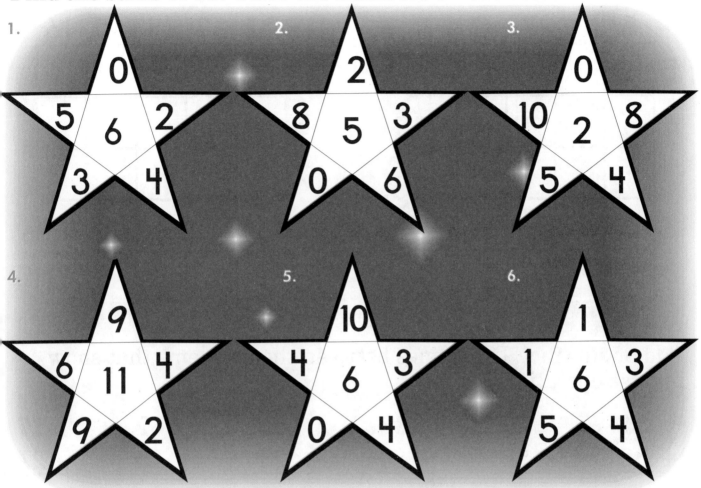

1. 0 5 6 2 3 4
2. 2 8 5 3 0 6
3. 0 10 2 8 5 4
4. 9 6 11 4 9 2
5. 10 4 6 3 0 4
6. 1 1 6 3 5 4

Add or subtract. Write the number of tens and ones.

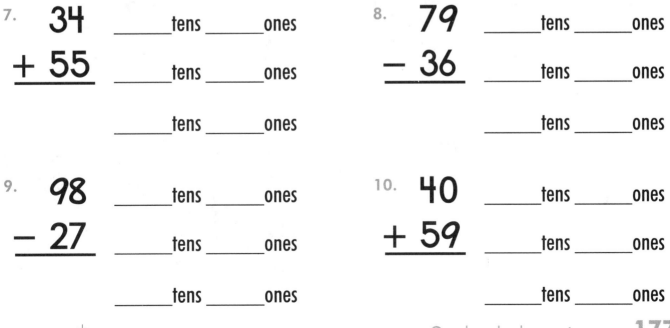

7. 34
  + 55

_____tens _____ones

_____tens _____ones

_____tens _____ones

8. 79
  − 36

_____tens _____ones

_____tens _____ones

_____tens _____ones

9. 98
  − 27

_____tens _____ones

_____tens _____ones

_____tens _____ones

10. 40
   + 59

_____tens _____ones

_____tens _____ones

_____tens _____ones

© Copyright 1999 Mathematics Grade 2

11. Add.

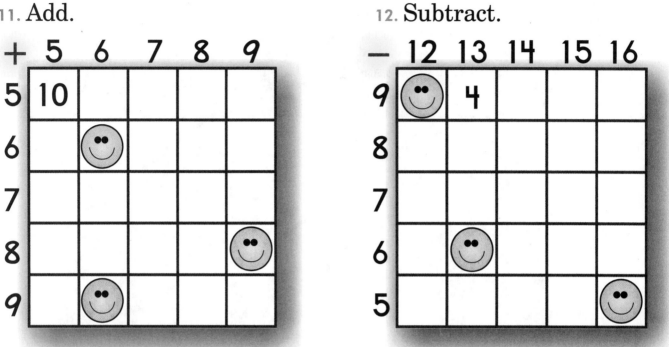

+	5	6	7	8	9
5	10				
6		☺			
7					
8				☺	
9		☺			

12. Subtract.

−	12	13	14	15	16
9	☺	4			
8					
7					
6			☺		
5					☺

Add or subtract. Draw lines between the problems that show inverse operations.

13. 34
+ 55

14. 72
− 51

15. 83
− 60

16. 51
+ 28

17. 62
+ 35

18. 49
− 27

19. 79
− 28

20. 89
− 55

21. 21
+ 51

22. 97
− 35

23. 22
+ 27

24. 23
+ 60

25. Six silly sheep are jumping the fence. Five more sheep jump the fence, then 4 more, then 3, then 2, and finally, 1 more. How many sheep are jumping the fence?

_____ sheep

© Copyright 1999 ACSI Mathematics Grade 2

CHAPTER 7

Fractions and Measurement

Therefore, if anyone is in Christ, he is a new creation; old things have passed away; behold, all things have become new.

2 Corinthians 5:17

Dear Parents,

The Chapter Seven divider page uses one of God's most beautiful creatures —the butterfly— to remind us of the transforming power of Christ. You may want to read the verse with your child and explain that the butterfly's transformation is similar to what happens when we accept Christ. We become new creatures because we allow Christ to change us. This transformation is more miraculous than the changes in the butterfly! Once we accept Christ as Savior, we will never be the same, just as the butterfly will never again be a caterpillar.

Our new chapter concentrates on fractions and measurement. The idea of fractions as <u>part of a whole</u> object was introduced in first grade. Your child will review the concept of equal parts, and study halves, thirds, fourths, and sixths. He or she will also learn about fractions as <u>part of a group</u> of things. For example, if asked to consider a group of four rabbits, your child will recognize that one of the four rabbits is one fourth. He or she may also be asked, "If you had four rabbits and gave half of them to your friend, how many rabbits would you have left?" Your child will come to understand that two rabbits are one half of four rabbits.

You can help your child learn more about fractions by making him or her aware of fractions in real-life activities. Discuss times when you might want to divide things in equal parts: sharing snacks, cooking, weighing, or wood-working. Point out to your child that fractions, or parts of things, are of everyday importance.

We will also study customary measurement (cup, pint, quart, gallon, ounce, pound, and Fahrenheit temperature) and metric measurement (gram and kilogram). You may have your child estimate the capacity of containers in your kitchen, especially containers of equal capacity but of a different shape. Have your child predict which container will hold more water, then measure. Second graders can measure laundry detergent, measure ingredients for recipes, and read the thermometer to report on the temperature.

We hope to make mathematics "pounds" of fun in Chapter Seven!

© Copyright 1999

Symmetry and Equal Parts   Lesson 90

A figure is <u>symmetrical</u> if you can fold it so the two parts match.

The fold line is the <u>line of symmetry</u>.

The two parts of this hat match.
They are the same shape and size.

The two parts of this hat do <u>not</u> match.
They are <u>not</u> the same shape and size.

Is the red line a line of symmetry? Circle <u>yes</u> or <u>no</u>.

1.

yes or no

2.

yes or no

3.

yes or no

Draw a line of symmetry.

4.

5.

6.

7.

8.

9.

© Copyright 1999   Mathematics Grade 2

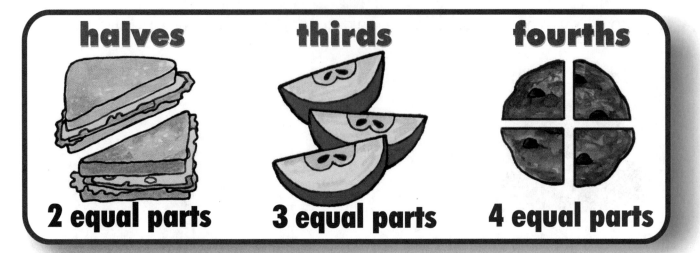

halves   **thirds**   **fourths**

2 equal parts   **3 equal parts**   **4 equal parts**

10. Circle the objects that show 2 equal parts.

11. Circle the objects that show 3 equal parts.

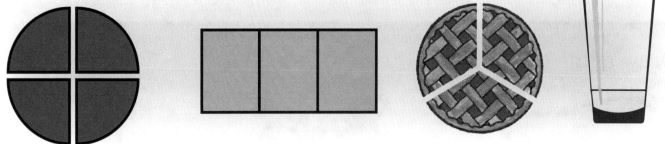

12. Circle the objects that show 4 equal parts.

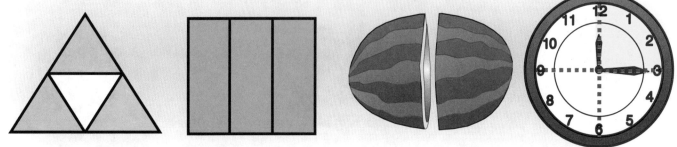

© Copyright 1999   Mathematics Grade 2

Writing Fractions — Lesson 91

A fraction is a number that names part of a whole.

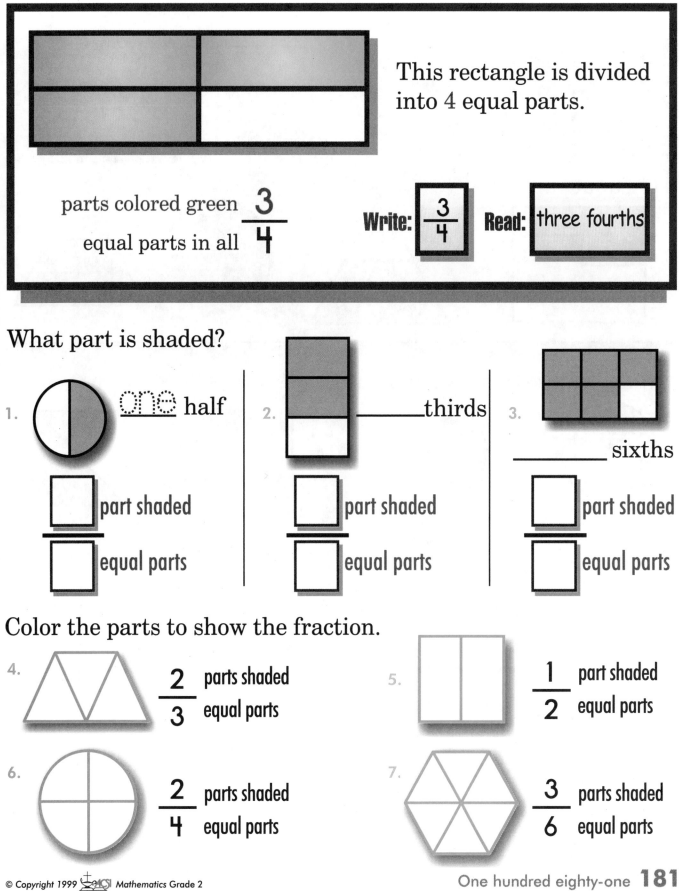

This rectangle is divided into 4 equal parts.

parts colored green $\dfrac{3}{4}$ equal parts in all

Write: $\dfrac{3}{4}$ **Read:** three fourths

What part is shaded?

1. _one_ half

   ☐ part shaded
   ─────
   ☐ equal parts

2. _____ thirds

   ☐ part shaded
   ─────
   ☐ equal parts

3. _____ sixths

   ☐ part shaded
   ─────
   ☐ equal parts

Color the parts to show the fraction.

4. $\dfrac{2}{3}$ parts shaded / equal parts

5. $\dfrac{1}{2}$ part shaded / equal parts

6. $\dfrac{2}{4}$ parts shaded / equal parts

7. $\dfrac{3}{6}$ parts shaded / equal parts

Circle each shape that shows equal parts.

8. 5 equal parts

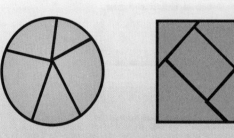

9. 4 equal parts

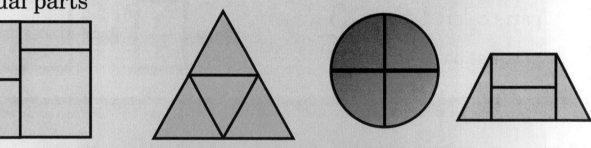

Which is more? Circle the fraction.

10.

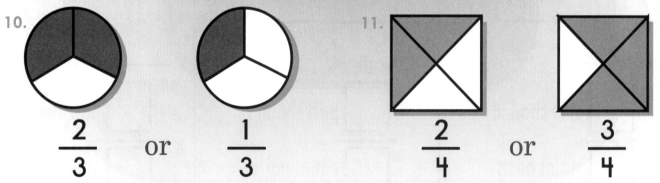

$\dfrac{2}{3}$ or $\dfrac{1}{3}$

11.

$\dfrac{2}{4}$ or $\dfrac{3}{4}$

12. In a fraction all parts must be equal. The top number tells how many parts are shaded. The bottom number tells how many equal parts there are in all. <u>Draw a picture that shows one third.</u> <u>Write the fraction</u>.

© Copyright 1999 Mathematics Grade 2

Halves, Thirds, and Sixths — Lesson 92

1. Circle pictures that show $\frac{1}{2}$.

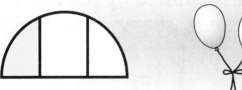

2. Circle pictures that show $\frac{1}{3}$.

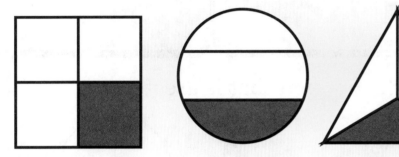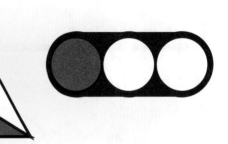

3. Circle pictures that show $\frac{1}{6}$.

4. Help Math Dog get to the pizza shop. Color parts of the blue circles to match the fractions you used to get through the maze. Put all the colored parts together on the yellow circle. What do you have?

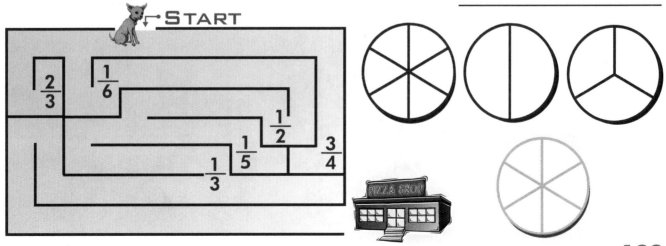

START

5. Draw a rectangle for each fraction. Draw lines to divide the shapes into equal parts. Color the parts named by the fraction.

$$\frac{2}{2}$$

$$\frac{2}{3}$$

$$\frac{5}{6}$$

6. Color the parts. Circle the fraction that is greater.

$$\frac{2}{6}$$ 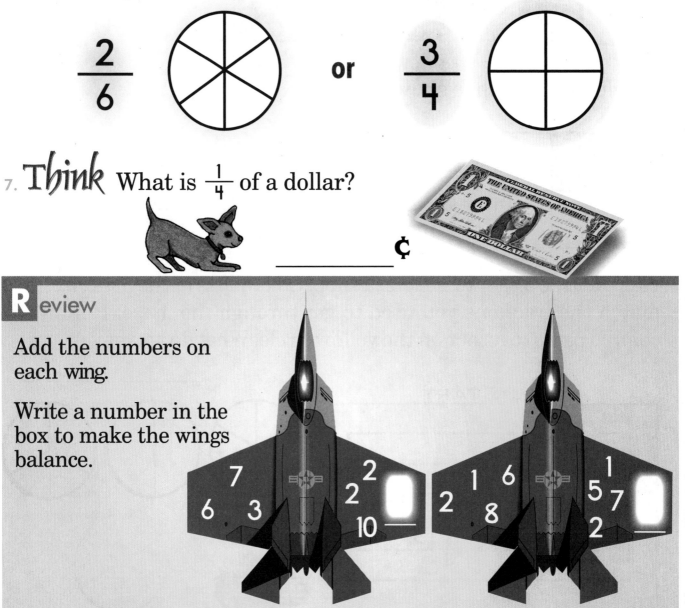 or $$\frac{3}{4}$$

7. **Think** What is $\frac{1}{4}$ of a dollar?

_____ ¢

Add the numbers on each wing.

Write a number in the box to make the wings balance.

7   2
6   3   2   2
10 ____

1   6   1
2   8   5   7
  2 ____

Coloring Fractions   Lesson 93

1. Color $\frac{1}{5}$ of the bug's body **blue**.

Color $\frac{3}{4}$ of the bug **yellow**.

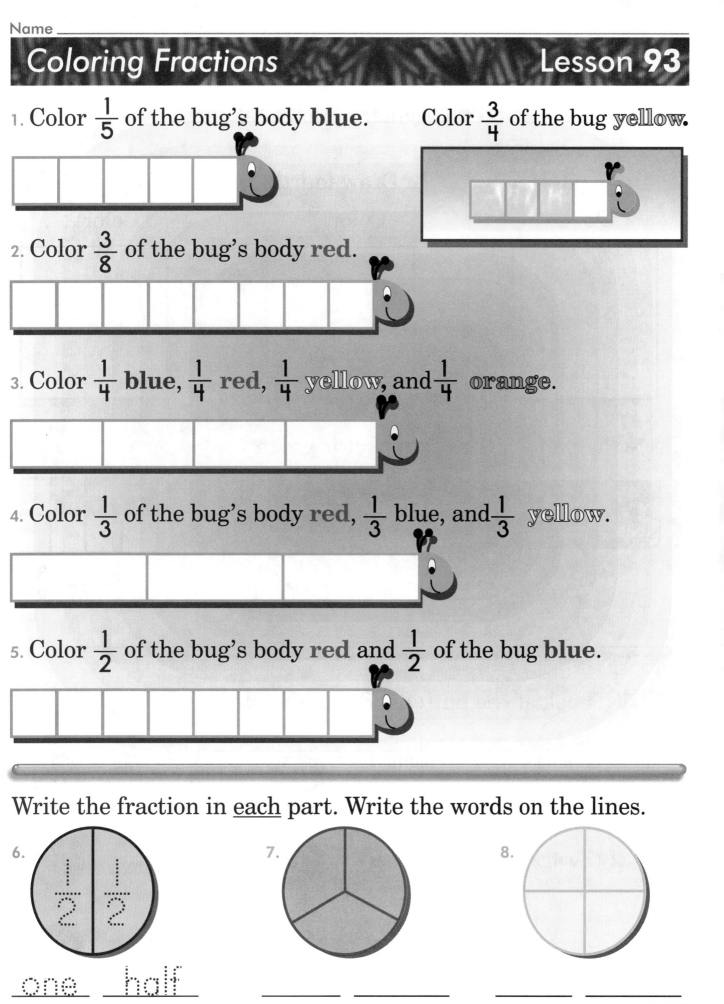

2. Color $\frac{3}{8}$ of the bug's body **red**.

3. Color $\frac{1}{4}$ **blue**, $\frac{1}{4}$ **red**, $\frac{1}{4}$ **yellow**, and $\frac{1}{4}$ **orange**.

4. Color $\frac{1}{3}$ of the bug's body **red**, $\frac{1}{3}$ **blue**, and $\frac{1}{3}$ **yellow**.

5. Color $\frac{1}{2}$ of the bug's body **red** and $\frac{1}{2}$ of the bug **blue**.

Write the fraction in <u>each</u> part. Write the words on the lines.

6.   7.   8.

$\frac{1}{2}$ $\frac{1}{2}$

<u>one</u>   <u>half</u>   _____ _____   _____ _____

Draw lines to divide each square into equal parts.
Color the fractions.

9. Draw halves.
   Color $\frac{1}{2}$.

10. Draw fourths.
    Color $\frac{3}{4}$.

11. Draw thirds.
    Color $\frac{2}{3}$.

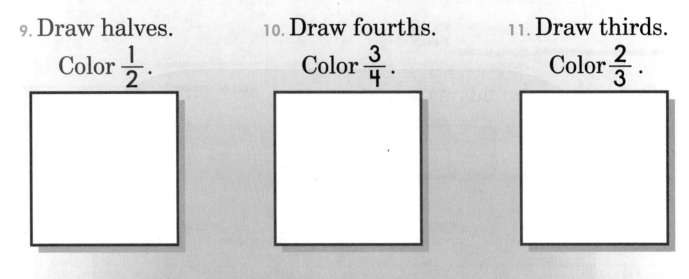

Circle the name for the part that is green.

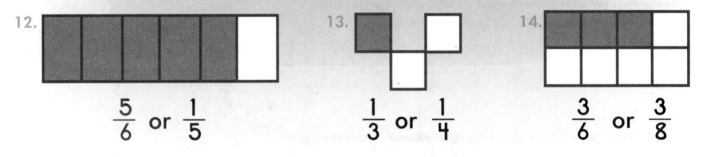

12.

$\frac{5}{6}$ or $\frac{1}{5}$

13.

$\frac{1}{3}$ or $\frac{1}{4}$

14.

$\frac{3}{6}$ or $\frac{3}{8}$

Think Look at the buttons. Fill in the blanks.

15. $\frac{1}{2}$ of 12 buttons = _____ buttons

16. $\frac{1}{3}$ of 12 buttons = _____ buttons

17. $\frac{1}{4}$ of 12 buttons = _____ buttons

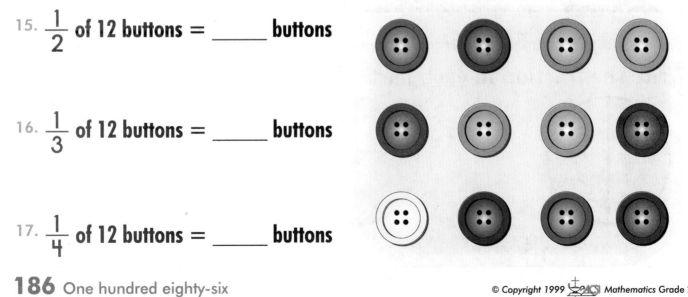

© Copyright 1999   Mathematics Grade 2

Comparing Fractions

Circle the fraction that is greater.

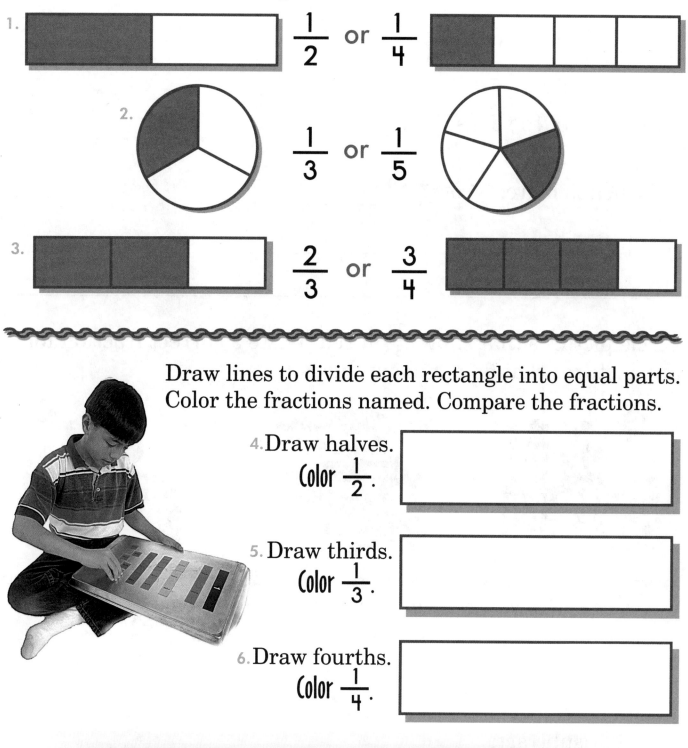

1. $\dfrac{1}{2}$ or $\dfrac{1}{4}$

2. $\dfrac{1}{3}$ or $\dfrac{1}{5}$

3. $\dfrac{2}{3}$ or $\dfrac{3}{4}$

Draw lines to divide each rectangle into equal parts. Color the fractions named. Compare the fractions.

4. Draw halves. Color $\dfrac{1}{2}$.

5. Draw thirds. Color $\dfrac{1}{3}$.

6. Draw fourths. Color $\dfrac{1}{4}$.

7. Which is greatest: $\dfrac{1}{2}$, $\dfrac{1}{4}$, or $\dfrac{1}{3}$? _____

© Copyright 1999 Mathematics Grade 2

Color the dogs. Compare the fractions.

8. Color $\frac{1}{2}$ of the dogs.

9. Color $\frac{1}{3}$ of the dogs.

10. Which is more, $\frac{1}{2}$ or $\frac{1}{3}$?_____

11. Why?_____

_____

Circle pictures that show $\frac{1}{3}$ in red. Write a correct fraction for any pictures that do <u>not</u> show thirds.

12.   13.   14.

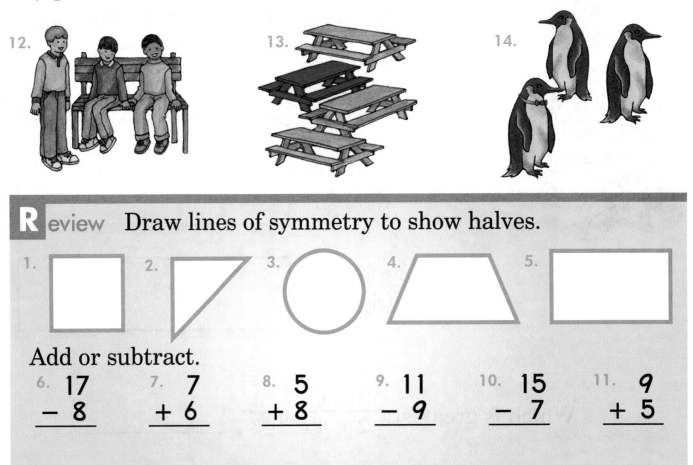

Review   Draw lines of symmetry to show halves.

1.   2.   3.   4.   5.

Add or subtract.

6.   17   7.   7   8.   5   9.   11   10.   15   11.   9
   − 8   + 6   + 8   − 9   − 7   + 5

© Copyright 1999   Mathematics Grade 2

Fraction Practice and Mixed Review   Lesson 95

Draw lines to divide the cakes for a party. Write the fractions.

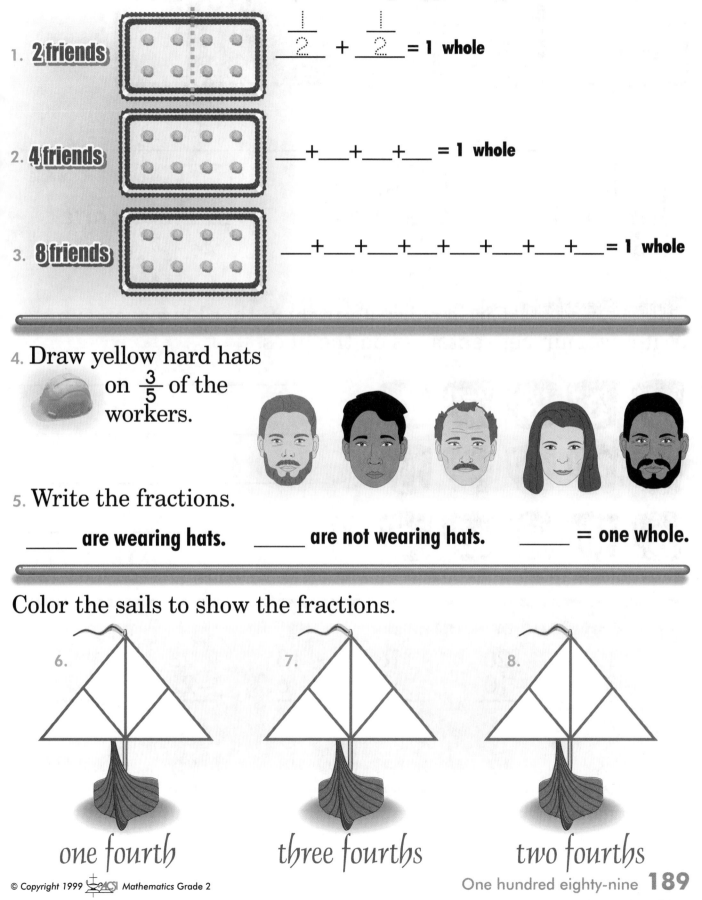

1. **2 friends** $\dfrac{1}{2}$ + $\dfrac{1}{2}$ = 1 **whole**

2. **4 friends**   ___+___+___+___ = 1 **whole**

3. **8 friends**   ___+___+___+___+___+___+___+___ = 1 **whole**

4. Draw yellow hard hats on $\dfrac{3}{5}$ of the workers.

5. Write the fractions.

_____ **are wearing hats.**   _____ **are not wearing hats.**   _____ **= one whole.**

Color the sails to show the fractions.

6.   7.   8.

one fourth   *three fourths*   *two fourths*

9. Write the fraction for each part.

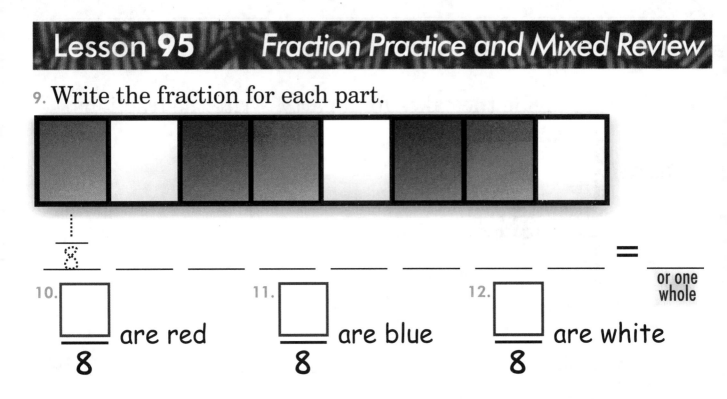

$$\frac{\ }{8} \_\_\_ \_\_\_ \_\_\_ \_\_\_ \_\_\_ \_\_\_ \_\_\_ = \frac{\ }{\ } \text{ or one whole}$$

10. $\dfrac{\Box}{8}$ are red

11. $\dfrac{\Box}{8}$ are blue

12. $\dfrac{\Box}{8}$ are white

Sum Search   Circle pairs of numbers that have <u>even</u> sums. Write five number sentences on the lines.

15 3 6 7 13

4 5 12 4 14

8 10 5 16 9

13. _____

14. _____

15. _____

16. _____

17. _____

Review   Add or subtract.

1. $\begin{array}{r} 12 \\ +37 \\ \hline \end{array}$
2. $\begin{array}{r} 20 \\ -10 \\ \hline \end{array}$
3. $\begin{array}{r} 16 \\ -\ 7 \\ \hline \end{array}$
4. $\begin{array}{r} 13 \\ +\ 6 \\ \hline \end{array}$
5. $\begin{array}{r} 28 \\ -22 \\ \hline \end{array}$
6. $\begin{array}{r} 43 \\ +21 \\ \hline \end{array}$

7. $\begin{array}{r} 16 \\ +42 \\ \hline \end{array}$
8. $\begin{array}{r} 17 \\ -\ 8 \\ \hline \end{array}$
9. $\begin{array}{r} 13 \\ -\ 9 \\ \hline \end{array}$
10. $\begin{array}{r} 14 \\ +13 \\ \hline \end{array}$
11. $\begin{array}{r} 33 \\ -23 \\ \hline \end{array}$
12. $\begin{array}{r} 30 \\ +30 \\ \hline \end{array}$

© Copyright 1999   Mathematics Grade 2

Fractions as Part of a Group — Lesson 96

Fraction Fruits

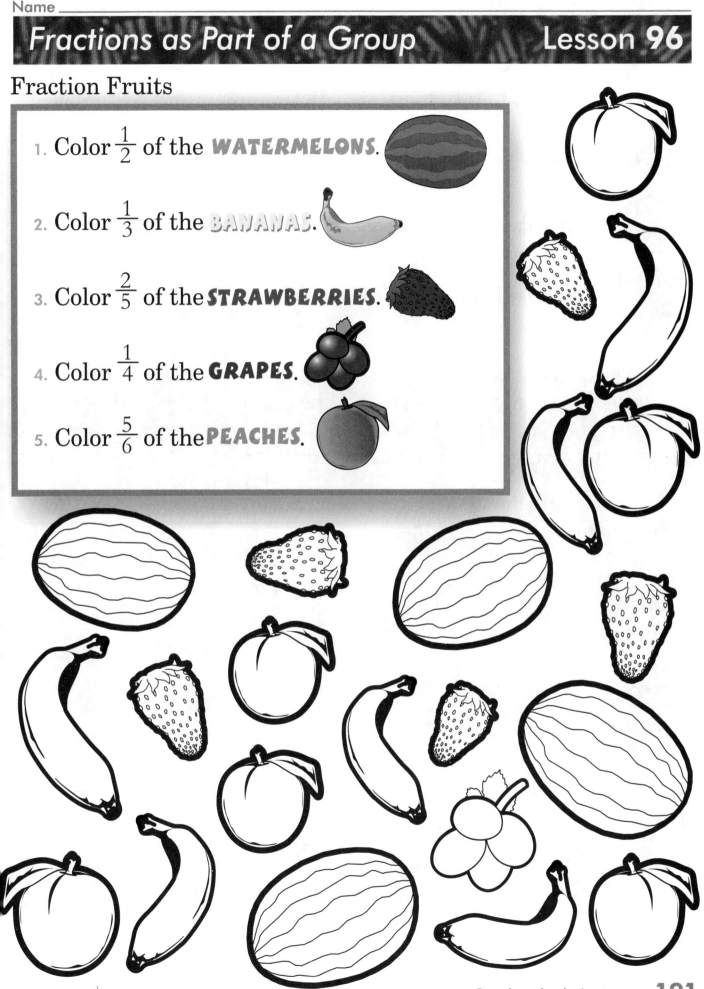

1. Color $\frac{1}{2}$ of the **WATERMELONS**.

2. Color $\frac{1}{3}$ of the **BANANAS**.

3. Color $\frac{2}{5}$ of the **STRAWBERRIES**.

4. Color $\frac{1}{4}$ of the **GRAPES**.

5. Color $\frac{5}{6}$ of the **PEACHES**.

Use the Fraction Fruits to answer these questions.

6. **Write the fraction of the strawberries that were <u>not</u> colored.** _____

7. **Write the fraction of the grapes that were <u>not</u> colored.** _____

8. **Write the fraction of the peaches that were <u>not</u> colored.** _____

Felipé and Rochelle went to the store and bought **8** oranges. Rochelle took $\frac{1}{2}$ of the oranges. Felipé took $\frac{1}{4}$ of the oranges. Their friends, Kate and Thom, each took $\frac{1}{8}$ of the oranges. How many oranges did each child have?

Oranges?	
9. **Rochelle**	
10. **Felipé**	
11. **Kate**	
12. **Thom**	
13. ***Total***	

14. **Think** If Rochelle cut each of her oranges in half, how many friends could she serve?

_____ friends

Review Use the bananas to count by 4's.

_____ _____ _____ _____ _____ _____ _____ _____

© Copyright 1999 Mathematics Grade 2

Fraction Review

Draw a line of symmetry in each letter.

1. 2. 3.

4. Circle drawings that show correct fractions.

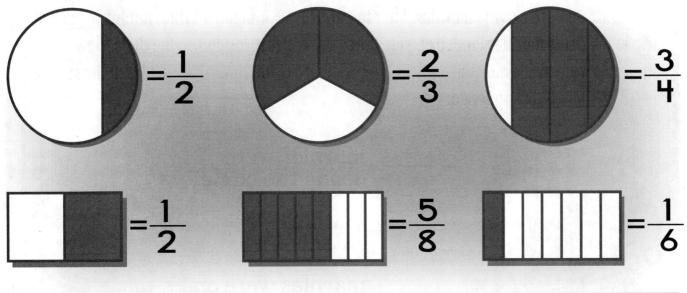

$= \frac{1}{2}$ $= \frac{2}{3}$ $= \frac{3}{4}$

$= \frac{1}{2}$ $= \frac{5}{8}$ $= \frac{1}{6}$

Draw and color each fraction.

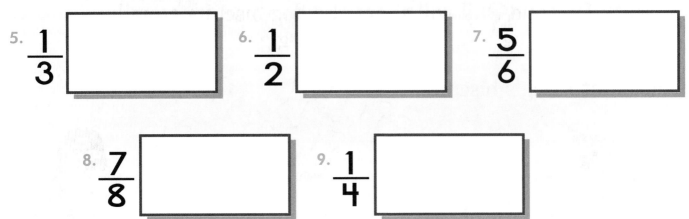

5. $\frac{1}{3}$

6. $\frac{1}{2}$

7. $\frac{5}{6}$

8. $\frac{7}{8}$

9. $\frac{1}{4}$

	Equal parts? *Write yes or no.*	What parts? *Write halves, thirds, or fourths.*	Write a fraction for the shaded parts.
	yes	fourths	$\frac{1}{4}$
10.			
11.			
12.			

Bill and Sue were playing marbles. After the first turn, $\frac{1}{2}$ of the marbles landed <u>inside</u> the circle. $\frac{1}{4}$ of the marbles landed <u>outside</u> the circle. The rest landed <u>on</u> the circle. How many marbles were inside, outside, and on the circle? Draw and color the marbles in the second circle to show what happened.

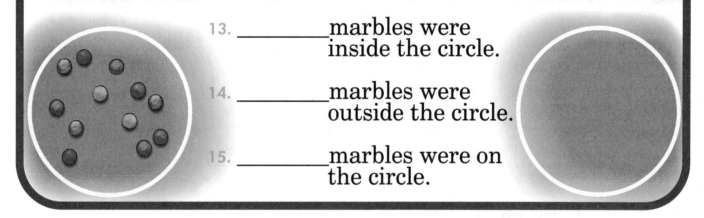

13. _____ marbles were inside the circle.

14. _____ marbles were outside the circle.

15. _____ marbles were on the circle.

16. Math Dog and Phil will share the dog biscuits equally. How many dog biscuits will each dog get? _____

Color Math Dog's biscuits.

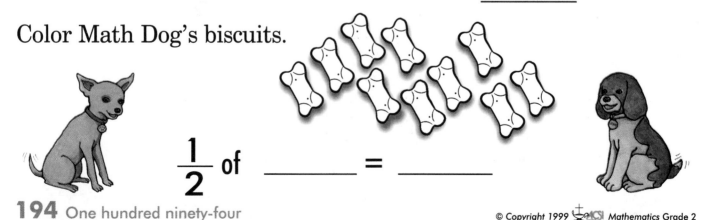

$\frac{1}{2}$ of _____ = _____

© Copyright 1999 Mathematics Grade 2

Capacity: Cup, Pint, Quart, Gallon — Lesson 98

Four friends are sharing one quart of juice. How much juice will each child receive?

2 cups = 1 pint   2 pints = 1 quart   4 quarts = 1 gallon

You can think of these units as fractions.

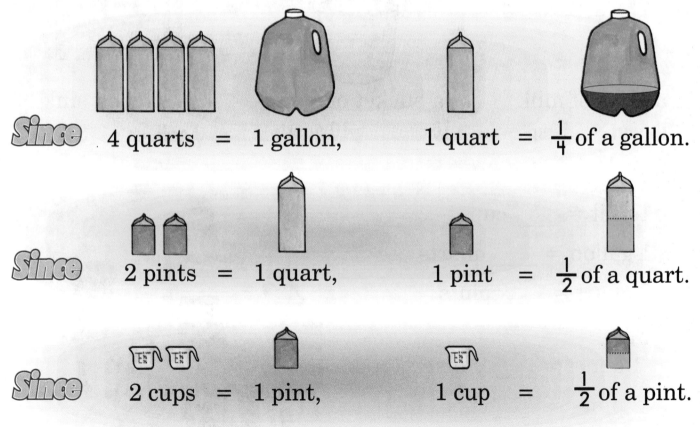

Since 4 quarts = 1 gallon,   1 quart = $\frac{1}{4}$ of a gallon.

Since 2 pints = 1 quart,   1 pint = $\frac{1}{2}$ of a quart.

Since 2 cups = 1 pint,   1 cup = $\frac{1}{2}$ of a pint.

Answer the question at the top of the page about the four friends.

_____

Match the containers that show the same amount.

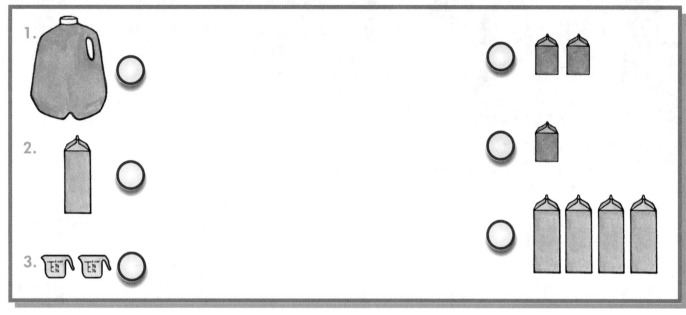

1.
2.
3.

Circle the better estimate.

4. a glass of milk
   1 quart   **1 cup**

5. a bucket of water
   10 cups   **10 quarts**

6. kitchen sink
   3 gallons   **3 pints**

Complete.

7. 1 pint = ____ cups

8. 1 gallon = ____ quarts

9. 1 quart = ____ pints

Think

10. 1 quart = ____ cups

11. 2 pints = ____ cups

12. 2 quarts = ____ pints

13. 2 gallons = ____ quarts

© Copyright 1999   Mathematics Grade 2

Comparing Containers Lesson 99

Circle all cup, pint, quart, and gallon containers.

Write two sets of equal amounts you found.

1. _____ = _____   2. _____ = _____

Circle the better estimate.

3. **cup or quart**   4. **pint or gallon**   5. **gallon or quart**   6. **quart or cup**

Complete.

7. 1 gallon = ____ quarts   8. 1 pint = ____ cups   9. 1 quart = ____ pints

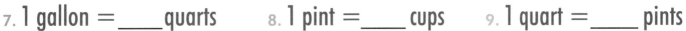

10. Math Dog's dish holds one pint of water. Phil's dish holds half as much. How much water does Phil's dish hold?_____

11. Help Math Dog reach Phil. Draw lines from one container to the other. You must follow this pattern: smaller, larger, smaller, larger. Try to make the shortest possible path.

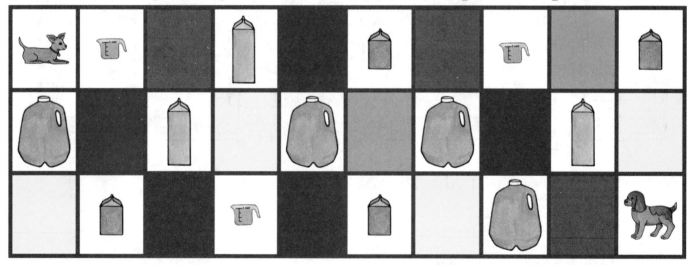

Review   Write two fractions for each picture.

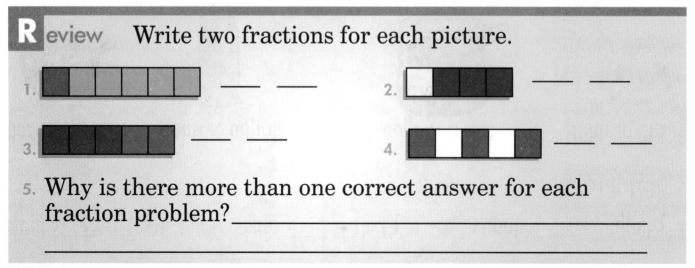

1. _____ _____

2. _____ _____

3. _____ _____

4. _____ _____

5. Why is there more than one correct answer for each fraction problem?_____

_____

© Copyright 1999   Mathematics Grade 2

Fahrenheit Temperature   Lesson 100

These are Fahrenheit thermometers. They measure temperature in degrees. Write the temperature.

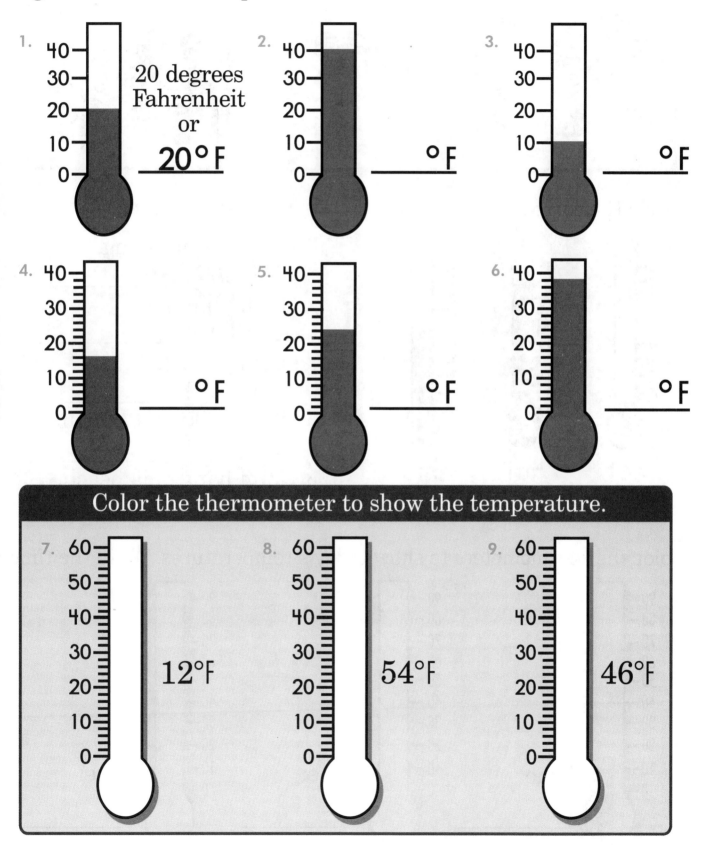

1. 20 degrees Fahrenheit
or
20° F

2. _____ °F

3. _____ °F

4. _____ °F

5. _____ °F

6. _____ °F

Color the thermometer to show the temperature.

7. 12°F

8. 54°F

9. 46°F

© Copyright 1999 ACSI Mathematics Grade 2

Which temperature is the better estimate? Fill in the oval.

10. 25° ○ 80° ○

11. 90° ○ 40° ○

12. 30° ○ 70° ○

Circle the correct answer.

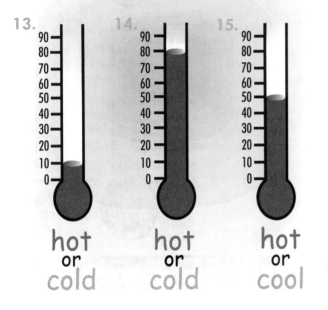

13. hot or cold

14. hot or cold

15. hot or cool

Write *True* or *False*.

16. I am water skiing, it is 40°F. _____

17. I am biking, it is 60°F. _____

18. I am picnicking, it is 85°F. _____

19. I am making a snowman, it is 30°F. _____

20. I am lying on a beach, it is 25°F. _____

Color the thermometers to show today's temperatures. Write the time.

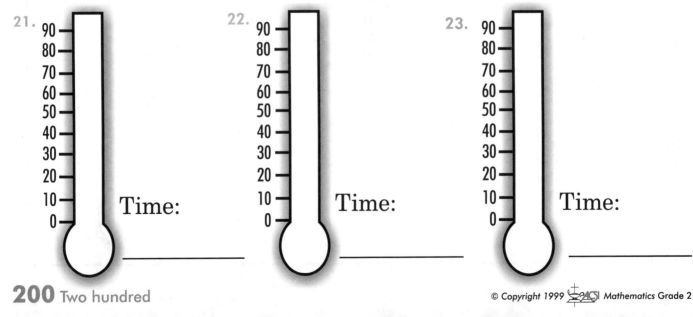

21. Time: _____

22. Time: _____

23. Time: _____

© Copyright 1999 — Mathematics Grade 2

Weight: Ounces and Pounds   Lesson 101

The ounce (oz) and the pound (lb) are customary units that are used to measure weight. Ten pennies weigh about one ounce.

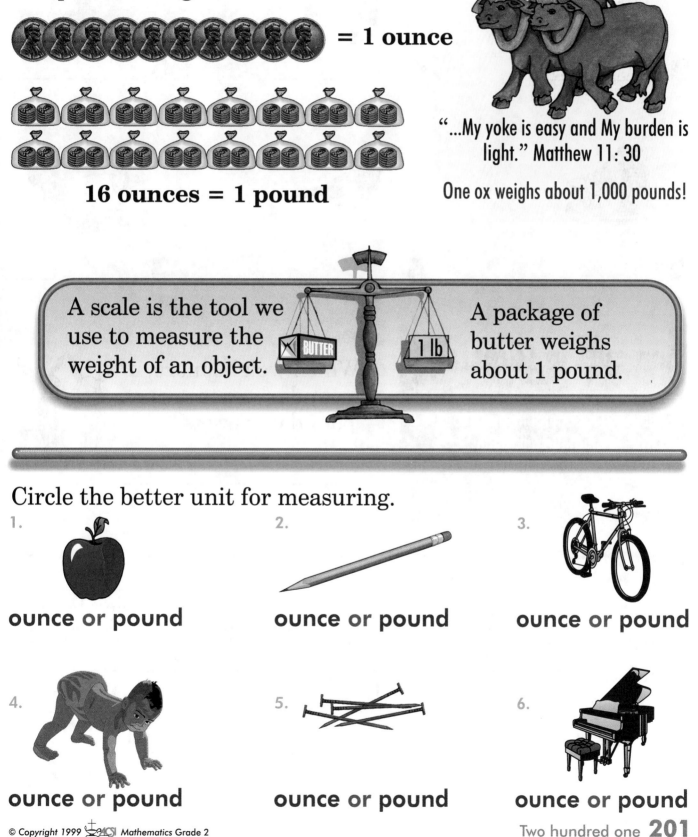

= 1 ounce

16 ounces = 1 pound

"...My yoke is easy and My burden is light." Matthew 11: 30

One ox weighs about 1,000 pounds!

A scale is the tool we use to measure the weight of an object.

A package of butter weighs about 1 pound.

Circle the better unit for measuring.

1.
ounce or pound

2.
ounce or pound

3.
ounce or pound

4.
ounce or pound

5.
ounce or pound

6.
ounce or pound

Choose the better unit. Write <u>ounces</u> or <u>pounds</u> after the number.

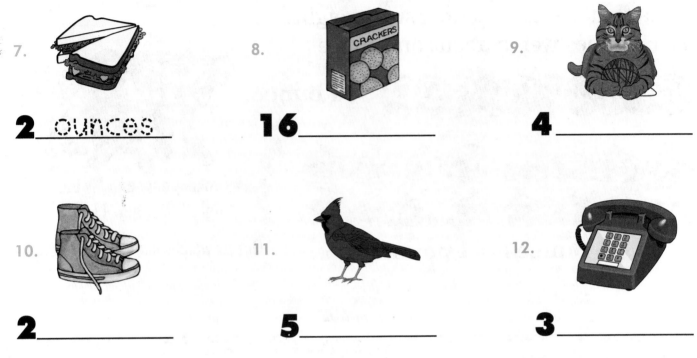

7. **2** ounces

8. **16**＿＿＿＿＿

9. **4**＿＿＿＿＿

10. **2**＿＿＿＿＿

11. **5**＿＿＿＿＿

12. **3**＿＿＿＿＿

Moments in Careers

"My dad works as a farmer. He uses math to figure out how much medicine to give a calf by how much the calf weighs."

Lee
Huron, SD

13. Which weighs more, a pound of pennies or a pound of carrots?

＿＿＿＿＿＿＿＿＿＿＿＿

Review

Find 2 or 3 numbers (across, down, or horizontally) that make the sum or difference given.

1. Sums equal to 20.

3	19	15	5
5	4	10	10
9	8	13	2
6	12	17	3

2. Differences equal to 8.

17	9	13	4
15	7	5	6
5	20	10	25
3	12	2	17

© Copyright 1999   Mathematics Grade 2

The gram (g) and the kilogram (kg) are metric units that are used to measure weight.

A paper clip weighs about one gram.

A dozen eggs weigh about one kilogram.

1,000 GRAMS = 1 KILOGRAM

Math Dog weighs about 3 kilograms.

A dime weighs about 4 grams.

A nickel weighs about 11 grams.

1. How much would 4 dimes and 2 nickels weigh? _____
2. What is the value? _____ ¢
3. How much would 3 dimes and 4 nickels weigh? _____
4. What is the value? _____ ¢

Think 5. If the value of the coins is the same, why is the weight different?

_____

Circle the better unit for measuring.

6.

gram or kilogram

7.

gram or kilogram

8.

gram or kilogram

9.

gram or kilogram

10.

gram or kilogram

11.

gram or kilogram

Circle the better unit for measuring.

12. one nickel
gram or kilogram

13. bag of flour
gram or kilogram

14. pickup truck
gram or kilogram

15. a canary
gram or kilogram

16. a letter
gram or kilogram

17. a second grade girl
gram or kilogram

Choose the better unit. Write **grams** or **kilograms** after the number.

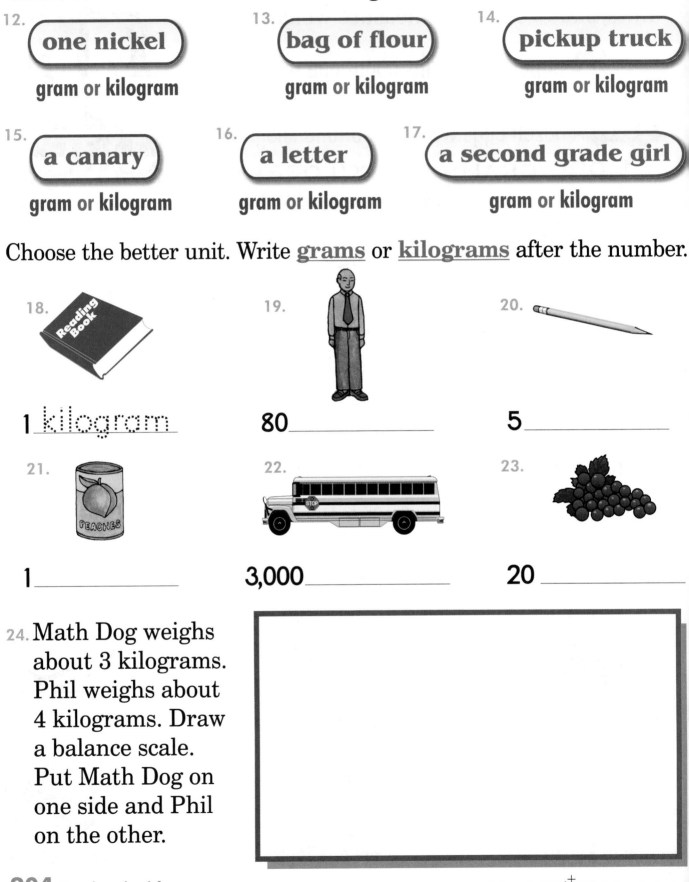

18. 1 kilogram

19. 80 _____

20. 5 _____

21. 1 _____

22. 3,000 _____

23. 20 _____

24. Math Dog weighs about 3 kilograms. Phil weighs about 4 kilograms. Draw a balance scale. Put Math Dog on one side and Phil on the other.

© Copyright 1999 Mathematics Grade 2

Measurement Review   Lesson 103

Write the best measurement tool. Use the word bank.

1. _____

2. _____

3. _____

Word Bank
cup
ruler
scale
yardstick

Write what is measured by each item. Use the word bank.

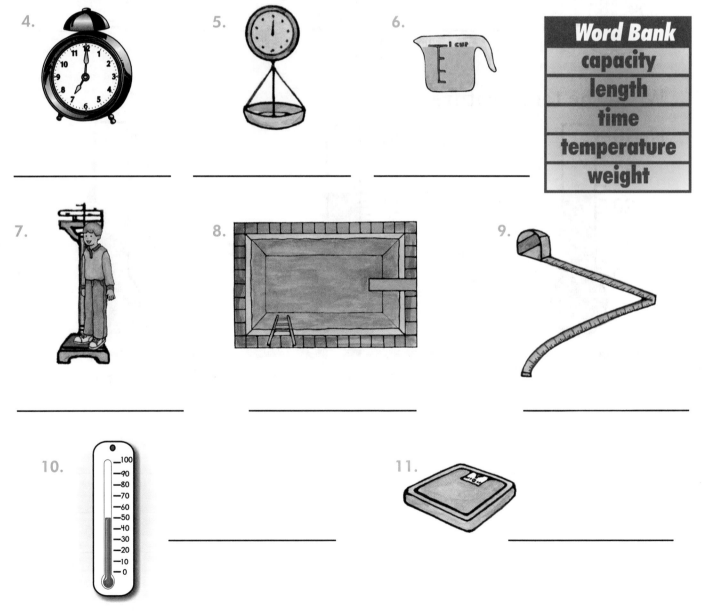

4. _____

5. _____

6. _____

Word Bank
capacity
length
time
temperature
weight

7. _____

8. _____

9. _____

10. _____

11. _____

Fill in the blanks. Write <u>inches</u>, <u>pounds</u>, or <u>gallons</u>.

12. Lauren's ribbon is 35 _____ long.

13. Aubrey's fish tank holds 25 _____.

14. Madison's weight is 30 _____.

15. The bag of flour is about 5 _____.

Fill in the blanks. Write <u>cups</u>, <u>pints</u>, or <u>quarts</u>.

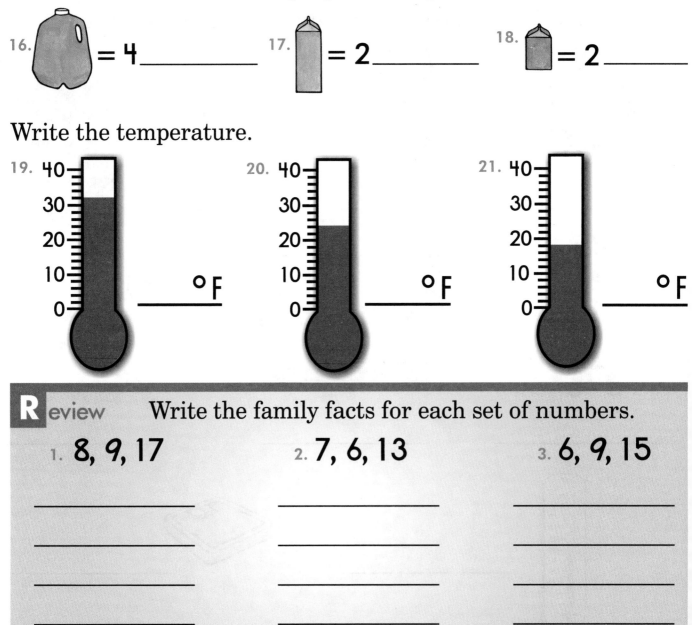

16. = 4 _____

17. = 2 _____

18. = 2 _____

Write the temperature.

19. _____ °F

20. _____ °F

21. _____ °F

Review   Write the family facts for each set of numbers.

1. 8, 9, 17

2. 7, 6, 13

3. 6, 9, 15

_____ _____ _____

_____ _____ _____

_____ _____ _____

_____ _____ _____

© Copyright 1999   Mathematics Grade 2

Chapter Seven Check-Up   Lesson 104

Draw a picture for each fraction word.

1.

thirds

2.

fourths

Write the fraction that shows what part is shaded.

3.

_____

4.

_____

5.

_____

6. Write the fraction name for each letter.

RABBIT   Total letters = _____

R = ___   A = ___   B = ___   I = ___   T = ___

7. Color the parts.

Color $\frac{1}{2}$ **red.**

Color $\frac{1}{4}$ **blue.**

Color $\frac{1}{8}$ yellow.

What part was
not colored? _____

Write the better unit for measuring. Write <u>gram</u> or <u>kilogram</u>.

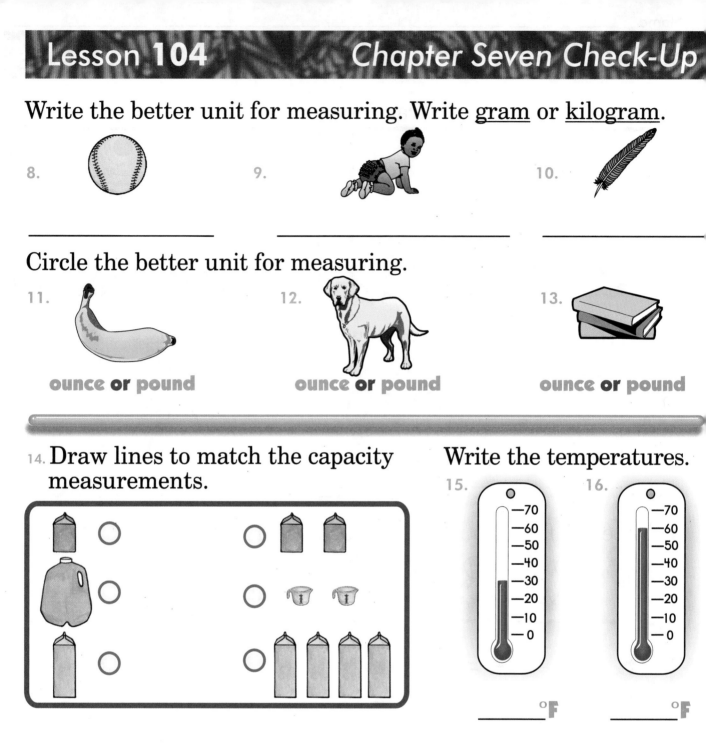

8. _____

9. _____

10. _____

Circle the better unit for measuring.

11.
ounce **or** pound

12.
ounce **or** pound

13.
ounce **or** pound

14. Draw lines to match the capacity measurements.

Write the temperatures.

15.   —70
       —60
       —50
       —40
       —30
       —20
       —10
       — 0

16.   —70
       —60
       —50
       —40
       —30
       —20
       —10
       — 0

_____°**F**   _____°**F**

17. Draw circles around the rabbits to solve the problem.

6 rabbits were playing. One half went home. One third went to dinner. The rest went to take a nap. How many went to each place?

_____ **Home**

_____ **Dinner**

_____ **Nap**

© Copyright 1999 ✝ACSI Mathematics Grade 2

CHAPTER 8

Two-Digit Addition with Regrouping

The judgments of the LORD are true and righteous altogether. More to be desired are they than gold, Yea, than much fine gold; Sweeter also than honey and the honeycomb. . . . And in keeping them there is great reward.

Psalm 19:9b-11

Dear Parents,

Chapter Eight of our math book covers a major concept taught in second grade: two-digit addition. Regrouping ones as tens is an essential skill for second graders to master, and is one that you can help your child practice at home.

One of the most effective math manipulatives can be found in your child's piggy bank! Dimes and pennies are perfect models for tens and ones place value concepts. A penny is one cent; a dime is the *regrouping* of 10 individual cents. You can use pennies and dimes to practice place value, trading ones for tens, and two-digit addition with regrouping.

• Write the number 45. Have your child model the number by placing 4 dimes under the <u>tens</u> column and 5 pennies under the <u>ones</u> column of the Tens and Ones Mat. When your child can show any two-digit number this way, you can move to trading ones for tens.

• Line up 23 pennies in the ones column. Have your child separate two groups of 10 pennies, replace them with dimes and place the dimes in the tens column. The three remaining pennies would be left in the ones column. Have your child verbalize what was done by stating that twenty-three ones is the same as 2 tens and 3 ones. Now for addition with regrouping . . .

• Write 27 + 18 in a vertical presentation. Have your child use dimes and pennies to first model 27 on the top of the mat and 18 on the bottom. There should now be a total of three dimes and 15 pennies on the mat. Have your child regroup ten of the 15 pennies by trading them for one dime, and read the sum as 45 (four dimes, five pennies).

Check your child's lessons to observe the way the paper-and-pencil skill of addition is being taught. Look for ways to demonstrate everyday uses of addition. Be careful, however, in having your child add money figures. Since decimals are not introduced in second grade, you will need to help with the placement of the decimal point if you add money amounts.

The picture of the honeybees and the words of Psalm 19:9b-11 reminds us of the "sweetness" of God's judgments and plans for our lives. Living according to His law yields sweet-as-honey rewards! Use this thought to encourage your child as you work through Chapter Eight.

© Copyright 1999 ACSI Mathematics Grade 2

Reviewing Two-Digit Addition   Lesson 105

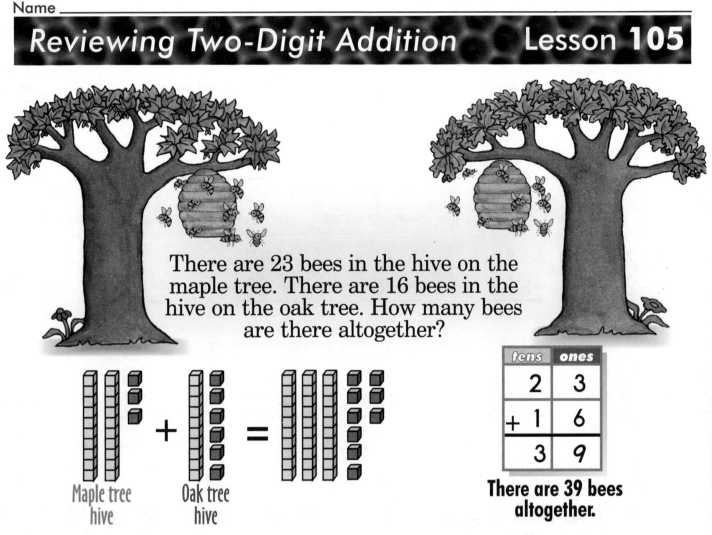

There are 23 bees in the hive on the maple tree. There are 16 bees in the hive on the oak tree. How many bees are there altogether?

Maple tree hive + Oak tree hive =

tens	ones
2	3
+ 1	6
3	9

There are 39 bees altogether.

Look at the tens and ones blocks. Write the addends. Find the sum.

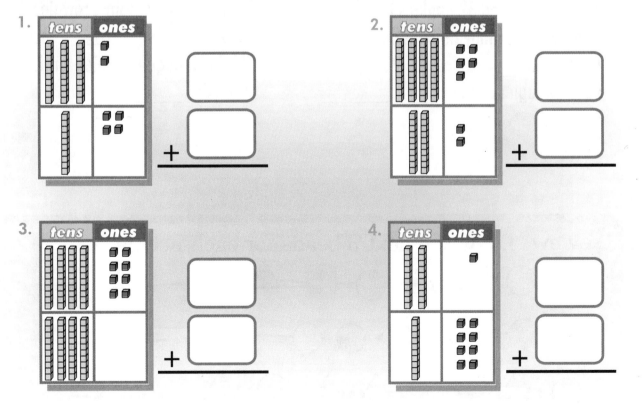

Add.

5.
tens	ones
1	5
+ 1	3

6.
tens	ones
4	3
+ 2	5

7.
tens	ones
8	2
+ 1	7

8.
tens	ones
5	4
+ 1	3

9. 74
   +21

10. 33
   +62

11. 61
   +18

12. 45
   +23

13. 24
   +12

14. 11
   +14

15. 83
   +14

16. 56
   +31

17. 76
   +12

18. 37
   +22

19. 60
   +34

20. 41
   +40

SOLVE.

21. Mrs. Baxter will serve 75 people at the church dinner. She has 50 napkins in one package and 32 napkins in another. How many napkins does she have in all? _____ napkins. Will she have enough napkins? _____

22. Mrs. Baxter baked one pan of 24 brownies and another pan of 32 brownies. How many brownies did she bake altogether? _____ brownies. Will this be enough brownies for the church dinner? _____

Review   Draw the next 3 beads for each necklace.

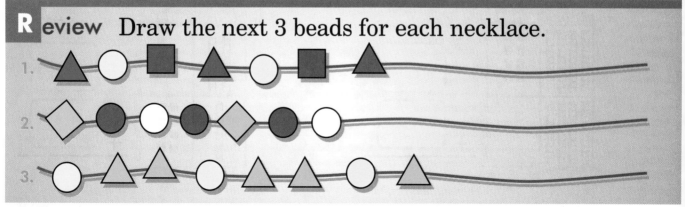

1.

2.

3.

© Copyright 1999   Mathematics Grade 2

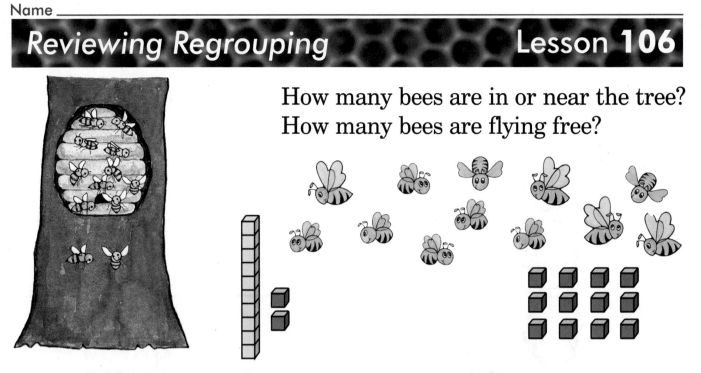

How many bees are in or near the tree?
How many bees are flying free?

10 bees in the hive + **2** on the bark **=** **12** bees flying free.

What does this **1** stand for?_____

1. Color 10 bees yellow. Put a circle around your ten yellow bees. Color the rest blue.

_____ yellow bees + _____ blue bees = _____ bees

Use counters and your Tens and Ones Mat to complete this chart.

	Show	Can you make 10?	How many?	New number
2.	6 + 8	___yes ___no	___ tens ___ones	
3.	9 + 3	___yes ___no	___ tens ___ones	
4.	7 + 7	___yes ___no	___ tens ___ones	

Add the numbers on each hive. Complete the chart.

	How many tens?	How many ones?	
5. 5 2 6	1	3	= 13
6. 8 0 9			=
7. 7 3 4			=
8. 9 7 5			=

Add.

9. 4
\+ 8

10. 6
\+ 7

11. 8
\+ 2

12. 9
\+ 9

13. 7
\+ 8

14. 6
\+ 9

15. 8
\+ 6

16. Look at your answers. Explain what the "1" means in each sum.

Look for the pattern in each box. Add mentally, then write the sum.

17.
   9   19   29
\+ 8   \+ 8   \+ 8
  17

18.
   5   15   25
\+ 8   \+ 8   \+ 8

Review Measure. Circle the objects that are <u>less than one inch</u>.

© Copyright 1999 Mathematics Grade 2

Kelly and her family are on a camping trip. Fireflies are everywhere! Kelly and her brother Brett have caught 16 fireflies. Their cousin Jack has caught 7 more. How many fireflies have been caught in all?

Kelly's and Brett's fireflies   **Jack's fireflies**

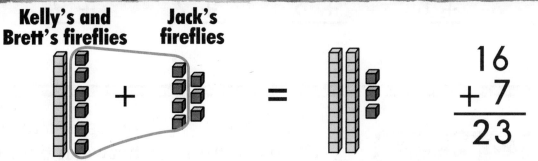

$$\begin{array}{r} 16 \\ + 7 \\ \hline 23 \end{array}$$

Use your Tens and Ones Mat and base ten blocks. Complete the chart.

Show	Regroup. How many...		Complete
---	Tens	Ones	---
1. 24 9	3	3	$\begin{array}{r} 24 \\ + 9 \\ \hline 33 \end{array}$
2. 18 7			$\begin{array}{r} 18 \\ + 7 \\ \hline \end{array}$
3. 27 3			$\begin{array}{r} 27 \\ + 3 \\ \hline \end{array}$
4. 14 8			$\begin{array}{r} 14 \\ + 8 \\ \hline \end{array}$

Add.

5.
$$\begin{array}{r} \square \\ + \\ 36 \\ + 5 \\ \hline \end{array}$$

6.
$$\begin{array}{r} \square \\ + \\ 42 \\ + 9 \\ \hline \end{array}$$

7.
$$\begin{array}{r} \square \\ + \\ 17 \\ + 7 \\ \hline \end{array}$$

8.
$$\begin{array}{r} \square \\ + \\ 28 \\ + 6 \\ \hline \end{array}$$

9.
$$\begin{array}{r} \square \\ + \\ 57 \\ + 3 \\ \hline \end{array}$$

10.
$$\begin{array}{r} \square \\ + \\ 48 \\ + 9 \\ \hline \end{array}$$

11.
$$\begin{array}{r} \square \\ + \\ 14 \\ + 7 \\ \hline \end{array}$$

12.
$$\begin{array}{r} \square \\ + \\ 37 \\ + 8 \\ \hline \end{array}$$

13.
$$\begin{array}{r} \square \\ + \\ 44 \\ + 6 \\ \hline \end{array}$$

14.
$$\begin{array}{r} \square \\ + \\ 26 \\ + 7 \\ \hline \end{array}$$

15.
$$\begin{array}{r} \square \\ + \\ 69 \\ + 9 \\ \hline \end{array}$$

16.
$$\begin{array}{r} \square \\ + \\ 56 \\ + 6 \\ \hline \end{array}$$

17.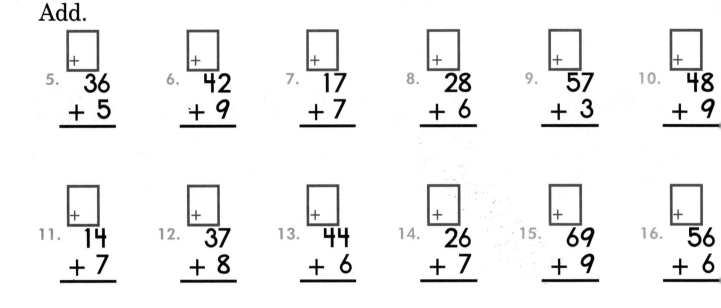

There are ____ fireflies in this jar. Choose a number between 6 and 9: ___. Draw that number of fireflies in the jar. Write an addition problem to show what you have added.

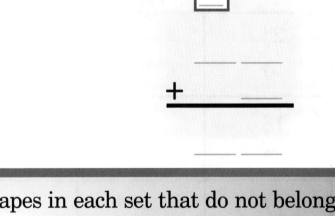

Review   Mark out the two shapes in each set that do not belong.

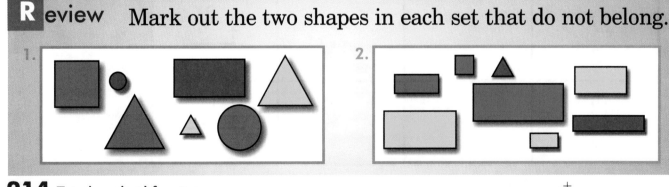

© Copyright 1999 | Mathematics Grade 2

Adding Two-Digit Numbers   Lesson **108**

SLAP! SLAP!

The family in campsite A has counted 15 mosquito bites during their weekend camp. The family in campsite B has counted 18 mosquito bites.

How many mosquito bites have both families had altogether?

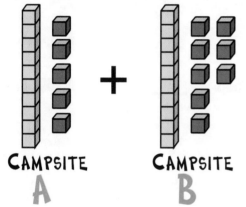   +   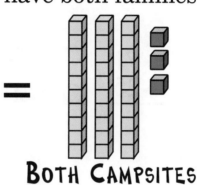   =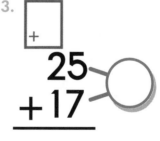

CAMPSITE **A**   CAMPSITE **B**   **BOTH CAMPSITES**

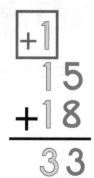

$$\begin{array}{r} +1 \\ 15 \\ +18 \\ \hline 33 \end{array}$$

The two families had 33 mosquito bites in all!

Add.

1.
$$\begin{array}{r} +1 \\ 46 \\ +38 \\ \hline 84 \end{array}$$ 14

2.
$$\begin{array}{r} + \\ 39 \\ +16 \\ \hline \end{array}$$ ◯

3.
$$\begin{array}{r} + \\ 25 \\ +17 \\ \hline \end{array}$$ ◯

4.
$$\begin{array}{r} + \\ 68 \\ +14 \\ \hline \end{array}$$ ◯

5.
$$\begin{array}{r} + \\ 18 \\ +18 \\ \hline \end{array}$$ ◯

6.
$$\begin{array}{r} + \\ 53 \\ +29 \\ \hline \end{array}$$ ◯

7.
$$\begin{array}{r} + \\ 76 \\ +14 \\ \hline \end{array}$$ ◯

8.
$$\begin{array}{r} + \\ 68 \\ +23 \\ \hline \end{array}$$ ◯

Shade the circle to show if regrouping is needed. Add the numbers.

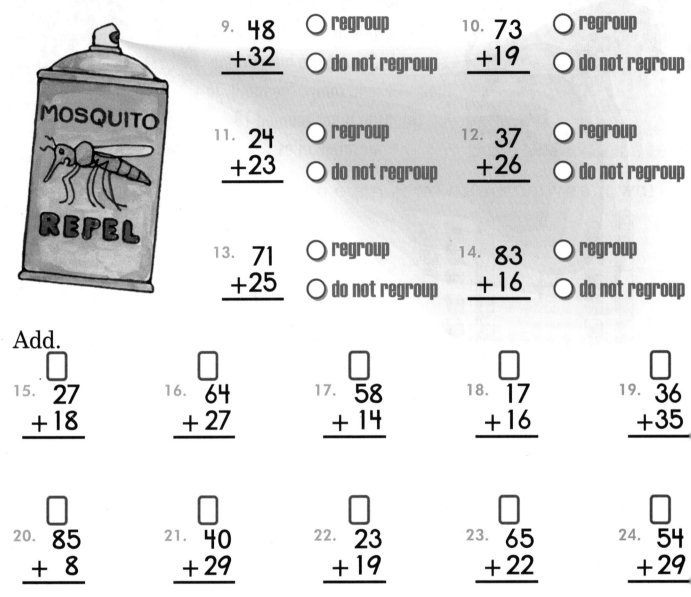

9. 48
+32
○ regroup
○ do not regroup

10. 73
+19
○ regroup
○ do not regroup

11. 24
+23
○ regroup
○ do not regroup

12. 37
+26
○ regroup
○ do not regroup

13. 71
+25
○ regroup
○ do not regroup

14. 83
+16
○ regroup
○ do not regroup

Add.

15. 27
+18

16. 64
+27

17. 58
+14

18. 17
+16

19. 36
+35

20. 85
+ 8

21. 40
+29

22. 23
+19

23. 65
+22

24. 54
+29

Review   Follow the mosquito's path.

9

+6

−7

+8

−2

+9

=_____

© Copyright 1999   Mathematics Grade 2

Practicing Two-Digit Addition   Lesson 109

Bees love Maggie's garden! This year Maggie planted 14 roses and 38 petunias. How many flowers did she plant in all?

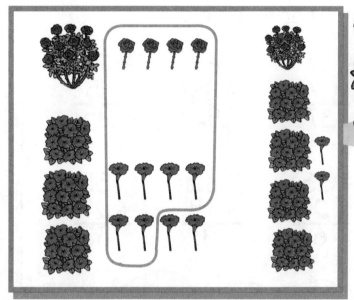

"BEE" CAREFUL! REMEMBER, IF THERE ARE 10 OR MORE ONES YOU NEED TO REGROUP!

14 + 38 = 52 flowers

Add. Circle any ones that need to be regrouped.

1. $\begin{array}{r} 17 \\ +15 \\ \hline \end{array}$

2. $\begin{array}{r} 26 \\ +14 \\ \hline \end{array}$

3. $\begin{array}{r} 28 \\ +11 \\ \hline \end{array}$

Add.

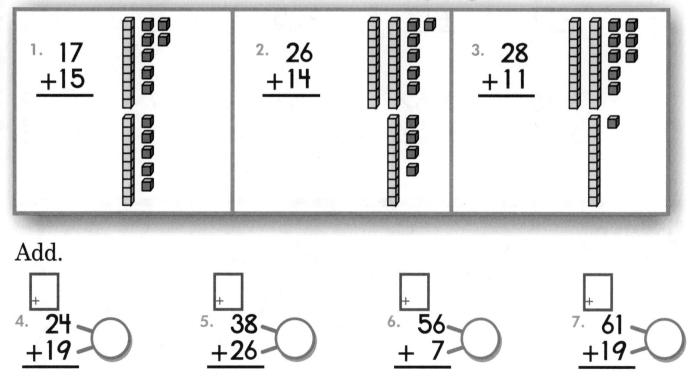

4. $\begin{array}{r} 24 \\ +19 \\ \hline \end{array}$

5. $\begin{array}{r} 38 \\ +26 \\ \hline \end{array}$

6. $\begin{array}{r} 56 \\ + 7 \\ \hline \end{array}$

7. $\begin{array}{r} 61 \\ +19 \\ \hline \end{array}$

Place a ✔ next to the incorrect answers. Write the total number of correct and incorrect answers in the blanks. Correct the errors.

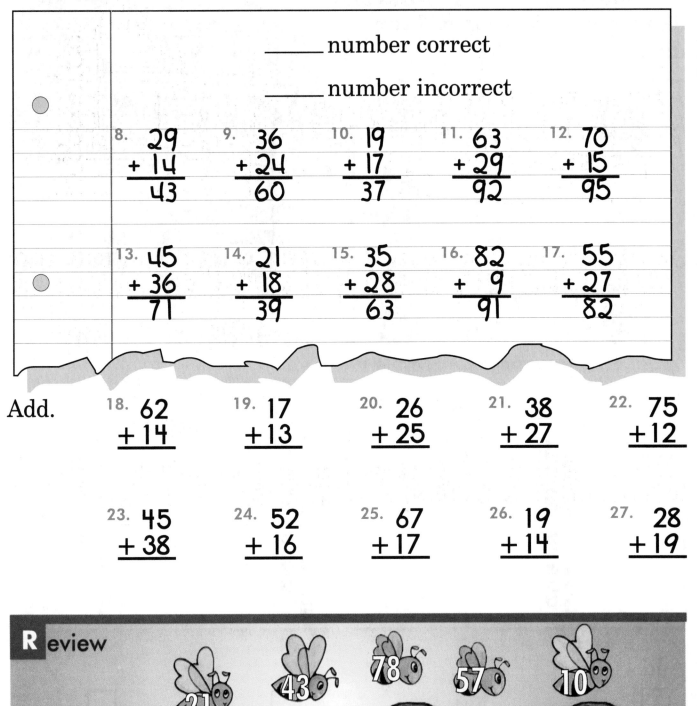

_____ number correct

_____ number incorrect

8.
```
  29
+ 14
  43
```

9.
```
  36
+ 24
  60
```

10.
```
  19
+ 17
  37
```

11.
```
  63
+ 29
  92
```

12.
```
  70
+ 15
  95
```

13.
```
  45
+ 36
  71
```

14.
```
  21
+ 18
  39
```

15.
```
  35
+ 28
  63
```

16.
```
  82
+  9
  91
```

17.
```
  55
+ 27
  82
```

Add.

18.
```
  62
+ 14
```

19.
```
  17
+ 13
```

20.
```
  26
+ 25
```

21.
```
  38
+ 27
```

22.
```
  75
+ 12
```

23.
```
  45
+ 38
```

24.
```
  52
+ 16
```

25.
```
  67
+ 17
```

26.
```
  19
+ 14
```

27.
```
  28
+ 19
```

Review

Write the numbers in the correct hive.

21   43   78   57   10   84

Even
_____
_____

Odd
_____
_____

© Copyright 1999   Mathematics Grade 2

Alyssa saw 4 dragonflies and 6 mosquitos buzzing near the lake shore. She counted 17 red canoes and 15 blue canoes on the beach.

$$\begin{array}{r} 4 \\ +6 \\ \hline 10 \end{array}$$

You know that $4 + 6 = 10$ can be written as

You also know that the order property means $4 + 6$ has the same sum as $6 + 4$.

The same rules apply to 2-digit addends.

How many canoes did Alyssa see altogether?

You can find the answer by adding four different ways:

$$17 + 15 = \underline{32}$$
$$15 + 17 = \underline{32}$$

$$\begin{array}{r} 17 \\ +15 \\ \hline 32 \end{array} \qquad \begin{array}{r} 15 \\ +17 \\ \hline 32 \end{array}$$

Rewrite these addition problems. Add.

1. $36 + 21 = $ $\begin{array}{r} 36 \\ +21 \\ \hline 57 \end{array}$

2. $49 + 30 = $ $+$ ____

3. $58 + 16 = $ $+$ ____

4. $25 + 17 = $ $+$ ____

5. $76 + 6 = $ $+$ ____

6. $43 + 9 = $ $+$ ____

Write the addition problems your teacher reads. Solve.

7.

$+$ _____

8.

$+$ _____

9.

$+$ _____

10.

$+$ _____

Use the numbers on these dragonflies to write addition problems. Write each problem two different ways.

11. **46** **25** ___ $+$ ___ $=$ ___ $+$ ___

12. **18** **34** ___ $+$ ___ $=$ ___ $+$ ___

SOLVE.

13. Alyssa counted 42 adult life jackets and 29 children's life jackets. How many life jackets did Alyssa count altogether?

_____

14. In the morning 36 people rented canoes. In the afternoon 55 people rented canoes. How many people rented canoes in all?

_____

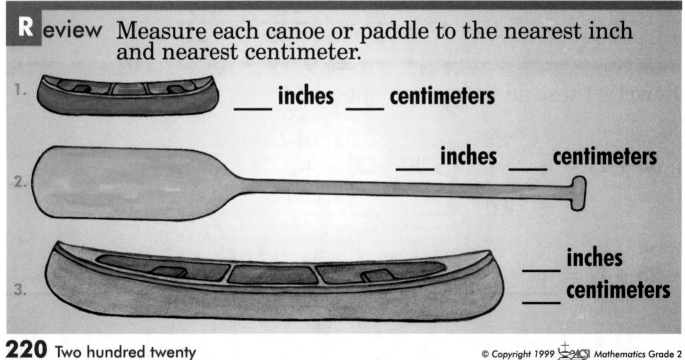

Review Measure each canoe or paddle to the nearest inch and nearest centimeter.

1. ___ **inches** ___ **centimeters**

2. ___ **inches** ___ **centimeters**

3. ___ **inches** ___ **centimeters**

© Copyright 1999 ACSI Mathematics Grade 2

Rounding Two-Digit Numbers   Lesson 111

17 hornets buzzed around their nest.

We could also say: about 20 hornets were near the nest.

17 is between 10 and 20. It is 7 away from 10. It is 3 away from 20.

10 11 12 13 14 15 16 17 18 19 20

Because 17 is closer to 20 than to 10, we round 17 to 20.

If a number is less than 5, round down.

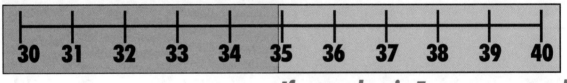

30 31 32 33 34 35 36 37 38 39 40

If a number is 5 or more, round up.

Circle the number on each number line. Round to the nearest ten.

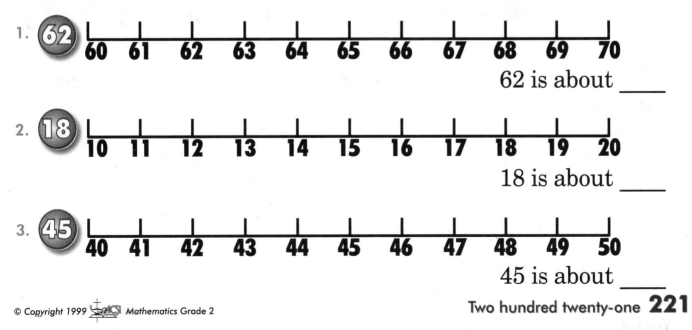

1. 62

60 61 62 63 64 65 66 67 68 69 70

62 is about _____

2. 18

10 11 12 13 14 15 16 17 18 19 20

18 is about _____

3. 45

40 41 42 43 44 45 46 47 48 49 50

45 is about _____

Write the tens before and after each number. Round to the nearest ten.

4. __80__ 84 __90__

84 is about __80__

5. ____ 71 ____

71 is about ____

6. ____ 29 ____

29 is about ____

7. ____ 15 ____

15 is about ____

8. ____ 43 ____

43 is about ____

9. ____ 66 ____

66 is about ____

Round each number to the nearest ten.

10. 32 _____   11. 57 _____   12. 98 _____   13. 21 _____   14. 76 _____

15. 89 _____   16. 44 _____   17. 12 _____   18. 65 _____   19. 37 _____

SOLVE.

20. There will be 87 people at the family reunion. About how many plates will be needed?

_____

21. Luke's team scored 11 points. About how many points did they score?

_____

22. The meteorologist predicts a high temperature of 54°F. About how many degrees will the high temperature reach?

_____

23. There are 26 children in Ashley's class. About how many birthday treats should she bring?

_____

Review Subtract.

| 1. $\begin{array}{r} 17 \\ -\ 9 \\ \hline \end{array}$ | 2. $\begin{array}{r} 15 \\ -\ 7 \\ \hline \end{array}$ | 3. $\begin{array}{r} 11 \\ -\ 2 \\ \hline \end{array}$ | 4. $\begin{array}{r} 16 \\ -\ 8 \\ \hline \end{array}$ | 5. $\begin{array}{r} 18 \\ -\ 9 \\ \hline \end{array}$ | 6. $\begin{array}{r} 12 \\ -\ 5 \\ \hline \end{array}$ |
| 7. $\begin{array}{r} 10 \\ -\ 4 \\ \hline \end{array}$ | 8. $\begin{array}{r} 14 \\ -\ 8 \\ \hline \end{array}$ | 9. $\begin{array}{r} 17 \\ -\ 8 \\ \hline \end{array}$ | 10. $\begin{array}{r} 13 \\ -\ 7 \\ \hline \end{array}$ | 11. $\begin{array}{r} 15 \\ -\ 9 \\ \hline \end{array}$ | 12. $\begin{array}{r} 11 \\ -\ 5 \\ \hline \end{array}$ |

© Copyright 1999 *Mathematics Grade 2*

Estimating Sums

Mrs. Nunez, Elisa, and Stephan are counting art supplies for Sunday School. In one box they found 48 scissors. In another box they found 33. About 80 scissors are needed. Are there enough?

We can estimate the sum of 48 + 33. Estimating is a quick way to get a close answer. To estimate the sum:

round the addends and add the tens

$$48 \longrightarrow 50$$
$$33 \longrightarrow 30$$

$$50 + 30 = 80 \text{ scissors}$$

Mrs. Nunez and her children found about 80 scissors. Yes, the church has enough for its Sunday School program.

Read the chart. The target number tells how many are needed. Estimate the sum and answer <u>yes</u> or <u>no</u>.

Item	Box 1	Box 2	Target Number
paint brushes	37	21	40
glue sticks	52	17	80
glitter tubes	9	15	20
watercolor sets	13	34	50

1. Paint brushes

$$\begin{array}{r} 40 \\ + 20 \\ \hline 60 \end{array}$$

Are there enough?
(yes) no

2. Glue sticks

$$+ \underline{}$$

Are there enough?
yes no

3. Glitter tubes

$$+ \underline{}$$

Are there enough?
yes no

4. Watercolor sets

$$+ \underline{}$$

Are there enough?
yes no

Write the estimated sum.

5. | 23 + 28 |

$$\begin{array}{r} 20 \\ + 30 \\ \hline 50 \end{array}$$

6. | 72 + 19 |

$$+ \over $$

7. | 56 + 11 |

$$+ \over $$

8. | 42 + 27 |

$$+ \over $$

Solve by estimating the sum.

9. Mrs. Nunez counted 13 boxes of crayons in one drawer and 22 boxes in another. About how many boxes of crayons were there altogether?

_____

10. Stephan found 17 bottles of poster paint. He saw a delivery man bring 24 more bottles. About how many bottles of poster paint are there now?

_____

11. Elisa found a box of 24 glue sticks. She found another box just like it. About how many glue sticks did Elisa find altogether?

_____

12. Mrs. Nunez needs 35 sets of colored tissue paper. She found 13 sets in one box and 14 in another. About how many sets did she find? Are there enough?

_____

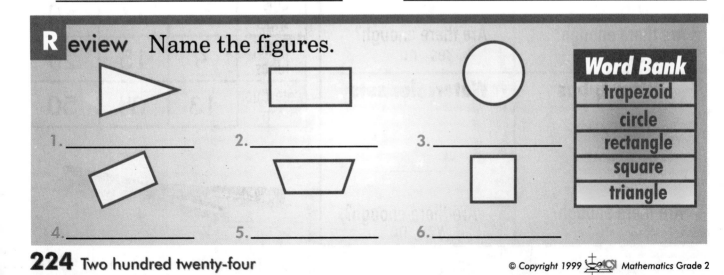

Review   Name the figures.

1._____

2._____

3._____

4._____

5._____

6._____

Word Bank

| trapezoid |
| circle |
| rectangle |
| square |
| triangle |

Two-Digit Addition Review — Lesson 113

Alice and Alan are 8-year-old twins. They live in eastern Nebraska. The twins like to identify butterflies. They have recorded seeing 27 white admirals and 16 eyed browns. How many butterflies of these two kinds have they seen?

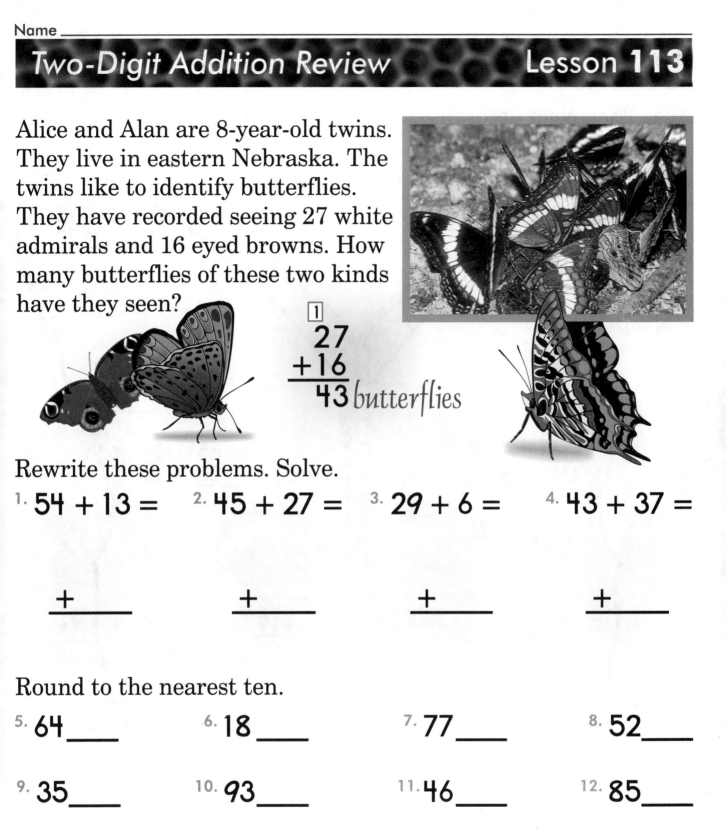

```
  1
  27
+16
  43 butterflies
```

Rewrite these problems. Solve.

1. $54 + 13 =$

2. $45 + 27 =$

3. $29 + 6 =$

4. $43 + 37 =$

+_____ +_____ +_____ +_____

Round to the nearest ten.

5. 64 ____

6. 18 ____

7. 77 ____

8. 52 ____

9. 35 ____

10. 93 ____

11. 46 ____

12. 85 ____

Estimate the sums.

13.
```
 41 →
+27 → +
```
_____

14.
```
 45 →
+39 → +
```
_____

15.
```
 62 →
+19 → +
```
_____

16.
```
 53 →
+36 → +
```
_____

Add. Then color according to the key below.

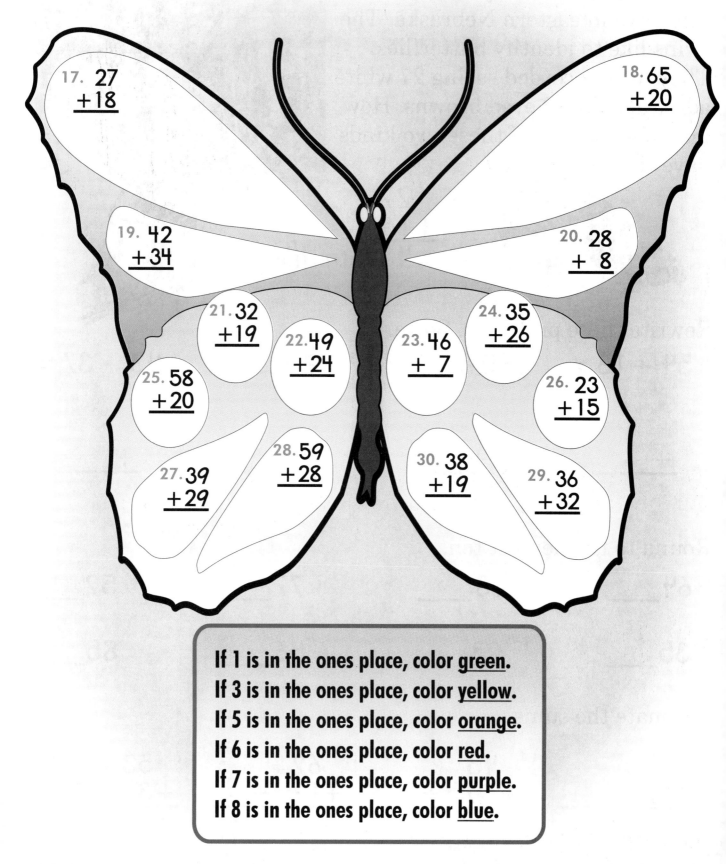

17. 27 +18

18. 65 +20

19. 42 +34

20. 28 + 8

21. 32 +19

22. 49 +24

23. 46 + 7

24. 35 +26

25. 58 +20

26. 23 +15

27. 39 +29

28. 59 +28

29. 36 +32

30. 38 +19

If 1 is in the ones place, color <u>green</u>.
If 3 is in the ones place, color <u>yellow</u>.
If 5 is in the ones place, color <u>orange</u>.
If 6 is in the ones place, color <u>red</u>.
If 7 is in the ones place, color <u>purple</u>.
If 8 is in the ones place, color <u>blue</u>.

© Copyright 1999   Mathematics Grade 2

Adding Money

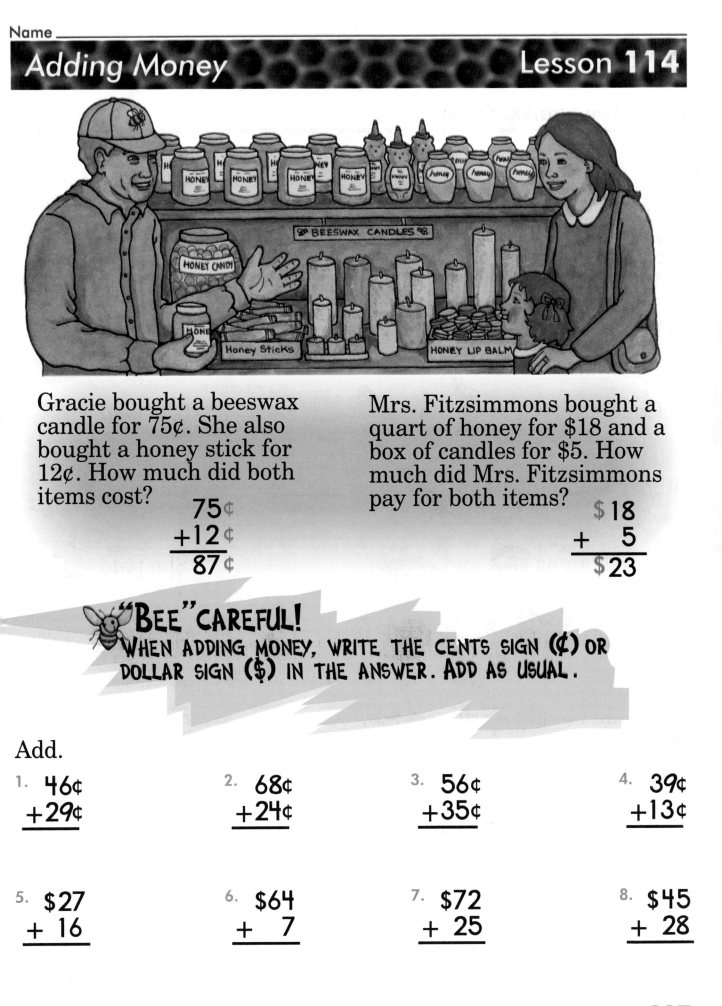

Gracie bought a beeswax candle for 75¢. She also bought a honey stick for 12¢. How much did both items cost?

$$\begin{array}{r} 75¢ \\ +12¢ \\ \hline 87¢ \end{array}$$

Mrs. Fitzsimmons bought a quart of honey for $18 and a box of candles for $5. How much did Mrs. Fitzsimmons pay for both items?

$$\begin{array}{r} \$18 \\ + \ 5 \\ \hline \$23 \end{array}$$

"BEE" CAREFUL!

WHEN ADDING MONEY, WRITE THE CENTS SIGN (¢) OR DOLLAR SIGN ($) IN THE ANSWER. ADD AS USUAL.

Add.

1. $$\begin{array}{r} 46¢ \\ +29¢ \\ \hline \end{array}$$

2. $$\begin{array}{r} 68¢ \\ +24¢ \\ \hline \end{array}$$

3. $$\begin{array}{r} 56¢ \\ +35¢ \\ \hline \end{array}$$

4. $$\begin{array}{r} 39¢ \\ +13¢ \\ \hline \end{array}$$

5. $$\begin{array}{r} \$27 \\ + \ 16 \\ \hline \end{array}$$

6. $$\begin{array}{r} \$64 \\ + \ 7 \\ \hline \end{array}$$

7. $$\begin{array}{r} \$72 \\ + \ 25 \\ \hline \end{array}$$

8. $$\begin{array}{r} \$45 \\ + \ 28 \\ \hline \end{array}$$

Fill in the blanks. Solve.

honey ice-cream cone	honey lemonade	honey candy bar	honey stick	honey lip balm	beeswax candle
75¢	56¢	38¢	16¢	27¢	49¢

9. Adam bought ▭ and (HONEY LIPS). _38¢_ + _27¢_ He paid _65¢_.

10. Hyacinth bought 🥤 and ▬. _____ + _____ She paid _____.

11. Joey bought 🍦 and ▬. _____ + _____ He paid _____.

12. Kyla bought 🕯 and ▭. _____ + _____ She paid _____.

13. Baxter bought 🥤 and (HONEY LIPS). _____ + _____ He paid _____.

14. Jordan bought 🥤 and ▭. _____ + _____ She paid _____.

Add. Watch the signs!

15. 49¢
   +27¢
   ─────

16. 83¢
   +13¢
   ─────

17. $35
   + 6
   ─────

18. 16¢
   +14¢
   ─────

19. 62¢
   +19¢
   ─────

20. $25
   + 18
   ─────

21. 58¢
   +26¢
   ─────

22. $73
   + 18
   ─────

© Copyright 1999 Mathematics Grade 2

Column Addition

Scientists watched as fish fed on mayflies at the pond.

The first hour, the fish ate 27 mayflies. The next hour, 23 mayflies were eaten.

The last hour, scientists observed 16 mayflies being eaten. How many mayflies were eaten in the three hours?

$$\begin{array}{r} \boxed{+1} \\ 27 \\ 23 \\ +16 \\ \hline 66 \end{array}$$

Adding three or more addends is called **column addition**.

Looking for 10's can make column addition easier.

$$\begin{array}{r} \boxed{+1} \\ 32 \\ 24 \\ +16 \\ \hline 72 \end{array}$$

$4 + 6 = 10$
$10 + 2 = 12$

Counting on can also make column addition easier.

$$\begin{array}{r} \boxed{+1} \\ 48 \\ 21 \\ +\ \ 8 \\ \hline 77 \end{array}$$

$8 + 8 = 16$, count on 1
16, <u>17</u>

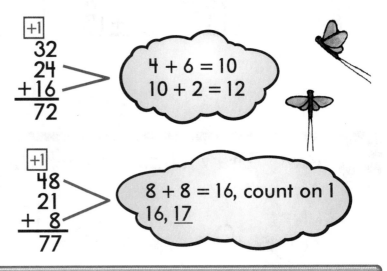

Circle the digits in the ones column that make a 10. Add.

1.
$$\begin{array}{r} 25 \\ 15 \\ +13 \\ \hline 53 \end{array}$$

2.
$$\begin{array}{r} 36 \\ 18 \\ +24 \\ \hline \end{array}$$

3.
$$\begin{array}{r} 17 \\ 7 \\ +23 \\ \hline \end{array}$$

4.
$$\begin{array}{r} 42 \\ 11 \\ +28 \\ \hline \end{array}$$

5.
$$\begin{array}{r} 51 \\ 9 \\ +16 \\ \hline \end{array}$$

Add the larger digits in the ones column first, then count on.
Add the tens column.

6. $\begin{array}{r} +1 \\ 38 \\ 18 \\ +11 \\ \hline 67 \end{array}$ > (16)

7. $\begin{array}{r} 25 \\ 29 \\ +13 \\ \hline \end{array}$ > ◯

8. $\begin{array}{r} 27 \\ 14 \\ + 8 \\ \hline \end{array}$ > ◯

9. $\begin{array}{r} 35 \\ 3 \\ +16 \\ \hline \end{array}$ > ◯

Add.

10. $\begin{array}{r} 27 \\ 32 \\ +11 \\ \hline \end{array}$

11. $\begin{array}{r} 16 \\ 12 \\ +25 \\ \hline \end{array}$

12. $\begin{array}{r} 28 \\ 9 \\ +12 \\ \hline \end{array}$

13. $\begin{array}{r} 35 \\ 22 \\ +15 \\ \hline \end{array}$

14. $\begin{array}{r} 64 \\ 6 \\ +23 \\ \hline \end{array}$

15. $\begin{array}{r} 43 \\ 17 \\ +24 \\ \hline \end{array}$

16. $\begin{array}{r} 38 \\ 13 \\ + 8 \\ \hline \end{array}$

17. $\begin{array}{r} 26 \\ 25 \\ +18 \\ \hline \end{array}$

18. $\begin{array}{r} 24 \\ 6 \\ +15 \\ \hline \end{array}$

19. $\begin{array}{r} 19 \\ 24 \\ +13 \\ \hline \end{array}$

20. $\begin{array}{r} 27 \\ 18 \\ +12 \\ \hline \end{array}$

21. $\begin{array}{r} 62 \\ 8 \\ +13 \\ \hline \end{array}$

Review   Draw a line to match the coins to the correct amount.

1. ◯   ◯26¢

2. ◯   ◯23¢

3. ◯   ◯28¢

4. ◯   ◯26¢

5. ◯   ◯31¢

6. ◯   ◯36¢

© Copyright 1999 ACSI Mathematics Grade 2

Oops! Honey has dripped on this piece of bread! Can you guess what number is under the honey?

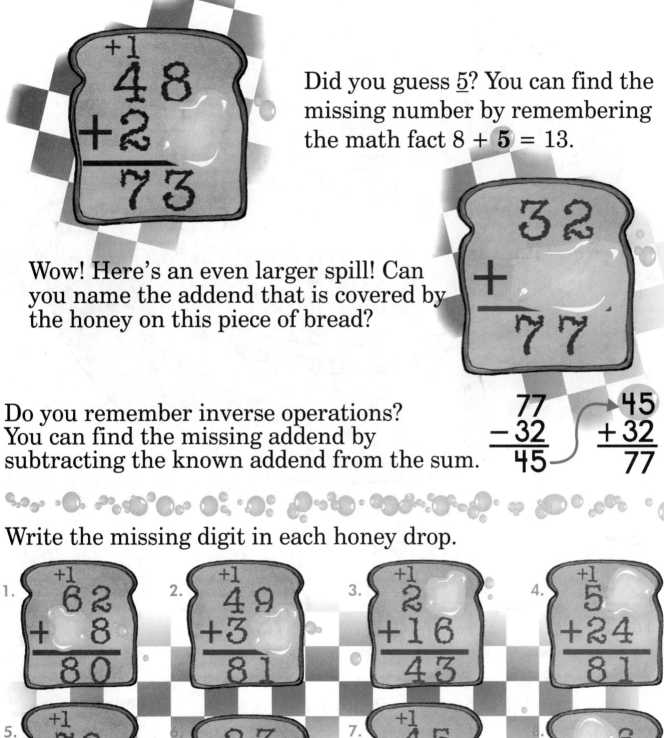

$$\begin{array}{r} {}^{+1} \\ 4\,8 \\ +\,2 \\ \hline 7\,3 \end{array}$$

Did you guess <u>5</u>? You can find the missing number by remembering the math fact 8 + **5** = 13.

Wow! Here's an even larger spill! Can you name the addend that is covered by the honey on this piece of bread?

$$\begin{array}{r} 3\,2 \\ + \\ \hline 7\,7 \end{array}$$

Do you remember inverse operations? You can find the missing addend by subtracting the known addend from the sum.

$$\begin{array}{r} 7\,7 \\ -\,3\,2 \\ \hline 4\,5 \end{array} \qquad \begin{array}{r} 4\,5 \\ +\,3\,2 \\ \hline 7\,7 \end{array}$$

Write the missing digit in each honey drop.

1.
$$\begin{array}{r} {}^{+1} \\ 6\,2 \\ +8 \\ \hline 8\,0 \end{array}$$

2.
$$\begin{array}{r} {}^{+1} \\ 4\,9 \\ +\,3 \\ \hline 8\,1 \end{array}$$

3.
$$\begin{array}{r} {}^{+1} \\ 2 \\ +1\,6 \\ \hline 4\,3 \end{array}$$

4.
$$\begin{array}{r} {}^{+1} \\ 5 \\ +2\,4 \\ \hline 8\,1 \end{array}$$

5.
$$\begin{array}{r} {}^{+1} \\ 7\,9 \\ +\,1 \\ \hline 9\,3 \end{array}$$

6.
$$\begin{array}{r} 2\,3 \\ +4 \\ \hline 7\,7 \end{array}$$

7.
$$\begin{array}{r} {}^{+1} \\ 4\,5 \\ +6 \\ \hline 8\,1 \end{array}$$

8.
$$\begin{array}{r} 6 \\ +5\,3 \\ \hline 8\,9 \end{array}$$

© Copyright 1999   Mathematics Grade 2

Write the missing addends in each honey drop.

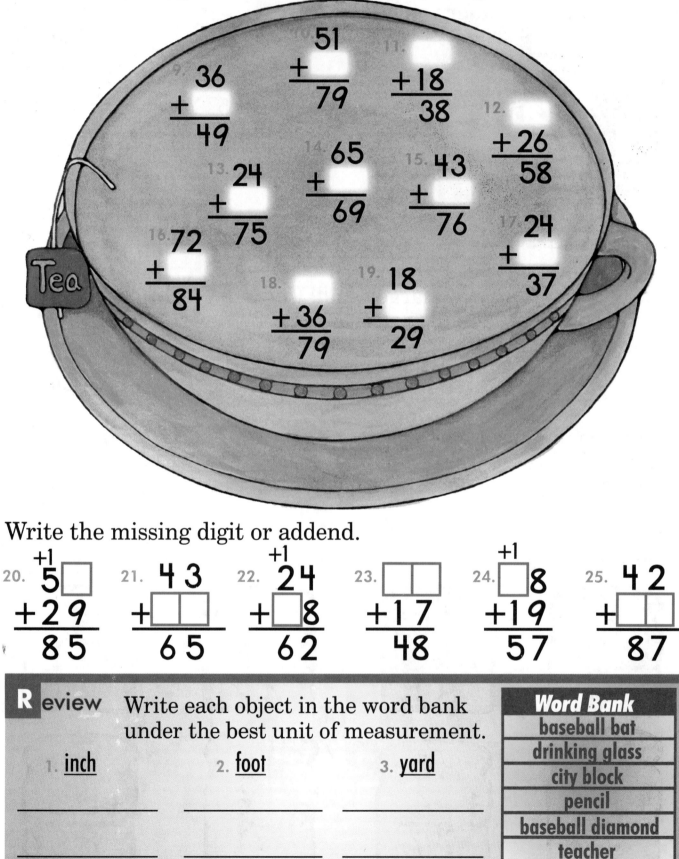

9.
$$\begin{array}{r} 36 \\ + \\ \hline 49 \end{array}$$

10.
$$\begin{array}{r} 51 \\ + \\ \hline 79 \end{array}$$

11.
$$\begin{array}{r} \\ +18 \\ \hline 38 \end{array}$$

12.
$$\begin{array}{r} \\ +26 \\ \hline 58 \end{array}$$

13.
$$\begin{array}{r} 24 \\ + \\ \hline 75 \end{array}$$

14.
$$\begin{array}{r} 65 \\ + \\ \hline 69 \end{array}$$

15.
$$\begin{array}{r} 43 \\ + \\ \hline 76 \end{array}$$

16.
$$\begin{array}{r} 72 \\ + \\ \hline 84 \end{array}$$

17.
$$\begin{array}{r} 24 \\ + \\ \hline 37 \end{array}$$

18.
$$\begin{array}{r} \\ +36 \\ \hline 79 \end{array}$$

19.
$$\begin{array}{r} 18 \\ + \\ \hline 29 \end{array}$$

Write the missing digit or addend.

20.
$$\begin{array}{r} +1 \\ 5\square \\ +29 \\ \hline 85 \end{array}$$

21.
$$\begin{array}{r} 43 \\ +\square\square \\ \hline 65 \end{array}$$

22.
$$\begin{array}{r} +1 \\ 24 \\ +\square 8 \\ \hline 62 \end{array}$$

23.
$$\begin{array}{r} \square\square \\ +17 \\ \hline 48 \end{array}$$

24.
$$\begin{array}{r} +1 \\ \square 8 \\ +19 \\ \hline 57 \end{array}$$

25.
$$\begin{array}{r} 42 \\ +\square\square \\ \hline 87 \end{array}$$

Review   Write each object in the word bank under the best unit of measurement.

1. <u>inch</u>   2. <u>foot</u>   3. <u>yard</u>

_____   _____   _____

_____   _____   _____

Word Bank
baseball bat
drinking glass
city block
pencil
baseball diamond
teacher

© Copyright 1999   Mathematics Grade 2

Problem Solving: Reading Tables   Lesson 117

Annelise made a table to show how many of each kind of cookie was made for the school bake sale.

Cookie	Number Made
Chocolate chip	48
Sugar	37
Oatmeal	55
Ginger snap	23

A <u>table</u> is an easy-to-read way of organizing information.

Use this table to answer the following questions.

Class	Sales During the First Hour	Sales During the Second Hour
1st Grade	45¢	52¢
2nd Grade	12¢	49¢
3rd Grade	27¢	38¢
4th Grade	60¢	15¢

BAKE SALE!

1. Which class made the most money during the first hour of the bake sale?_____

2. How much did the 2nd grade class make during both hours of the bake sale?_____

3. Did the 3rd grade class make more money during the first or second hour of the bake sale?_____

4. How much money did grades 1 and 4 make together during the second hour of the bake sale?_____

This table, a <u>tally chart</u>, shows the students' votes for favorite cookie. Use it to answer the following questions.

Cookie	Number of Votes
Chocolate chip	卌 卌 卌 卌 卌 卌
Peanut butter	卌 卌 卌 卌 ‖
Oatmeal	卌 卌 卌 ‖‖
Sugar	卌 卌 卌 ‖‖‖

5. Which kind of cookie received the most votes?

_____

6. How many votes did the oatmeal cookie receive?

_____

7. How many total votes did the peanut butter and the sugar cookie receive?

_____

8. How many total votes did the chocolate chip and the oatmeal cookie receive?

_____

9. Which kind of cookie received the least votes?

_____

10. If you were voting for favorite cookie, which one of these would you choose?

_____

Review   Circle the name of the figure.

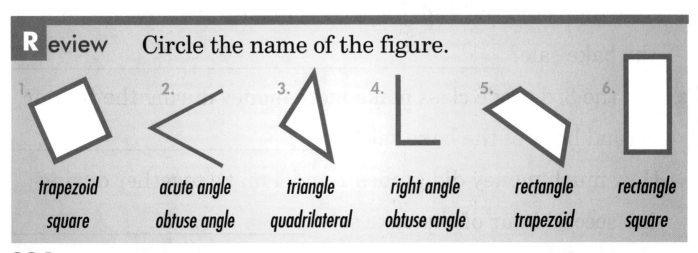

1.	2.	3.	4.	5.	6.
trapezoid	acute angle	triangle	right angle	rectangle	rectangle
square	obtuse angle	quadrilateral	obtuse angle	trapezoid	square

© Copyright 1999 ACSI Mathematics Grade 2

Some primary students volunteered to make an exhibit for the school Science Fair. Students in grades 4-6 were required to take part. How many students in each class made a Science Fair exhibit?

Graphs help us organize information. They use pictures or bars to tell how many.

👤 = 2 students

Students Who Made a Science Fair Exhibit

Class	Number of Students
1st Grade	👤👤
2nd Grade	👤👤👤
3rd Grade	👤👤👤
4th Grade	👤👤👤👤👤👤
5th Grade	👤👤👤👤👤👤👤👤
6th Grade	👤👤👤👤👤👤👤👤👤👤

Read the graph to find the answers.

1. How many 2nd graders took part in the Science Fair?_____

2. Which class had the most students take part?_____

3. How many 1st, 2nd, and 3rd graders took part in all?_____

4. If 👤 = 2 students, how many students do you think ⅃ equals?

_____

5. Which had more students involved, 6th grade, or 4th and 5th grades together?_____

This graph tells the kind of science shown by the exhibits. Read the graph to find the answers.

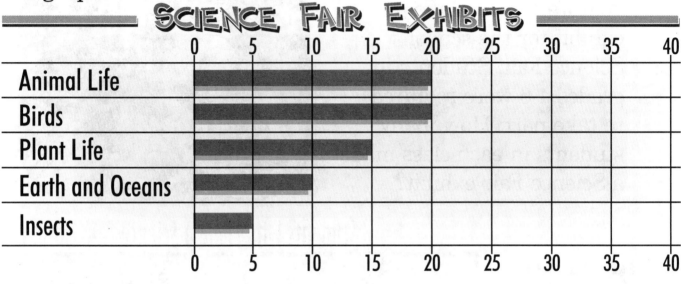

SCIENCE FAIR EXHIBITS

6. How many exhibits were about Plant Life?

_____

7. How many exhibits were about Animal Life and Birds?

_____

8. Which type of science had the fewest exhibits?

_____

9. Which had less: Animal Life, or Plant Life plus Earth and Oceans?

_____

10. Six of the Earth and Oceans exhibits were about volcanoes. How many were not about volcanoes?

_____

11. How many total exhibits were there for Birds, Plant Life, and Insects?

_____

Review Complete.

		$+$	$+$	$-$	$=$
1.	4	2	3	5	___
2.	3	3	5	7	___
3.	5	1	7	4	___

© Copyright 1999 *Mathematics Grade 2*

Chapter Eight Check-Up   Lesson 119

Add.

1. 41
  +36

2. 25
  +14

3. 46
  + 4

4. 59
  + 6

5. 68
  +17

6. 24
  +19

7. 36
  +26

8. 42
  +38

9. 65
  +27

10. 55
  +39

Round each number to the nearest ten.

11. 29 _____

12. 13 _____

13. 72 _____

14. 56 _____

15. 35 _____

16. 44 _____

17. 78 _____

18. 27 _____

Round each addend. Estimate the sums.

19. 45   _____
   +28 + _____
        _____

20. 23   _____
   +17 + _____
        _____

21. 67   _____
   +14 + _____
        _____

Find the prices. Add.

rock candy

18¢

lollipop

stick candy

6¢

32¢

45¢

57¢

button candy

licorice lace

22. lollipop and rock candy

23. licorice lace and stick candy

24. button candy and lollipop

25. rock candy and button candy

+ _____
¢

+ _____

+ _____

+ _____

© Copyright 1999 Mathematics Grade 2

Add. Fill in the circle to identify the strategy you used.

26.
```
   23    ○ making a ten
   17    ○ counting on
 + 12    ○ neither
```

27.
```
   38    ○ making a ten
   18    ○ counting on
 + 11    ○ neither
```

28.
```
   45    ○ making a ten
   24    ○ counting on
 + 13    ○ neither
```

29.
```
   27    ○ making a ten
   26    ○ counting on
 + 13    ○ neither
```

30.
```
   24    ○ making a ten
    6    ○ counting on
 + 15    ○ neither
```

31.
```
   25    ○ making a ten
   18    ○ counting on
 + 13    ○ neither
```

Answer the questions about this table.

Allowance Money Earned

Name	Week 1	Week 2
Brandon	55¢	62¢
James	47¢	34¢
Laura	29¢	51¢
Emily	43¢	36¢
Brian	33¢	59¢

32. Who earned the most money during Week 1?_____

33. How much money did Brian earn in both weeks?_____

34. Who earned the most money during Week 2?_____

35. Did Emily or Laura earn more money for both weeks?_____

Candy Sold 🍬 = 2 candies

lollipops 🍬🍬
rock candy 🍬🍬🍬🍬🍬
licorice laces 🍬🍬🍬🍬
button candy 🍬🍬🍬🍬🍬🍬
stick candy 🍬🍬🍬🍬🍬🍬🍬🍬

36. How many licorice laces were sold?_____

37. How many total rock candies and button candies were sold?

_____

CHAPTER 9

Two-Digit Subtraction with Regrouping

These all wait for You, that You may give them their food in due season. What You give them they gather in; You open Your hand, they are filled with good.

Psalm 104:27-28

Dear Parents,

Chapter Nine of our math book is a "sequel" to the material in Chapter Eight. Because subtraction is the reverse operation of addition, you'll find that the coming lessons closely parallel the flow of lessons in Chapter Eight.

The skill of regrouping is critical to the understanding of addition and subtraction. In Chapter Eight we suggested you help your child conceptualize the process of regrouping ones as tens. Now you can help practice regrouping in the other direction, tens as ones. An easy way to do this is to bundle (with rubber bands) groups of ten drinking straws, popsicle sticks, or toothpicks. Here is a pattern for the way you can use these manipulatives to practice a subtraction problem.

- Model the number 32 with three bundles of 10 straws and two single straws.

- Ask your child to take away (subtract) 14. In order to do this, one of the bundles will have to be separated into individual straws. Then four single straws can be removed, along with another bundle of 10.

- Have your child "read" the number that is left. One bundle and eight single straws equal 18.

You may find practice like this especially helpful for Lessons 121-124. As your child's proficiency with subtraction grows, the need for manipulatives will decrease.

The assistance you give your child will serve as a wonderful model of Chapter Nine's spiritual theme of God's provision. On these pages you will see pictures of eagles, hawks, owls, and other birds of prey to remind your child that God provides for every part of His creation. As God provides you with energy and love, you provide your child with the reinforcement he or she needs to experience success.

© Copyright 1999 Mathematics Grade 2

Reviewing Two-Digit Subtraction   Lesson 120

The park rangers at Glen Haven Nature Preserve have counted 27 birds of prey. 12 of them are eagles. How many are other types of birds?

tens	ones
2	7
− 1	2
1	5

Begin with 27. Take away 12. 15 are left.

15 birds are other types of birds of prey.

Subtract.

1. 45	2. 24	3. 67	4. 25	5. 39
− 23	− 3	− 14	− 11	− 25

6. 58	7. 74	8. 48	9. 87	10. 95
− 5	− 52	− 15	− 51	− 64

Subtract. Write the difference at the top of the next problem.

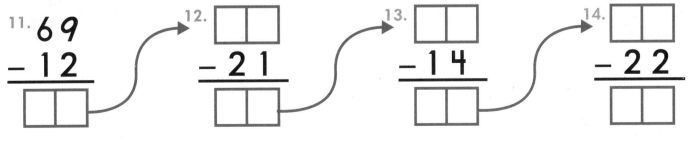

11. 69
− 12

12.
− 21

13.
− 14

14.
− 22

15. Help the eagle find his prey. Color the dots on each correct problem.
Draw a path by connecting the colored dots. Do not lift your pencil.

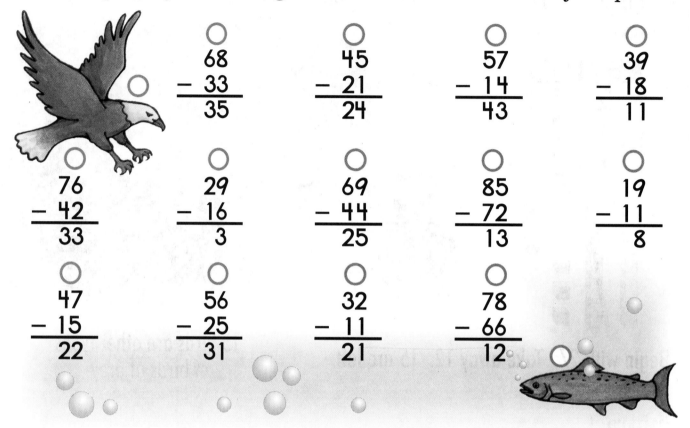

$$\begin{array}{r} 68 \\ -33 \\ \hline 35 \end{array}$$

$$\begin{array}{r} 45 \\ -21 \\ \hline 24 \end{array}$$

$$\begin{array}{r} 57 \\ -14 \\ \hline 43 \end{array}$$

$$\begin{array}{r} 39 \\ -18 \\ \hline 11 \end{array}$$

$$\begin{array}{r} 76 \\ -42 \\ \hline 33 \end{array}$$

$$\begin{array}{r} 29 \\ -16 \\ \hline 3 \end{array}$$

$$\begin{array}{r} 69 \\ -44 \\ \hline 25 \end{array}$$

$$\begin{array}{r} 85 \\ -72 \\ \hline 13 \end{array}$$

$$\begin{array}{r} 19 \\ -11 \\ \hline 8 \end{array}$$

$$\begin{array}{r} 47 \\ -15 \\ \hline 22 \end{array}$$

$$\begin{array}{r} 56 \\ -25 \\ \hline 31 \end{array}$$

$$\begin{array}{r} 32 \\ -11 \\ \hline 21 \end{array}$$

$$\begin{array}{r} 78 \\ -66 \\ \hline 12 \end{array}$$

16. Brad's family drove 96 miles to Bible camp. They drove 54 miles before making a stop. How many miles did they drive after the stop?

_____

17. Kerry had 48 baseball cards in her collection. She gave 15 duplicate cards to Marcus. How many cards does Kerry have left?

_____

Review   Write the time shown on each clock.

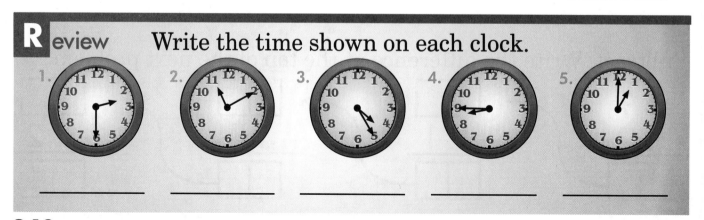

1. _____ _____ _____ _____ _____

© Copyright 1999   Mathematics Grade 2

Regrouping Tens as Ones — Lesson 121

24 can be shown as
2 tens and 4 ones.

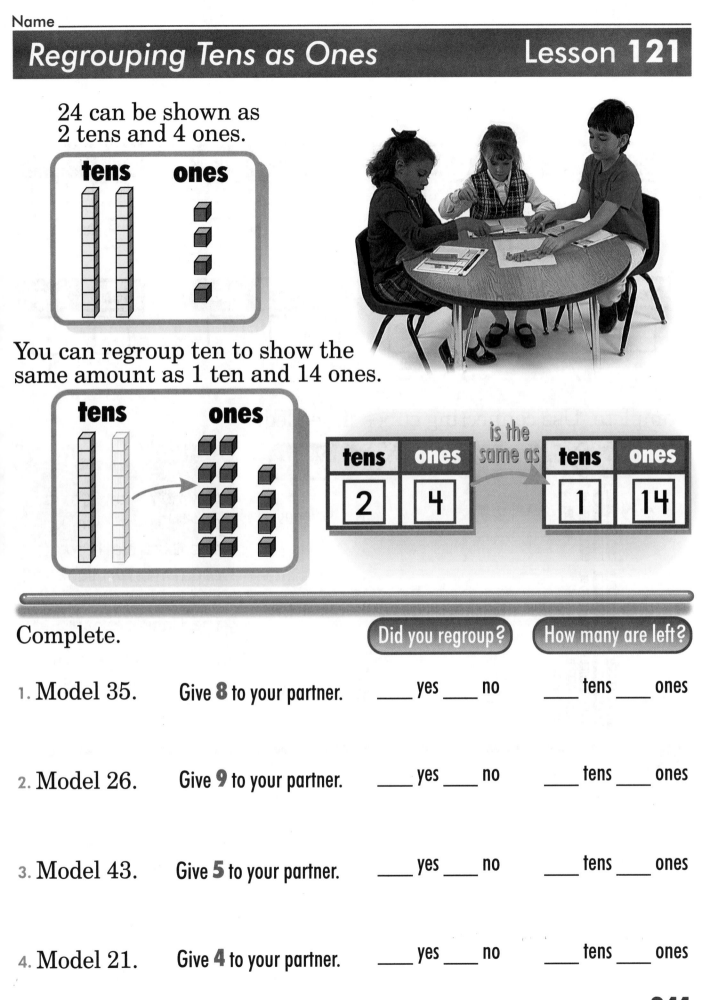

tens   ones

You can regroup ten to show the
same amount as 1 ten and 14 ones.

tens   ones

tens	ones
2	4

is the same as

tens	ones
1	14

Complete.

Did you regroup?   **How many are left?**

1. Model 35.   Give **8** to your partner.   ____ yes ____ no   ____ tens ____ ones

2. Model 26.   Give **9** to your partner.   ____ yes ____ no   ____ tens ____ ones

3. Model 43.   Give **5** to your partner.   ____ yes ____ no   ____ tens ____ ones

4. Model 21.   Give **4** to your partner.   ____ yes ____ no   ____ tens ____ ones

Regroup the tens in each number.

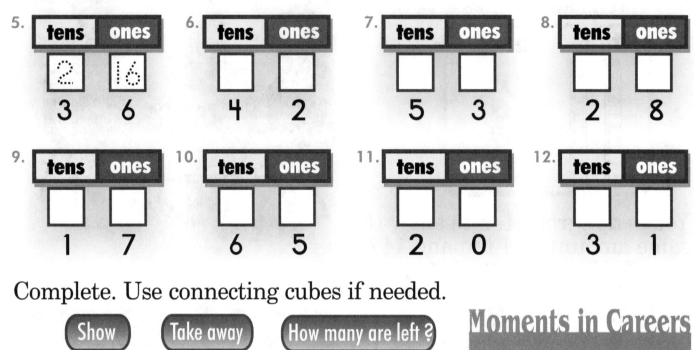

5. | tens | ones |
   |------|------|
   | 2 | 16 |
   | 3 | 6 |

6. | tens | ones |
   |------|------|
   | | |
   | 4 | 2 |

7. | tens | ones |
   |------|------|
   | | |
   | 5 | 3 |

8. | tens | ones |
   |------|------|
   | | |
   | 2 | 8 |

9. | tens | ones |
   |------|------|
   | | |
   | 1 | 7 |

10. | tens | ones |
    |------|------|
    | | |
    | 6 | 5 |

11. | tens | ones |
    |------|------|
    | | |
    | 2 | 0 |

12. | tens | ones |
    |------|------|
    | | |
    | 3 | 1 |

Complete. Use connecting cubes if needed.

Show	Take away	How many are left?
13. **32**	6	____ tens ____ ones
14. **25**	8	____ tens ____ ones
15. **44**	7	____ tens ____ ones

Moments in Careers

My mom works as a clerk. In her work she uses math to count money, subtract, and add numbers for the bank deposit.

Elizabeth
Huron, S.D.

Review   Subtract.

1. 12
  − 8

2. 15
  − 7

3. 18
  − 9

4. 17
  − 8

5. 14
  − 7

6. 11
  − 5

7. 10
  − 6

8. 12
  − 9

9. 13
  − 5

10. 15
  − 6

11. 14
  − 8

12. 16
  − 8

© Copyright 1999   Mathematics Grade 2

Using Regrouping to Subtract — Lesson 122

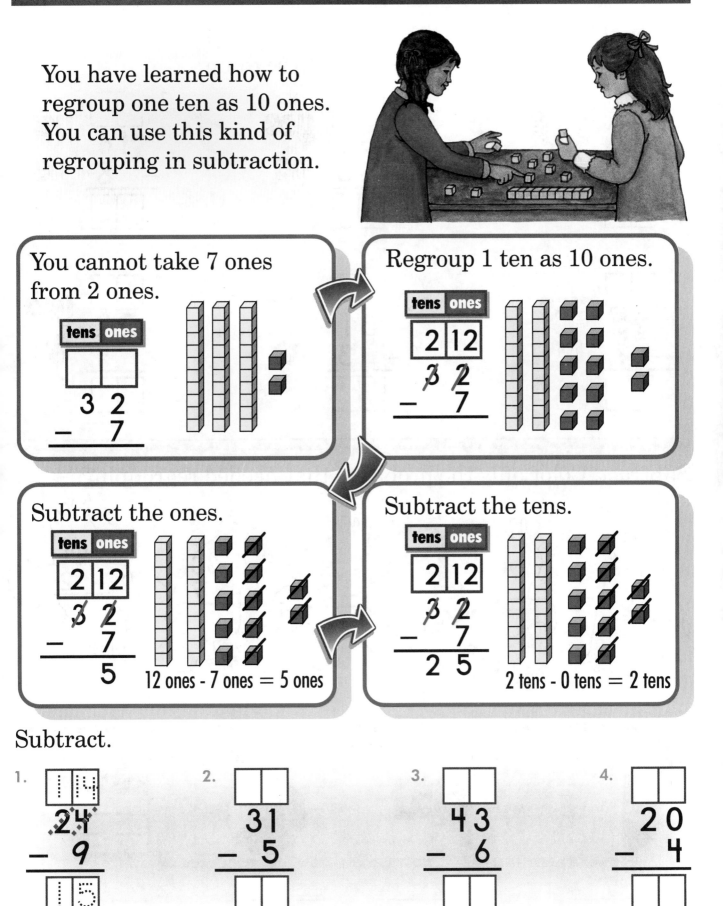

You have learned how to regroup one ten as 10 ones. You can use this kind of regrouping in subtraction.

You cannot take 7 ones from 2 ones.

tens	ones
3	2
−	7

Regroup 1 ten as 10 ones.

tens	ones
2	12
3	2
−	7

Subtract the ones.

tens	ones
2	12
3	2
−	7
	5

12 ones − 7 ones = 5 ones

Subtract the tens.

tens	ones
2	12
3	2
−	7
2	5

2 tens − 0 tens = 2 tens

Subtract.

1.
```
 14
 2 4
−  9
 1 5
```

2.
```
  3 1
−   5
```

3.
```
  4 3
−   6
```

4.
```
  2 0
−   4
```

Subtract.
Circle <u>yes</u> or <u>no</u> to show if you need to regroup.

5.
```
  3 12
  4 2   yes
-   6   no
  0 6
```

6.
```
  3 8   yes
-   5   no
```

7.
```
  4 6   yes
-   8   no
```

8.
```
  2 5   yes
-   9   no
```

9.
```
  3 1   yes
-   3   no
```

10.
```
  2 2   yes
-   4   no
```

Subtract. Color only the problems that needed regrouping.

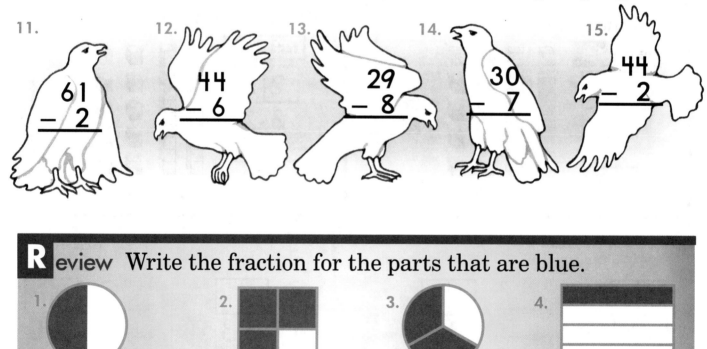

11.
```
  6 1
- 2
```

12.
```
  4 4
- 6
```

13.
```
  2 9
- 8
```

14.
```
  3 0
- 7
```

15.
```
  4 4
- 2
```

Review   Write the fraction for the parts that are blue.

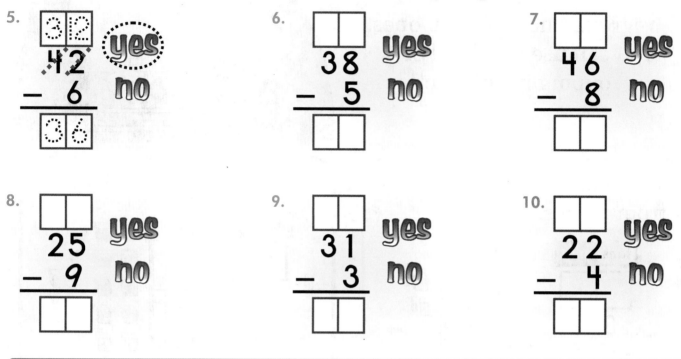

1. _____ 2. _____ 3. _____ 4. _____

© Copyright 1999   Mathematics Grade 2

Name _____

Subtracting Two-Digit Numbers   Lesson 123

The Raptor Center is an international medical facility for birds of prey. In one month 16 of the Center's 42 patients were owls. How many were other birds of prey?

Use the same three steps you already know to subtract a two-digit number from another two-digit number.

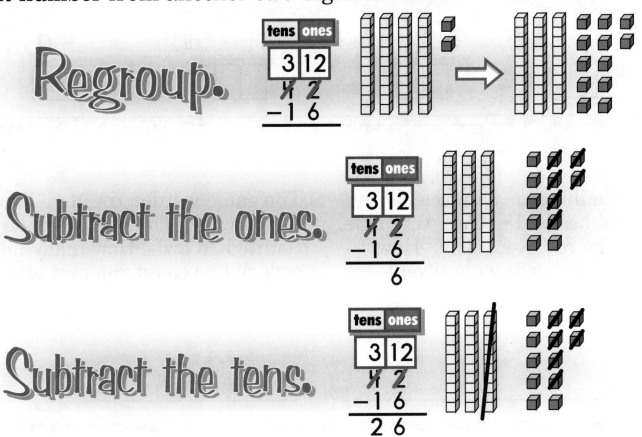

Regroup.

tens	ones
3	12

  4̶ 2̶
− 1 6

Subtract the ones.

tens	ones
3	12

  4̶ 2̶
− 1 6
_____
      6

Subtract the tens.

tens	ones
3	12

  4̶ 2̶
− 1 6
_____
    2 6

Subtract.

1.
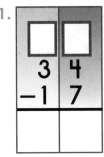
  3 4
− 1 7

2.
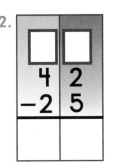
  4 2
− 2 5

3.
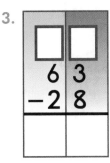
  6 3
− 2 8

4.
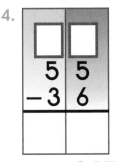
  5 5
− 3 6

© Copyright 1999 ACSI Mathematics Grade 2

Two hundred forty-five **245**

Circle <u>yes</u> or <u>no</u> to show if you need to regroup. Subtract.

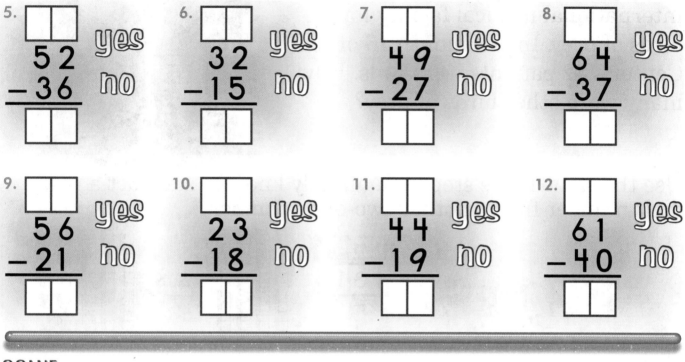

5.
52
−36
yes
no

6.
32
−15
yes
no

7.
49
−27
yes
no

8.
64
−37
yes
no

9.
56
−21
yes
no

10.
23
−18
yes
no

11.
44
−19
yes
no

12.
61
−40
yes
no

SOLVE.

13. Emily made a bracelet with 34 beads. 18 beads were blue. The rest were silver. How many beads were silver?

14. The game warden counted 23 owls in one week. The next week he counted 16 owls. How many more owls did he count the first week?

_____   _____

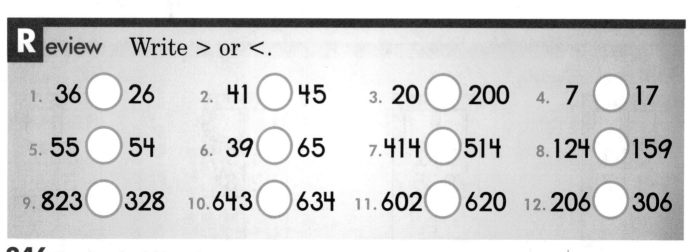

Review   Write > or <.

1. 36 ◯ 26   2. 41 ◯ 45   3. 20 ◯ 200   4. 7 ◯ 17

5. 55 ◯ 54   6. 39 ◯ 65   7. 414 ◯ 514   8. 124 ◯ 159

9. 823 ◯ 328   10. 643 ◯ 634   11. 602 ◯ 620   12. 206 ◯ 306

© Copyright 1999 Mathematics Grade 2

Practicing Two-Digit Subtraction   Lesson 124

The park rangers counted 34 barn owls in the fall. 16 were not found the next spring. <u>How many</u> barn owls <u>are left</u>?

```
  2 14
  3̶4̶
- 16
─────
  18 barn owls left
```

The rangers counted 27 great horned owls. They counted 82 mice. <u>How many more</u> mice were counted than owls?

```
  7 12
  8̶2̶
- 27
─────
  55 more mice
```

Subtraction can answer <u>how many are left</u> or <u>how many more</u>.

Solve. Fill in the circle to show how subtraction is used.

1. Micah collected 53 baseball cards. He gave away 18 duplicate cards. How many cards does Micah have left?

   _____

   ○ **How many are left?**
   ○ **How many more?**

2. Last year 31 hawks were counted. This year there were 25. How many more hawks were counted last year than this year?

   _____

   ○ **How many are left?**
   ○ **How many more?**

3. The park rangers counted 26 screech owls. They found 13 nests. How many more owls than nests were counted?

   _____

   ○ **How many are left?**
   ○ **How many more?**

Subtract to help the owl find its prey. Color the dots on problems that needed to be regrouped. Draw a path by connecting the colored dots. Do not lift your pencil.

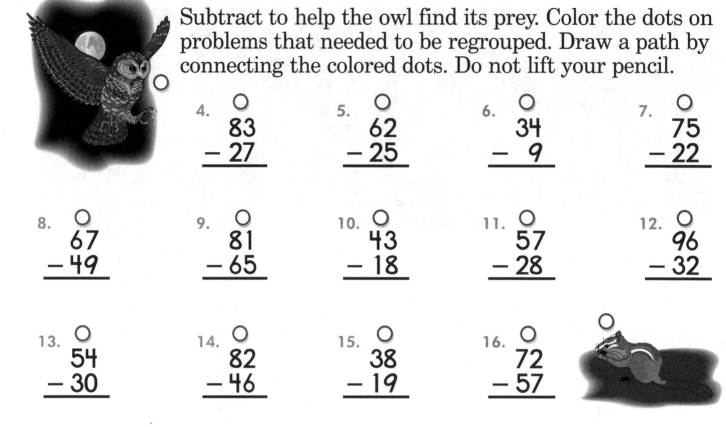

4. ○
```
  83
- 27
```

5. ○
```
  62
- 25
```

6. ○
```
  34
-  9
```

7. ○
```
  75
- 22
```

8. ○
```
  67
- 49
```

9. ○
```
  81
- 65
```

10. ○
```
  43
- 18
```

11. ○
```
  57
- 28
```

12. ○
```
  96
- 32
```

13. ○
```
  54
- 30
```

14. ○
```
  82
- 46
```

15. ○
```
  38
- 19
```

16. ○
```
  72
- 57
```

Subtract. Write > or < for each pair of differences.

17.
```
  41          83
- 17   ○    - 35
```

18.
```
  65          32
- 42   ○    - 14
```

19.
```
  54          76
- 29   ○    - 49
```

Review   Mark off the correct amount of money.

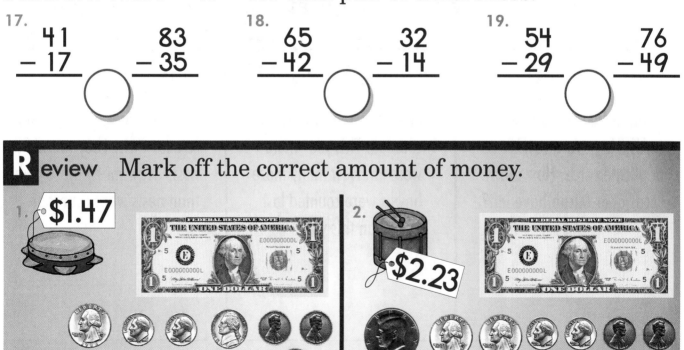

1. $1.47

2. $2.23

© Copyright 1999 ACSI *Mathematics Grade 2*

Writing Subtraction Problems Lesson 125

attic

2nd floor

1st floor

foundation

Houses are built in a certain way, from the foundation at the bottom to the roof at the top.

Subtraction has to be done in a certain way, too.

$14 - 6 = 8$ <u>but</u> $6 - 14$ is not 8!

Subtraction problems can be written <u>horizontally</u> or <u>vertically</u>,

$$53 - 27 = 26 \qquad \begin{array}{r} 53 \\ -27 \\ \hline 26 \end{array}$$

but the numbers must be in the right place.

Rewrite the problems. Line up the tens and ones columns. Subtract.

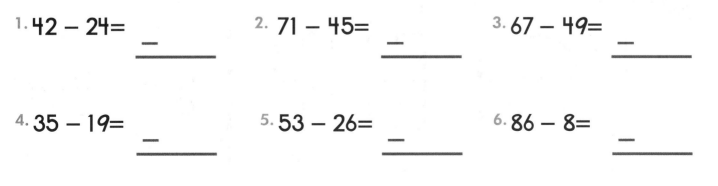

1. $42 - 24 =$ _____

2. $71 - 45 =$ _____

3. $67 - 49 =$ _____

4. $35 - 19 =$ _____

5. $53 - 26 =$ _____

6. $86 - 8 =$ _____

Write the subtraction problems your teacher reads. Subtract.

7.

8.

9.

10.

$$-$$ $$-$$ $$-$$ $$-$$

Use the numbers to write subtraction problems. Solve.

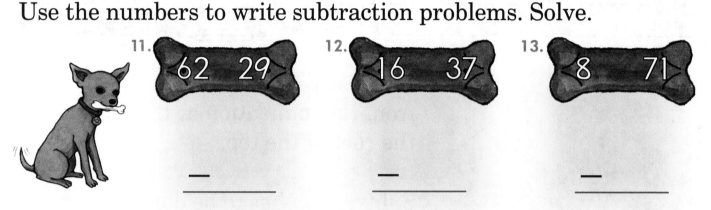

11. 62 29

12. 16 37

13. 8 71

$$-$$ $$-$$ $$-$$

SOLVE.

14. Lizzie strung 46 beads to make a necklace. 17 beads fell off the end of the string. How many beads were left?

15. One wall is 33 meters long. The other wall is 27 meters long. How much longer is the first wall than the second?

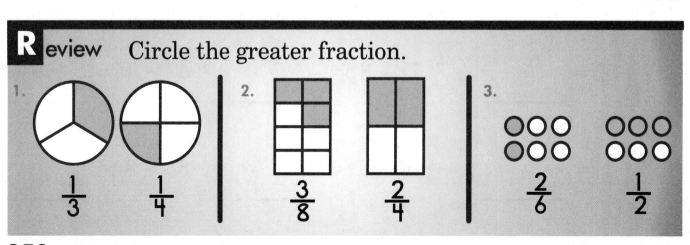

Review   Circle the greater fraction.

1. $\frac{1}{3}$ $\frac{1}{4}$

2. $\frac{3}{8}$ $\frac{2}{4}$

3. $\frac{2}{6}$ $\frac{1}{2}$

© Copyright 1999   Mathematics Grade 2

Checking Subtraction with Addition   Lesson 126

54 falcons were trained to hunt.

25 were sent as a gift to the king.

How many falcons were left?

_____ falcons

Numbers form fact families. Larger numbers work the same way. You can check subtraction by using addition:

Add the **difference** and the bottom number of the subtraction problem. They should equal the **top number** of the subtraction problem.

29 falcons were left.

Match subtraction problems to the addition "checks."

1.
$$\begin{array}{r} 42 \\ -11 \\ \hline 31 \end{array}$$
○

○
①
$$\begin{array}{r} 26 \\ +25 \\ \hline 51 \end{array}$$

2.
$$\begin{array}{r} {}^{2}\;{}^{16} \\ \cancel{36} \\ -18 \\ \hline 18 \end{array}$$
○

○
$$\begin{array}{r} 31 \\ +11 \\ \hline 42 \end{array}$$

3.
$$\begin{array}{r} {}^{4}\;{}^{11} \\ \cancel{51} \\ -25 \\ \hline 26 \end{array}$$
○

○
①
$$\begin{array}{r} 18 \\ +18 \\ \hline 36 \end{array}$$

Complete.

4.
```
  64  ⟶ ☐
- 19    + 19
 ☐ ⟫⟫ ____
```

5.
```
  85  ⟶ ☐
- 37    + 37
 ☐ ⟫⟫ ____
```

6.
```
  73  ⟶ ☐
- 52    + 52
 ☐ ⟫⟫ ____
```

Subtract. Add to check.

7.
```
 93  ____
-47  + ____

____  ____
```

8.
```
 86  ____
-32  + ____

____  ____
```

9.
```
 72  ____
-57  + ____

____  ____
```

10.
```
 82  ____
-46  + ____

____  ____
```

11.
```
 65  ____
-24  + ____

____  ____
```

12.
```
 84  ____
-38  + ____

____  ____
```

13.
```
 38  ____
-19  + ____

____  ____
```

14.
```
 97  ____
-66  + ____

____  ____
```

Review   Measure the arrows to the nearest inch or centimeter.

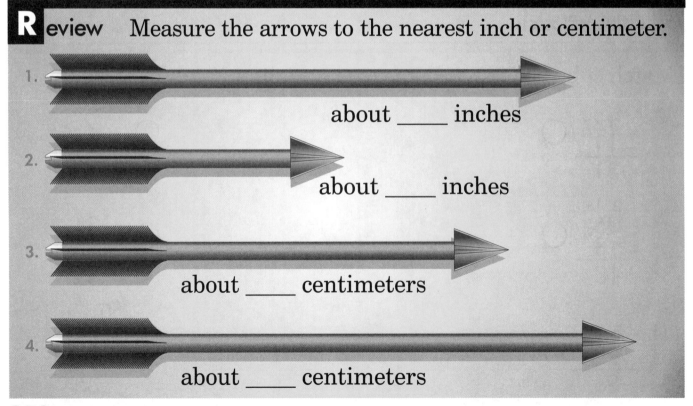

1. about ____ inches

2. about ____ inches

3. about ____ centimeters

4. about ____ centimeters

© Copyright 1999   Mathematics Grade 2

Subtracting from Zero Ones   Lesson 127

Freddy's Drive-In makes the best fries in town! Mrs. Connor ordered 2 small packages of French fries. There are 10 fries in each package.

She gave 7 fries to Billy.
How many does she have left?

$$\begin{array}{r} {\scriptstyle 1 \;\; 10} \\ 2\cancel{0} \\ -\;\; 7 \\ \hline 13 \end{array}$$

13 fries are left.

These fries are regrouped. Mark off to subtract. Write the numbers.

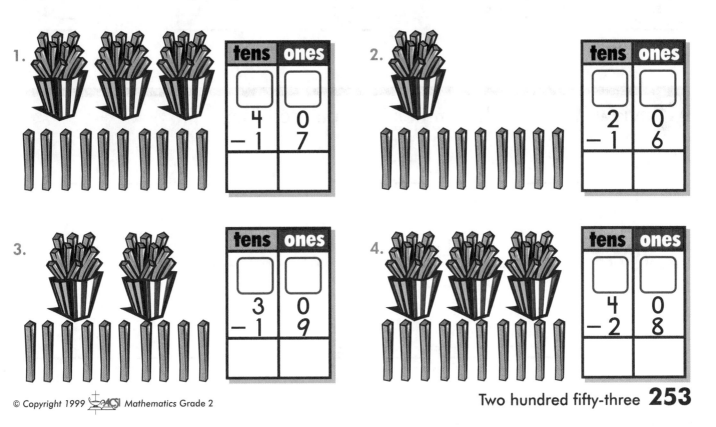

1.

tens	ones
4	0
− 1	7

2.

tens	ones
2	0
− 1	6

3.

tens	ones
3	0
− 1	9

4.

tens	ones
4	0
− 2	8

© Copyright 1999 ᴬᶜˢ Mathematics Grade 2

Subtract.

5.

tens	ones
□	□
6	0
− 4	2

6.

tens	ones
□	□
3	0
− 1	3

7.

tens	ones
□	□
7	0
− 4	9

8.

tens	ones
□	□
6	0
− 3	7

9. 52
   − 26

10. 40
   − 18

11. 81
   − 67

12. 60
   − 21

13. 44
   − 23

14. 65
   − 37

15. 20
   − 5

16. 42
   − 26

17. 30
   − 14

18. 50
   − 36

19. 71
   − 55

20. 80
   − 65

21. 90
   − 17

22. 65
   − 44

23. 80
   − 47

Review Write each number in expanded form.

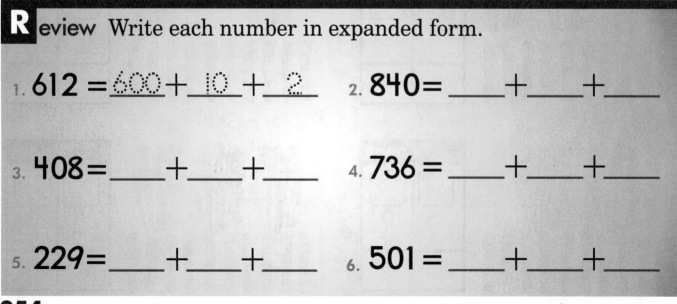

1. 612 = 600 + 10 + 2   2. 840 = ___ + ___ + ___

3. 408 = ___ + ___ + ___   4. 736 = ___ + ___ + ___

5. 229 = ___ + ___ + ___   6. 501 = ___ + ___ + ___

 © Copyright 1999 *Mathematics Grade 2*

Mid-Chapter Review

Use connecting cubes. Complete this chart.

	Model with Cubes	Take Away	How Many Are Left? Tens	Ones
1.	32	6	2	6
2.	43	8		
3.	21	3		
4.	55	7		

Rewrite these problems. Subtract.

5. $29 - 13 =$ 6. $42 - 26 =$ 7. $51 - 4 =$

Subtract. Check your work with addition.

8.
$$\begin{array}{r} 64 \\ -39 \\ \hline 25 \end{array} \quad \begin{array}{r} 25 \\ +39 \\ \hline 64 \end{array}$$

9.
$$\begin{array}{r} 35 \\ -17 \\ \hline \end{array} \quad +$$

10.
$$\begin{array}{r} 61 \\ -43 \\ \hline \end{array} \quad +$$

11.
$$\begin{array}{r} 92 \\ -63 \\ \hline \end{array} \quad +$$

Subtract.

12.
$$\begin{array}{r} 20 \\ -8 \\ \hline \end{array}$$

13.
$$\begin{array}{r} 50 \\ -26 \\ \hline \end{array}$$

14.
$$\begin{array}{r} 40 \\ -23 \\ \hline \end{array}$$

15.
$$\begin{array}{r} 70 \\ -47 \\ \hline \end{array}$$

Circle the owl if the problem needs regrouping. Subtract.

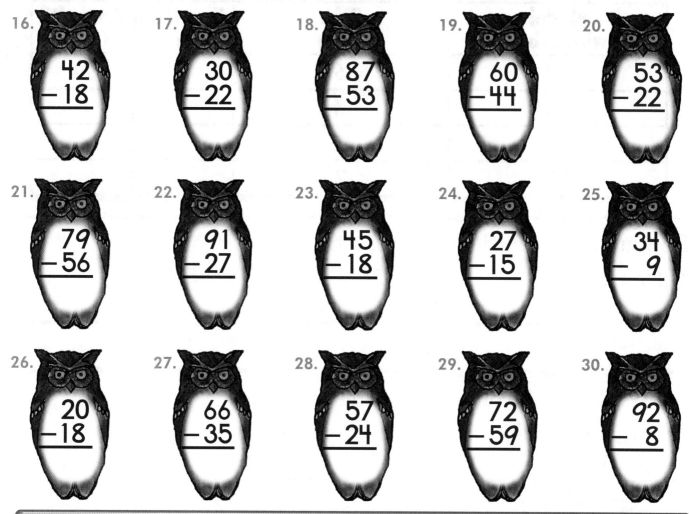

16.
$$42 - 18$$

17.
$$30 - 22$$

18.
$$87 - 53$$

19.
$$60 - 44$$

20.
$$53 - 22$$

21.
$$79 - 56$$

22.
$$91 - 27$$

23.
$$45 - 18$$

24.
$$27 - 15$$

25.
$$34 - 9$$

26.
$$20 - 18$$

27.
$$66 - 35$$

28.
$$57 - 24$$

29.
$$72 - 59$$

30.
$$92 - 8$$

Use the differences to fill in the spaces of this puzzle.

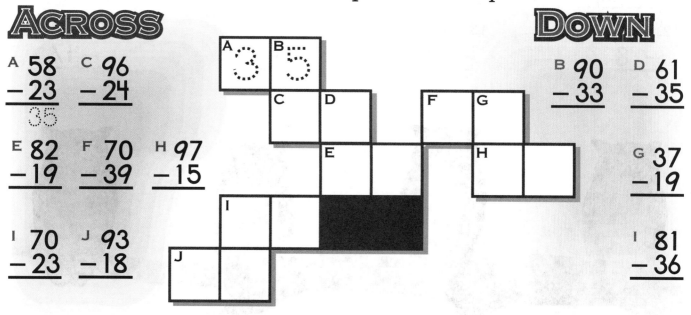

ACROSS

A
$$58 - 23$$
35

C
$$96 - 24$$

E
$$82 - 19$$

F
$$70 - 39$$

H
$$97 - 15$$

I
$$70 - 23$$

J
$$93 - 18$$

DOWN

B
$$90 - 33$$

D
$$61 - 35$$

G
$$37 - 19$$

I
$$81 - 36$$

© Copyright 1999   Mathematics Grade 2

Problem Solving: Estimating Differences   Lesson 129

Sir Reginald and Sir Edward are training their falcons. Sir Reginald's falcon flew 88 feet before returning. Sir Edward's falcon flew 63 feet. About how much farther did Sir Reginald's falcon fly than Sir Edward's?

We can estimate the difference by

rounding the numbers   and   subtracting the tens

$$88 \longrightarrow 90$$
$$63 \longrightarrow 60$$

$$\begin{array}{r} 90 \\ -\ 60 \\ \hline 30 \end{array}$$

> **Sir Reginald's falcon flew about 30 feet farther than Sir Edward's falcon.**

Estimate differences to solve these problems.

1. About how much farther did Sir Gerald's falcon fly than Sir George's falcon?   — _____

_____

2. About how much farther did Sir Edward's falcon fly than Sir Philip's falcon?   — _____

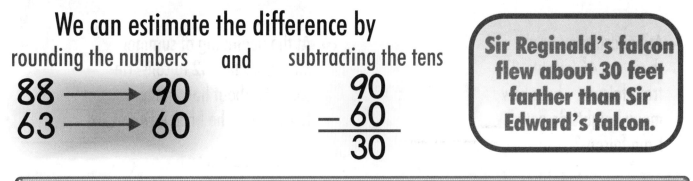

Length of Falcon Training Flights

Sir Reginald's 🦅—88 feet
Sir Gerald's 🦅—76 feet
Sir Edward's 🦅— 63 feet
Sir George's 🦅— 55 feet
Sir Philip's 🦅— 43 feet

Estimate the differences.

| 78 42 | 64 19 | 52 36 | 81 17 |

3.
$$78 \rightarrow 80$$
$$-42 \rightarrow -40$$
$$\overline{40}$$

4.
$$\rightarrow$$
$$- \rightarrow -$$

5.
$$\rightarrow$$
$$- \rightarrow -$$

6.
$$\rightarrow$$
$$- \rightarrow -$$

Solve by estimating the difference.

7. The falcons captured 23 grouse and 12 partridge. About how many more grouse were captured than partridge?

_____

_____ more grouse

8. Sir Reginald is 38 years old. Sir Philip is 19. About how much older is Sir Reginald than Sir Philip?

_____

_____ years older

9. At Sandrington Castle there are 46 knights. 27 train falcons. About how many knights do not train falcons?

_____

_____ knights

10. At the beginning of summer Mr. James had 42 falcons. He sold 26. About how many falcons does he have now?

_____

_____ falcons

Review Write the times.

1. One half hour after
2. 15 minutes after
3. One hour before
4. 20 minutes before
5. One hour and a half after

_____ _____ _____ _____ _____

© Copyright 1999 *Mathematics Grade 2*

Subtracting Money — Lesson 130

Edie has 78¢. She buys a small popcorn for 45¢. About how much money will she have left?

Estimating the difference first can help you know what to expect. It will give you a close answer.

78 cents ⟶ 80 cents

45 cents ⟶ _ 50 cents

30 cents

```
  78 ¢
- 45 ¢
  33 ¢
```

When subtracting money amounts, remember to write the cents sign (¢) or the dollar sign ($).

Subtract.

1. 49¢
   − 27¢

2. 62¢
   − 15¢

3. 53¢
   − 26¢

4. 84¢
   − 38¢

5. 71¢
   − 59¢

6. $33
   − 6

7. $95
   − 77

8. $29
   − 15

9. $41
   − 18

10. $63
    − 44

Solve. Fill in the blanks.

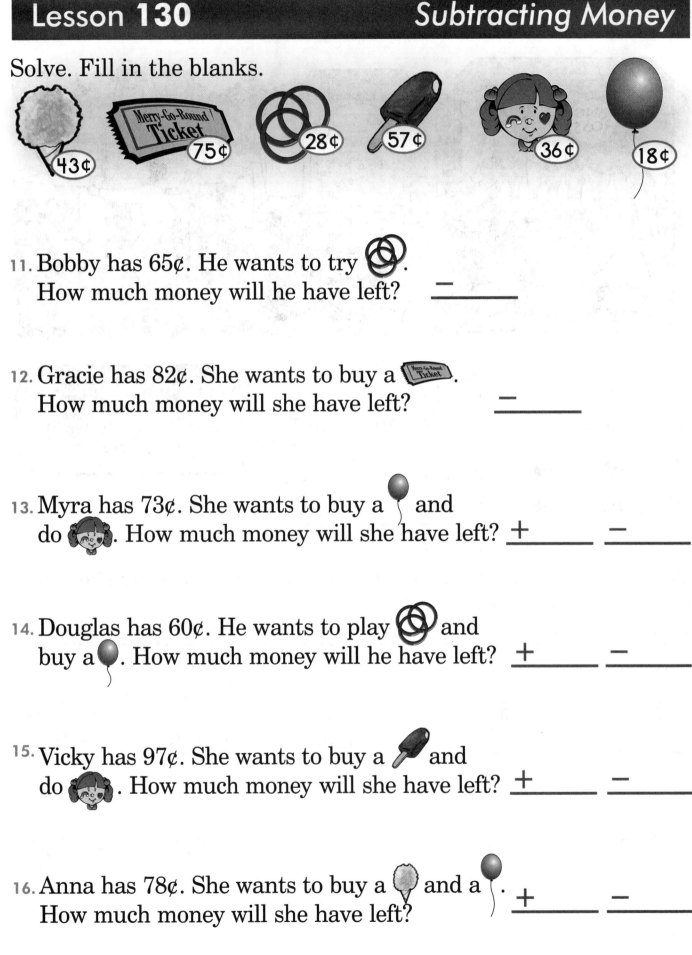

43¢   75¢   28¢   57¢   36¢   18¢

11. Bobby has 65¢. He wants to try ⬤.
    How much money will he have left?   − _____

12. Gracie has 82¢. She wants to buy a Ticket.
    How much money will she have left?   − _____

13. Myra has 73¢. She wants to buy a 🎈 and
    do 👧. How much money will she have left? + _____ − _____

14. Douglas has 60¢. He wants to play ⬤ and
    buy a 🎈. How much money will he have left? + _____ − _____

15. Vicky has 97¢. She wants to buy a 🍦 and
    do 👧. How much money will she have left?   + _____ − _____

16. Anna has 78¢. She wants to buy a 🍦 and a 🎈.
    How much money will she have left?   + _____ − _____

© Copyright 1999   Mathematics Grade 2

Solving for the Missing Number   Lesson **131**

Uh-oh! Someone let go of a balloon bouquet! Can you figure out the numbers hidden by these balloons?

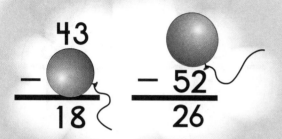

In subtraction the whole is the number we are subtracting from. It is written on top.

$$\begin{array}{r} \textbf{whole} \\ - \ \textbf{part} \\ \hline \textbf{part} \end{array}$$

If one <u>part</u> is missing, we can find it by subtracting the other part.

$$\begin{array}{r} 43 \\ - \\ \hline 18 \end{array} \qquad \begin{array}{r} {}^{3\ 13} \\ \cancel{43} \\ -18 \\ \hline 25 \end{array}$$

25 is the missing part.

If the <u>whole</u> is missing, we can find it by adding the parts.

$$\begin{array}{r} \\ -52 \\ \hline 26 \end{array} \qquad \begin{array}{r} 26 \\ +52 \\ \hline 78 \end{array}$$

78 is the missing whole.

$$\begin{array}{r} {}^{5\ 11} \\ \cancel{6}\ \cancel{1} \\ -3 \\ \hline 27 \end{array}$$

You can find a missing digit by remembering a subtraction fact.

$$11 - \underline{4} = 7$$

Write the missing part in each balloon.

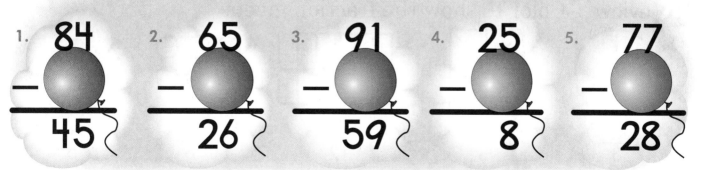

1. $\begin{array}{r} 84 \\ - \\ \hline 45 \end{array}$ 2. $\begin{array}{r} 65 \\ - \\ \hline 26 \end{array}$ 3. $\begin{array}{r} 91 \\ - \\ \hline 59 \end{array}$ 4. $\begin{array}{r} 25 \\ - \\ \hline 8 \end{array}$ 5. $\begin{array}{r} 77 \\ - \\ \hline 28 \end{array}$

Write the missing whole in each balloon.

6.
$$-\,25$$
$$\overline{29}$$

7.
$$-\,15$$
$$\overline{50}$$

8.
$$-\,33$$
$$\overline{27}$$

9.
$$-\,62$$
$$\overline{21}$$

10.
$$-\,8$$
$$\overline{34}$$

Write the missing digit.

11. ⁷8̸ ¹⁴
  − 5 9
  2 5

12. ² ¹⁰ 0̸
  − 1 3
  1 7

13. 4
  − 1 8
  3 0

14. ³4̸ ¹¹1̸
  − 2
  1 3

15. ⁶7̸ ¹³8̸
  − 7
  5 6

16. ⁵6̸ ¹⁷7̸
  − 9
  3 8

17. ¹¹1̸
  − 6 7
  1 4

18. ¹2̸ ¹⁴4̸
  − 6
  8

19. 7
  − 4 5
  4 2

20. ⁶7̸ ¹²2̸
  − 3
  3 7

Write the missing digits.

21. 2 8
  − □ 2
  1 6

22. □ □
  − 4 8
  2 8

23. 8 □
  − 1 5
  6 7

24. 5 0
  − □ □
  2 2

25. 6 2
  − □ 9
  4 3

Review Color to show the fraction given.

1. $\dfrac{2}{3}$

2. $\dfrac{3}{8}$

3. $\dfrac{5}{12}$

4. $\dfrac{2}{6}$

5. $\dfrac{1}{5}$

© Copyright 1999 *Mathematics Grade 2*

Problem Solving: Mixed Practice   Lesson **132**

Mr. Weaver has 33 tropical birds in his store. Nineteen of these birds are parrots. How many of these birds are other types?

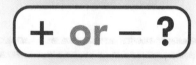

+ or − ?

Sometimes it helps to model a word problem in order to solve it.

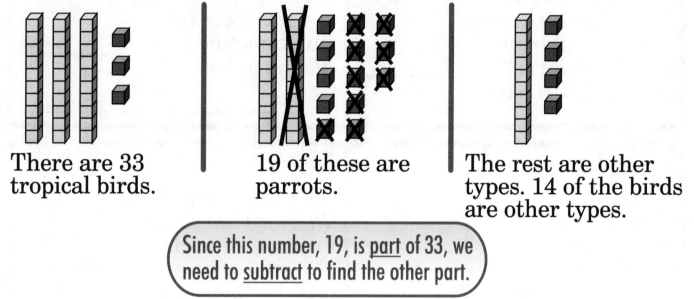

There are 33 tropical birds.

19 of these are parrots.

The rest are other types. 14 of the birds are other types.

Since this number, 19, is <u>part</u> of 33, we need to <u>subtract</u> to find the other part.

Circle + or −. Write the problem and solve it.

1. Mr. Weaver had 27 goldfish in a tank. He placed 15 more fish in the same tank. Now how many fish are in the tank?	2. There are 28 gerbils in the pet store. There are 34 hamsters. How many more hamsters are there than gerbils?	3. Alicia had 80¢. She spent 55¢ on a box of fish food. How much money does she have left?

⊕ or −   27
        +15
        ‾‾‾‾
         42
	+ or − _____	+ or − _____

Some problems take two steps to solve. Show your work for each step.

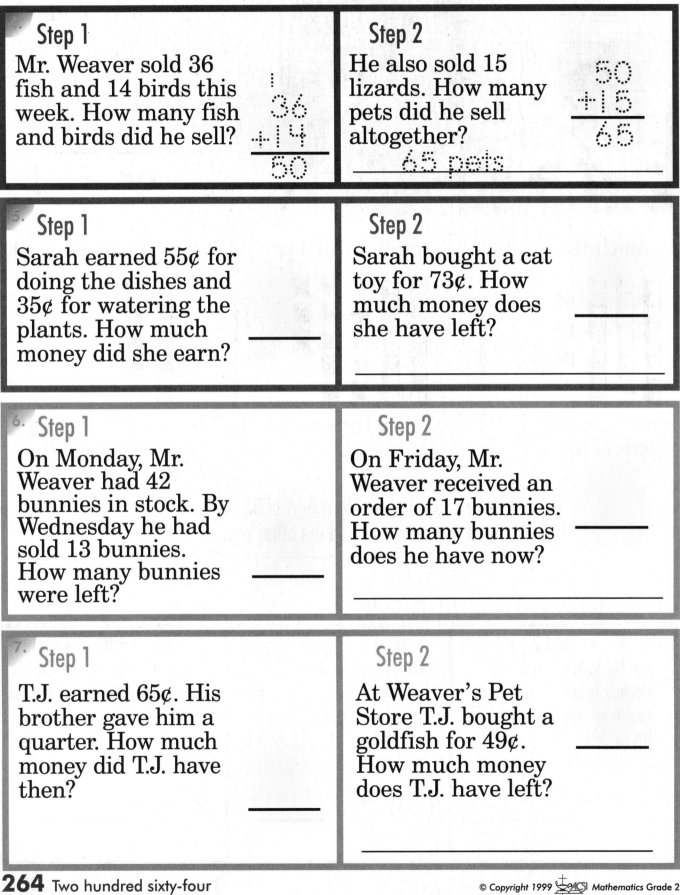

Step 1
Mr. Weaver sold 36 fish and 14 birds this week. How many fish and birds did he sell?

$$\begin{array}{r} 36 \\ + 14 \\ \hline 50 \end{array}$$

Step 2
He also sold 15 lizards. How many pets did he sell altogether?

$$\begin{array}{r} 50 \\ + 15 \\ \hline 65 \end{array}$$

_____ 65 pets

5.

Step 1
Sarah earned 55¢ for doing the dishes and 35¢ for watering the plants. How much money did she earn?

_____

Step 2
Sarah bought a cat toy for 73¢. How much money does she have left?

_____

6.

Step 1
On Monday, Mr. Weaver had 42 bunnies in stock. By Wednesday he had sold 13 bunnies. How many bunnies were left?

_____

Step 2
On Friday, Mr. Weaver received an order of 17 bunnies. How many bunnies does he have now?

_____

7.

Step 1
T.J. earned 65¢. His brother gave him a quarter. How much money did T.J. have then?

_____

Step 2
At Weaver's Pet Store T.J. bought a goldfish for 49¢. How much money does T.J. have left?

_____

© Copyright 1999 — Mathematics Grade 2

Problem Solving: Graphing Lesson 133

Maria's class is having a **POPCORN OLYMPICS!** They have made a graph to compare the scores for each event.

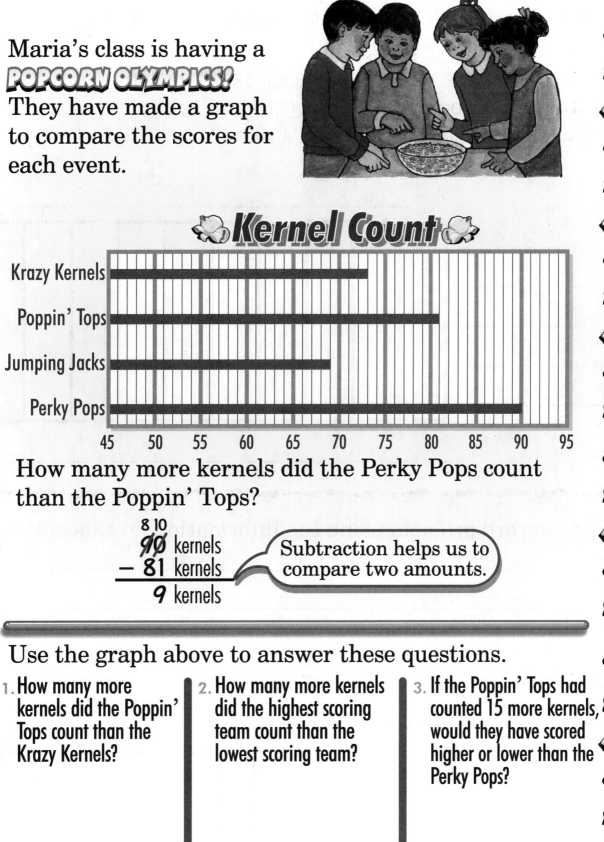

Kernel Count

Krazy Kernels		
Poppin' Tops		
Jumping Jacks		
Perky Pops		

45 50 55 60 65 70 75 80 85 90 95

How many more kernels did the Perky Pops count than the Poppin' Tops?

```
  8 10
   9̶0̶  kernels
 − 81   kernels
   9    kernels
```

Subtraction helps us to compare two amounts.

Use the graph above to answer these questions.

1. How many more kernels did the Poppin' Tops count than the Krazy Kernels?

2. How many more kernels did the highest scoring team count than the lowest scoring team?

3. If the Poppin' Tops had counted 15 more kernels, would they have scored higher or lower than the Perky Pops?

4. Design a graph using information from your own class.
- Write a title <u>above</u> the graph.
- Write the teams' names <u>on the side</u> of the graph.
- Write the numbers <u>along the bottom</u> of the graph.
- Draw a bar to show each team's score.

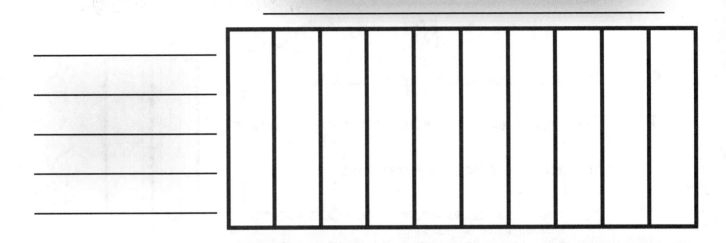

5. Write a word problem using the information on this graph.

_____

_____

_____

6. Now, trade papers with a classmate. Solve each other's word problem here.

7. Add the 2 lowest scores on the graph. Is their total <u>more</u> or <u>less</u> than the highest score? Circle the word.

more

+ _____   less

© Copyright 1999   *Mathematics Grade 2*

Chapter Nine Check-Up

Subtract.

1. 52
  − 11

2. 82
  − 7

3. 41
  − 32

4. 60
  − 24

5. 24
  − 9

6. 36
  − 15

7. 76
  − 49

8. 90
  − 58

9. 55
  − 27

10. 81
  − 4

11. 47
  − 33

Rewrite these subtraction problems. Subtract.

12. 39 − 14 =

13. 52 − 25 =

14. 84 − 6 =

Subtract. Check your work by addition.

15. 72
  − 49 +

16. 35
  − 8 +

17. 61
  − 19 +

Round each number to the nearest ten. Estimate the difference.

18. 57
  − 14 −

19. 82
  − 58 −

20. 25
  − 19 −

Find the amount of money each customer has left.

 47¢    29¢    35¢   56¢    37¢

21. Jim has 62¢. He buys the bubbles.   – _____

22. Mary Lou has 75¢. She buys the pinwheel.   – _____

23. Don has 50¢. He buys the jacks.   – _____

24. Bessie has 42¢. She buys the glider.   – _____

25. Jerry has 83¢. He buys the glider and the ball.   + _____   – _____

Fill in the missing numbers.

26.
```
  □□
- 1 6
-----
  3 2
```

27.
```
  6 0
- □□
-----
  4 5
```

28.
```
  □□
- 5 3
-----
  2 7
```

29.
```
  7 15
  8̶ 5̶
- □ 6
-----
  4 9
```

30. Nan lives 23 miles from school. Bob lives 18 miles from school. How much farther away does Nan live than Bob?   – _____

31. Joelle has 32 ballet stickers. She gave 5 to her sister. How many does she have left?   – _____

© Copyright 1999   *Mathematics Grade 2*

CHAPTER 10

Place Value, Addition, and Subtraction

Sing to the LORD a new song,
And His praise from the ends of the earth,
You who go down to the sea, and all that is in it,
You coastlands and you inhabitants of them!

Isaiah 42:10

Dear Parents,

Chapter Ten expands your child's knowledge of place value to the thousands place. We will be reading, writing, and comparing the value of numbers up to 9,999. As you page through the newspaper or browse in the mall, look for examples of four-digit numbers. Have your child read the number, using proper place value vocabulary, and explain the number in its context (i.e., a price tag, a mileage sign, a year). We will also be learning to add and subtract three-digit numbers.

Here's a simple tool you can make to reinforce the concept of four-digit numbers. You will need a spiral notebook, scissors, and four different colors of markers. Holding the notebook horizontally, with the spiral on top, flip up the cover. Make three vertical cuts in the first page, forming four narrow sections of paper. (See Figure A.) Do the same for nine more consecutive pages of the notebook. These four sections represent the four places from ones to thousands. Using a different color marker for each place, number each section, beginning with 0 on the top paper to 9 on the last paper. If you want to display the number *2,418*, flip the thousands section to the number 2, the hundreds section to the number 4, the tens section to the number 1, and the ones section to the number 8. (See Figure B.)

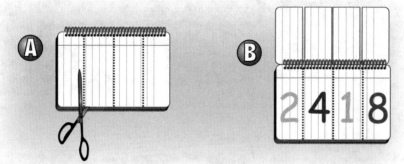

Have your child read each number you display. Then challenge him or her to flip the pages to form a number that you dictate. The flip chart can also be used for counting. If the chart is set to *2,418*, have your child flip the ones section to read *2,419*. Flip again, and you run out of numbers! Show your child how to flip the tens section to 2 and the ones section to 0 to form *2,420*.

Our visual theme for this chapter is coastal birds. As they glide on the air currents above the restless water, they remind us of the way God carries us over the troubled times as well as the calm. *Then they cry out to the LORD in their trouble, And He brings them out of their distresses (Psalm 107:28).*

God bless you and your child as you learn together!

© Copyright 1999

Exploring Four-Digit Numbers — Lesson 135

You know that 10 ones make one ten

and that 10 tens make one hundred.

<u>Ten hundreds</u> make <u>one thousand</u>.

=

Thousands are the next greatest place in place value.

thousands,	hundreds	tens	ones
2 ,	3	5	6

=

A thousand is how many hundreds? _____

Write the thousands.

1. __1__ __thousand__

2. ___ _____

3. ___ _____

4. ___ _____

5. ___ _____

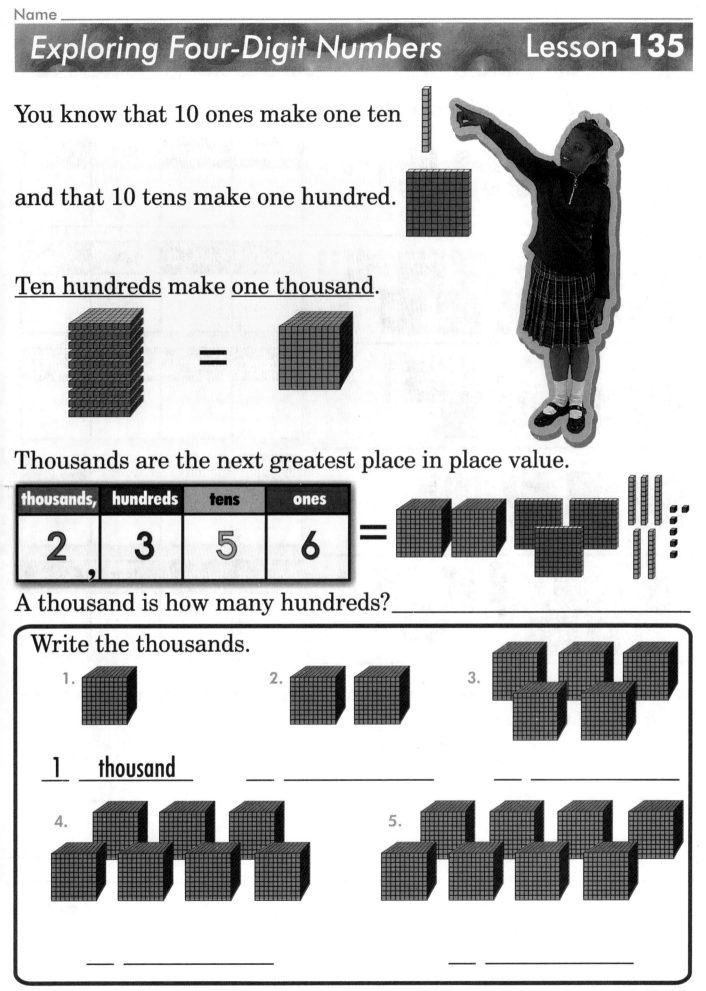

Write the four-digit numbers in the place value charts.

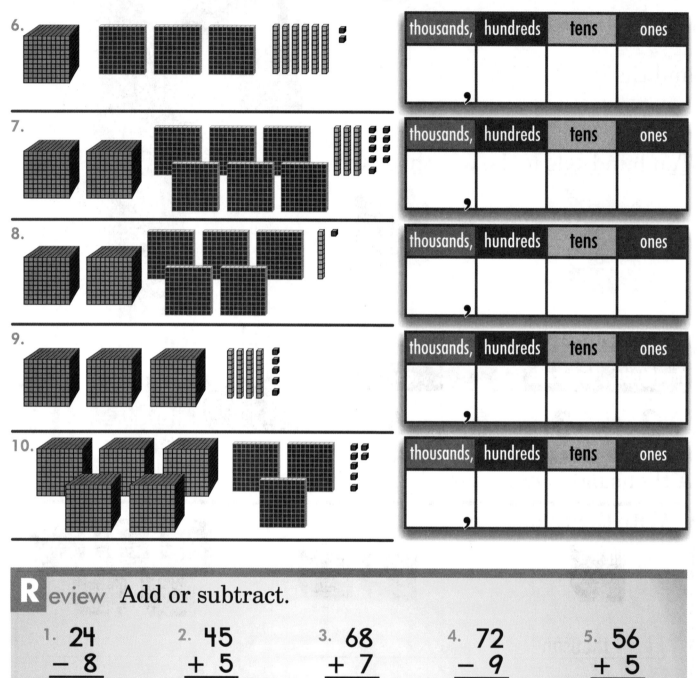

6.

thousands,	hundreds	tens	ones
,			

7.

thousands,	hundreds	tens	ones
,			

8.

thousands,	hundreds	tens	ones
,			

9.

thousands,	hundreds	tens	ones
,			

10.

thousands,	hundreds	tens	ones
,			

Review   Add or subtract.

1. 24
    − 8

2. 45
    + 5

3. 68
    + 7

4. 72
    − 9

5. 56
    + 5

6. 93
    −75

7. 54
    +37

8. 39
    + 26

9. 88
    −45

10. 70
    −38

© Copyright 1999   Mathematics Grade 2

Understanding Four-Digit Place Value   Lesson 136

There are <u>2,358</u> pelicans along the California coast.
What does this number mean?

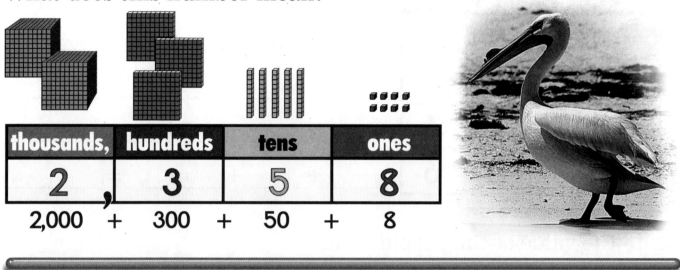

thousands,	hundreds	tens	ones
2 ,	**3**	**5**	**8**

2,000 + 300 + 50 + 8

Write these numbers in expanded form.

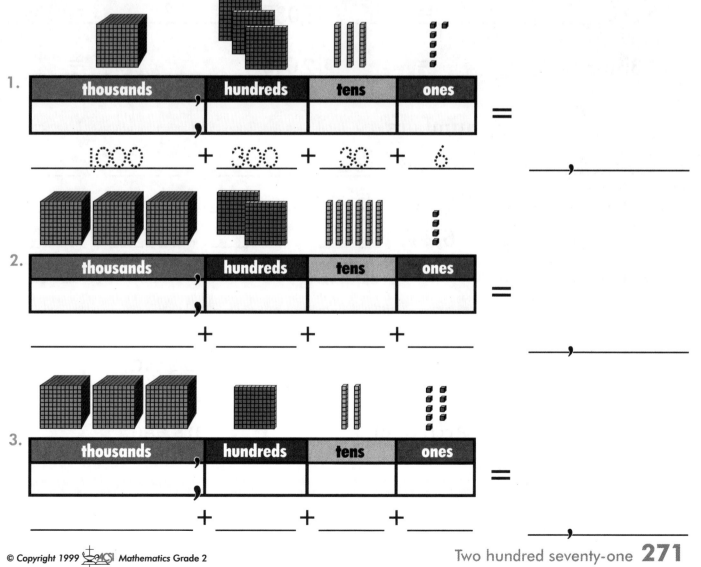

1.

thousands	,	hundreds	tens	ones

= _____

____1,000____ + ___300___ + ___30___ + __6__   ____,____

2.

thousands	,	hundreds	tens	ones

= _____

_____ + _____ + _____ + _____   ____,____

3.

thousands	,	hundreds	tens	ones

= _____

_____ + _____ + _____ + _____   ____,____

© Copyright 1999 SAXON Mathematics Grade 2

Write the numbers in expanded and standard form.

th	h	t	o
7,	2	9	0
4,	3	1	1
5,	8	2	6
1,	0	5	6

4. $7000 + 200 + 90 + 0 = 7,290$

5. ___ + ___ + ___ + ___ = ___

6. ___ + ___ + ___ + ___ = ___

7. ___ + ___ + ___ + ___ = ___

Write the value of the purple digit.

8. 3,124 __2 tens__ = 20

9. 4,515 _____ = ___

10. 5,280 _____ = ___

11. 1,035 _____ = ___

12. 6,351 _____ = ___

13. 2,049 _____ = ___

Write the next four numbers.

14. Count by 1's: 1,286   1287 ____ ____ ____

15. Count by 10's: 2,443   2453 ____ ____ ____

16. Count by 100's: 6,285   ____ ____ ____ ____

17. Count by 1,000's: 3,267   ____ ____ ____ ____

Circle the most sensible number.

18. Stephen's younger brother is _____ years old.

   7   70   700   7,000

19. Jesus walked on earth about _____ years ago.

   2   20   200   2,000

20. Lindsay's mom is about _____ years old.

   4   40   400   4,000

© Copyright 1999   Mathematics Grade 2

Numbers Before and After — Lesson 137

These pelicans have caught 2,174 fish this month. What number comes next? What number comes just before 2,174?

You know the numbers that come before and after 4.
...<u>3</u>, 4, <u>5</u>...

You know the numbers that come before and after 74.
...<u>73</u>, 74, <u>75</u>...

You also know the numbers before and after 174.
...<u>173</u>, 174, <u>175</u>...

Name the numbers before and after 2,174.
...<u>2,173</u>, 2,174, <u>2,175</u>...

Fill in this chart.

1,200	1,201	1,202	1,203	1,204		1,206	1,207		1,209
1,210		1,212	1,213		1,215	1,216		1,218	
1,220	1,221		1,223	1,224		1,226		1,228	1,229
	1,231	1,232			1,235	1,236			1,239
1,240			1,243	1,244			1,247	1,248	
		1,252			1,255			1,258	
	1,261					1,266			
1,270				1,274					1,279
		1,282					1,287		
									1,299

© Copyright 1999 Mathematics Grade 2

Write the number <u>before</u>, <u>between</u>, or <u>after</u>.

	Before	
1.	1,458	1,459
2.		5,207
3.		4,361
4.		8,211
5.		9,600
6.		2,754
7.		3,038

	Between		
8.	6,247		6,249
9.	7,192		7,194
10.	1,583		1,585
11.	5,964		5,966
12.	4,310		4,312
13.	8,021		8,023
14.	3,299		3,301

	After	
15.	9,825	
16.	2,640	
17.	3,029	
18.	6,737	
19.	7,776	
20.	1,219	
21.	5,462	

Write these numbers in the correct order.

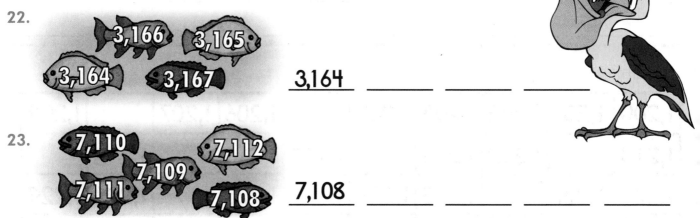

22. 3,166 3,165 3,164 3,167

3,164 _____ _____ _____

23. 7,110 7,112 7,109 7,111 7,108

7,108 _____ _____ _____ _____

24. Pages **1,157**; **1,159**; **1,160**; and **1,158** have fallen out of Andy's phone book. Help him put them in the correct order.

_____ _____ _____ _____

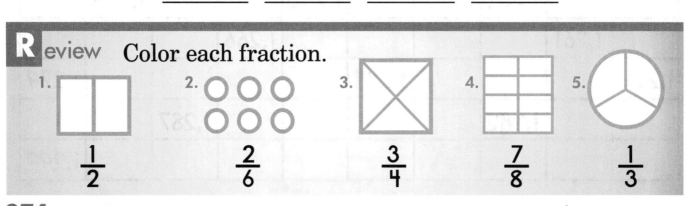

Review Color each fraction.

1. $\frac{1}{2}$ 2. $\frac{2}{6}$ 3. $\frac{3}{4}$ 4. $\frac{7}{8}$ 5. $\frac{1}{3}$

© Copyright 1999 Mathematics Grade 2

Comparing Four-Digit Numbers   Lesson 138

2,316 sea gulls

1,243 sandpipers

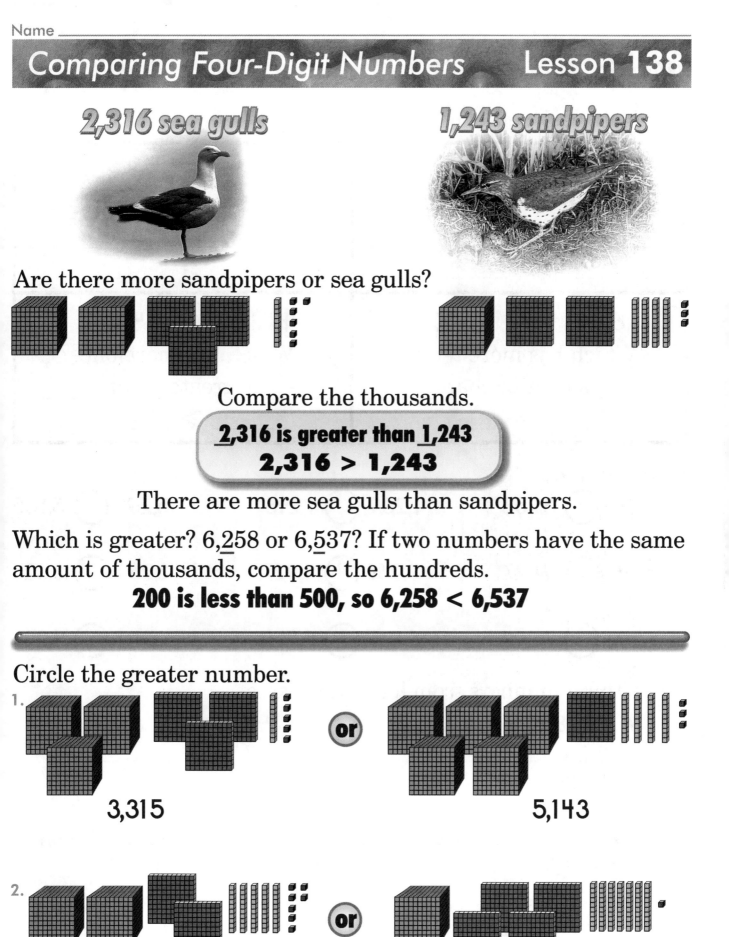

Are there more sandpipers or sea gulls?

Compare the thousands.

2,316 is greater than 1,243
2,316 > 1,243

There are more sea gulls than sandpipers.

Which is greater? 6,2̲58 or 6,5̲37? If two numbers have the same amount of thousands, compare the hundreds.

200 is less than 500, so 6,258 < 6,537

Circle the greater number.

1.   3,315   **or**   5,143

2.   2,257   **or**   1,471

Complete each sentence.

3. 4,628 5,713 Which has more thousands? _____ is greater than _____ _____ > _____	**4.** 8,594 8,267 Which has more hundreds? _____ is greater than _____ _____ > _____
5. 6,248 6,221 Which has more tens? _____ is greater than _____ _____ > _____	**6.** 4,124 4,129 Which has more ones? _____ is greater than _____ _____ > _____

Write > or <.

7. 6,249 ◯ 3,258   **8.** 1,269 ◯ 1,246   **9.** 5,293 ◯ 5,105

10. 9,014 ◯ 9,027   **11.** 2,268 ◯ 4,927   **12.** 3,264 ◯ 3,624

13. 7,293 ◯ 7,299   **14.** 8,126 ◯ 8,216   **15.** 4,210 ◯ 4,201

Write these numbers from least to greatest.

16. 2,458 _____   **17.** 6,349 _____
2,216 _____   6,327 _____
2,698 _____   6,388 _____
2,571 _____   6,310 _____

Review Add or subtract.

1. 32 + 49	**2.** 81 − 56	**3.** 74 − 67	**4.** 27 − 15	**5.** 29 + 19	**6.** 68 + 29

© Copyright 1999   Mathematics Grade 2

Graphing Four-Digit Numbers   Lesson 139

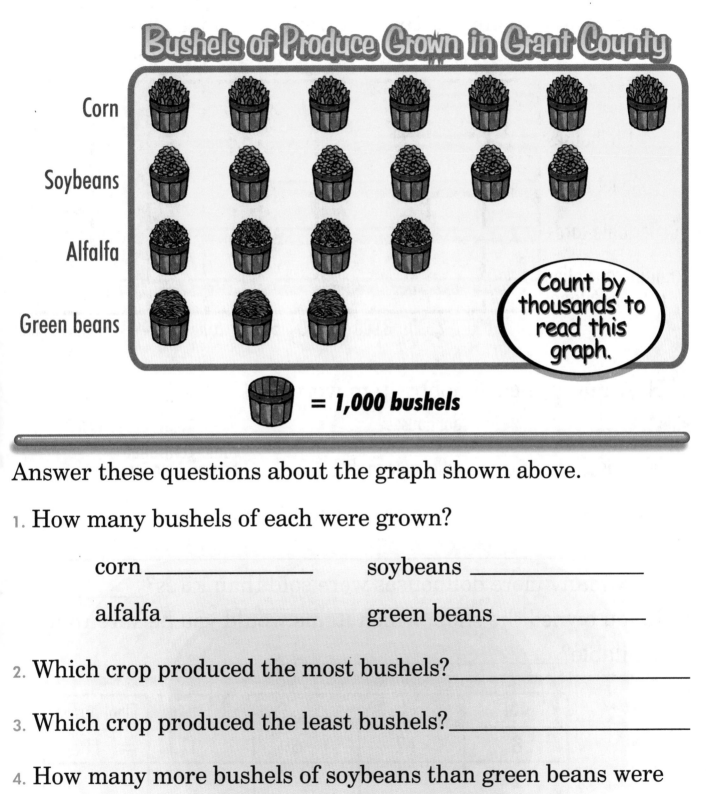

Bushels of Produce Grown in Grant County

Corn

Soybeans

Alfalfa

Green beans

Count by thousands to read this graph.

= 1,000 bushels

Answer these questions about the graph shown above.

1. How many bushels of each were grown?

corn _____   soybeans _____

alfalfa _____   green beans _____

2. Which crop produced the most bushels? _____

3. Which crop produced the least bushels? _____

4. How many more bushels of soybeans than green beans were grown? _____

5. How many bushels of green beans and alfalfa were produced altogether? _____

Use this graph to answer the following questions.

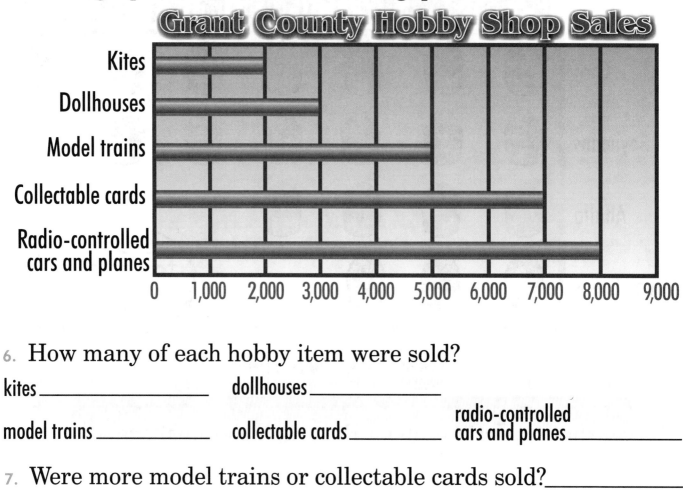

Grant County Hobby Shop Sales

6. How many of each hobby item were sold?

kites _____   dollhouses _____

model trains _____   collectable cards _____   radio-controlled cars and planes _____

7. Were more model trains or collectable cards sold?_____

_____

8. How many more dollhouses were sold than kites? _____

9. If you owned the shop, which items would you be sure to have available?_____

Review

	start	+4	−6	+5	Final Answer
1.	8	12	6	11	= 11
2.	2				=
3.	5				=
4.	9				=
5.	6				=

© Copyright 1999   Mathematics Grade 2

Adding Three-Digit Numbers Lesson 140

John and Lisa tried to count the birds at Budd Beach.
John counted 215 sandpipers
Lisa counted 143 terns.
How many birds were counted in all?

215 sandpipers

143 terns

How many birds?

hundreds	tens	ones
2	1	5
+ 1	4	3
3	5	8

Add the ones.

Add the tens.

Add the hundreds.

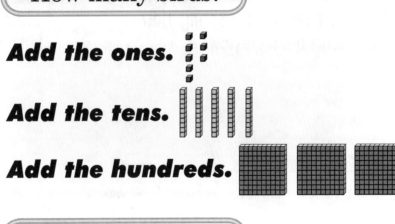

358 birds in all.

Add.

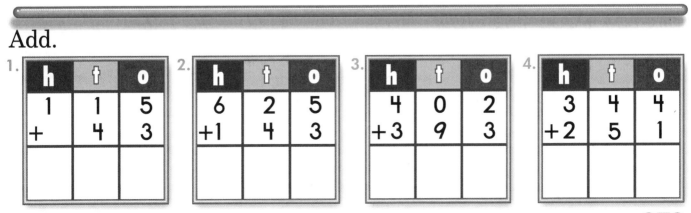

1.

h	t	o
1	1	5
+	4	3

2.

h	t	o
6	2	5
+1	4	3

3.

h	t	o
4	0	2
+3	9	3

4.

h	t	o
3	4	4
+2	5	1

Add.

5. 514
+ 231

6. 161
+ 325

7. 625
+ 174

8. 528
+ 471

9. 724
+ 230

10. 316
+ 71

11. 500
+ 237

12. 418
+ 231

13. 112
+ 35

14. 612
+ 27

15. 819
+ 110

16. 514
+ 263

SOLVE.

17. 328 terns live on the coast. 61 young terns were hatched this spring. How many terns are there now?

18. Mrs. Stoll baked 124 brownies. She baked 110 cupcakes. How many desserts did she bake in all?

_____

_____

Review   Write the following numbers.

1. $3,000 + 500 + 10 + 6 =$ _____

2. $2,000 + 400 + 8 =$ _____

3. $3,000 + 200 + 20 + 7 =$ _____

4. $4,000 + 70 + 2 =$ _____

5. $8,000 + 100 + 50 =$ _____

6. $9,000 + 800 + 2 =$ _____

Write > or <.

7. 6,324 ◯ 5,899

8. 4,325 ◯ 4,384

9. 3,216 ◯ 3,261

10. 3,264 ◯ 3,268

© Copyright 1999 ACSI Mathematics Grade 2

Adding, Regrouping Ones

In the new park 237 acres will be used for a lake. 115 acres will be grass, woods, and trails. How large will the new park be?

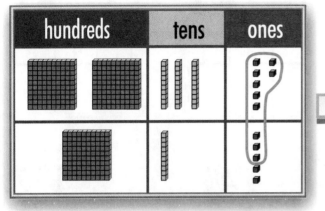 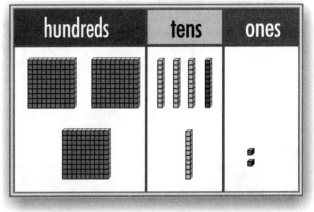

$$237$$
$$+115$$

Because 7 + 5 = 12, we need to regroup the ones.

$$\overset{1}{237}$$
$$+115$$
$$\overline{352}$$

Circle ones to regroup as tens. Add.

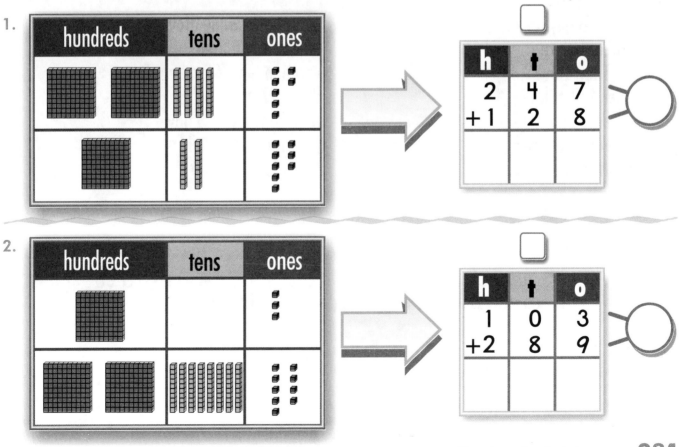

1.

h	t	o
2	4	7
+1	2	8

2.

h	t	o
1	0	3
+2	8	9

© Copyright 1999 Mathematics Grade 2

Add.

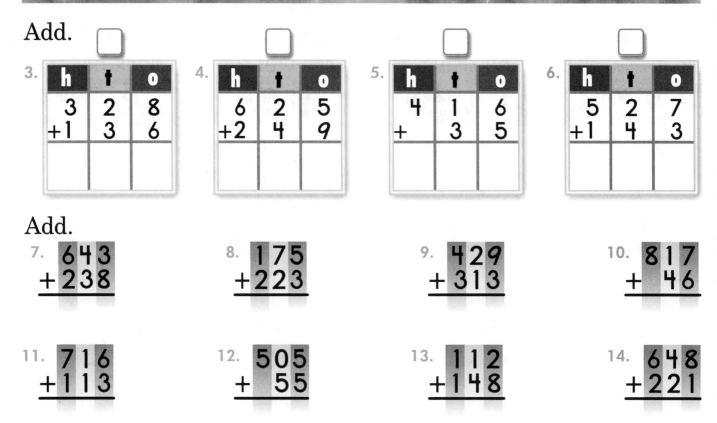

3.
h	t	o
3	2	8
+1	3	6

4.
h	t	o
6	2	5
+2	4	9

5.
h	t	o
4	1	6
+	3	5

6.
h	t	o
5	2	7
+1	4	3

Add.

7. 643
  +238

8. 175
  +223

9. 429
  +313

10. 817
  + 46

11. 716
  +113

12. 505
  + 55

13. 112
  +148

14. 648
  +221

SOLVE.

15. Chrissy's family drove 214 miles before lunch. They drove another 139 miles in the afternoon. How many miles did they drive altogether?

_____ miles

16. Terriann's family drove 247 miles on their vacation. Ken's family drove 27 more miles than Terriann's family. How many miles did Ken's family drive?

_____ miles

Review   Measure the length of each set of waves to the nearest inch and nearest centimeter.

1. _____in. ____cm

2. _____in. ____cm

3. _____in. ____cm

© Copyright 1999 Mathematics Grade 2

Adding, Regrouping Tens

Lesson 142

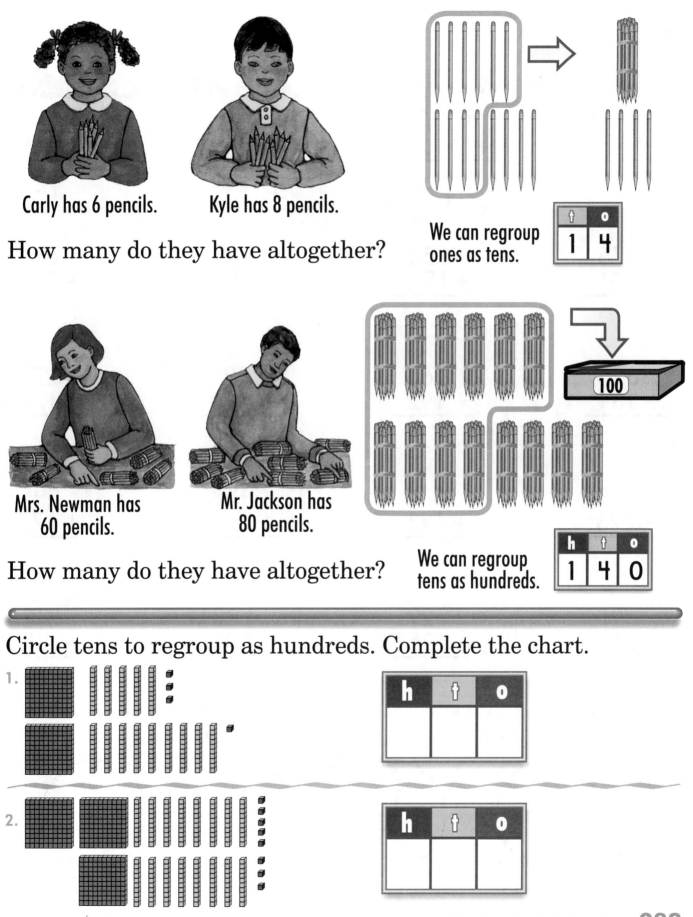

Carly has 6 pencils.   Kyle has 8 pencils.

How many do they have altogether?

We can regroup ones as tens.

t	o
1	4

Mrs. Newman has 60 pencils.   Mr. Jackson has 80 pencils.

How many do they have altogether?

We can regroup tens as hundreds.

h	t	o
1	4	0

Circle tens to regroup as hundreds. Complete the chart.

1.

h	t	o

2.

h	t	o

Add.

	h	t	o
3.	3	6	4
	+1	7	2

	h	t	o
4.	6	9	3
	+1	2	3

	h	t	o
5.	2	4	1
	+1	9	0

	h	t	o
6.	5	8	2
	+2	8	4

7. 275
   +281

8. 156
   +151

9. 734
   +183

10. 389
    +220

11. 625
    +181

12. 263
    +192

13. 591
    + 20

14. 277
    +171

15. 458
    + 226

16. 372
    +193

17. 458
    + 121

18. 245
    + 173

19. 721
    +116

20. 527
    +125

21. 188
    +301

22. 418
    +214

Review Write the time shown on each clock.

1.

2.

3.

4.

_____   _____   _____   _____

© Copyright 1999 · Mathematics Grade 2

The naturalists at Carrington Beach Nature Center counted 177 kittiwakes last summer. They counted 146 more terns than kittiwakes. How many terns did the naturalists count?

First, regroup the ones.

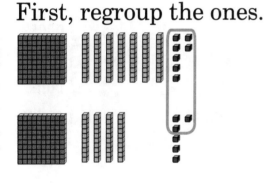

	1	
h	**t**	**o**
1	7	7
+1	4	6
		3

Next, regroup the tens.

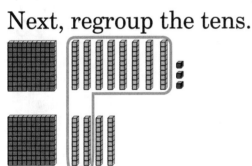

1	**1**	
h	**t**	**o**
1	7	7
+1	4	6
	2	**3**

Add the hundreds.

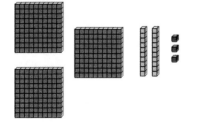

1	**1**	
h	**t**	**o**
1	7	7
+1	4	6
3	**2**	**3**

The naturalists counted 323 terns.

Add.

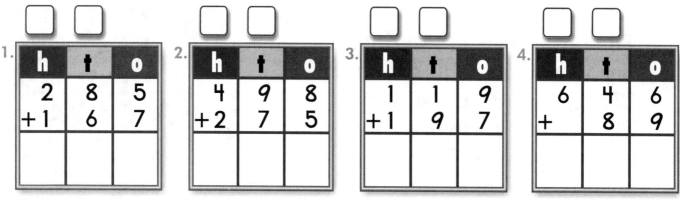

1.
h	t	o
2	8	5
+1	6	7

2.
h	t	o
4	9	8
+2	7	5

3.
h	t	o
1	1	9
+1	9	7

4.
h	t	o
6	4	6
+	8	9

Check the kind of regrouping needed. Add.

5. 345
 + 268
 ☐ ones
 ☐ tens
 ☐ both
 ☐ neither

6. 716
 + 123
 ☐ ones
 ☐ tens
 ☐ both
 ☐ neither

7. 539
 + 146
 ☐ ones
 ☐ tens
 ☐ both
 ☐ neither

8. 263
 + 183
 ☐ ones
 ☐ tens
 ☐ both
 ☐ neither

Add.

9. 452
 + 369

10. 214
 + 311

11. 412
 + 393

12. 819
 + 23

13. 188
 + 125

14. 287
 + 281

15. 348
 + 129

16. 621
 + 118

Review Subtract.

1. 45
 − 12

2. 82
 − 17

3. 64
 − 9

4. 24
 − 13

5. 56
 − 29

© Copyright 1999 *Mathematics Grade 2*

Subtracting Three-Digit Numbers Lesson **144**

Did you know that albatrosses can fly up to 300 miles in one day?

One albatross flew 238 miles yesterday.
Another albatross flew 114 miles.
How much farther did the first albatross fly than the second?

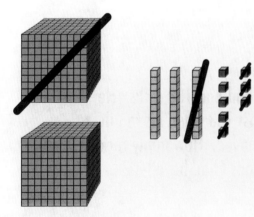

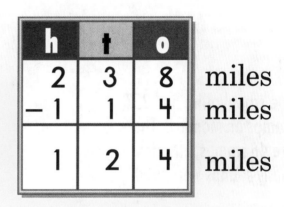

h	t	o	
2	3	8	miles
− 1	1	4	miles
1	2	4	miles

Take away 4 ones, 1 ten and 1 hundred.

The first albatross flew 124 more miles than the second.

Find the difference.

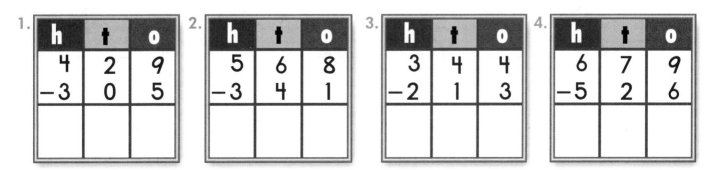

1.

h	t	o
4	2	9
−3	0	5

2.

h	t	o
5	6	8
−3	4	1

3.

h	t	o
3	4	4
−2	1	3

4.

h	t	o
6	7	9
−5	2	6

Subtract.

5. $\begin{array}{r} 619 \\ -204 \\ \hline \end{array}$ 6. $\begin{array}{r} 522 \\ -10 \\ \hline \end{array}$ 7. $\begin{array}{r} 746 \\ -313 \\ \hline \end{array}$ 8. $\begin{array}{r} 829 \\ -614 \\ \hline \end{array}$

9. $\begin{array}{r} 187 \\ -52 \\ \hline \end{array}$ 10. $\begin{array}{r} 948 \\ -715 \\ \hline \end{array}$ 11. $\begin{array}{r} 268 \\ -135 \\ \hline \end{array}$ 12. $\begin{array}{r} 304 \\ -102 \\ \hline \end{array}$

13. $\begin{array}{r} 498 \\ -268 \\ \hline \end{array}$ 14. $\begin{array}{r} 676 \\ -433 \\ \hline \end{array}$ 15. $\begin{array}{r} 587 \\ -425 \\ \hline \end{array}$ 16. $\begin{array}{r} 786 \\ -75 \\ \hline \end{array}$

SOLVE.

17. The school office had 257 stamps on Monday. There are 46 stamps left. How many stamps were used?

_____

18. Chad had 168 rocks. He lost 108 when his family moved. How many rocks does Chad have left?

_____

19. It is 284 miles to Rockford. The Hall's have driven 53 of those miles. How many miles are left to drive?

_____

20. Jason wrote 178 words. Tara wrote 199. How many more words did Tara write than Jason?

_____

Review Rewrite these groups of numbers from least to greatest.

1. 429 _____	2. 711 _____	3. 2,041 _____
31 _____	2,008 _____	2,044 _____
785 _____	987 _____	2,011 _____
98 _____	1,013 _____	2,104 _____
114 _____	1,122 _____	2,014 _____

© Copyright 1999 Mathematics Grade 2

There are 385 penguins. There are 117 American sheathbills. How many more penguins are there than American sheathbills?

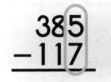

Since we cannot take 7 from 5, we need to regroup 1 <u>ten</u> as 10 <u>ones</u>.

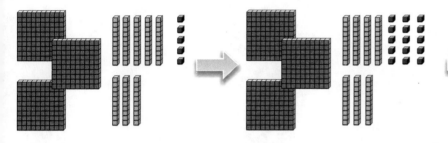

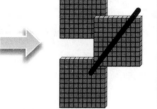

There are 268 more penguins than American sheathbills.

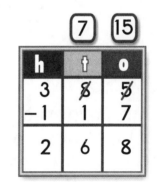

	7	15
h	t	o
3	8̸	5̸
−1	1	7
2	6	8

Use manipulatives to find the difference.

1.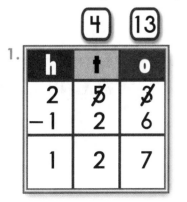

	4	13
h	t	o
2	5̸	3̸
−1	2	6
1	2	7

2.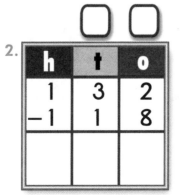

	◯	◯
h	t	o
1	3	2
−1	1	8

3.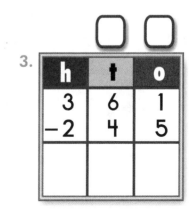

	◯	◯
h	t	o
3	6	1
−2	4	5

© Copyright 1999 ACSI Mathematics Grade 2

Subtract.

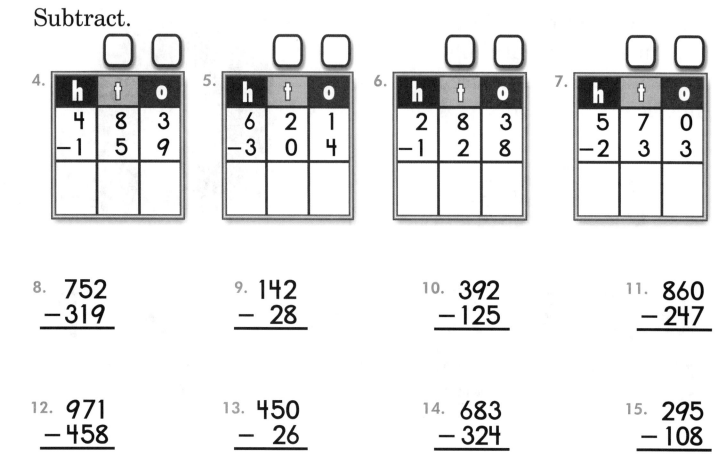

4.
h	t	o
4	8	3
−1	5	9

5.
h	t	o
6	2	1
−3	0	4

6.
h	t	o
2	8	3
−1	2	8

7.
h	t	o
5	7	0
−2	3	3

8. 752
   −319

9. 142
   − 28

10. 392
   −125

11. 860
   − 247

12. 971
   −458

13. 450
   − 26

14. 683
   − 324

15. 295
   −108

16. Mr. Martino ordered 264 cans of soda for the church picnic. 137 cans are cola. The rest of the cans are other flavors. How many cans of soda are other flavors?

_____

Review   Name the shape you see in each picture: circle, rectangle, square, triangle.

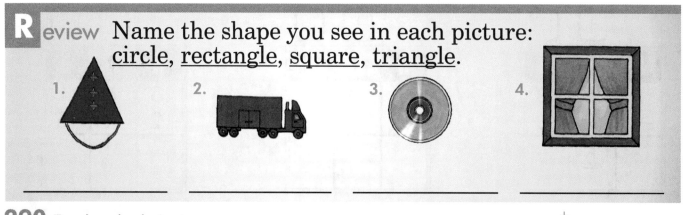

1.   2.   3.   4.

_____   _____   _____   _____

    © Copyright 1999 ACSI *Mathematics Grade 2*

The school secretary buys postage stamps in sheets of 100. She began the week with 315 stamps. She has 172 left. How many postage stamps did she use?

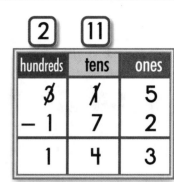

| | 2 | 11 |
hundreds	tens	ones
̶3̶	̶1̶	5
− 1	7	2
1	4	3

When one hundred is regrouped as 10 tens, we can subtract. 143 postage stamps were used during the week.

Mark out ones, tens, and hundreds from these regrouped models. Subtract.

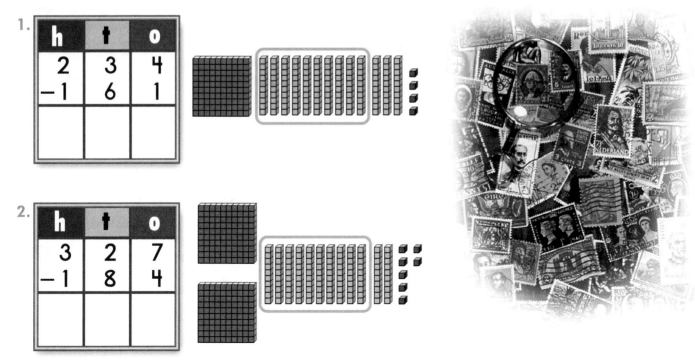

1.

h	t	o
2	3	4
−1	6	1

2.

h	t	o
3	2	7
−1	8	4

Subtract.

3.
h	t	o
5	1	8
−2	6	3

4.
h	t	o
8	4	9
−3	5	2

5.
h	t	o
6	0	6
−4	5	4

6.
h	t	o
9	5	6
−6	9	1

7.
```
  724
−241
```

8.
```
  268
−  93
```

9.
```
  127
−  84
```

10.
```
  448
−276
```

11.
```
  362
−180
```

12.
```
  559
−384
```

13.
```
  809
−626
```

14.
```
  637
−256
```

15.
```
  841
−635
```

16.
```
  211
−106
```

17.
```
  495
−263
```

18.
```
  927
−382
```

19.
```
  759
−346
```

20.
```
  638
−252
```

21.
```
  387
−124
```

22.
```
  538
−274
```

Review　Answer these questions.

JULY						
S	M	T	W	Th	F	S
		1	2	3	4	5
6	7	8	9	10	11	12
13	14	15	16	17	18	19
20	21	22	23	24	25	26
27	28	29	30	31		

1. Which day of the week is July 11?

2. What date is one week before July 22?

3. On what day was June 30?

© Copyright 1999 Mathematics Grade 2

Subtracting, Regrouping Tens and Hundreds   Lesson 147

Ricardo has hurt his leg. Maria is helping by carrying his bookbag.

There are 325 steps from the bus to the second grade classroom.

They have walked 148 steps.

How many more steps do they need to walk?

You have regrouped tens to subtract. You have regrouped hundreds. Some problems, however, require the regrouping of both tens and hundreds.

First, regroup the tens. Subtract the ones.

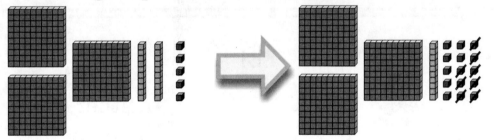

	1	15
hundreds	tens	ones
3	2̶	5̶
− 1	4	8
		7

Then, regroup the hundreds. Subtract the tens.

2	11	15
hundreds	tens	ones
3̶	2̶	5̶
− 1	4	8
	7	7

Finally, subtract the hundreds.

2	11	15
hundreds	tens	ones
3̶	2̶	5̶
− 1	4	8
1	7	7

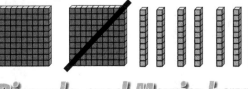

Ricardo and Maria have 177 more steps to go.

© Copyright 1999 Mathematics Grade 2

Subtract.

1.
☐ ☐ ☐

hundreds	tens	ones
5	1	2
− 3	8	7

2.
☐ ☐ ☐

hundreds	tens	ones
4	3	6
− 1	5	9

3.
☐ ☐ ☐

hundreds	tens	ones
2	1	0
−	7	6

4.
☐ ☐ ☐

hundreds	tens	ones
8	2	3
− 5	5	7

Check the kind of regrouping needed. Subtract.

5.
$$427$$
$$-291$$
☐ tens
☐ hundreds
☐ neither
☐ both

6.
$$653$$
$$-421$$
☐ tens
☐ hundreds
☐ neither
☐ both

7.
$$264$$
$$- 89$$
☐ tens
☐ hundreds
☐ neither
☐ both

8.
$$861$$
$$-335$$
☐ tens
☐ hundreds
☐ neither
☐ both

Subtract.

9.
$$624$$
$$-305$$

10.
$$425$$
$$-162$$

11.
$$876$$
$$-521$$

12.
$$732$$
$$-485$$

13.
$$743$$
$$-368$$

14.
$$216$$
$$- 57$$

15.
$$941$$
$$-623$$

16.
$$118$$
$$- 62$$

© Copyright 1999 *Mathematics Grade 2*

Remember the problem-solving STAR:

  Seek to understand.
  Think of a plan.
  Act on your plan.
  Review the plan.

When you think of a plan, you need to ask yourself:

  What do I already know?
  What do I need to know?
  What operation do I use? + or −

Look at this problem:

> Mr. Nelson served 837 snow cones during the three days of Tidal Fest.
> 319 of these were served on the first day.
> How many snow cones were served on the other days of the festival?

What do I already know? ⟹ 837 snow cones were served in all.
319 were served on the first day.

What do I need to know? ⟹ the number of snow cones served the other days of the festival

What operation do I use? ⟹ subtraction: $837 - 319 = 518$ snow cones

Write + or − in the ☐ . Solve each problem.

1. One team designed a ship and anchor for the sand-sculpting contest. They used 349 pounds of sand to make the ship and 105 pounds to make the anchor. How many pounds of sand did they use altogether?

☐ _____

_____

_____

2. 623 pieces of candy were buried in the sand for the "buried treasure game." 215 pieces of candy have been found so far. How many pieces are still buried?

☐ _____

_____

_____

3. Mrs. Rusco sold 142 wooden sea gulls. She sold 69 more wooden lighthouses than sea gulls. How many lighthouses did Mrs. Rusco sell?

☐ _____

_____

_____

4. The largest sand sculpture was 104 feet long. The winning sculpture was 32 feet shorter. How many feet long was the winning sculpture?

☐ _____

_____

_____

SOLVE.

5. 756 dinners were served. 312 were clambake dinners. How many dinners were not clambake dinners?

_____ dinners

6. The Nature Center displayed a collection of 257 shells. They had the same number of sea life specimens. How many items were displayed altogether?

_____ items

© Copyright 1999 ACSI Mathematics Grade 2

Name _____

Write the number shown by these base ten blocks.

1. 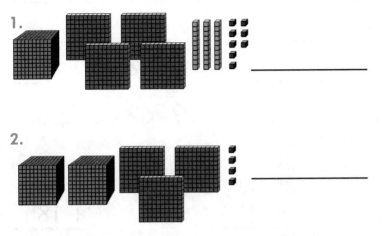 _____

2. _____

3. Mr. Lowell had 167 wooden ducks to sell. He had 29 left at the end of the craft fair. How many ducks did he sell?

_____

Write these numbers in expanded form.

thousands,	hundreds	tens	ones
3,	2	1	6
8,	0	2	5
4,	3	0	9
7,	0	6	1

4. 3,000 + 200 + 10 + 6 _____
5. _____
6. _____
7. _____

Write the number before and after each of these numbers.

8. _____ 4,023 _____

9. _____ 2,119 _____

10. _____ 3,999 _____

11. _____ 8,059 _____

12. _____ 6,453 _____

13. _____ 1,010 _____

Write > or < to compare each pair of numbers.

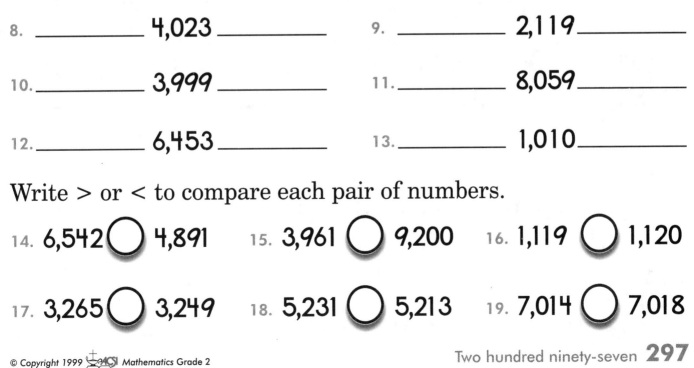

14. 6,542 ◯ 4,891   15. 3,961 ◯ 9,200   16. 1,119 ◯ 1,120

17. 3,265 ◯ 3,249   18. 5,231 ◯ 5,213   19. 7,014 ◯ 7,018

Rewrite these numbers from least to greatest.

20. 5,438 _____   21. 1,110 _____   22. 9,260 _____

    5,460 _____   1,312 _____   9,261 _____

    5,449 _____   1,230 _____   9,259 _____

    5,468 _____   1,132 _____   9,262 _____

Add.

23. 345	24. 629	25. 489	26. 293
+ 231	+ 155	+ 263	+ 184

27. 627	28. 724	29. 529	30. 452
+ 295	+ 254	+ 314	+ 159

Subtract.

31. 857	32. 638	33. 128	34. 932
− 234	− 265	− 19	− 546

35. 324	36. 456	37. 261	38. 742
− 109	− 135	− 159	− 98

SOLVE.

39. Lindsay's family lives 216 miles north of the state boundary. Kayla's family lives 58 miles north of Lindsay's family. How many miles north of the state boundary does Kayla's family live? _____

© Copyright 1999 ACSI Mathematics Grade 2

CHAPTER 11

Multiplication and Division

He has made everything beautiful in its time.

Ecclesiastes 3:11a

Dear Parents,

How can we help but be completely awed by the beauty of the peacock on the Chapter Eleven divider page? Read the Scripture verse with your child: *"He has made everything beautiful in its time"* (Ecclesiastes 3:11a). Assure your child that it takes time to grow physically, to grow in knowledge of math concepts, and to grow in understanding of godly principles.

Chapter Eleven will introduce your child to God's multiplication, as well as standard multiplication and division concepts. He or she will understand that the more love you give, the more love you have to give away. Your child will understand the story of the loaves and fishes as a miracle of multiplication. Jesus "multiplied" the amount of food brought to Him in order that 5,000 people could be fed (Matthew 14:17-21).

Multiplication will be introduced through repeated addition. The children will multiply by two, three, four, five, and ten. Division will be introduced through making equal groups with counters. Relating division to repeated subtraction, and to multiplication, will establish a foundation of understanding that will be developed further in grade three.

Thank you for the privilege of teaching your child. Thank you for your continued diligence in helping your child learn and grow. Your dedication and commitment to your child will be rewarded in "His" time!

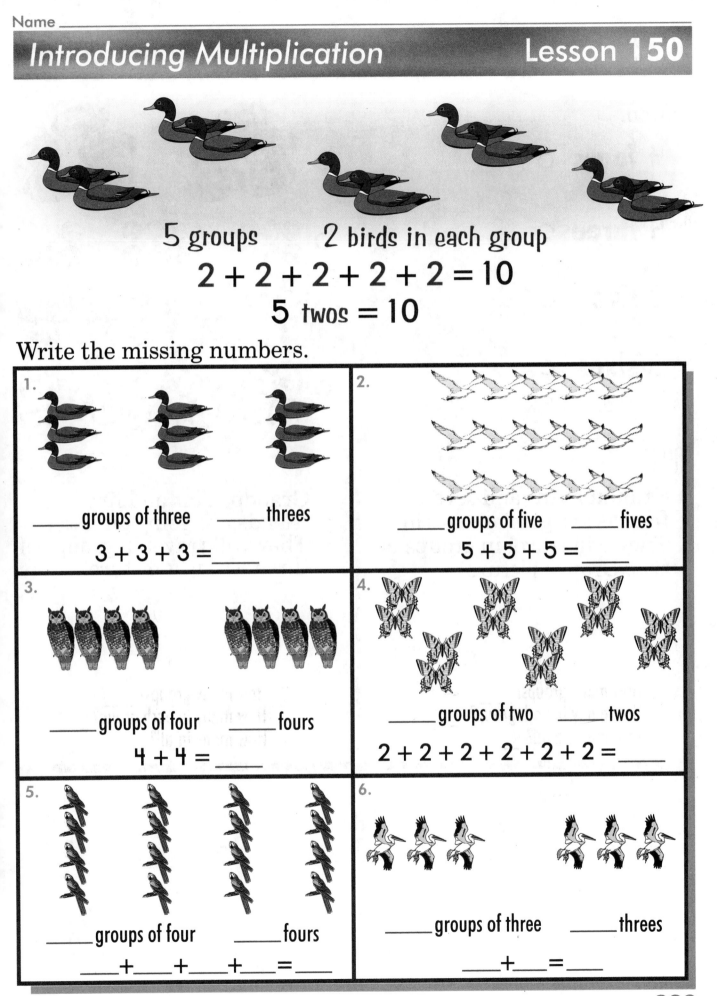

5 groups   2 birds in each group

$$2 + 2 + 2 + 2 + 2 = 10$$

5 twos = 10

Write the missing numbers.

1.

_____ groups of three   _____ threes

$$3 + 3 + 3 = \_\_\_\_$$

2.

_____ groups of five   _____ fives

$$5 + 5 + 5 = \_\_\_\_$$

3.

_____ groups of four   _____ fours

$$4 + 4 = \_\_\_\_$$

4.

_____ groups of two   _____ twos

$$2 + 2 + 2 + 2 + 2 + 2 = \_\_\_\_$$

5.

_____ groups of four   _____ fours

$$\_\_\_ + \_\_\_ + \_\_\_ + \_\_\_ = \_\_\_$$

6.

_____ groups of three   _____ threes

$$\_\_\_ + \_\_\_ = \_\_\_$$

Match.

7. **4 fours** ○

8. **4 threes** ○

9. **2 fives** ○

10. **3 sixes** ○

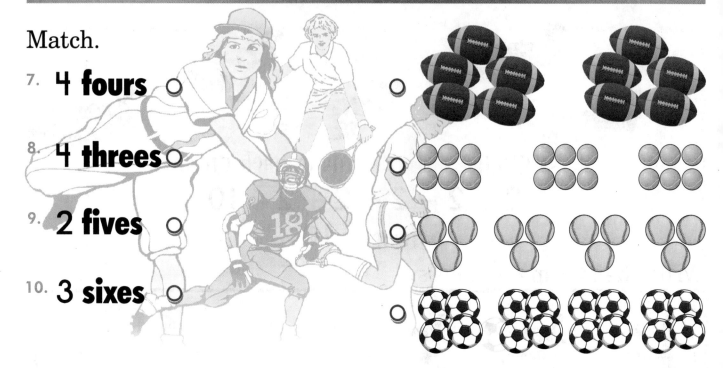

SOLVE.

11. Grandma Ant and seven friends are going on a trip. They will travel in groups of two. Draw a picture.

How many groups? ____
How many in each group? ____
How many in all? ____

12. Grandpa Ant and five friends are going on a trip. They will travel in groups of three. Draw a picture.

How many groups? ____
How many in each group? ____
How many in all? ____

Review   Add or subtract.

1.	2.	3.	4.	5.
52 +18	36 +42	86 −29	78 −65	49 +43

6.	7.	8.	9.	10.
27 − 8	64 +29	96 −78	35 +58	80 − 5

© Copyright 1999   Mathematics Grade 2

Multiplying with 2 as a Factor   Lesson 151

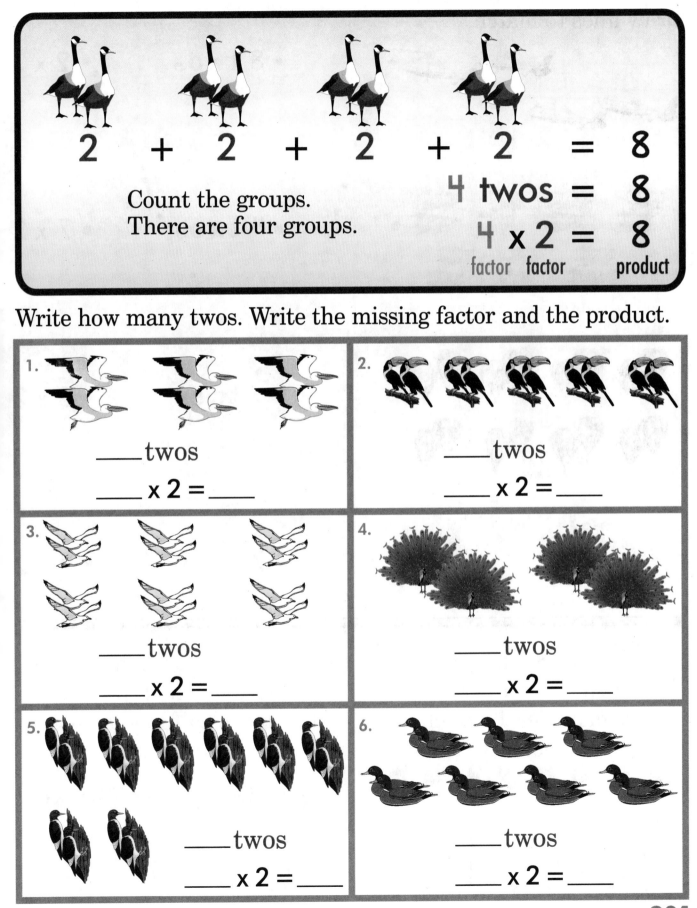

2 + 2 + 2 + 2 = 8

Count the groups.
There are four groups.

4 twos = 8

4 x 2 = 8

factor   factor   product

Write how many twos. Write the missing factor and the product.

1.

_____ twos

_____ x 2 = _____

2.

_____ twos

_____ x 2 = _____

3.

_____ twos

_____ x 2 = _____

4.

_____ twos

_____ x 2 = _____

5.

_____ twos

_____ x 2 = _____

6.

_____ twos

_____ x 2 = _____

Draw lines to match.

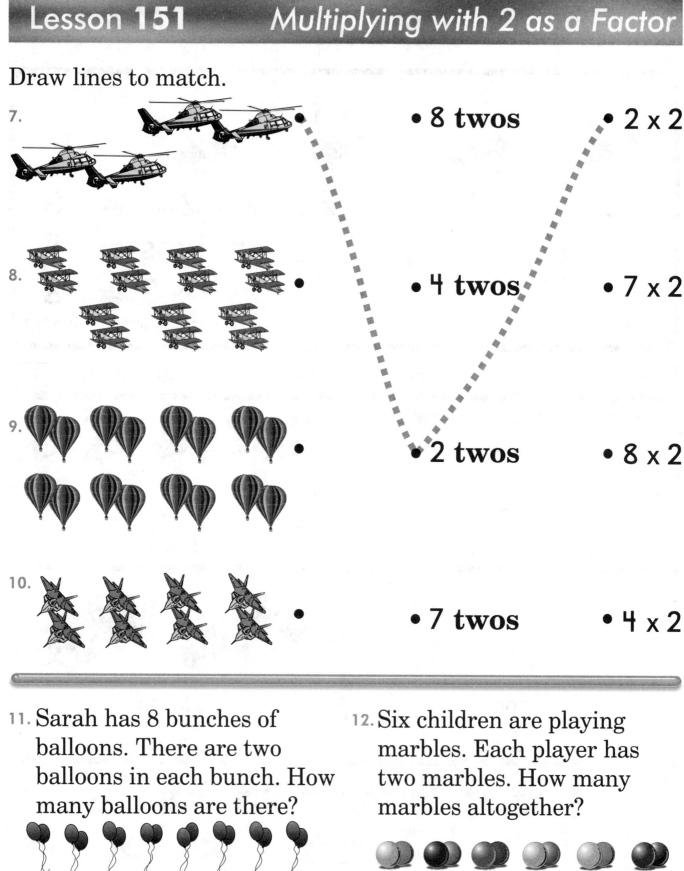

7.

8.

9.

10.

• 8 twos

• 4 twos

• 2 twos

• 7 twos

• 2 x 2

• 7 x 2

• 8 x 2

• 4 x 2

11. Sarah has 8 bunches of balloons. There are two balloons in each bunch. How many balloons are there?

□ x □ = □

12. Six children are playing marbles. Each player has two marbles. How many marbles altogether?

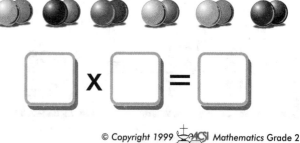

□ x □ = □

© Copyright 1999   Mathematics Grade 2

Multiplying with 3 as a Factor Lesson 152

1. Count the sides of the triangles. Fill in the blanks. Add.

△ △ △ △

_____ + _____ + _____ + _____ = _____

Write a multiplication sentence. ⬜ x ⬜ = _____

Number of triangles   Number of sides on each triangle

2. Write the products.

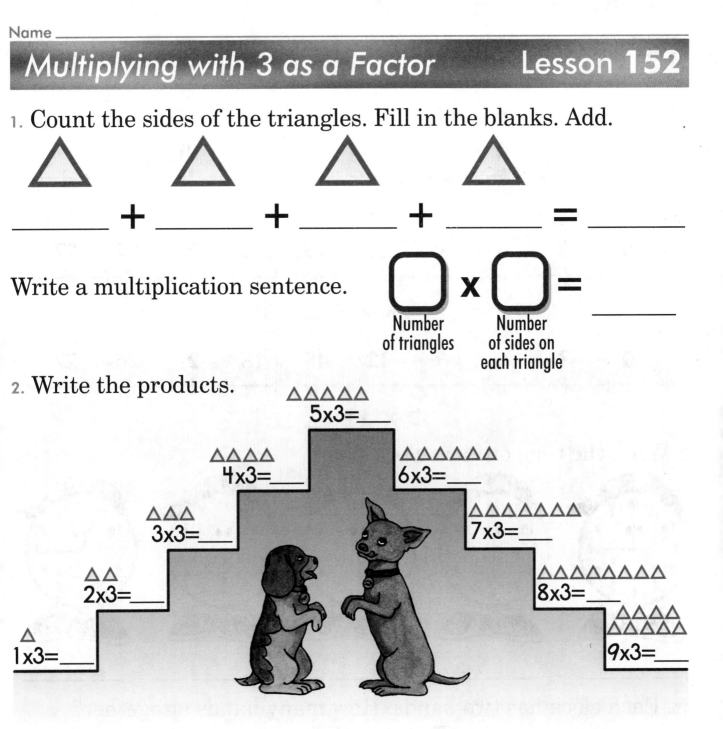

5x3=____

4x3=____   6x3=____

3x3=____   7x3=____

2x3=____   8x3=____

1x3=____   9x3=____

Math Dog and Phil are testing new treats for a dog food company. They each get 3 treats a day for one week. How many treats will <u>each</u> dog get? How many treats will the dogs get altogether?

Write an addition sentence.   Write a multiplication sentence.

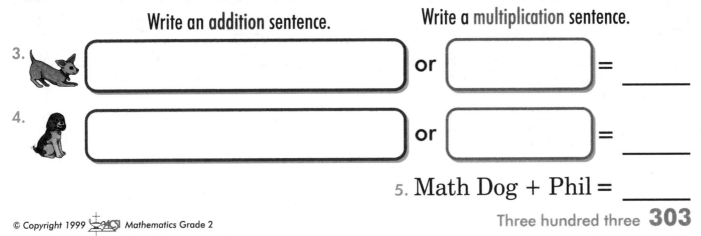

3. [_____] or [_____] = ____

4. [_____] or [_____] = ____

5. Math Dog + Phil = ____

Use the number lines to find the products.

6.
| 0 | 3 | 6 | 9 | 12 | 15 | 18 | 21 | 24 | 27 |

4 x 3 = ____

7.
| 0 | 3 | 6 | 9 | 12 | 15 | 18 | 21 | 24 | 27 |

8 x 3 = ____

8.
| 0 | 3 | 6 | 9 | 12 | 15 | 18 | 21 | 24 | 27 |

5 x 3 = ____

9. Write the time on each clock.

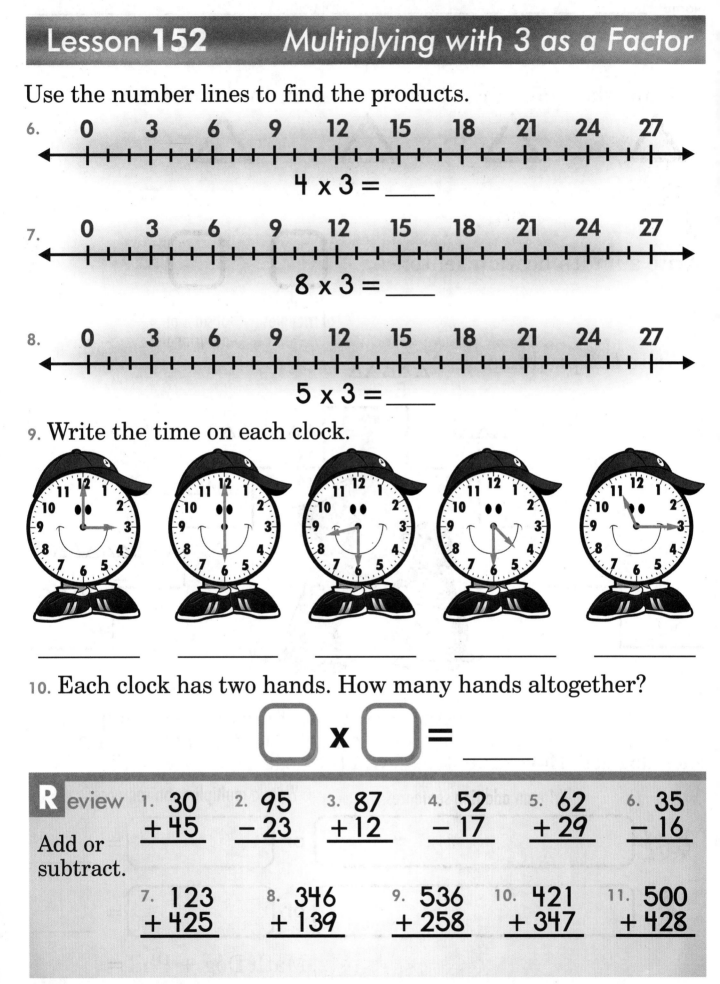

____   ____   ____   ____   ____

10. Each clock has two hands. How many hands altogether?

◯ x ◯ = ____

Review
Add or subtract.

1. 30	2. 95	3. 87	4. 52	5. 62	6. 35
+ 45	− 23	+ 12	− 17	+ 29	− 16

7. 123	8. 346	9. 536	10. 421	11. 500
+ 425	+ 139	+ 258	+ 347	+ 428

© Copyright 1999 ACSI Mathematics Grade 2

Multiplying with 4 as a Factor Lesson 153

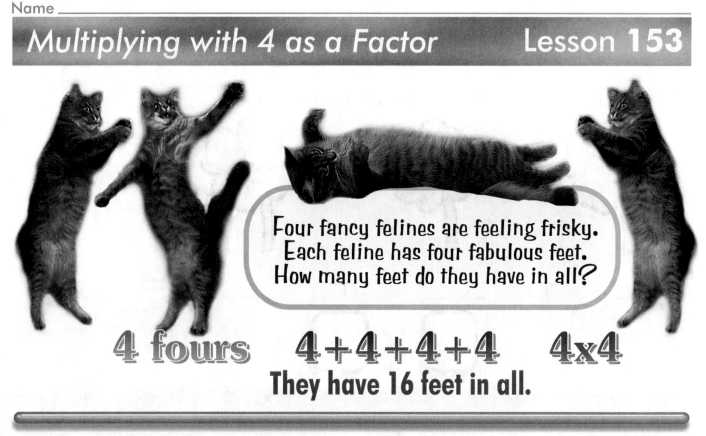

Four fancy felines are feeling frisky.
Each feline has four fabulous feet.
How many feet do they have in all?

4 fours   4+4+4+4   4x4

They have 16 feet in all.

Fill in the missing numbers.

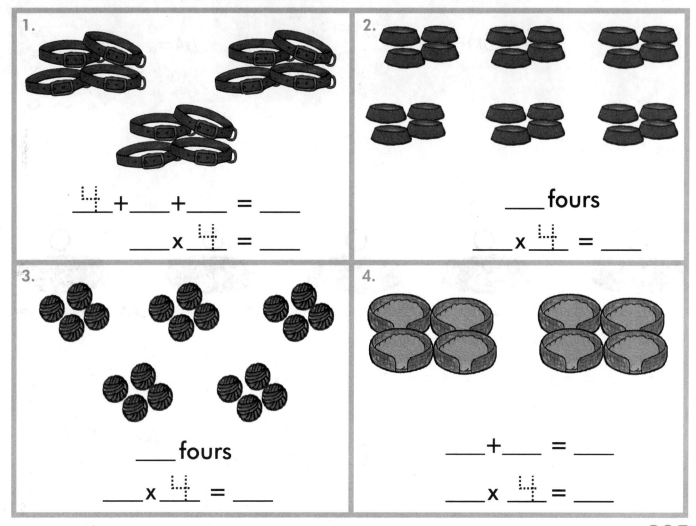

1.

__4__ + ___ + ___ = ___

___ x __4__ = ___

2.

___ fours

___ x __4__ = ___

3.

___ fours

___ x __4__ = ___

4.

___ + ___ = ___

___ x __4__ = ___

How many leaves are on the four-leaf clovers?

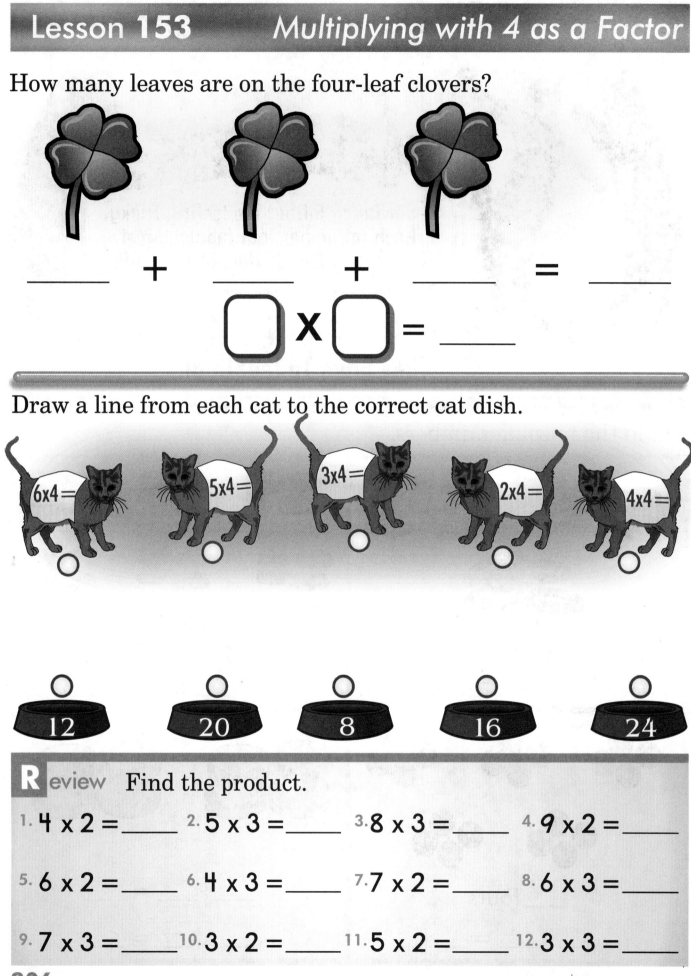

_____ + _____ + _____ = _____

$\boxed{} \times \boxed{} =$ _____

Draw a line from each cat to the correct cat dish.

6x4=   5x4=   3x4=   2x4=   4x4=

12   20   8   16   24

Review   Find the product.

1. $4 \times 2 =$ _____   2. $5 \times 3 =$ _____   3. $8 \times 3 =$ _____   4. $9 \times 2 =$ _____

5. $6 \times 2 =$ _____   6. $4 \times 3 =$ _____   7. $7 \times 2 =$ _____   8. $6 \times 3 =$ _____

9. $7 \times 3 =$ _____   10. $3 \times 2 =$ _____   11. $5 \times 2 =$ _____   12. $3 \times 3 =$ _____

© Copyright 1999   Mathematics Grade 2

Multiplying with 5 as a Factor   Lesson 154

The Taylor triplets each have 5 teeth.
How many teeth do the babies have altogether?

How many babies? How many teeth each?
The Taylor triplets have 15 teeth altogether.

3 fives = 15
3 x 5 = 15

Fill in the missing numbers.

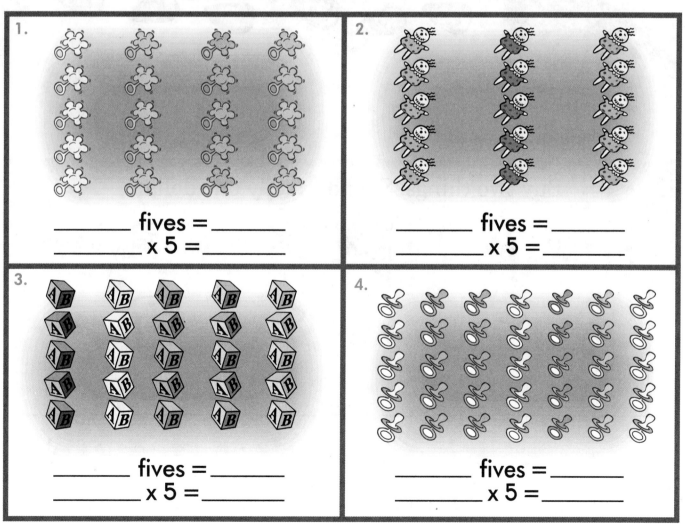

1.

_____ fives = _____
_____ x 5 = _____

2.

_____ fives = _____
_____ x 5 = _____

3.

_____ fives = _____
_____ x 5 = _____

4.

_____ fives = _____
_____ x 5 = _____

© Copyright 1999 ACSI Mathematics Grade 2

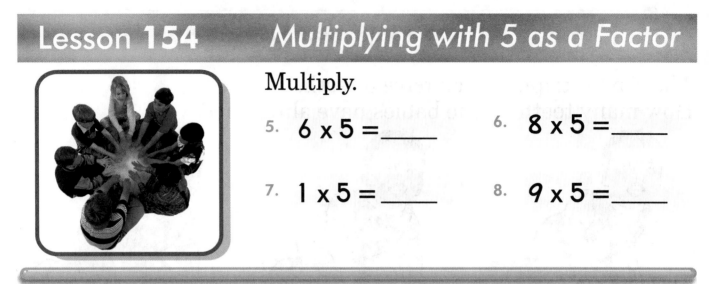

Multiply.

5. $6 \times 5 = \underline{}$

6. $8 \times 5 = \underline{}$

7. $1 \times 5 = \underline{}$

8. $9 \times 5 = \underline{}$

9. Help the cardinal find sunflower seeds with facts of five. Draw his path by choosing the correct facts in order.

7   14   18   24   38   35   40
5   8   15   19   25   30   37   45
10   12   20   21   34   50

Review   Buy two things. Spend exactly one dollar.

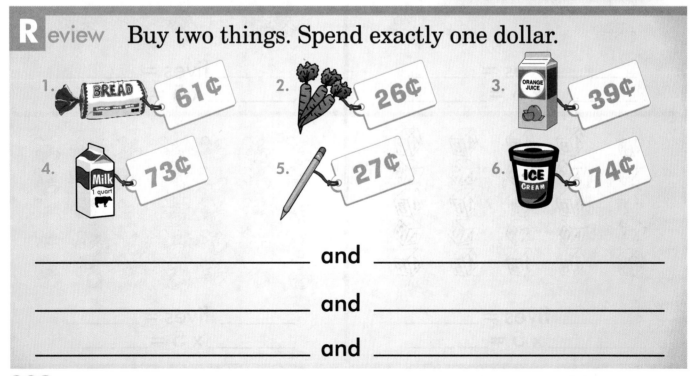

1. BREAD 61¢
2. carrots 26¢
3. ORANGE JUICE 39¢
4. Milk 1 quart 73¢
5. pencil 27¢
6. ICE CREAM 74¢

_____ and _____

_____ and _____

_____ and _____

© Copyright 1999   Mathematics Grade 2

Multiplying with 10 as a Factor — Lesson 155

Math Dog has invited 3 friends to a party. He wants to give each friend 10 small biscuits. Help Math Dog "wrap" the biscuits in tens.

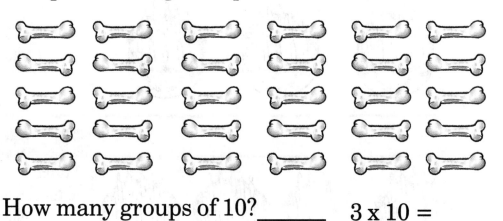

How many groups of 10? _____   3 x 10 = _____

After counting by tens to 30, Math Dog learned a "cool rule."

1. Write the problem: 8 x 10 = ___
2. Remember: the first factor tells how many <u>times</u> to add the second factor.
3. Think: 8 x 10 is 8 tens
   Write the number for 8 tens.
   8 x 10 = <u>80</u>

1. Write the facts for 10 using the "cool rule."

1 x 10 = __10__   6 x 10 = _____

2 x 10 = _____   7 x 10 = _____

3 x 10 = _____   8 x 10 = _____

4 x 10 = _____   9 x 10 = _____

5 x 10 = _____

Some cakes are shown. Some cakes are still in the kitchen.
Fill in the blanks.

2.

Seen	Unseen
3 cakes 10 candles each ____ candles in all	2 more cakes 10 candles each ____ more candles
_____ candles altogether	

3.

Seen	Unseen
4 cakes 10 candles each ____ candles in all	3 more cakes 10 candles each ____ more candles
_____ candles altogether	

4.

Seen	Unseen
2 cakes 10 candles each ____ candles in all	5 more cakes 10 candles each ____ more candles
____ candles altogether	

Review   Read the story.
Draw lines to match the city to the temperature.

San Diego, San Francisco, and San Jose, California have three different
temperatures. San Francisco is colder than San Diego. San Jose's temperature
is between the other two cities' temperatures.

San Diego	70°F
San Francisco	72°F
San Jose	68°F

© Copyright 1999 ACSI Mathematics Grade 2

Problem Solving: Multiplication — Lesson 156

Glue or tape the woodpeckers to the correct multiplication fact tree.

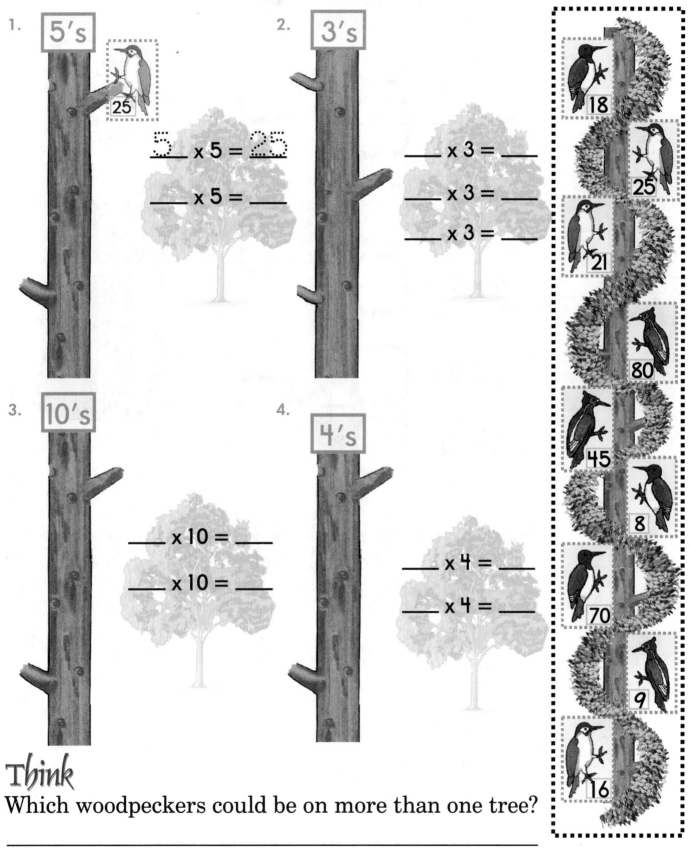

1. 5's

$\_\_ \times 5 = 25$

$\_\_ \times 5 = \_\_$

2. 3's

$\_\_ \times 3 = \_\_$

$\_\_ \times 3 = \_\_$

$\_\_ \times 3 = \_\_$

3. 10's

$\_\_ \times 10 = \_\_$

$\_\_ \times 10 = \_\_$

4. 4's

$\_\_ \times 4 = \_\_$

$\_\_ \times 4 = \_\_$

Woodpecker numbers: 18, 25, 21, 80, 45, 8, 70, 9, 16

Think

Which woodpeckers could be on more than one tree?

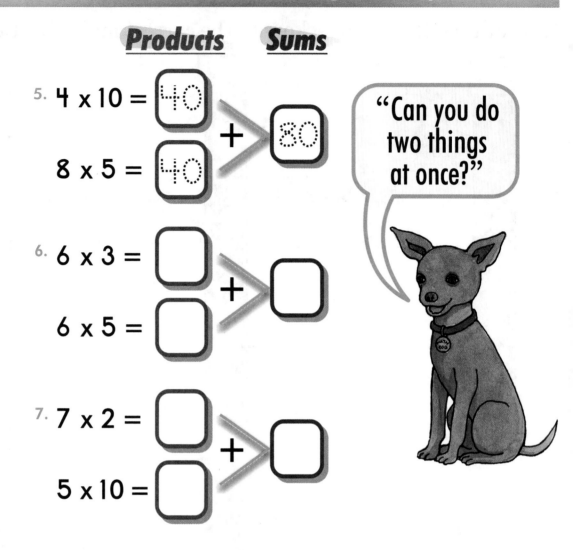

Products   **Sums**

5. $4 \times 10 =$ [40]

$+$ > [80]

$8 \times 5 =$ [40]

6. $6 \times 3 =$ [ ]

$+$ > [ ]

$6 \times 5 =$ [ ]

7. $7 \times 2 =$ [ ]

$+$ > [ ]

$5 \times 10 =$ [ ]

"Can you do two things at once?"

Review   Add or subtract <u>only</u> the problems that need to be regrouped.

1.   34
   + 48

2.   60
   − 29

3.   54
   + 32

4.   143
   + 29

5.   269
   − 148

6.   95
   + 38

7.   99
   − 26

8.   87
   − 38

9.   152
   + 378

10. 146
   − 98

© Copyright 1999   Mathematics Grade 2

Multiplication Review

Math Dog is having a party for 3 friends. He wants 2 doggie treats, one party hat, and slippers for himself and each friend. Write a fact to show:

1. How many treats? _____

2. How many hats? _____

3. How many slippers? _____

Fill in the answer that matches the picture.

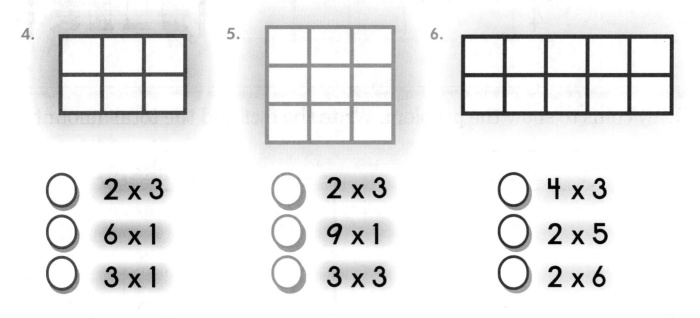

4.

   ○ **2 x 3**

   ○ **6 x 1**

   ○ **3 x 1**

5.

   ○ **2 x 3**

   ○ **9 x 1**

   ○ **3 x 3**

6.

   ○ **4 x 3**

   ○ **2 x 5**

   ○ **2 x 6**

Match facts that have the same answer.

7. 3 x 4 _____

8. 5 x 4 _____

9. 2 x 3 _____

10. 6 x 4 _____

11. 5 x 6 _____

a. 8 x 3

b. 6 x 1

c. 3 x 10

d. 10 x 2

e. 6 x 2

© Copyright 1999 Mathematics Grade 2

12. Write 3 x <u>4</u> with repeated addition.

[ ] + [ ] + [ ] = [ ]

13. Write 4 x <u>3</u> with repeated addition.

[ ] + [ ] + [ ] + [ ] = [ ]

14. Fill in the boxes on the chart. Each swing set has 4 swings.

Swing sets	1	2	3			
Swings	4					

Draw coins to show the problem. Write the fact and the total amount.

15. **9 dimes**

[ ] X [ ] = [ ]

16. **6 nickels**

[ ] X [ ] = [ ]

Multiply.

17. 5 x 2 = _____

18. 4 x 4 = _____

19. 7 x 2 = _____

20. 6 x 3 = _____

21. 9 x 2 = _____

22. 8 x 10 = _____

23. 7 x 10 = _____

24. 7 x 5 = _____

25. 7 x 3 = _____

© Copyright 1999   Mathematics Grade 2

Exploring Division
Lesson 158

Use counters to make equal groups.
Write how many in each group.

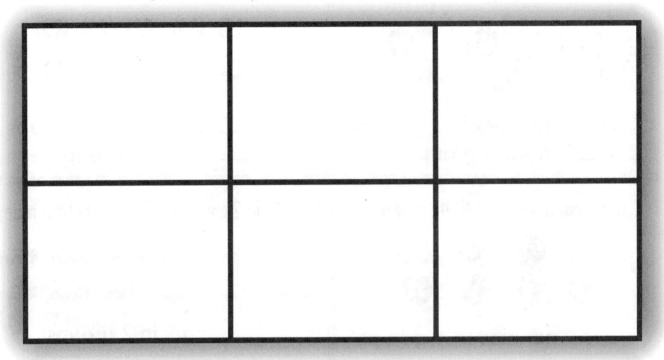

1. Use 6 counters. Make 2 equal groups. _____ in each group.

2. Use 6 counters. Make 3 equal groups. _____ in each group.

3. Use 8 counters. Make 2 equal groups. _____ in each group.

4. Use 8 counters. Make 4 equal groups. _____ in each group.

5. Use 10 counters. Make 2 equal groups. _____ in each group.

6. Use 10 counters. Make 5 equal groups. _____ in each group.

7. Use 12 counters. Make 2 equal groups. _____ in each group.

8. Use 12 counters. Make 3 equal groups. _____ in each group.

Make equal groups.

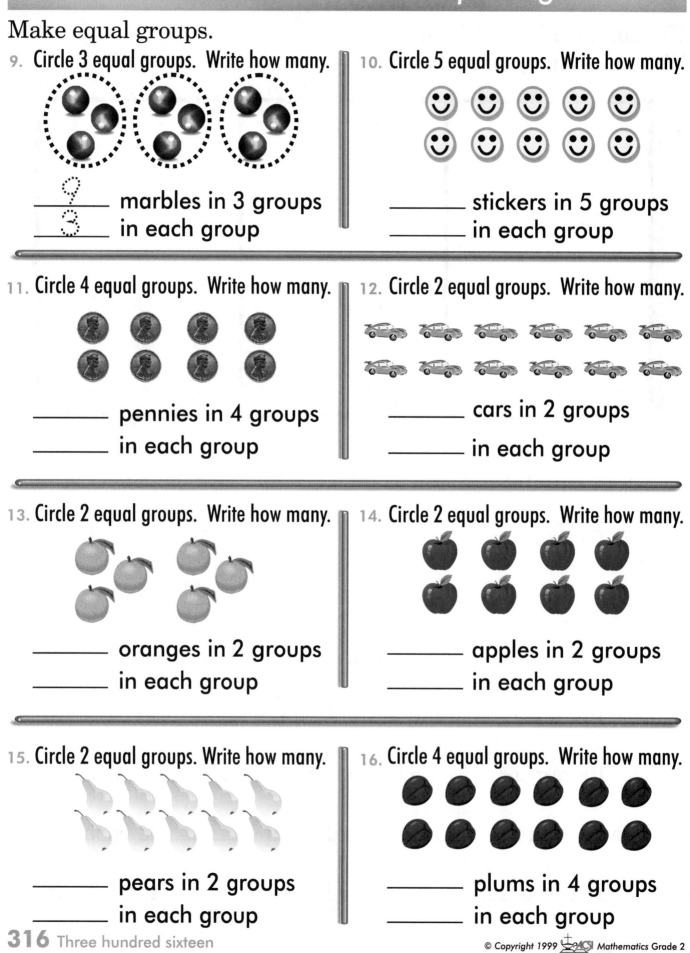

9. Circle 3 equal groups. Write how many.

___3___ marbles in 3 groups
___3___ in each group

10. Circle 5 equal groups. Write how many.

_____ stickers in 5 groups
_____ in each group

11. Circle 4 equal groups. Write how many.

_____ pennies in 4 groups
_____ in each group

12. Circle 2 equal groups. Write how many.

_____ cars in 2 groups
_____ in each group

13. Circle 2 equal groups. Write how many.

_____ oranges in 2 groups
_____ in each group

14. Circle 2 equal groups. Write how many.

_____ apples in 2 groups
_____ in each group

15. Circle 2 equal groups. Write how many.

_____ pears in 2 groups
_____ in each group

16. Circle 4 equal groups. Write how many.

_____ plums in 4 groups
_____ in each group

© Copyright 1999   Mathematics Grade 2

Relating Division to Subtraction   Lesson 159

Jordyn has 20 crackers to feed the parrots. She wants to give each parrot five crackers. Will she have enough? Start with 20. How many times can you subtract 5?

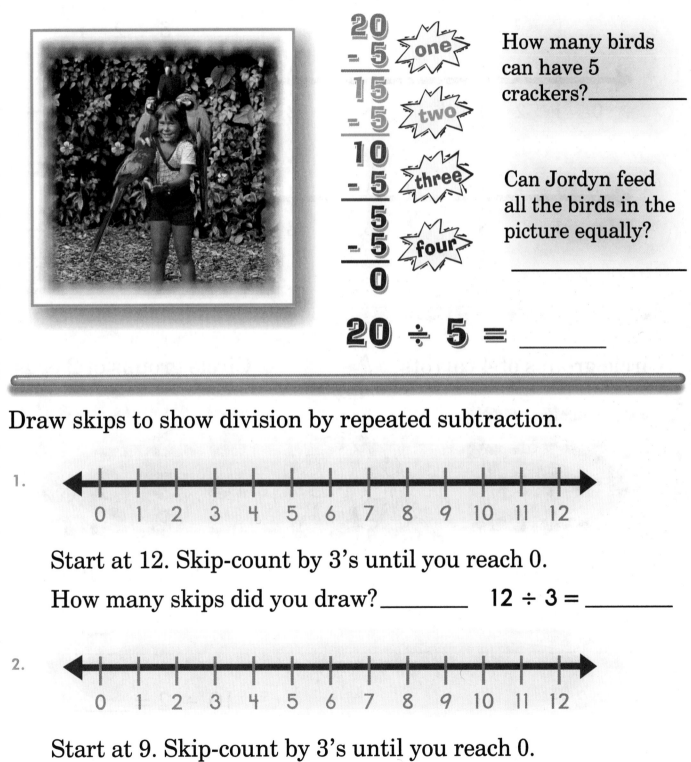

$$20 - 5 \quad \text{one}$$
$$15 - 5 \quad \text{two}$$
$$10 - 5 \quad \text{three}$$
$$5 - 5 \quad \text{four}$$
$$0$$

How many birds can have 5 crackers?_____

Can Jordyn feed all the birds in the picture equally?

_____

$$20 \div 5 = \underline{\hspace{2cm}}$$

Draw skips to show division by repeated subtraction.

1.

0 1 2 3 4 5 6 7 8 9 10 11 12

Start at 12. Skip-count by 3's until you reach 0.

How many skips did you draw? _____ $12 \div 3 =$ _____

2.

0 1 2 3 4 5 6 7 8 9 10 11 12

Start at 9. Skip-count by 3's until you reach 0.

How many skips did you draw? _____ $9 \div 3 =$ _____

Draw skips to show division. Write the numbers.

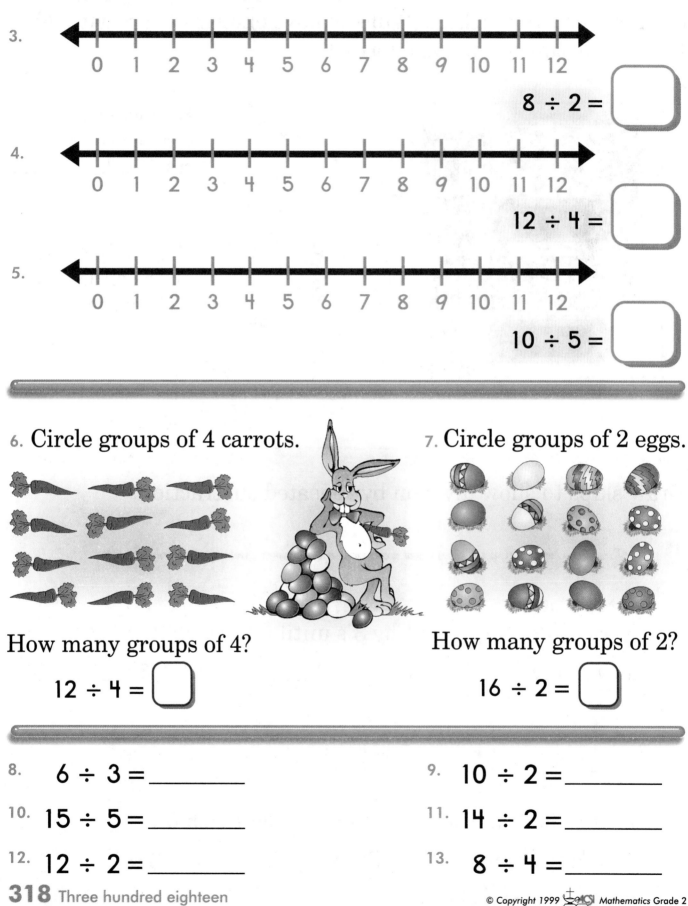

3.

$8 \div 2 =$ ☐

4.

$12 \div 4 =$ ☐

5.

$10 \div 5 =$ ☐

6. Circle groups of 4 carrots.

How many groups of 4?

$12 \div 4 =$ ☐

7. Circle groups of 2 eggs.

How many groups of 2?

$16 \div 2 =$ ☐

8. $6 \div 3 =$ _____

9. $10 \div 2 =$ _____

10. $15 \div 5 =$ _____

11. $14 \div 2 =$ _____

12. $12 \div 2 =$ _____

13. $8 \div 4 =$ _____

© Copyright 1999   Mathematics Grade 2

Write the rest of the family facts.

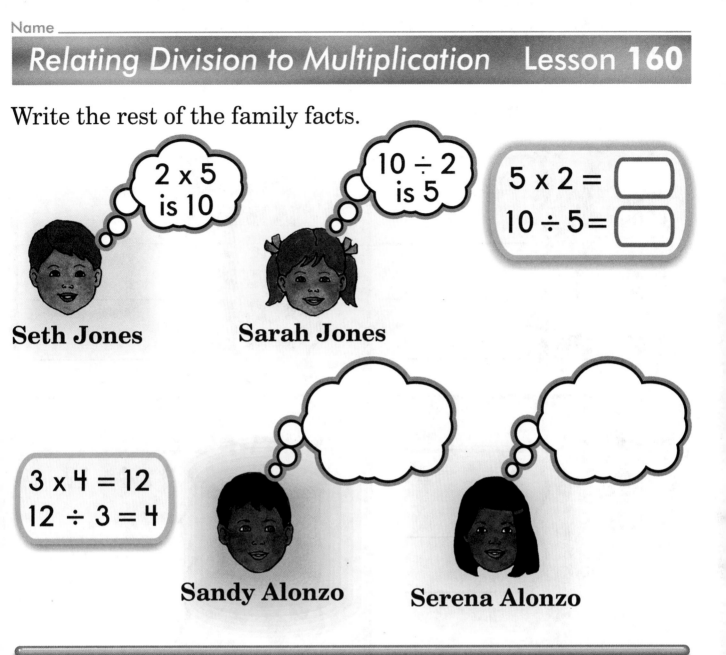

Seth Jones — 2 x 5 is 10

Sarah Jones — 10 ÷ 2 is 5

$5 \times 2 = \boxed{}$
$10 \div 5 = \boxed{}$

$3 \times 4 = 12$
$12 \div 3 = 4$

Sandy Alonzo

Serena Alonzo

Fill in the boxes to complete the family of facts.

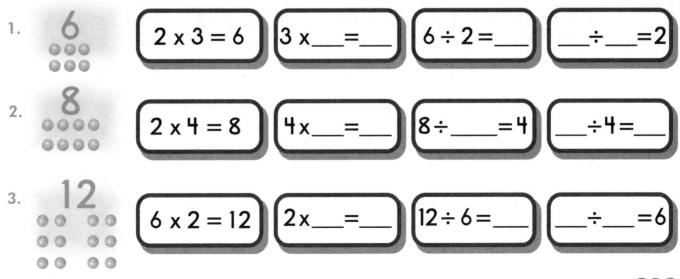

1. **6** $2 \times 3 = 6$ $3 \times \underline{\quad} = \underline{\quad}$ $6 \div 2 = \underline{\quad}$ $\underline{\quad} \div \underline{\quad} = 2$

2. **8** $2 \times 4 = 8$ $4 \times \underline{\quad} = \underline{\quad}$ $8 \div \underline{\quad} = 4$ $\underline{\quad} \div 4 = \underline{\quad}$

3. **12** $6 \times 2 = 12$ $2 \times \underline{\quad} = \underline{\quad}$ $12 \div 6 = \underline{\quad}$ $\underline{\quad} \div \underline{\quad} = 6$

Write the fact families.

4.

$2 \times 2 = 4$

_____

_____

_____

5.

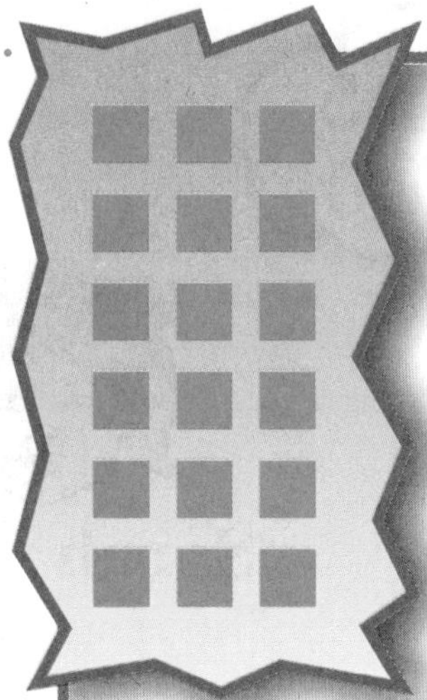

$6 \times 3 = 18$

_____

_____

_____

6.

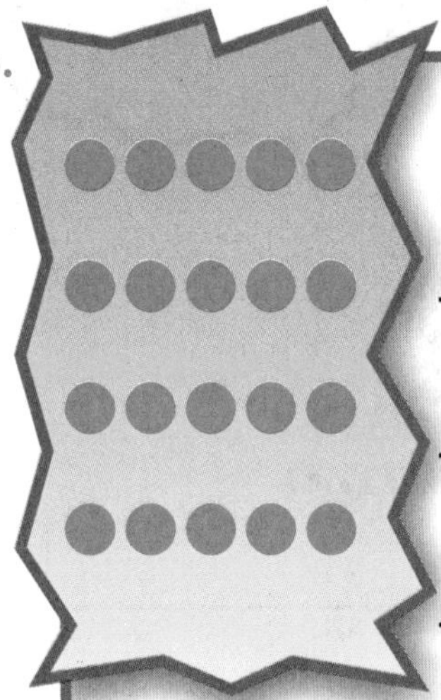

$4 \times 5 = 20$

_____

_____

_____

7.

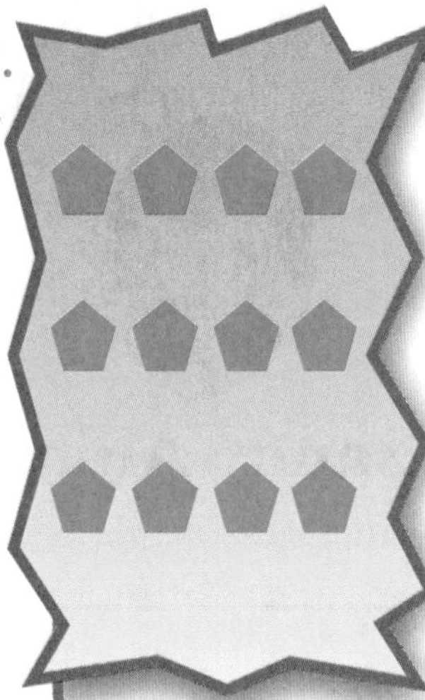

$3 \times 4 = 12$

_____

_____

_____

Review   Write <u>between</u>, <u>before</u>, or <u>after</u> on the line.

1. 36 is _____ 22 and 35.

2. 42 is _____ 49 and 68.

3. 18 is _____ 27 and 35.

4. 24 is _____ 15 and 36.

5. 75 is _____ 60 and 71.

© Copyright 1999   Mathematics Grade 2

Problem Solving: Multiplication and Division   Lesson **161**

At Riverside Hospital Mrs. Jackson and Mrs. Roberts had twins.
Mrs. Craig and Mrs. Tower had triplets.

1. Complete the problem.

How many mothers had twins? _____   **How many had triplets?** _____

⬜ X ⬜ = ⬜ twin
babies   ⬜ X ⬜ = ⬜ triplet
babies

total number of babies = _____

2.

> 20 students were awarded a trip to the amusement park.
> 4 children could ride in the Matterhorn car at one time.
> How many cars would be needed?

Write the numbers in the boxes.
Circle the correct operation.

⬜   X
÷   ⬜   =   ⬜

Number of   **Choose**   **Number of**   **Number of**
students   **riders**   **cars needed**

3. Tim, Tom, Ted, and Todd will share this pizza equally. How many pieces will each boy take?

How many pieces of pepperoni will each boy have?

Write a division problem to show how many pieces of pizza each boy will take.

$$\boxed{} \div \boxed{} = \boxed{}$$ **pieces of pizza**

Write a multiplication problem to show how many pieces of pepperoni each boy will have.

$$\boxed{} \times \boxed{} = \boxed{}$$ **pieces of pepperoni**

Review **Place Value Match**

Read the numbers in the center column. Circle the digits in the columns on either side that match the shaded digits (same number in the same place). Draw lines between the matches.

2,463	5̲47	1,800
1,562	67̲8	2,611
4,928	2̲,751	1,593
872	8̲34	348

© Copyright 1999 ACSI *Mathematics Grade 2*

More Problem Solving   Lesson **162**

Alex and his friends are working at the school fair. They get 3 free go-cart rides for every hour worked. How many free rides does each student get?

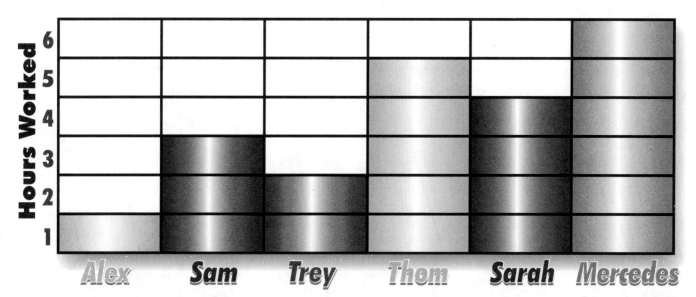

How many free rides for:

1. Alex _____   2. Sam _____   3. Trey _____

4. Thom _____   5. Sarah _____   6. Mercedes _____

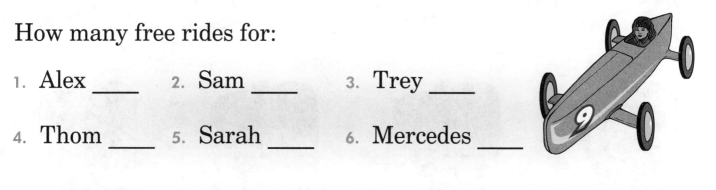

7. 30 prizes were given out at the bowling game. Five small awards were given to each student. How many students won prizes?

Write a number sentence for the problem. _____

Write > or < in the ⬜.

8. 3 x 4 ⬜ 5 x 2

9. 6 x 5 ⬜ 9 x 4

10. 4 x 4 ⬜ 3 x 5

11. 7 x 3 ⬜ 5 x 5

Match socks to boots that help solve the problems.
Write the missing numbers.

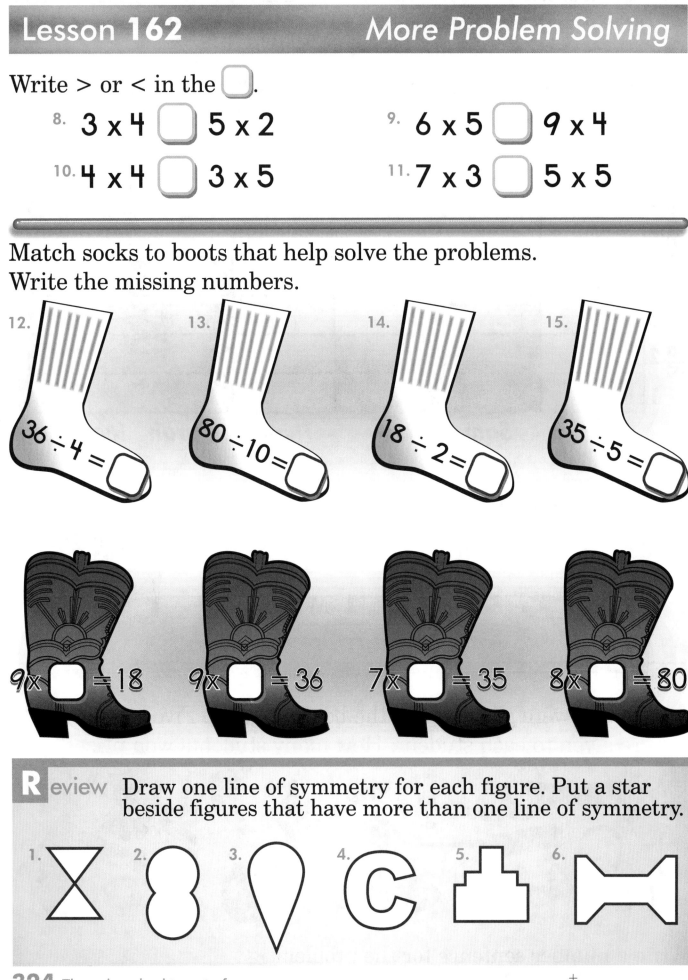

12. 36 ÷ 4 = ⬜

13. 80 ÷ 10 = ⬜

14. 18 ÷ 2 = ⬜

15. 35 ÷ 5 = ⬜

9 x ⬜ = 18

9 x ⬜ = 36

7 x ⬜ = 35

8 x ⬜ = 80

Review Draw one line of symmetry for each figure. Put a star beside figures that have more than one line of symmetry.

1. 2. 3. 4. 5. 6.

© Copyright 1999   Mathematics Grade 2

Chapter Eleven Check-Up   Lesson 163

Write a multiplication sentence for each figure.

1.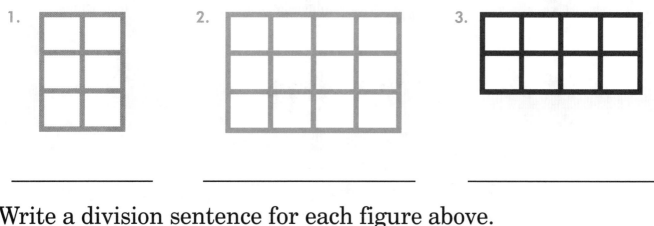

2.

3.

_____   _____   _____

Write a division sentence for each figure above.

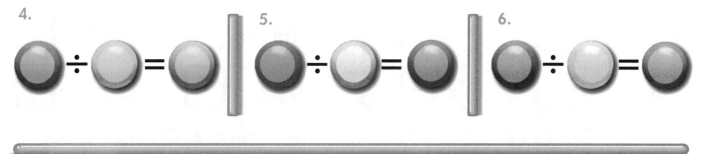

4.   5.   6.

_____

7. Circle groups of five berries. How many groups? _____
   Write a division sentence.

Write a multiplication sentence for each picture.

8.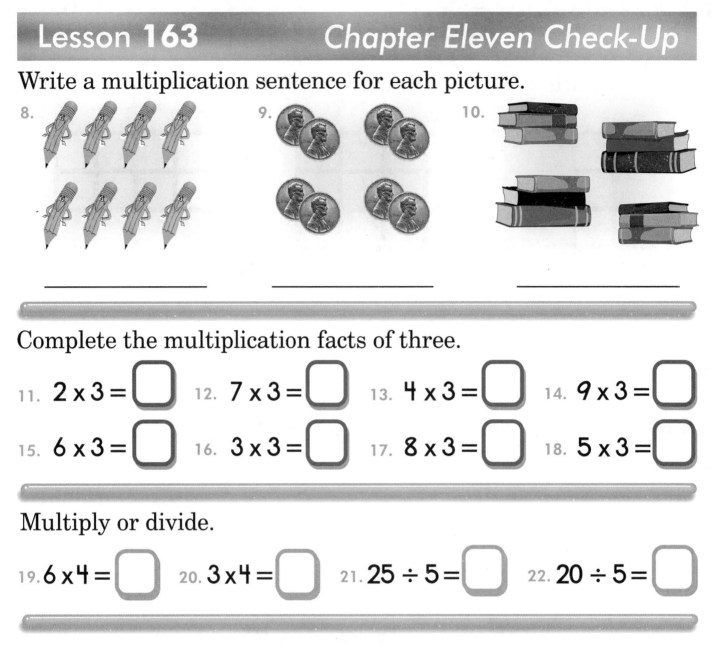

9.

10.

_____   _____   _____

Complete the multiplication facts of three.

11. **2 x 3 =** ◯   12. **7 x 3 =** ◯   13. **4 x 3 =** ◯   14. ***9 x 3 =*** ◯

15. **6 x 3 =** ◯   16. **3 x 3 =** ◯   17. **8 x 3 =** ◯   18. **5 x 3 =** ◯

Multiply or divide.

19. **6 x 4 =** ◯   20. **3 x 4 =** ◯   21. **25 ÷ 5 =** ◯   22. **20 ÷ 5 =** ◯

Solve.

23. Nine buses drove 3 miles each. How many total miles?

_____

24. 15 chairs in 3 rows. Draw the rest of the chairs. How many in each row?_____

© Copyright 1999   Mathematics Grade 2

CHAPTER 12

Mixed Review

Look at the birds of the air, for they neither sow nor reap nor gather into barns; yet your heavenly Father feeds them. Are you not of more value than they?

Matthew 6:26

Dear Parents,

We have arrived at the last chapter in our math book. In Chapter 12 we will review many concepts your child has studied during the year. We have tried to help your child have fun while learning the necessary math concepts. We hope you have enjoyed helping your child succeed in this important effort.

Remember that it is essential your child continue to think about, and practice, mathematics in daily life. Ask your child pertinent questions, such as:

"How many hours until breakfast (or dinner)?"
"If you have ten dollars, how much more money will you need to save before you can buy _____ for $25.00?"
"Is it possible for you and a friend to eat all you want at a fast food restaurant if you have $6.00?"

Have your child explain his or her thinking about the answers given. Such questions will help your child understand the importance of mathematics in daily life.

The world of mathematics is reflected throughout the Scriptures. The Bible discusses number, time, shapes, design, measurement, size relationships, adding, subtracting, multiplying, dividing, and much, much more. Part of the design of this series has been to reveal God's attention to mathematics. It is a joy to consider the wonder of His plan for this aspect of our daily lives. God is great, God is good, and God is powerful. We believe that your child has increased in mathematical power because we have studied mathematics as part of God's design!

© Copyright 1999

Patterns   Lesson 164

1. Complete the patterns.

The Wright Brothers' Flyer was built and flown in 1903. Complete the patterns on the wings. Number the planes in the correct order from 1 to 4.

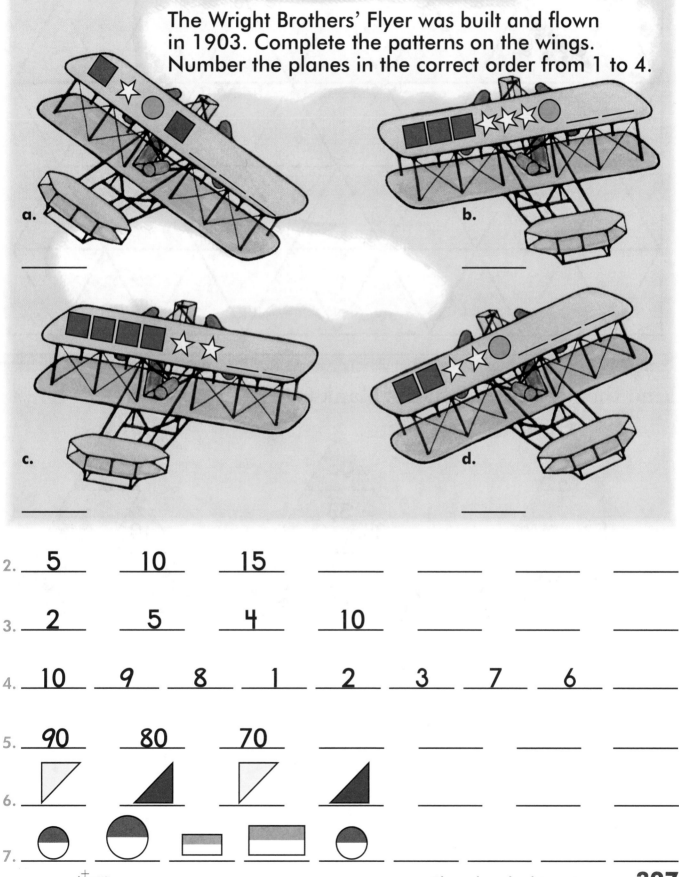

a. _____

b. _____

c. _____

d. _____

2. __5__   __10__   __15__   ____   ____   ____   ____

3. __2__   __5__   __4__   __10__   ____   ____   ____

4. __10__   __9__   __8__   __1__   __2__   __3__   __7__   __6__   ____

5. __90__   __80__   __70__   ____   ____   ____   ____

6.

7.

8. Color pattern block shapes to make a symmetrical pattern.

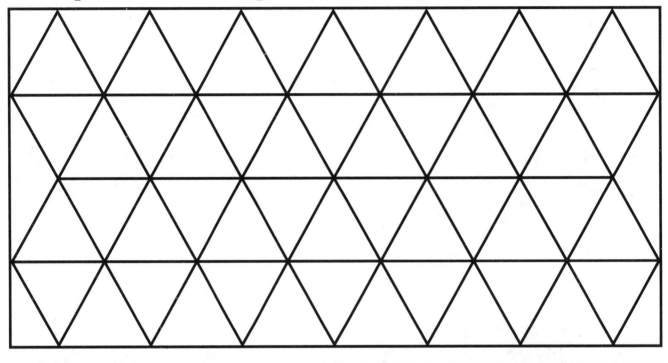

Find the pattern. Fill in the blanks.

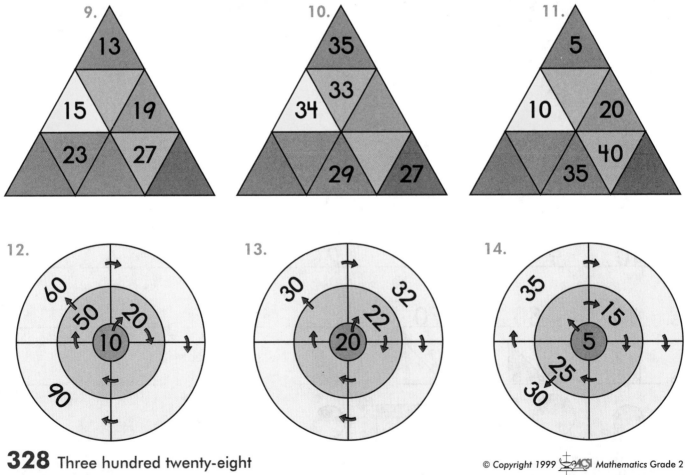

1. Count by hundreds. Number the helicopters.

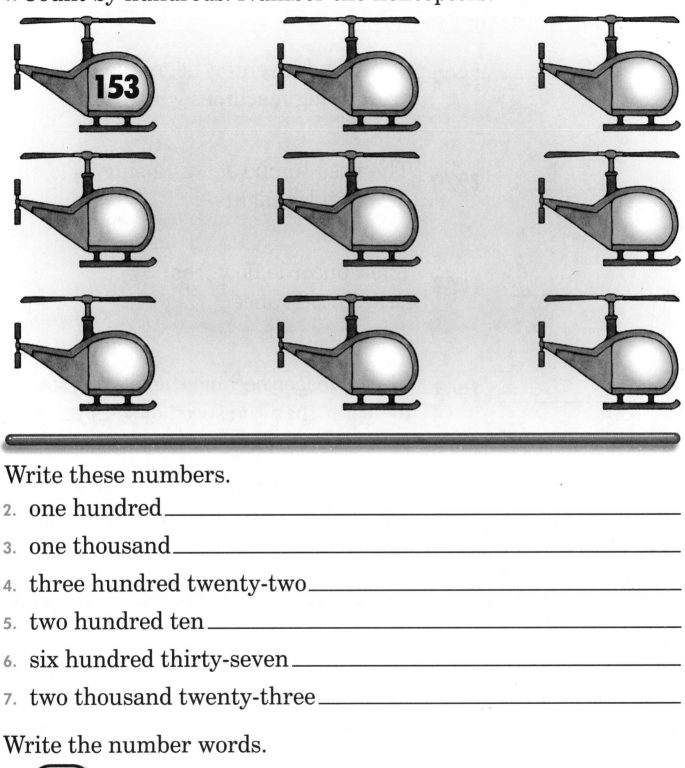

Write these numbers.

2. one hundred _____

3. one thousand _____

4. three hundred twenty-two _____

5. two hundred ten _____

6. six hundred thirty-seven _____

7. two thousand twenty-three _____

Write the number words.

8. _____

9. 523 _____

© Copyright 1999 ACSI Mathematics Grade 2

10. Put these airplane history facts in order.
Use the words <u>first</u> to <u>fifth</u>.

_____ **1500**   Artist and inventor, Leonardo da Vinci, drew flying machines with wings.

_____ **1970**   The first Jumbo Jet, a Boeing 747, flew regular flights.

_____ **1969**   The Concorde flew from Britain to France.

_____ **1947**   Chuck Yeager became the first person to fly faster than the speed of sound.

_____ **1903**   Orville and Wilbur Wright flew the world's first successful airplane.

Think 11. How many 100's make 1,000?_____

Review   Draw the coins needed to make a total of $1.00.

1.

2.

3.

© Copyright 1999 Mathematics Grade 2

ACSI Airline – **Departing San Diego**

FLIGHT #	DESTINATION	DEPARTURE	ARRIVAL
160	BIRMINGHAM	9:00 a.m.	1:30 p.m.
270	CINCINNATI	10:00 a.m.	2:00 p.m.
340	COLORADO SPRINGS	11:20 a.m.	1:20 p.m.

Draw hands on the clock to show departure and arrival times.
Write how much time has passed from departure to arrival.

Departure   **Arrival**

1. **From** San Diego
   To Birmingham
   Time passed:

   ____ hours ____ minutes

2. **From** San Diego
   To Cincinnati
   Time passed:

   ____ hours ____ minutes

3. **From** San Diego
   To Colorado Springs
   Time passed:

   ____ hours ____ minutes

Look at the time on the digital clocks. Draw hands on the clock faces to show the time it will be 2 hours later.

4. `12:05`

5. `6:15`

6. `8:35`

7. It costs $100.00 an hour to rent a helicopter. How much would it cost if you left at 6:00 a.m. and returned at 10:30 a.m.?

_____

8. You can make $1.00 an hour walking Math Dog. You start walking at 3:30 p.m. You must be home for dinner by 6:00 p.m. How much money would you make?

_____

Add or subtract. Write the numbers in the correct places.

9.
$$\$3.48$$
$$+\ 4.53$$
$\$\ \underline{\quad}.\underline{\quad}$

10.
$$\$9.65$$
$$-\ 7.58$$
$\$\ \underline{\quad}.\underline{\quad}$

11.
$$\$6.84$$
$$+\ 2.38$$
$\$\ \underline{\quad}.\underline{\quad}$

12.
$$\$7.52$$
$$-\ 1.38$$
$\$\ \underline{\quad}.\underline{\quad}$

© Copyright 1999   *Mathematics Grade 2*

Write the name of the month on the jet's wings.

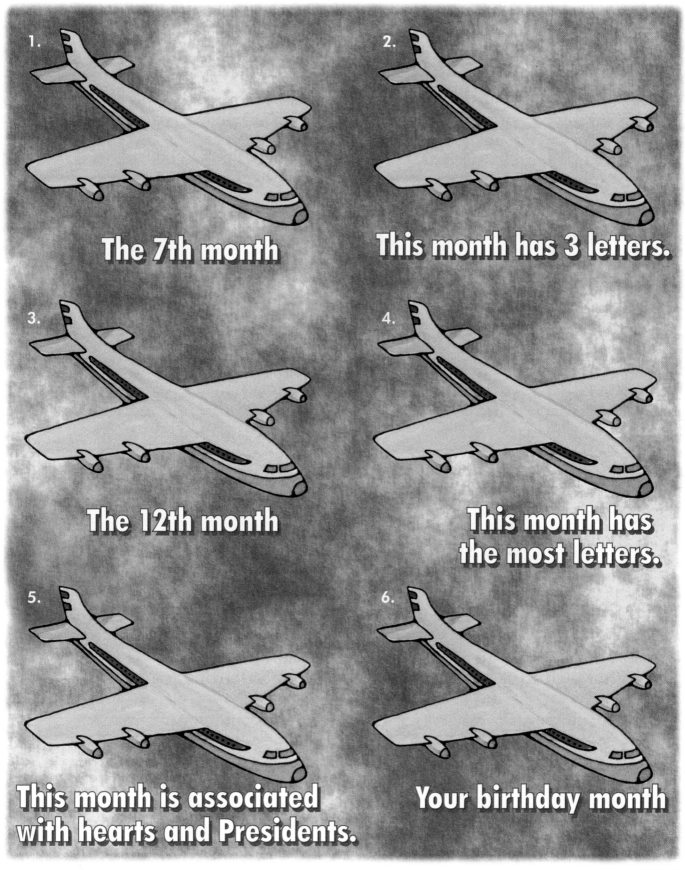

1. The 7th month

2. This month has 3 letters.

3. The 12th month

4. This month has the most letters.

5. This month is associated with hearts and Presidents.

6. Your birthday month

Use the calendar to answer questions 7-11.

Sunday	Monday	Tuesday	Wednesday	Thursday	Friday	Saturday
11	12	13	14	15	16	17

7. What will the date be 2 weeks after Sunday?_____

8. What day of the week was the first day of this month?_____

9. What will the date be two days after Saturday?_____

10. Math Dog is planning a birthday party for Phil during this week. To find Phil's birthday, count by fives. _____

11. During this week you made $5.00 each even-numbered day and $4.00 each odd-numbered day. How much money did you make?

_____

Think Which month does not belong in this group?

_____

Why not?_____

April   November   September   June   December

© Copyright 1999 Mathematics Grade 2

Comparing Fractions   Lesson 168

Write the fraction for the part that is <u>green</u>.

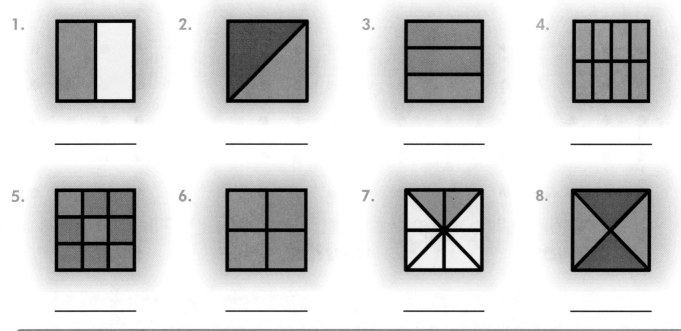

1. _____

2. _____

3. _____

4. _____

5. _____

6. _____

7. _____

8. _____

Write the fraction for the <u>colored</u> <u>part</u> of each group.

9. _____

10. _____

11. _____

12. _____

Draw lines to show these fractions.

13.

halves

14.

fourths

15.

eighths

Use the chart to show which fraction is greater. Write < or >.

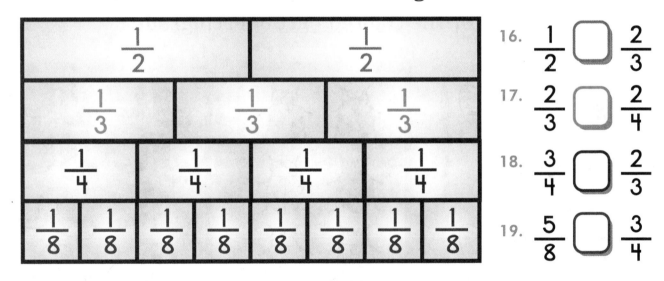

16. $\dfrac{1}{2} \bigcirc \dfrac{2}{3}$

17. $\dfrac{2}{3} \bigcirc \dfrac{2}{4}$

18. $\dfrac{3}{4} \bigcirc \dfrac{2}{3}$

19. $\dfrac{5}{8} \bigcirc \dfrac{3}{4}$

Use the chart to write equal fractions.

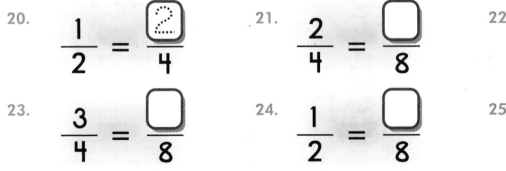

20. $\dfrac{1}{2} = \dfrac{2}{4}$

21. $\dfrac{2}{4} = \dfrac{}{8}$

22. $\dfrac{1}{4} = \dfrac{}{8}$

23. $\dfrac{3}{4} = \dfrac{}{8}$

24. $\dfrac{1}{2} = \dfrac{}{8}$

25. $\dfrac{8}{8} = \dfrac{}{4}$

© Copyright 1999 ACSI Mathematics Grade 2

Addition Review

Complete the problems.

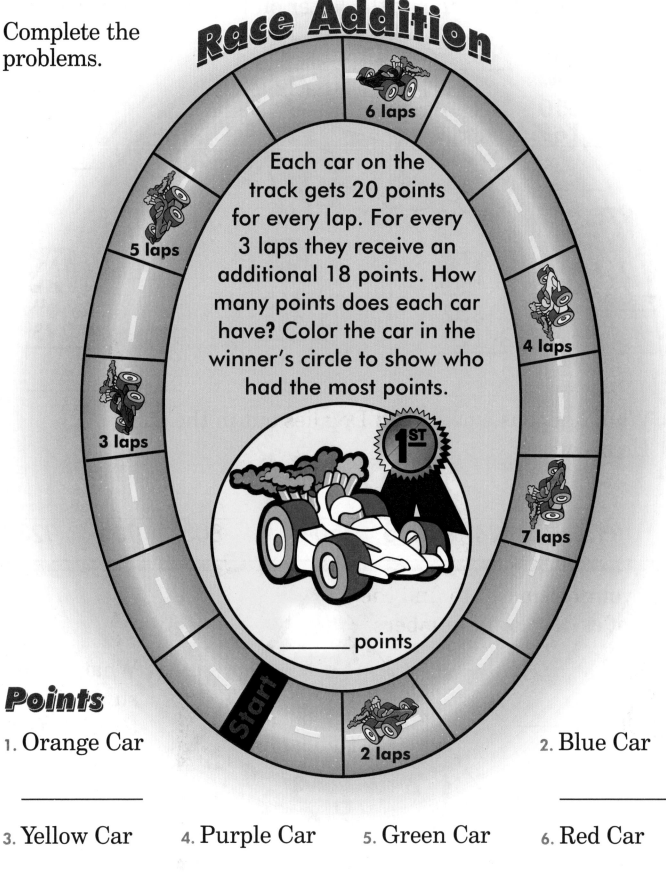

Race Addition

Each car on the track gets 20 points for every lap. For every 3 laps they receive an additional 18 points. How many points does each car have? Color the car in the winner's circle to show who had the most points.

6 laps

5 laps

4 laps

3 laps

7 laps

2 laps

_____ points

Points

1. Orange Car

_____

2. Blue Car

_____

3. Yellow Car

_____

4. Purple Car

_____

5. Green Car

_____

6. Red Car

_____

Solve each problem and put the letter on the correct line below.
Add.

T
7. 340
+ 169
_____

O
8. 447
+ 458
_____

G
12. 687
+ 236
_____

O
9. 268
+ 637
_____

H
10. 852
+ 129
_____

D
11. 465
+ 338
_____

A
13. 654
+ 293
_____

14. What happens when Math Dog lies out in the sun?
He becomes

_____ _____ _____ _____ _____ _____ _____
947   981   905   509   803   905   923

Use your calculator to find the
sum of each color of numbers.

15. **Red** _____

16. **Green** _____

17. **Blue** _____

18. **Purple** _____

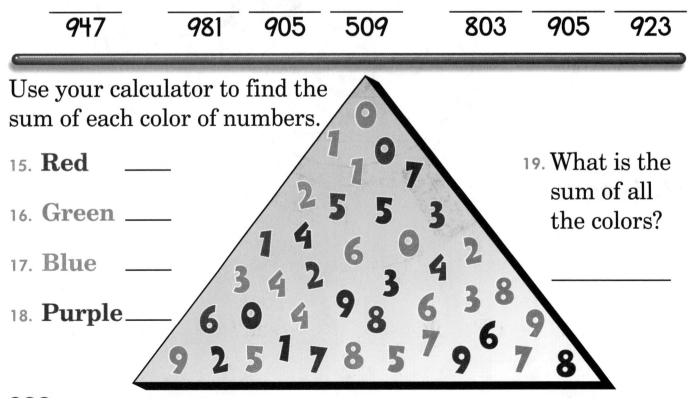

19. What is the
sum of all
the colors?

_____

© Copyright 1999 ACSI Mathematics Grade 2

Subtraction Review   Lesson 170

The Boeing 747 was the first jumbo jet. It was bigger, flew farther, and carried more people than any other airplane.

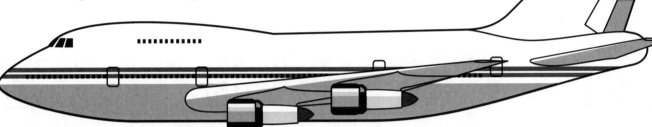

The chart below has information on three jumbo jets. Use the chart to answer the questions.

Jet	First Year in Service	Approximate Number of Passengers	Length
Boeing 747	1969	374 – 416	231 feet
Boeing 767	1981	201 – 304	159 feet
Boeing 777	1995	305 – 386	209 feet

1. Which is the newest jet?_____

2. How many years passed between the <u>newest</u> and the <u>first</u> jumbo jet?_____

3. Which jet carries the fewest passengers?_____

4. Find the range between the least number of passengers and the greatest number of passengers that can be carried on any of these planes. _____ to _____

5. What is the difference in feet between the shortest and longest jets?_____ feet

Subtract.

6.
$$\begin{array}{r} 168 \\ -94 \\ \hline \end{array}$$

7.
$$\begin{array}{r} 276 \\ -84 \\ \hline \end{array}$$

8.
$$\begin{array}{r} 378 \\ -163 \\ \hline \end{array}$$

9.
$$\begin{array}{r} 477 \\ -229 \\ \hline \end{array}$$

10.
$$\begin{array}{r} 583 \\ -279 \\ \hline \end{array}$$

11.
$$\begin{array}{r} 643 \\ -252 \\ \hline \end{array}$$

12.
$$\begin{array}{r} 876 \\ -157 \\ \hline \end{array}$$

13.
$$\begin{array}{r} 752 \\ -334 \\ \hline \end{array}$$

14.

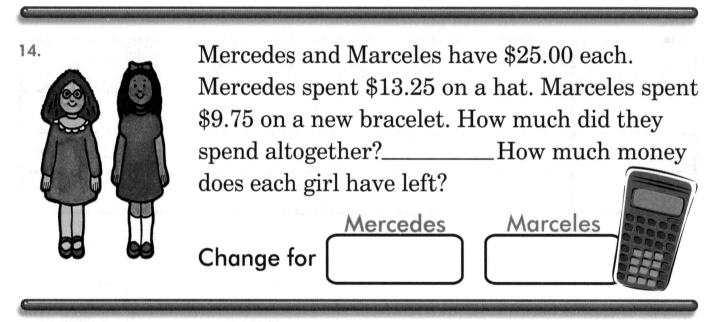

Mercedes and Marceles have $25.00 each. Mercedes spent $13.25 on a hat. Marceles spent $9.75 on a new bracelet. How much did they spend altogether?_____ How much money does each girl have left?

Change for   Mercedes [ ]   Marceles [ ]

BUG SUBTRACTION.

Draw the path the bug should follow to solve the subtraction problems. Connect the blocks that make correct problems.

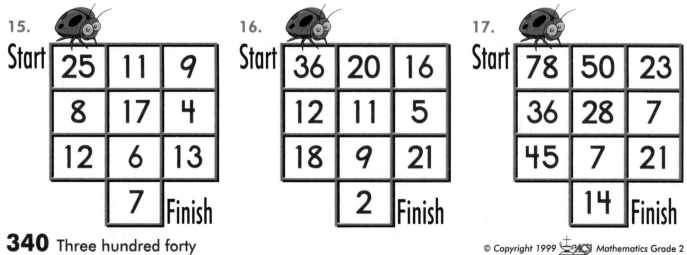

15. Start

25	11	9
8	17	4
12	6	13
	7	Finish

16. Start

36	20	16
12	11	5
18	9	21
	2	Finish

17. Start

78	50	23
36	28	7
45	7	21
	14	Finish

© Copyright 1999 ACSI Mathematics Grade 2

Read the clock.

Write the answers in digital time.

1. What time will it be in 20 minutes? _____

2. What time will it be in one hour? _____

3. What time will it be in 40 minutes? _____

Match. Where can you find this item?

4. **a minute hand**_____   **a. on a ruler**
5. **days of the week** _____   **b. on a triangle**
6. **an addend** _____   **c. on a clock**
7. **a centimeter** _____   **d. in a subtraction problem**
8. **a difference** _____   **e. in an addition problem**
9. **three equal sides** _____   **f. on a calendar**

Write signs to complete the quilt problems.

10.

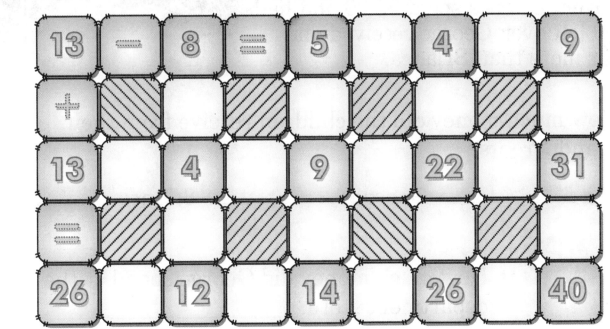

Add or subtract.

11. $\begin{array}{r} 345 \\ -138 \\ \hline \end{array}$　　12. $\begin{array}{r} 538 \\ +276 \\ \hline \end{array}$　　13. $\begin{array}{r} 986 \\ -296 \\ \hline \end{array}$　　14. $\begin{array}{r} 382 \\ +487 \\ \hline \end{array}$

Look at each number. Read and solve the problem.

3,658　15. What number will be in the hundreds place if you add 300?_____

9,235　16. Subtract 10. What number is in the tens place?_____

Think

Susan, George, and Brianca received money from their grandparents for their birthdays. At the department store Susan spent $3.50, and had $3.50 left over. Brianca spent $5.00 and had $2.50 left over. George received one dollar more than Brianca.

17. How much money did the children receive from their grandparents?

Susan _____　George_____　Brianca _____

18. How much money did George spend at the department store?_____

© Copyright 1999　Mathematics Grade 2

Geometry Review   Lesson 172

Use the Word Bank to name the shapes.

> The famous Pentagon in Washington D.C. was built with **5** sides.

1. four sides

_____

2. five sides

_____

3. three sides

_____

4. six sides

_____

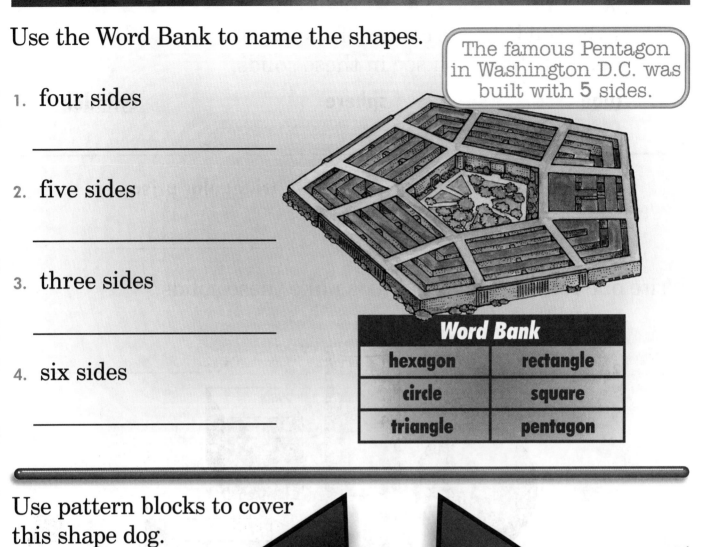

Word Bank	
hexagon	rectangle
circle	square
triangle	pentagon

Use pattern blocks to cover this shape dog.

5. How many triangles will fit? _____

6. Find other ways to cover the dog. Write the name and number of the blocks you used.

_____

_____

_____

Look at the solids in the center of the page.
Name one flat shape you see in these solids.

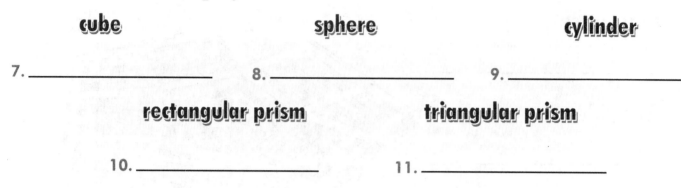

cube   **sphere**   **cylinder**

7. _____   8. _____   9. _____

rectangular prism   **triangular prism**

10. _____   11. _____

Write one real-life item that looks like these solids.

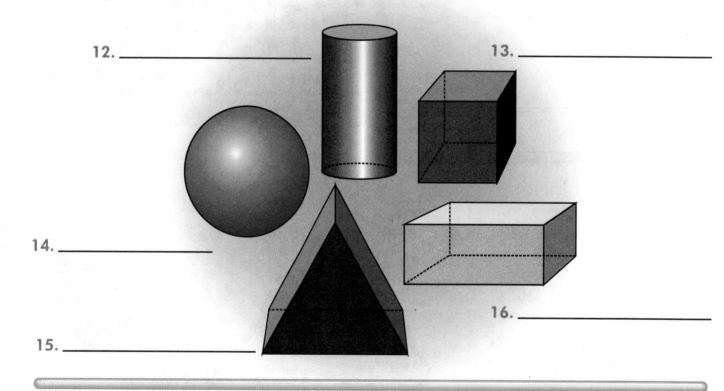

12. _____   13. _____

14. _____

16. _____

15. _____

17. Put two or three triangles together to form other shapes.
What is the name of the new shape? Draw two shapes.

_____

Measurement Review

1. Estimate the number of popcorn pieces pictured around this page. _____

2. Now count! How many pieces? _____

3. What is the difference between your guess and the actual answer? _____

4. This cup of popcorn has about 95 pieces. About how many pieces would there be in 6 cups?

_____

Estimate first, then measure with an inch or centimeter ruler. Find the difference between the estimate and the actual numbers.

	Estimate	Answer	Difference
5. the length of your desk in <u>inches</u>			
6. the length of your shoe in <u>centimeters</u>			
7. the length of your hand in <u>centimeters</u>			
8. the width of your math book in <u>inches</u>			
9. the length of your pencil in <u>centimeters</u>			

10. Add the numbers in your Difference column. _____

© Copyright 1999 Mathematics Grade 2

Use the graph to answer the shark questions.

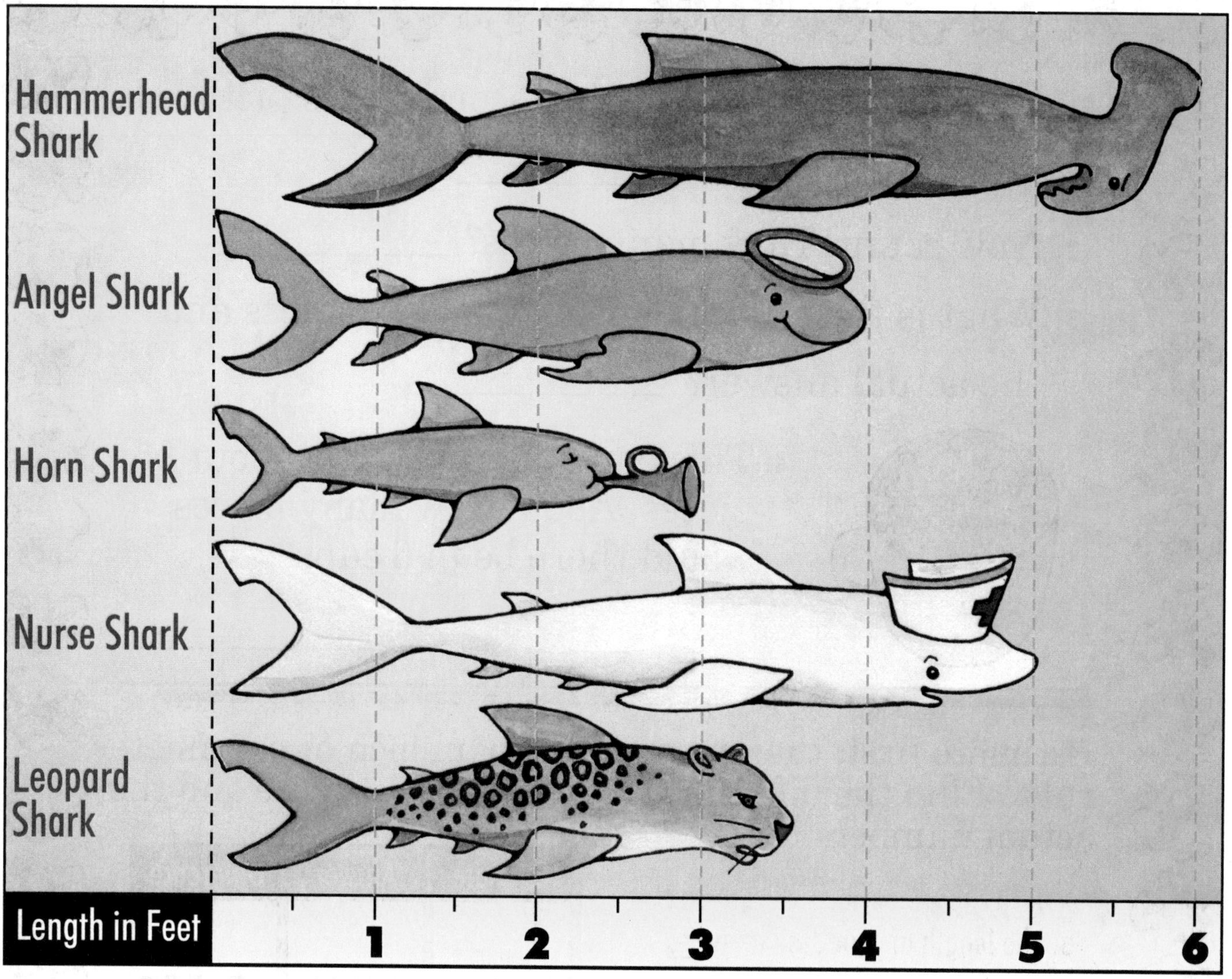

| | | **Length in Feet** | 1 | 2 | 3 | 4 | 5 | 6 |

- Hammerhead Shark
- Angel Shark
- Horn Shark
- Nurse Shark
- Leopard Shark

                                                   Name   **Size**

11. Which is the longest shark? _____ _____

12. Which is the shortest shark? _____ _____

13. Which shark is shorter than the hammerhead, but longer than the angel shark? _____ _____

14. Which two sharks together would equal seven and one-half feet?   **and** _____

© Copyright 1999   Mathematics Grade 2

Multiplication Review   Lesson **174**

Write a multiplication sentence for each array.

1.

2.

3.

_____   _____   _____

4. Draw a picture of 6 x 4 = ☐

5. **"Multiplying by 10 is easy."**

Step 1 Write the problem.
6 x 10 =

Step 2 Remember that the first factor tells how many <u>times</u> to add the second factor. Think:
6 x 10 is 6 tens

Step 3 Write the number for 6 tens.
6 x 10 = _____

Follow the rules to multiply.

6. 7 x 10 = _____   7. 4 x 10 = _____   8. 5 x 10 = _____

9. 8 x 10 = _____   10. 3 x 10 = _____   11. 9 x 10 = _____

12. There are 5 spots on each of 7 worms. How many spots are there altogether? _____worms x _____spots = _____spots

13. There are 4 groups of 4 students using the connecting cubes to multiply. How many students are there altogether? _____students

14. You can travel 10 miles on each gallon of gas. How far can you travel on 5 gallons of gas? _____miles

Multiply.

15.	16.	17.	18.	19.	20.
8 x 3	7 x 2	6 x 5	6 x 3	9 x 2	7 x 3

21. 4 + 4 + 4 + 4 + 4 = ☐ x ☐ = ☐

© Copyright 1999   Mathematics Grade 2

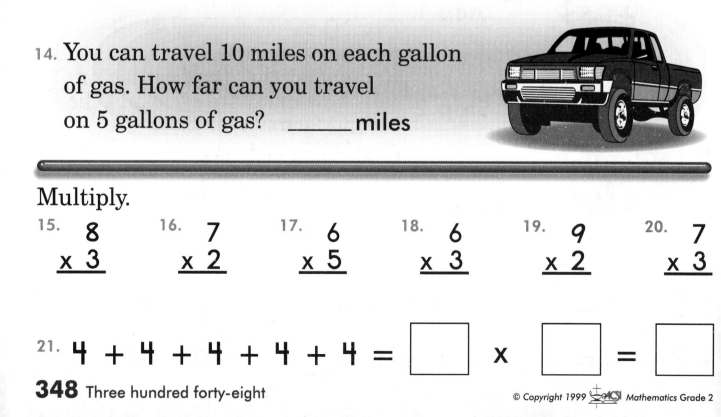

Division Review

Write how many in each group.

1. 12 lollipops are in 3 groups. How many in each group? ___4___

2. 12 lollipops are in 4 groups. How many in each group? _____

3. 12 lollipops are in 2 groups. How many in each group? _____

4. 12 lollipops are in 6 groups. How many in each group? _____

5. 12 lollipops are in 1 group. How many in each group? _____

Write a division sentence for each problem above.

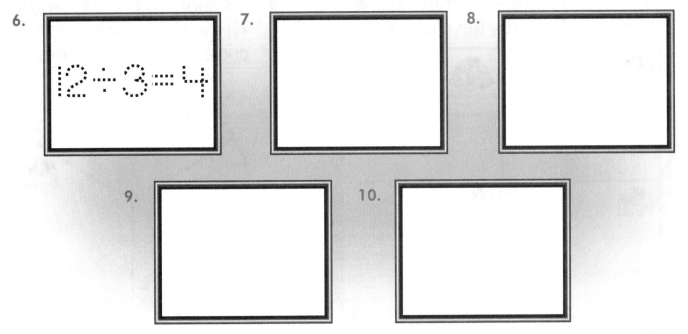

6. $12 \div 3 = 4$

7.

8.

9.

10.

Match each division problem with its correct answer.

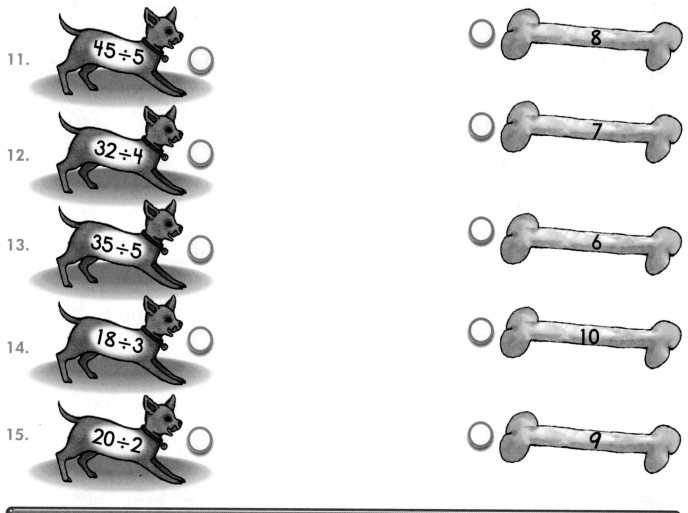

11. $45 \div 5$

12. $32 \div 4$

13. $35 \div 5$

14. $18 \div 3$

15. $20 \div 2$

8

7

6

10

9

16. 16 airplanes for 4 friends. Draw the number of planes for each friend.

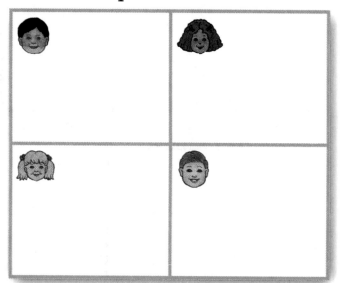

17. 18 cookies for 3 friends. Draw the number of cookies for each friend.

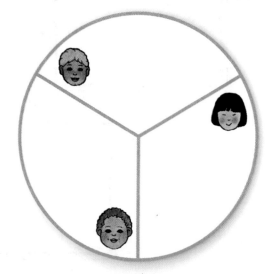

© Copyright 1999 ACSI Mathematics Grade 2

Chapter Twelve Check-Up   Lesson 176

Add across and down.

1.

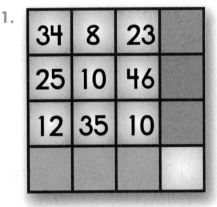

Continue the pattern.

2.

Color to show the fraction.

3. $\frac{5}{8}$

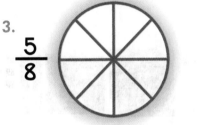

4. $\frac{4}{9}$

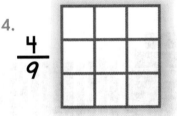

5. $\frac{2}{3}$

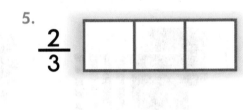

Draw and color shapes to show these fractions.

6. $\frac{3}{4}$

7. $\frac{2}{5}$

8. $\frac{1}{3}$

Think 9. Name the dogs. Phil's problem has an answer that rounds to 80. Math Dog's answer is a multiple of ten. Sam's answer has an 8 in the tens place.

Name: _____ _____ _____

Answer: _____ _____ _____

Add or subtract.

10. 345
 + 386

11. 780
 − 279

12. 649
 + 258

13. 875
 − 637

14. 957
 + 41

Write the numbers.

15. **723** = _____ hundreds _____ tens _____ ones

16. **645** = _____ hundreds _____ tens _____ ones

17. _____

18. _____

19. _____

20. Fill in the chart to show the number of paws on 1, 2, 3, and 4 dogs. Label the chart. Record the answers.

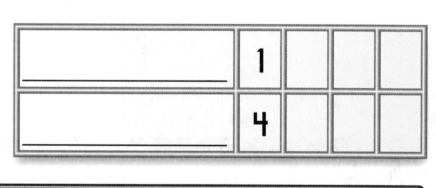

	1			
	4			

Write the letter for the best measure.

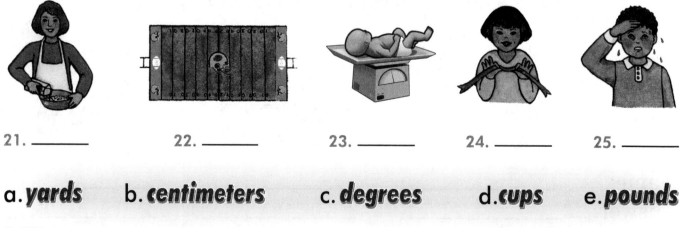

21. _____   22. _____   23. _____   24. _____   25. _____

a. **yards**   b. **centimeters**   c. **degrees**   d. **cups**   e. **pounds**

© Copyright 1999   Mathematics Grade 2

Time

1 hour = 60 minutes
1 day = 24 hours
1 week = 7 days
1 year = 12 months,
        or 52 weeks,
        or 365 days

Metric Units

Length
1 decimeter = 10 centimeters (cm)
1 meter = 100 centimeters
1 meter = 10 decimeters

Weight
1 kilogram = 1,000 grams

United States Customary Units

Length
1 foot = 12 inches
1 yard = 36 inches, or 3 feet

Weight
1 pound = 16 ounces

Capacity
1 pint = 2 cups
1 quart = 2 pints, or 4 cups
1 gallon = 4 quarts

Temperature
32° Fahrenheit (F) - water freezes
212° Fahrenheit (F) - water boils

Money

1 penny = 1 cent (¢)
1 nickel = 5 cents
1 dime = 10 cents
1 quarter = 25 cents
1 half dollar = 50 cents
1 dollar ($) = 100 cents

Symbols

<   is less than
>   is greater than
=   is equal to
°F   degrees Fahrenheit

© Copyright 1999 Mathematics

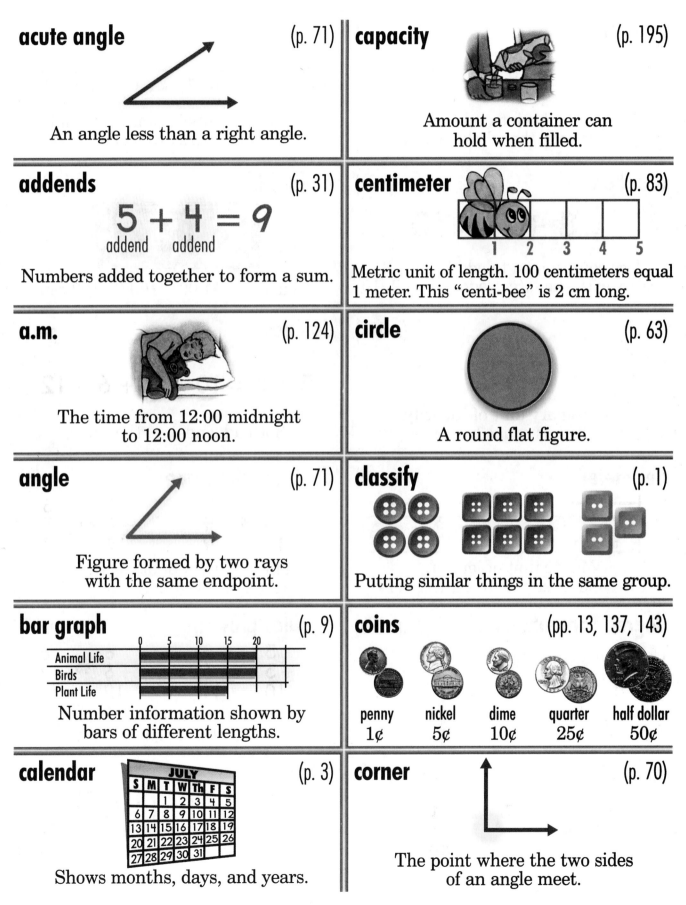

acute angle (p. 71)

An angle less than a right angle.

addends (p. 31)

$$5 + 4 = 9$$
addend   addend

Numbers added together to form a sum.

a.m. (p. 124)

The time from 12:00 midnight to 12:00 noon.

angle (p. 71)

Figure formed by two rays with the same endpoint.

bar graph (p. 9)

	0	5	10	15	20
Animal Life					
Birds					
Plant Life					

Number information shown by bars of different lengths.

calendar (p. 3)

JULY

S	M	T	W	Th	F	S
		1	2	3	4	5
6	7	8	9	10	11	12
13	14	15	16	17	18	19
20	21	22	23	24	25	26
27	28	29	30	31		

Shows months, days, and years.

capacity (p. 195)

Amount a container can hold when filled.

centimeter (p. 83)

1 2 3 4 5

Metric unit of length. 100 centimeters equal 1 meter. This "centi-bee" is 2 cm long.

circle (p. 63)

A round flat figure.

classify (p. 1)

Putting similar things in the same group.

coins (pp. 13, 137, 143)

penny   nickel   dime   quarter   half dollar
1¢   5¢   10¢   25¢   50¢

corner (p. 70)

The point where the two sides of an angle meet.

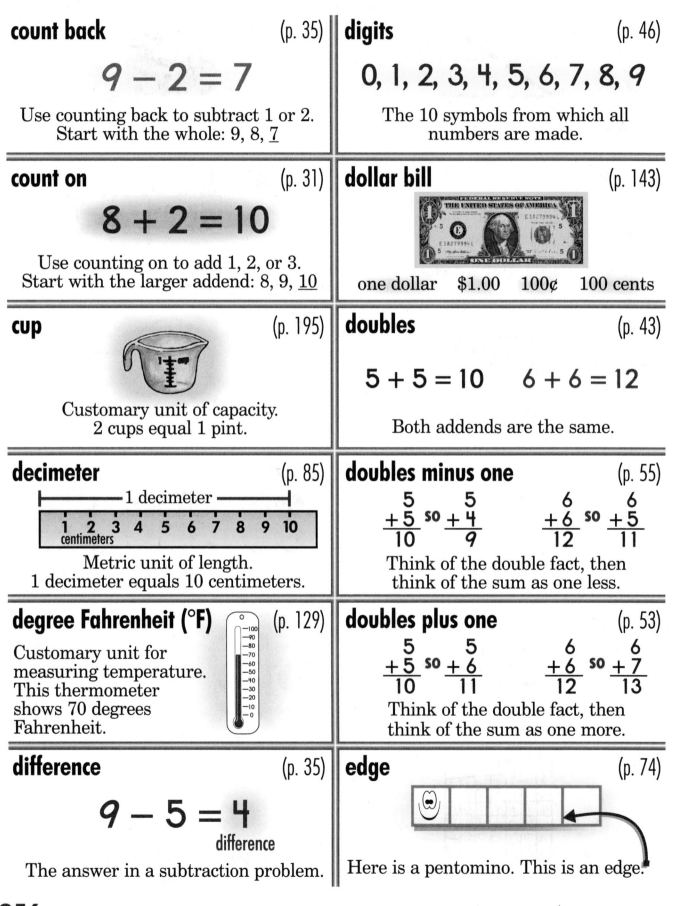

count back (p. 35)

$$9 - 2 = 7$$

Use counting back to subtract 1 or 2.
Start with the whole: 9, 8, 7

count on (p. 31)

$$8 + 2 = 10$$

Use counting on to add 1, 2, or 3.
Start with the larger addend: 8, 9, 10

cup (p. 195)

Customary unit of capacity.
2 cups equal 1 pint.

decimeter (p. 85)

1 decimeter
1 2 3 4 5 6 7 8 9 10
centimeters

Metric unit of length.
1 decimeter equals 10 centimeters.

degree Fahrenheit (°F) (p. 129)

Customary unit for
measuring temperature.
This thermometer
shows 70 degrees
Fahrenheit.

difference (p. 35)

$$9 - 5 = 4$$
difference

The answer in a subtraction problem.

digits (p. 46)

0, 1, 2, 3, 4, 5, 6, 7, 8, 9

The 10 symbols from which all
numbers are made.

dollar bill (p. 143)

one dollar $1.00   100¢   100 cents

doubles (p. 43)

$$5 + 5 = 10 \qquad 6 + 6 = 12$$

Both addends are the same.

doubles minus one (p. 55)

$$\begin{array}{c} 5 \\ +5 \\ \hline 10 \end{array} \text{ so } \begin{array}{c} 5 \\ +4 \\ \hline 9 \end{array} \qquad \begin{array}{c} 6 \\ +6 \\ \hline 12 \end{array} \text{ so } \begin{array}{c} 6 \\ +5 \\ \hline 11 \end{array}$$

Think of the double fact, then
think of the sum as one less.

doubles plus one (p. 53)

$$\begin{array}{c} 5 \\ +5 \\ \hline 10 \end{array} \text{ so } \begin{array}{c} 5 \\ +6 \\ \hline 11 \end{array} \qquad \begin{array}{c} 6 \\ +6 \\ \hline 12 \end{array} \text{ so } \begin{array}{c} 6 \\ +7 \\ \hline 13 \end{array}$$

Think of the double fact, then
think of the sum as one more.

edge (p. 74)

Here is a pentomino. This is an edge.

© Copyright 1999   Mathematics Grade 2

elapsed time (p. 122)

5:00   9:00

Time that has passed.
4 hours have elapsed.

fact family (p. 41)

$$6 + 3 = 9 \qquad 9 - 6 = 3$$
$$3 + 6 = 9 \qquad 9 - 3 = 6$$

A set of related facts that uses
the same set of digits.

equal groups (p. 316)

9 marbles in 3 groups.
3 in each group.

factors (p. 301)

$$6 \times 2 = 12$$
factor   factor

Numbers that are multiplied
together to form a product.

equal parts (p. 180)

two
equal parts   three
equal parts   four
equal parts

foot (p. 79)

1 foot

1 2 3 4 5 6 7 8 9 10 11 12
inches

Customary unit of length.
1 foot equals 12 inches.

estimating sums (p. 223)

$$63 \longrightarrow 60$$
$$+19 \longrightarrow 20$$
$$\overline{80}$$

To find an answer that is close to the
exact answer, round the addends and add.

fraction (p. 181)

$\frac{2}{3}$ $\frac{3}{4}$

Number used to name parts of
a whole or parts of a group.

even number (p. 17)

2, 4, 6, 8, 10 . . .

Any number that has 0, 2, 4, 6,
or 8 in the ones place.

gallon (p. 195)

1 gallon   =   4 quarts

Customary unit of capacity.
1 gallon equals 4 quarts.

expanded form (p. 95)

$$347 = 300 + 40 + 7$$

Shows the value of each digit.

gram (p. 203)

1 gram

Metric unit of weight.
A paper clip weighs about 1 gram.

graph (p. 9)

Information shown by using pictures or bars.

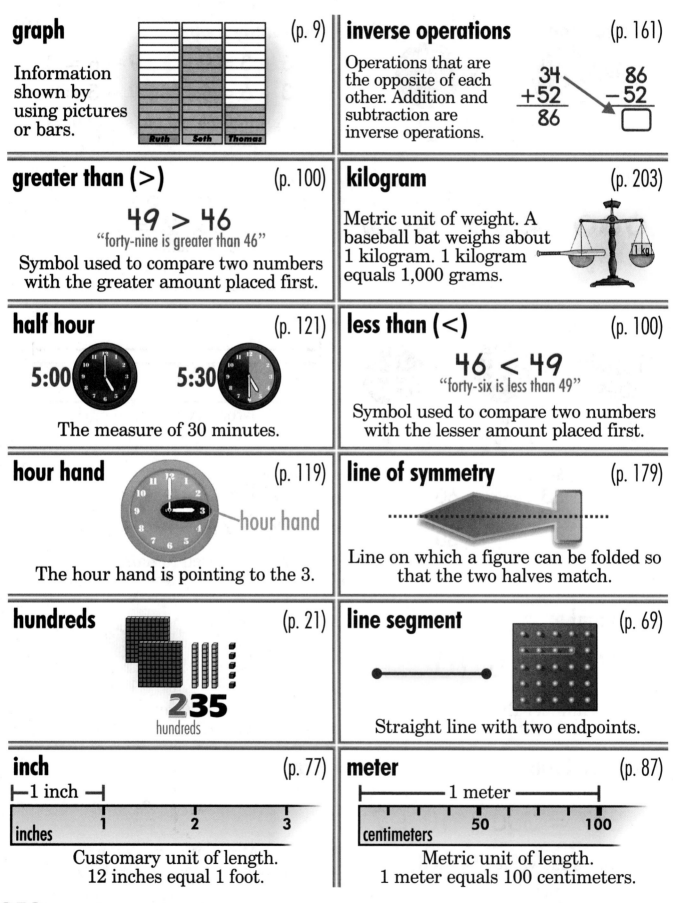

Ruth   Seth   Thomas

inverse operations (p. 161)

Operations that are the opposite of each other. Addition and subtraction are inverse operations.

$$34 + 52 = 86$$

$$86 - 52 = \square$$

greater than (>) (p. 100)

$$49 > 46$$

"forty-nine is greater than 46"

Symbol used to compare two numbers with the greater amount placed first.

kilogram (p. 203)

Metric unit of weight. A baseball bat weighs about 1 kilogram. 1 kilogram equals 1,000 grams.

1 kg

half hour (p. 121)

5:00   5:30

The measure of 30 minutes.

less than (<) (p. 100)

$$46 < 49$$

"forty-six is less than 49"

Symbol used to compare two numbers with the lesser amount placed first.

hour hand (p. 119)

hour hand

The hour hand is pointing to the 3.

line of symmetry (p. 179)

Line on which a figure can be folded so that the two halves match.

hundreds (p. 21)

235
hundreds

line segment (p. 69)

Straight line with two endpoints.

inch (p. 77)

⊢1 inch⊣

inches   1   2   3

Customary unit of length. 12 inches equal 1 foot.

meter (p. 87)

⊢———— 1 meter ————⊣

centimeters   50   100

Metric unit of length. 1 meter equals 100 centimeters.

© Copyright 1999 ACSI Mathematics Grade 2

minute hand (p. 119)

When the minute hand points to 12, it is "o'clock" time.

minute hand

number line (p. 31)

0 1 2 3 4 5 6 7 8 9 10 11 12 13 14

A line that shows numbers in order.

number sentence (p. 169)

$4 + 3 = 7$ $8 - 5 = 3$

Shows the relationship between numbers.

obtuse angle (p. 71)

An angle greater than a right angle.

odd number (p. 17)

$1, 3, 5, 7, 9 \ldots$

Any number that has 1, 3, 5, 7, or 9 in the ones place.

one fourth (p. 181)

$\frac{1}{4}$ part shaded equal parts

one half (p. 181)

$\frac{1}{2}$ part shaded equal parts

one third (p. 181)

$\frac{1}{3}$ part shaded equal parts

ones (p. 23)

23**5**
ones

order property for addition (p. 39)

$4 + 2 = 6$ $2 + 4 = 6$

Changing the order of the addends does not change the sum.

ordinal numbers (p. 4)

1st first   2nd second   3rd third   4th fourth   5th fifth

Numbers that tell order or position.

ounce (p. 201)

Customary unit of weight. A slice of bread weighs about 1 ounce. 16 ounces equal 1 pound.

one ounce

p.m. (p. 124)

The time from 12:00 noon to 12:00 midnight.

pound (p. 201)

Customary unit of weight. 1 pound equals 16 ounces.

part/whole (p. 41)

Part + Part = Whole
Whole – Part = Part

Whole 7	
Part 5	Part 2

product (p. 301)

$$5 \times 4 = 20$$
product

The answer in a multiplication problem.

pattern (p. 2)

2 4 6 8 10
60 50 40 30 20

Objects or numbers in a certain order.

quadrilateral (p. 67)

quadrilateral   parallelogram   rectangle   trapezoid   square

Any four-sided figure.

pictograph (p. 10)

Favorite Flavors	
vanilla	
chocolate	
mint chocolate chip	

A graph that uses pictures to show and compare information.

quart (p. 195)

1 quart = 2 pints

Customary unit of capacity. 1 quart equals 2 pints.

pint (p. 195)

1 pint = 2 cups

Customary unit of capacity. 1 pint equals 2 cups.

quarter hour (p. 123)

7:00   7:15   7:30   7:45

place value (p. 21)

thousands,	hundreds	tens	ones
4,	9	0	1

Value given to the place a digit holds in a number.

rectangle (p. 61)

A flat shape with two pairs of same-length sides and four right angles.

© Copyright 1999   Mathematics Grade

right angle (p. 71)

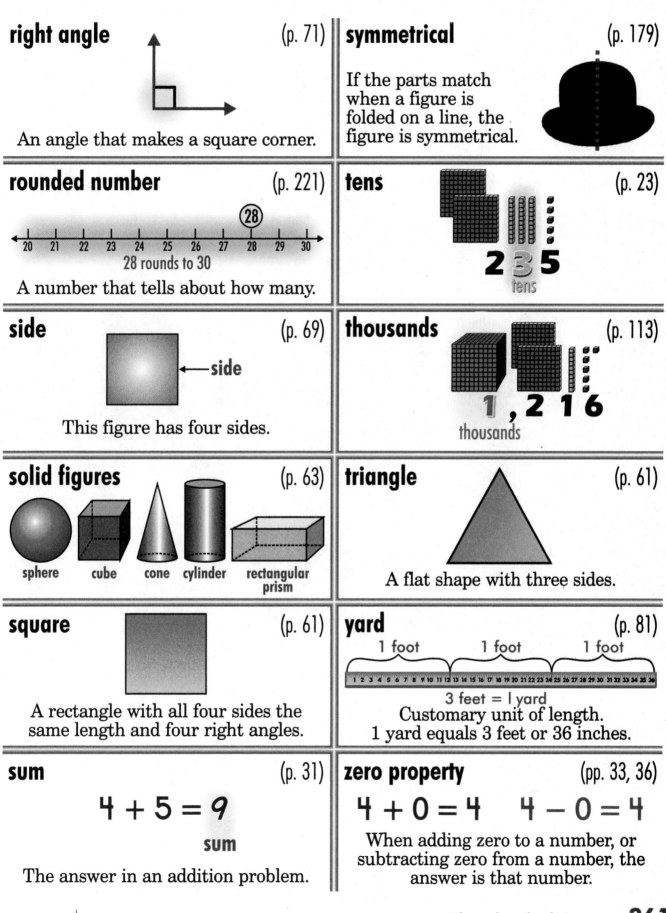

An angle that makes a square corner.

symmetrical (p. 179)

If the parts match when a figure is folded on a line, the figure is symmetrical.

rounded number (p. 221)

28 rounds to 30

A number that tells about how many.

tens (p. 23)

2 3 5
tens

side (p. 69)

←side

This figure has four sides.

thousands (p. 113)

1 , 2 1 6
thousands

solid figures (p. 63)

sphere   cube   cone   cylinder   rectangular prism

triangle (p. 61)

A flat shape with three sides.

square (p. 61)

A rectangle with all four sides the same length and four right angles.

yard (p. 81)

1 foot   1 foot   1 foot

3 feet = 1 yard
Customary unit of length.
1 yard equals 3 feet or 36 inches.

sum (p. 31)

$$4 + 5 = 9$$
sum

The answer in an addition problem.

zero property (pp. 33, 36)

$$4 + 0 = 4 \quad 4 - 0 = 4$$

When adding zero to a number, or subtracting zero from a number, the answer is that number.

© Copyright 1999

© Copyright 1999 Mathematics Grade

© Copyright 1999 Mathematics Grade 2

© Copyright 1999 Mathematics Grade

© Copyright 1999 Mathematics Grade 2

© Copyright 1999 Mathematics Grade 2